SAGE Readings

for Introductory Sociology

Second Edition

SAGE Readings
for Introductory Sociology
Second Edition

Kimberly McGann, Editor
Nazareth College

Los Angeles | London | New Delhi
Singapore | Washington DC | Melbourne

FOR INFORMATION:

SAGE Publications, Inc.
2455 Teller Road
Thousand Oaks, California 91320
E-mail: order@sagepub.com

SAGE Publications Ltd.
1 Oliver's Yard
55 City Road
London, EC1Y 1SP
United Kingdom

SAGE Publications India Pvt. Ltd.
B 1/I 1 Mohan Cooperative Industrial Area
Mathura Road, New Delhi 110 044
India

SAGE Publications Asia-Pacific Pte. Ltd.
3 Church Street
#10-04 Samsung Hub
Singapore 049483

Printed in the United States of America

Cataloging-in-publication data is available for this title from the Library of Congress.

ISBN 978-1-5443-0043-6

Names: McGann, Kimberly, editor.

Title: SAGE readings for introductory sociology / Kimberly McGann, Nazareth College, USA.

Description: Second Edition. | Thousand Oaks : SAGE Publications, [2017] | Revised edition of Sage readings for introductory sociology, [2016]

Identifiers: LCCN 2017050506 | ISBN 9781544300436 (pbk. : alk. paper)

Subjects: LCSH: Sociology.

Classification: LCC HM585 .S24 2017 | DDC 301—dc23 LC record available at https://lccn.loc.gov/2017050506

This book is printed on acid-free paper.

Acquisitions Editor: Jeff Lasser
Editorial Assistant: Adeline Wilson
Production Editor: Karen Wiley
Copy Editor: Tammy Giesmann
Typesetter: Hurix Digital
Proofreader: Sue Irwin
Cover Designer: Anupama Krishnan
Marketing Manager: Kara Kindstrom

17 18 19 20 21 10 9 8 7 6 5 4 3 2 1

Contents

PART III CONSTRUCTING DEVIANCE AND NORMALITY

PART IV GENDER

PART V RACE

PART VI   SOCIAL CLASS

Contents by Theme

SYMBOLIC INTERACTIONISM

Preface

Why Should I Read What's in This Book?

The morning after the 2016 presidential election is one that will not be forgotten anytime soon, whether you were thrilled or terrified by the outcome. The election of Donald Trump as the 45th president of the United States sent shockwaves through not just the country, but the world. "How could he have won?" was a question asked by both supporters and detractors. Reliable polling organizations all showed Hillary Clinton with a lead going into Election Day and Trump's victory was a surprise even to him, telling a crowd in Wisconsin in December that partway through the evening of election day he thought he had lost. While there is no question Trump won the electoral college to become president, there are many, many questions about why his win was not predicted, why those who voted for him did so, and what his presidency means for the country and the world.

"Wait a minute," you might be thinking, "why are you talking about politics at the beginning of a sociology book?" It's because the kinds of issues and beliefs that figure into any election, but especially those in 2016, are exactly the kinds of things that sociologists excel at studying and explaining. Elections are inherently sociological—they are about who will represent society and who will shape the public policies that in turn greatly influence our day to day lives. When you cast a vote, you're giving a hat tip to one of the main premises of sociology—that larger social forces affects what happens to people. We vote for the candidate that we think will shape public policy in a way that will do good for ourselves and our community. For example, if you take the subway to work, you might vote for a candidate who says they support public transportation. But you don't expect them to personally drive your subway car if elected, you expect them to enact policies that make public transportation efficient and affordable. By casting a vote (for or against) a candidate, you're acknowledging that what happens in social institutions, like government, shapes the opportunities and obstacles that you'll face everyday. This link between larger social forces and personal experience is one of the hallmarks of sociological thinking.

Sociological thinking can help you in your day-to-day life as well. Have you ever gone home to visit your family on break and found yourself completely at odds with someone on some social or political issue? We all sometimes encounter people whose values and beliefs are so different from our own that we can't wrap our head around why they think the way they do. To figure that out, you have to look beyond any one person. Our most personal values and beliefs aren't products of our individual life experiences alone, they are always shaped by culture. Understanding how *where you are* (geographic location or social situation) and *when you are* (from the time of day to the moment in history you're at) affects *who you are* (what you believe, how you behave) is a cornerstone of sociology. If you want to sway someone's opinion, you have to understand not just *what they think*, but *why they think that way*. The answer to the why question will always have a sociological component to it.

Learning sociological ideas can also help in your day-to-day life in ways completely unrelated to politics. Understanding how your *life chances*—the odds that certain obstacles and opportunities will present themselves to you—are shaped by social forces can alleviate a lot of stress and help with solving problems. For example, a former student came back to visit me and while his job was going well, he was beamoaning the fact that he was having a hard time meeting someone. He was worried that there was something about him that made him unappealing to potential partners, and he was especially confused because he hadn't had much trouble in college getting dates. I suggested that we look up the town he now lived in on the American Fact Finder page of the US Census Bureau.[1] It turns out that he was living in a town with an exceptionally high number of married people with kids, and very few single people his age. His problem was not that nobody wanted to date him, the problem was that there was no one available for him to date in the first place. College had been full of demographically appropriate potential partners, his new home was not. His solution? He started making the drive to a larger city about 30 minutes away to play in a kickball league—a hobby with lots of single folks his age, and there he met his significant other. Where you are (in a small town with few people your age or a large city with lots of them) and when you are (in your mid-20s or in your mid-70s) affects who you are (a single person or a coupled person.) This kind of thinking can help with everything from finding a job to losing weight to getting really good at a hobby you enjoy.

So whether you are interested in understanding why American society looks the way it does or you'd just like to get through this class and continue on your way to a degree in an unrelated field, there is something in this book for you that will help you in your future endeavors.

What's in This Book?

Sociology is a broad discipline whose boundaries are defined less by subject and more by perspective. This volume gathers in one place some of the classic readings in sociology, as well as contemporary articles that examine common sociological themes in an engaging and accessible fashion. This

---

[1] https://factfinder.census.gov/faces/nav/jsf/pages/index.xhtml

range is reflected here in readings covering topics from how the culture of college hookups can be unavoidable and stratification among sex workers in Vietnam to how and why societies sometimes vilify groups during moral panics and the experience of transgender individuals in the workplace. You'll find a range of readings that deal with big-picture (what sociologists call macro level) issues and also readings that examine the nitty-gritty micro level details of social life and interaction. This book also reflects a concerted effort to be gender and racially inclusive. There is an even split between male and female authors, and almost one-third of the authors are minorities. Researchers bring their own life experiences into their work, even if just at the level of the topics they chose to study, and sociology as a discipline is in part about being able to see the world from another person's vantage point. Reading from a wide range of authors is an important part of that ability.

How Should I Read This Book?

This book was designed to be appropriate for use either in conjunction with a traditional textbook or as a stand-alone text for an introduction to sociology course. Whether your instructor has assigned this book as a supplement or your only text, there are additional materials included to help you get the most from each article. Each reading has a brief introduction that places it in perspective for you and suggests an approach to reading the piece. There are also discussion questions or activities to accompany each piece that may be used as the basis of class discussion by your teacher or simply as thought-provoking exercises for you to do on your own. The writing styles of the readings vary widely, and you will likely find many of the pieces accessible and enjoyable to read. However, there are some that are likely to present more of a challenge, and I encourage you not to give up on these! Think of writing like wrapping paper: just because you don't think it's attractive or it's hard to take apart doesn't mean that what's inside isn't really enjoyable! All these articles have something important and interesting to say about the social world we live in. Just as we shouldn't judge a book by its cover, I encourage you not to judge an article's ideas by its writing style!

I Like This! What Do I Do Now?

If you find yourself intrigued with some of the ideas you encounter in this book, you might consider majoring or minoring in sociology if you aren't already. Many students over the years have found a sociological perspective to be a compelling, useful, and meaningful way to understand the world around them but are unsure what exactly to do with those skills and ideas once they graduate. Your professor and the chair of the sociology department should be your first stop. They will have a good idea of the types of jobs that majors and minors from your school have found. The American Sociological Association also has an excellent set of resources for those interested in using a sociology major or minor on the job market. Just visit asanet.org and type *sociology major* into the search box (or visit directly at http://www.asanet.org/teaching-learning/undergraduate-student-resources).

Finally, remember that you don't have to major or minor in sociology to put the ideas from these readings to work in your own life and the world around you. A sociological perspective is a valuable tool for understanding how the context of the social world has consequences (good and bad) for what happens to individuals. Not only can this help you make informed decisions about your own life choices, but you'll be able to see how social forces also influence your life chances and plan accordingly.

Acknowledgments

I was lucky enough to have Donileen Loseke and Spencer Cahill introduce me to sociology at Skidmore College when I was an undergraduate, and I am still grateful for their dedication and talent as both sociologists and teachers. My experiences with them set the standard that I still aspire to as a teacher and scholar.

Contrary to popular belief, one does not magically age out of writer's block or fits of procrastination. Ginger Jacobson listened to more than her fair share of grumbling about writer's block and challenged me to think far more critically about issues of race and privilege in my own scholarly efforts. Rachel Bailey Jones again provided both moral support and inspiration for what a truly productive and engaged scholar looks like. My dean, Dianne Oliver, kindly let me rearrange my schedule in the Spring 2017 semester so I could have time to work on this project, and I'm especially grateful for her support in all things academic.

I'd like to thank Jeff Lasser at SAGE Publications for offering me the chance to do a second edition and for having a wonderfully collaborative and straightforward approach to this process. This has again been a thoroughly enjoyable project to work on.

Finally, I am most grateful to all of the students who have taken classes with me in the past 10 years. Their insights and feedback have vastly improved my teaching, and I have learned as much from them as they have from me. Their goodwill and willingness to put up with (and often embrace) my wacky analogies, stick figure drawings, and bad jokes always amazes me. College students are interesting people at an interesting time in their lives, and I feel lucky to have a job that lets me be a part of that.

Thinking
Sociologically

The Sociological Imagination

The Promise

C. Wright Mills

Students often enroll in an introduction to sociology course without having any idea what sociology is. Oftentimes, the course description sounded interesting or the class fulfilled a requirement or a friend recommended the class. And sometimes, students leave class at the end of the semester having learned a great deal about poverty, social norms, culture, race, and gender but perhaps still a little fuzzy on what makes sociology "sociology." This is not just understandable, but it also should be of no great surprise given that many of the topics that sociologists study are also studied by other disciplines. Social workers and economists also study the distribution of wealth and the effects of poverty. Psychologists are interested in how social norms affect people's behavior. Anthropologists study culture. Historians look at how gender roles and race relations have changed over time. If there's so much overlap in what different disciplines study, what is it that makes sociology unique as discipline?

The answer lies not in *what* sociologists study, but in how they study the world around them. This unique sociological perspective is described in this classic piece by C. Wright Mills. He uses the term *sociological imagination* to describe a way of studying the world that connects what happens to individuals to larger social, cultural, political, and economic forces. Or as he puts it, "Neither the life of an individual nor the history of a society can be understood without understanding both" (p. 3). What Mills is arguing is that sociology provides a perspective that lets people see how what happens to them is influenced by events, policies, and interactions that make up the social structure of a society. It's important to note that he's not at all arguing that we as individuals have no autonomy and that our own individual actions and efforts don't matter in what happens to us. Instead, he's urging us to be aware of the social and historical context in which our lives unfold and to think about how those social and historical forces shape our individual life chances. (Life chances are the

---

odds that some opportunity or obstacle will present itself to you.) To give one example—college students who graduated between 2008 and 2014 are much more likely to be unemployed or underemployed than students who graduated before 2008. Why might this be? From an individual perspective, we might argue that these particular students are less motivated or not as smart or qualified as those who graduated before 2008. Perhaps they just didn't try as hard to get jobs. These are all individual-level explanations, and none of them explain why these graduates were so much less likely to find good jobs. But if we employ Mills's sociological imagination, it immediately becomes clear that the number of jobs available in the U.S. economy shrank drastically in 2008 due to the financial crisis. It certainly mattered for students graduating in that time period if they were smart, qualified, and motivated to find a job. But it also mattered that there weren't enough jobs in the economy for all the qualified candidates. This is an example of linking what's happening at the social and historical level (the economy shrank and had fewer jobs available) to what happens to individuals (the 2008—2014 cohort of college graduates were less likely to find good jobs.) This is the underpinning of sociological imagination, and it is this way of thinking about the world that defines sociology.

As you read this article, think about what aspects of your life are shaped by where and when you are living. The sociological imagination is the underpinning of sociology as a discipline, but it's also incredibly useful in understanding how and why life unfolds the way it does for you and those around you. Once you start to be able to see the connections between what happens to individuals and larger social forces, you're well on your way to having a better understanding of the social world and being able to see the world from a sociological perspective.

Nowadays men often feel that their private lives are a series of traps. They sense that within their everyday worlds, they cannot overcome their troubles, and in this feeling, they are often quite correct: What ordinary men are directly aware of and what they try to do are bounded by the private orbits in which they live; their visions and their powers are limited to the close-up scenes of job, family, neighborhood; in other milieux, they move vicariously and remain spectators. And the more aware they become, however vaguely, of ambitions and of threats which transcend their immediate locales, the more trapped they seem to feel.

Underlying this sense of being trapped are seemingly impersonal changes in the very structure of continent-wide societies. The facts of contemporary history are also facts about the success and the failure of individual men and women. When a society is industrialized, a peasant becomes a worker; a feudal lord is liquidated or becomes a businessman. When classes rise or fall, a man is employed or unemployed; when the rate of investment goes up or down, a man takes new heart or goes broke. When wars happen, an insurance salesman becomes a rocket launcher; a store clerk, a radar man; a wife lives alone; a child grows up without a father. Neither the life of an individual nor the history of a society can be understood without understanding both.

Yet men do not usually define the troubles they endure in terms of historical change and institutional contradiction. The well-being they enjoy, they do not usually impute to the big ups and downs of the societies in which they live. Seldom aware of the intricate connection between the patterns of their own lives and the course of world history, ordinary men do not usually know what this connection means for the kinds of men they are becoming and for the kinds of history-making in which they might take part. They do not possess the quality of mind essential to grasp the interplay of man and society, of biography and history, of self and world. They cannot cope with their personal troubles in such ways as to control the structural transformations that usually lie behind them.

What they need, and what they feel they need, is a quality of mind that will help them to use information and to develop reason in order to achieve lucid summations of what is going on in the world and of what may be happening within themselves. It is this quality, I am going to contend, that journalists and scholars, artists and publics, scientists and editors are coming to expect of what may be called the sociological imagination.

1

The sociological imagination enables its possessor to understand the larger historical scene in terms of its meaning for the inner life and the external career of a variety of individuals. It enables him to take into account how individuals, in the welter of their daily experience, often become falsely conscious of their social positions. Within that welter, the framework of modern society is sought, and within that framework the psychologies of a variety of men and women are formulated. By such means the personal uneasiness of individuals is focused upon explicit troubles and the indifference of publics is transformed into involvement with public issues.

The first fruit of this imagination—and the first lesson of the social science that embodies it—is the idea that the individual can understand his own experience and gauge his own fate only by locating himself within his period, that he can know his own chances in life only by becoming aware of those of all individuals in his circumstances. In many ways it is a terrible lesson; in many ways a magnificent one. We do not know the limits of man's capacities for supreme effort or willing degradation, for agony or glee, for pleasurable brutality or the sweetness of reason. But in our time we have come to know that the limits of 'human nature' are frighteningly broad. We have come to know that every individual lives, from one generation to the next, in some society; that he lives out a biography, and that he lives it out within some historical sequence. By the fact of his living he contributes, however minutely, to the shaping of this society and to the course of its history, even as he is made by society and by its historical push and shove.

The sociological imagination enables us to grasp history and biography and the relations between the two within society. That is its task and its promise. To recognize this task and this promise is the mark of the classic social analyst. It is characteristic of Herbert Spencer—turgid, polysyllabic, comprehensive; of E. A. Ross—graceful, muckraking, upright; of Auguste Comte and Emile Durkheim; of the intricate and subtle Karl Mannheim. It is the quality of all that is intellectually excellent in Karl Marx; it is the clue to Thorstein Veblen's brilliant and ironic insight, to Joseph Schumpeter's many-sided constructions of reality; it is the basis of the psychological sweep of W. E. H. Lecky no less than of the profundity and clarity of Max Weber. And it is the signal of what is best in contemporary studies of man and society.

No social study that does not come back to the problems of biography, of history and of their intersections within a society has completed its intellectual journey. Whatever the specific problems of the classic social analysts, however limited or however broad the features of social reality they have examined, those who have been imaginatively aware of the promise of their work have consistently asked three sorts of questions:

1. What is the structure of this particular society as a whole? What are its essential components, and how are they related to one another? How does it differ from other varieties of social order? Within it, what is the meaning of any particular feature for its continuance and for its change?

2. Where does this society stand in human history? What are the mechanics by which it is changing? What is its place within and its meaning for the development of humanity as a whole? How does any particular feature we are examining affect, and how is it affected by, the historical period in which it moves? And this period—what are its essential features? How does it differ from other periods? What are its characteristic ways of history-making?

3. What varieties of men and women now prevail in this society and in this period? And what varieties are coming to prevail? In what

ways are they selected and formed, liberated and repressed, made sensitive and blunted? What kinds of 'human nature' are revealed in the conduct and character we observe in this society in this period? And what is the meaning for 'human nature' of each and every feature of the society we are examining?

Whether the point of interest is a great power state or a minor literary mood, a family, a prison, a creed—these are the kinds of questions the best social analysts have asked. They are the intellectual pivots of classic studies of man in society—and they are the questions inevitably raised by any mind possessing the sociological imagination. For that imagination is the capacity to shift from one perspective to another—from the political to the psychological; from examination of a single family to comparative assessment of the national budgets of the world; from the theological school to the military establishment; from considerations of an oil industry to studies of contemporary poetry. It is the capacity to range from the most impersonal and remote transformations to the most intimate features of the human self—and to see the relations between the two. Back of its use there is always the urge to know the social and historical meaning of the individual in the society and in the period in which he has his quality and his being.

That, in brief, is why it is by means of the sociological imagination that men now hope to grasp what is going on in the world, and to understand what is happening in themselves as minute points of the intersections of biography and history within society. In large part contemporary man's self-conscious view of himself as at least an outsider, if not a permanent stranger, rests upon an absorbed realization of social relativity and of the transformative power of history. The sociological imagination is the most fruitful form of this self-consciousness. By its use men whose mentalities have swept only a series of limited orbits often come to feel as if suddenly awakened in a house with which they had only supposed themselves to be familiar. Correctly or incorrectly, they often come to feel that they can now provide themselves with adequate summations, cohesive assessments, comprehensive orientations. Older decisions that once appeared sound now seem to them products of a mind unaccountably dense. Their capacity for astonishment is made lively again. They acquire a new way of thinking, they experience a transvaluation of values: in a word, by their reflection and by their sensibility, they realize the cultural meaning of the social sciences.

2

Perhaps the most fruitful distinction with which the sociological imagination works is between 'the personal troubles of milieu' and 'the public issues of social structure.' This distinction is an essential tool of the sociological imagination and a feature of all classic work in social science.

Troubles occur within the character of the individual and within the range of his immediate relations with others; they have to do with his self and with those limited areas of social life of which he is directly and personally aware. Accordingly, the statement and the resolution of troubles properly lie within the individual as a biographical entity and within the scope of his immediate milieu—the social setting that is directly open to his personal experience and to some extent his willful activity. A trouble is a private matter: values cherished by an individual are felt by him to be threatened.

Issues have to do with matters that transcend these local environments of the individual and the range of his inner life They have to do with the organization of many such milieux into the institutions of an historical society as a whole, with the ways in which various milieux overlap and interpenetrate to form the larger structure of social and historical life. An issue is a public matter: some value cherished by publics is felt to be threatened. Often there is a debate about what that value really is and about what it is that really threatens it. This debate is often without focus if only because it is the very nature of an issue, unlike even widespread trouble, that it cannot very well be defined in terms of the immediate and everyday environments of ordinary men. An issue, in fact, often involves a crisis in institutional arrangements, and often too it involves what Marxists call 'contradictions' or 'antagonisms.'

In these terms, consider unemployment. When, in a city of 100,000, only one man is unemployed, that is his personal trouble, and for its relief we properly look to the character of the man, his skills, and his immediate opportunities. But when in a nation of 50 million employees, 15 million men are unemployed, that is an issue, and we may not hope to find its solution within the range of opportunities open to any one individual. The very structure of opportunities has collapsed. Both the correct statement of the problem and the range of possible solutions require us to consider the economic and political institutions of the society, and not merely the personal situation and character of a scatter of individuals.

Consider war. The personal problem of war, when it occurs, may be how to survive it or how to die in it with honor; how to make money out of it; how to climb into the higher safety of the military apparatus; or how to contribute to the war's termination. In short, according to one's values, to find a set of milieux and within it to survive the war or make one's death in it meaningful. But the structural issues of war have to do with its causes; with what types of men it throws up into command; with its effects upon economic and political, family and religious institutions, with the unorganized irresponsibility of a world of nation-states.

Consider marriage. Inside a marriage a man and a woman may experience personal troubles, but when the divorce rate during the first four years of marriage is 250 out of every 1,000 attempts, this is an indication of a structural issue having to do with the institutions of marriage and the family and other institutions that bear upon them.

In so far as an economy is so arranged that slumps occur, the problem of unemployment becomes incapable of personal solution. In so far as war is inherent in the nation-state system and in the uneven industrialization of the world, the ordinary individual in his restricted milieu will be powerless—with or without psychiatric aid—to solve the troubles this system or lack of system imposes upon him. In so far as the family as an institution turns women into darling little slaves and men into their chief providers and unweaned dependents, the problem of a satisfactory marriage remains incapable of purely private solution.

What we experience in various and specific milieux, I have noted, is often caused by structural changes. Accordingly, to understand the changes of many personal milieux we are required to look beyond them. And the number and variety of such structural changes increase as the institutions within which we live become more embracing and more intricately connected with one another. To be aware of the idea of social structure and to use it with sensibility is to be capable of tracing such linkages among a great variety of milieux. To be able to do that is to possess the sociological imagination.

DISCUSSION QUESTIONS

1. Make a list of three to four important goals you would like to accomplish sometime in the future. What larger social forces will either facilitate your achieving these goals or make them more difficult to attain?

2. How do you think your life would be different if you had been born 75 years ago? What do you think would have been different about your childhood? Your diet and exercise habits? Your life expectancy? Your educational opportunities? Your career choices? Your fashion sense?

3. Friendship seems like a natural, freely chosen relationship that is based entirely on individual preferences. People who meet and enjoy each other's company often become friends. How do larger social forces influence our "choice" of friends? Does when and where you grow up affect who you might become friends with? Does your gender, race, or social class? What role do you think technology and social media might play in how people go about getting and maintaining friendships?

Lower Ed

Tressie McMillan Cottom

If you ask someone what discipline sociology has the most in common with, the typical answers are anthropology, psychology, or social work. And certainly sociology does have quite a bit in common with these disciplines, as well as many others. But if you think about this question a bit differently, and instead look not at what is being studied but why and how the studying is being done, it turns out that sociology has the greatest overlap with physics.

Physics?? You might be scratching your head at that—and on the surface it does seem a bit strange. After all, the physicists are the folks trying to find out how the universe came into existence (a really big "macro" level question) all the way down to quantum physics which studies the tiniest particles that make up the universe, a very micro-level question. But what sociology and physics have in common are their general goals and the types of challenges they face in doing research. Physicists are interested in understanding the rules and principles that govern the physical world. They develop theories that can explain why the physical world acts the way it does. Sociologists are interested in doing the same thing, except they are looking for the rules and principles that govern the social world. And just as physicists look at both a macro and micro level for this understanding, so do sociologists. Physicists also often encounter the same problem sociologists sometimes face in trying to gather data and test hypotheses—the data we need isn't always available. Just as some subatomic particles are extremely difficult to find and observe, many types of people aren't very forthcoming about making themselves available for researchers (e.g., how do you study all the child molesters who haven't been caught yet?).

In this article, sociologist Tressie McMillan Cottom has gathered data and come up with a theory that links the micro-level experience of individual students seeking credentials at for-profit colleges to macro-level social, political, and economic inequalities that are deeply embedded in our social institutions. Before returning to school to earn her PhD in sociology, Cottom worked as a recruiter for two different for-profit colleges. She introduces the idea of Lower Ed, which encompasses not just for-profit schools but also the expansion of credentialing and neglect of any societal obligation to alleviate social inequality through education. Throughout, she connects the opportunities and obstacles encountered by students at for-profit colleges to larger changes in the economy, our political system, and our cultural beliefs. It's an excellent example of sociological imagination in action.

The Education Gospel

In the first decade of the twenty-first century, as millions of Americans entered higher education, almost 30 percent of them went to for-profit colleges, and I enrolled at least a couple hundred of those students. I worked first at a cosmetology school and later at a technical college. I remember many of those students—their stories, their struggles, their daily successes—but Jason is the student who most changed my life. When I think of Jason now, I hope that he can't say the same of my impact on him.

When we met, Jason was in his early 20s. He was a local boy, born and raised in a rural suburb of Charlotte, North Carolina. At the time, Charlotte was a thriving urban core in the U.S. South. Its national stature, good quality of life, and strong labor markets relied significantly on the banking industry. As the banks went, so too went Charlotte's economic fortunes. When I met Jason, the banks were post-technology bubble but pre-global recession. I was an enrollment officer at the Technical College. It was one of a dozen for-profit colleges in the Charlotte area, each with slightly different branding. There was the for-profit college in high-end Southpark that only offered graduate degrees in business and technology. There was the all-male for-profit college over by the airport whose claim to fame was training mechanics to work at NASCAR. Then there were for-profit colleges in cosmetology, barbering, and what we would have once called secretarial programs. Like those other brands, the Technical College was located in a business park. This one was sandwiched between the high-end part of town and the growing middle-class subdivisions filling up with black and Hispanic families using low down-payment mortgages to escape the center city. The entire school occupied two floors of a six-story building. I had worked previously in a similar role at a cosmetology school. Unlike the cosmetology school, the Technical College offered degrees instead of certificates: associate's, bachelor's, and master's degrees in technology, business, and criminal justice. Technology and business were very broadly defined. Technology included a program in electrical engineering that emphasized electrical more than engineering. The students learned business technology and how to wire common electrical units like those in household appliances instead of learning the math of engineering a structure with electricity. The business degree was *applied*, meaning it included everything from how to write a business memo to how to use accounting software like Quicken. The master's in business also included case studies in common business problems like managing bad publicity. Only the criminal justice curriculum was occupationally specific. The course had to qualify students to take the police exam, and, as a result, it had the most valuable real estate in the building. One entire classroom was set up like a crime scene.

When students like Jason came to visit, anyone who couldn't name a specific occupational interest or degree program was steered to technology or business. Only students who specifically asked for criminal justice were given information about that program. If you didn't know what you wanted a degree in or what kind of job you hoped to have, technology and business were deemed suitably general enough to tell you how much you'd like them but specific enough to sound like something you heard on the news was a *good job*. Jason didn't know what he wanted a degree in, so I told him about technology and business. He chose technology because, he said, "I always upgrade my phone."

Jason was newly married to his high school sweetheart, Bree, who attended each of his appointments with him. They held hands and prayed together before he enrolled. He was eloquent and earnest. They were members of one of the area's non-denominational megachurches that met in shopping centers and played rock music during worship. Between them, Jason and Bree had one truck, three jobs, and one high school diploma. She was working part-time and hoping to work full-time. They wanted a family and thought God was leading them to adopt a Kenyan child with special needs, as friends in their congregation had done. Jason had graduated from high school but suffered from severe test anxiety, which had caught up with him when he once enrolled in community college.

Jason's test anxiety was common enough among prospective students at the Technical College. It was also a potential roadblock to the stated purpose of my job—closing the sale and helping the economy (more on this later)—because the Technical College required an online skills test during the enrollment process. This was fairly rare among for-profit colleges, most of which have very few admission criteria (they are typically called open-access schools). The Technical College used something called the Wonderlic Cognitive Ability Test, best known for being the test that the National Football League uses to assess the IQ of new players. The 50-question assessment purports to scale group intelligence scores and peg them to the average school grade. For example, a 20 on the Wonderlic is roughly equivalent to a 100 on an IQ test, or the baseline for *average intelligence.* The Technical College paid for a version of the Wonderlic that then correlated the IQ score with scholastic skill levels and provided a General Assessment of Instructional Needs (GAIN) score. For example, if this score were a 5, it meant that the test taker had the IQ of the typical fifth grader. To *pass*, prospective students at the Technical College had to score at least a 6. Prospective students could take the online assessment as many times as necessary to get a 6, and scores generally improved the more the test was taken. If all else failed, ambitious enrollment officers coached prospective students to make sure they passed. There was no real chance of failure. We never told the prospective student that. Instead, passing the Wonderlic became part of the motivational sales technique.

Jason was terrified of the Wonderlic. Per the instructions in the training manual, I told Jason that he could take the entrance test multiple times until he passed. On his first try, Jason just barely made the cut-off score. He was stunned. Bree beamed. Then I told him what my supervisor had instructed us to tell those who passed: even she, who was enrolled in an MBA program at another local for-profit college, had failed it her first time. The point was that someone like Jason should be proud of his accomplishment and confident enough in his academic future to complete the financial aid paperwork. Happy to have cleared an academic bar he'd previously failed and anxious to earn a degree for a good job to support a young family, Jason had toured the campus, paid his enrollment fee, been tested, and officially become a Technical College student in a single appointment. It was a slam dunk.

Now, we had only to hold Jason's hand until he completed his federal financial aid paperwork and showed up for the first day of classes. These were critical goalposts for both Jason and my employer. The Technical College didn't get paid unless Jason completed his financial aid paperwork, and the first installment check from the government on Jason's behalf was contingent on his showing up the first week of class. The enrollment staff was held accountable for the new students' showing up on the very first day so as to maximize our *tuition guaranteed* numbers.

At Jason's appointment with financial aid, he learned that after all his aid was applied he would have a tuition balance. The financial aid counselor gave him the standard options. He could make a payment plan. This was something like $400 or so a month, the equivalent of a car loan for a young couple that shared one truck. Needless to say, Jason and Bree could not afford the monthly bill. Frankly, the financial aid representative did not push the payment plan. That was deliberate. The Technical College wasn't fond of payment-plan students, because the staff had to spend valuable time chasing down those monthly payments. Plus, it was rumored that payment-plan students almost never showed up on the all-important first day of class. I don't have data on that or a clear-cut reason for why it might be true. But, for a whole host of reasons, it isn't hard to imagine that students who are likely to choose a for-profit college don't have significant cash on hand. If they do, their lives are likely to present good reasons to spend that money on something else: food, rent, repairs. As any salesperson or behavioral economist can tell you, every point at which someone exchanges money for a good or service is a moment for them to reconsider their commitment to that purchase. The down payment on that payment plan may be one too many decision points for the likely students at for-profit colleges. Regardless, Jason didn't have the money, the financial aid representative was glad, and off we went to the other options.

Jason could have a family member co-sign for an additional loan. He did not think anyone in his family, except for an aunt, would qualify. Unlike his student loan, the loan his aunt would be taking on had underwriting criteria. The aunt was elderly. She had good credit but was on Social Security. Jason and Bree worried that a loan payment would be too much stress for her. I thought the same thing about Jason and Bree. Sitting in on their financial aid appointments, I increasingly worried that Jason and Bree could not afford the tuition or the risk of the bachelor's degree program he was signing up for. But I was not there to counsel them on their best options. I was there to close. Jason and Bree were prayerful. Consequently, they wouldn't sign on to any of the options without a word from God. That meant they'd leave every appointment with nothing signed, but committed enough to make yet another financial aid appointment.

As the next start date loomed closer and Jason's financial aid package was still not finished, my supervisor, Lisa, pressured me to tell Jason to do what he had to do to make a better life. She pulled me into her office and fired off a set of questions. Had I called the aunt? Did I make Jason bring his aunt's Social Security number? Did I explain to Jason that if he doesn't start he'll never get his life on track? Dissatisfied with my answers—no, I hadn't called his aunt; no, I didn't ask for his aunt's Social Security number; and, no, I didn't tell Jason he was a loser—Lisa erased Jason's tick mark beside my name on the office sales board. She threw open her office door and gathered the entire staff around her. I would be an example: we closed leads, but unless the federal financial aid paperwork and loan agreements were signed off on to satisfy all the tuition, we would all be out of a job soon. She held an impromptu mock session for the whole staff to guide us in reminding those prospects who were dragging their feet that they had told us they wanted better for themselves. It was time to put up or shut up to prove that they really wanted this. To the enrollment staff she said, "I don't know about you, but I own stock. I need people working in this economy so my stocks do well and welfare doesn't drag down the economy." Closing helps the economy.

As a priest in the educational faith, I can tell you that no matter what Lisa's questionable applied economic theory said, Jason wasn't the economy. Jason was a good kid who had test anxiety and no family wealth to buy test prep, tutors, or anxiety medication. And without the good credit born of wealth, young Jason couldn't make the financial commitment he had to make in order for me to close. I wanted to help Jason, but the Technical College didn't allow us to be priests, only televangelists. We sold, we didn't counsel. We pushed the prayer cloth because a collection plate left too much profit to chance.

One day I turned to a colleague to try to make sense of how I felt. Wasn't I helping Jason change his life for the better? Michael was the most senior enrollment officer in the office. He had worked his way up to only conducting tours of area high school career fairs. He was spared the conversion statistics that ruled the rest of us, confined to the campus backroom where we shared office space. The rumor was that Michael was the only person who our supervisor, Lisa, was too afraid to *coach*. That could have been because he was a military veteran, which showed in ways both big and small. While the other enrollment officers' desks were always littered with leads and files stuffed with enrollment paperwork, Michael's desk had the minimalist order of someone who had once made hospital corners on a bed for the sake of national security. It was intimidating.

Michael also had two children preparing for college. One of our employee benefits allowed family members to take courses at the technical college at a discount. Another colleague, Mary, had taken the job precisely so that her husband could earn a degree on the benefits and quit his job as a plumber. I asked Michael if he was encouraging his eldest son to do the same. He glanced away and said that, while he had thought about it, he had worked hard so that his son had better options. Michael wouldn't stand in his son's way if his son wanted it, but enrolling in the technical college was not the family plan.

Not long after my conversation with Michael about the extent to which we were improving lives, the entire office was scheduled for an afternoon meeting with the bigwigs. The technical college's corporate director was coming to give us a state-of-company address. The director had an expensive-looking haircut and a crisp suit. He introduced himself by telling us that he had worked in finance for years and had never before witnessed what was currently happening in the economic markets. It was spring 2008. Access to credit was drying up, including the private student loans on which many of our students relied to cover the gap that Jason was struggling to fill. But, the director said, we shouldn't worry. The company had negotiated a short-term credit salutation that would allow us to offer company-backed loans to students like Jason. We should not expect the nosediving market to get in the way of closing.

Years later, I would also realize how Jason could think that the Technical College was God's will, as education gospels converge with our articles of faith in individual work ethic, self-sacrifice, and gendered norms about being the head of a household. A college education, whether it is a night class in auto mechanics or a graduate degree in physics, has become an individual good. This is in contrast to the way we once thought of higher (or post-secondary) education as a collective good, one that benefits society when people have the opportunity to develop their highest abilities through formal learning. Despite our shift to understanding higher education as a personal good, we have held on to the narrative of all education being inherently good and moral. Economists W. Norton Grubb and Marvin Lazerson call this the education gospel: our faith in education as moral, personally edifying, collectively beneficial, and a worthwhile investment no matter the cost, either individual or societal. Grubb and Lazerson aren't the only ones to allude to education as a faith-based institution. All institutions require our collective faith in them for them to work. We call that legitimacy. But I like Grubb and Lazerson's construction of the education gospel, in part because it speaks to the contradictions in that faith. The gospel was critical to higher education's shift to its vocational promise. That is, the idea that higher education is a moral good is allowable only insofar as higher education serves market interests. Education is good because a good job is good. The faith breaks down when we divorce higher education from jobs. The contradiction is that we don't like to talk about higher education in term of jobs, but rather in terms of citizenship and the public good, even when that isn't the basis of our faith.

Based on the education gospel, we increasingly demand more personal sacrifice from those who would pursue higher education: more loans, fewer grants; more choices, fewer practical options; more possibilities, more risk of failing to attain any of them. We justify that demand by pointing to the significant return in higher wages that those with higher education credentials enjoy. And we imply that this wage premium will continue in the *knowledge economy*, where twenty-first-century jobs will require everyone to have some post-secondary education to do highly cognitive work. The gap between the education gospel and the real options available to people—those who need a priest but who instead get a televangelist—is how we end up with *Lower Ed*.

Lower Ed refers to credential expansion created by structural changes in how we work, unequal group access to favorable higher education schemes, and the risk shift of job training, from states and companies to individuals and families, exclusively for profit. Lower Ed is the subsector of high-risk post-secondary schools and colleges that are part of the same system as the most elite institutions. In fact, Lower Ed can exist precisely because elite Higher Ed does. The latter legitimizes the education gospel while the former absorbs all manner of vulnerable groups who believe in it: single mothers, downsized workers, veterans, people of color, and people transitioning from welfare to work. Lower Ed is, first and foremost, a set of institutions organized to commodify social inequalities (see Chapters 3 and 4) and make no social contributions beyond the assumed indirect effect of greater individual human capital. But Lower Ed is not just a collection of schools or set of institutional practices like profit taking and credential granting. Lower Ed encompasses ail credential expansion that leverages our faith in education without challenging its market imperatives and that preserves the status quo of race, class, and gender inequalities in education and work. When we offer more credentials in lieu of a stronger social contract, it is Lower Ed. When we ask for social insurance and get workforce training, it is Lower Ed. When we ask for justice and get *opportunity*, it is Lower Ed.

The new economy makes one overriding demand of education: constantly and consistently retrain millions of workers, quickly and at little to no expense for the employer. The new economy is marked by four characteristic changes to the relationships that underpin our social contract: people are frequently changing jobs and employers over their working lifetimes (job mobility); firms place greater reliance on contract, term, and temporary labor (labor flexibility); there is less reliance on employers for income growth and career progression (declining internal labor markets); and workers are shouldering more responsibility for their job training, healthcare, and retirement (risk shift).

Yale political scientist Jacob S. Hacker says the new economy marks both an economic change and an ideological change, each characterized by the *great risk shift* of corporate responsibility to workers and families. Hacker's argument is that incomes have become spikier—they go up and down as workers experience job losses and more frequent changes in their job arrangements. At the same time, workers are expected to plan and invest for their own retirements (401ks and Individual Retirement Accounts), healthcare costs (e.g., Healthcare Savings Accounts), and periods of unemployment (e.g., savings). This risk shift has created an ascendant new work contract that provides fewer buffers to help workers navigate life shocks.

The new economy's work contract affects all workers, albeit differently due to job polarization. That's the phenomenon of highly educated workers pulling ahead financially and socially with near-exclusive access to a shrinking pool of good jobs while less-educated workers are concentrated in on-demand, low-wage jobs with little job security and few promotion ladders. Risk shift for those with good jobs means greater competition for less stability but still high status. Risk shift for those with bad jobs means more of the same poor labor market outcomes and fewer ways to work one's way into a good job.

Hacker identifies two major areas where American workers feel these effects: healthcare and retirement. He calls the shift from corporate responsibility for workers through pensions and health insurance to personal responsibility *risky healthcare* and *risky retirement*. To that I would add, *risky credentialing*, or Lower Ed. Declining investment in social insurance programs that, by design, diffused the individual risk of old age or health episodes exacerbates the risks associated with sickness and old age. In the same way, declining investment in public higher education exacerbates the risks associated with labor market shocks. As social insurance policies like healthcare and pensions declined, so too did public investment in higher education. Traditional colleges shifted more of the cost of a credential (or risk) to students and families with more loans and fewer grants offered, even as steep price discounting fought to hold individual costs down. The U.S. Federal Reserve explains that "the decline in state government support and increasing generosity of financial aid are both aspects of a broader paradigm shift from broad, publicly-subsidized higher education to greater reliance on tuition payments from students and their families." This pattern is true for all of higher education, but it is most true, in the extreme, at for-profit colleges that are by definition tuition dependent.

Despite the inevitableness of the rhetoric about how for-profit colleges serve a necessary market function, it did not have to be this way. The decision to encourage or allow expansion to happen in the private sector instead of in the public sector was a political choice to uphold neoliberal ideas of individualism, markets, and profit taking. Even when we deigned to offer new schemes to offset the cost of higher education we came up with individual education savings accounts, when 50 years ago we may have massively expanded federal grant programs, work training grants, or public-sector employment. The shareholder for-profit colleges that were responsible for the majority of the growth in the sector during its most profitable era said in their regulatory findings that this ideology, above all, guaranteed them access to federal student aid programs and relatively little competition for the millions of workers who had few options if they wanted a good job. And, should for-profit degrees not lead to a good job, our ideology of personal responsibility absolves the institutions. Essentially, we believe that Jason should have known better.

The Real

The questions surrounding for-profit higher education are endless. Are they real schools? Do their students get jobs? Do they prey on poor and minority students? Are they ripping off the taxpayer? Are they a beacon of hope for students whom traditional higher education cannot or will not serve?

The latest research in this area remains primarily interested in how employers view for-profit college credentials and how much for-profit college graduates earn. To revisit a point made previously, recall that employers do not show markedly better reads of the profit status of colleges than do students; however, anecdotal evidence abounds regarding how human resources professionals develop informal screening processes to weed out *diploma mills*. We don't know if a for-profit credential is just a poor status signal for employers or if it is a type of negative credential that marks workers as likely being poor, minority, female, or somehow low status. All of this research focuses on those who actually earn a for-profit credential, while the majority of those who enroll in for-profit colleges do not even graduate. We do not have good data on what happens to them in either education or the labor market. These kinds of data could go a long way toward explaining how for-profit colleges expanded, how new forms of Lower Ed might expand, and the cost of all these credentials in dollars and lives. Taken together, this set of facts signals a need for greater scrutiny than researchers have attempted thus far, and especially for deeper and more sustained qualitative research on the various aspects of how Lower Ed credentials are produced, taken up, and interpreted.

Nevertheless, there is plenty of working knowledge about this sector on which we can begin to build a much fuller picture of why this growth has come to pass. For-profit colleges are profit-seeking entities that produce credentials for the express purpose of generating profit for the colleges' owners. For-profit colleges "use the language of colleges and universities but operate like corporations or sole-proprietorships." For-profit colleges are precisely defined by their tax status, which allows them to generate profit that can be extracted and distributed to shareholders or owners. In contrast, traditional not-for-profit colleges can participate in revenue-generating activities (and they do; see: patents and collegiate sports teams), but their tax status dictates how they can extract profit and to what ends. For-profit colleges can extract excess revenue and distribute it as profit, whereas not-for-profit colleges cannot. The *for-profit college* designation has become a discursive distinction that represents differences in prestige (both institutional and among students enrolled), legitimacy, and functional value in the labor market.

Scholars and policymakers have paid greater attention to for-profit colleges because of their recent rapid growth, and I focus on this time period for the same reasons they do: scale and form. Two million students were enrolled at for-profit colleges in 2010, up from less than 400,000 in 2000, and that growth was not evenly distributed. While 1 in 20 of all students in higher education is enrolled in a for-profit college, 1 in 10 black students, 1 in 14 Latino students, and 1 in 14 first-generation college students is enrolled at a for-profit college. The typical for-profit college student is a woman and a parent. For-profit colleges dominate in producing black bachelor's degree holders. While there has been a lot made of the declining enrollments at for-profit colleges between 2012 and 2015, the fact remains that this is mostly related to rates of growth. Growth has, in fact, been declining during this more recent period. Save a few notable implosions, like the phased closure and eventual change in ownership of Corinthian-owned for-profit Everest Colleges in 2015, many for-profit colleges continue to enroll students, and the overall share of the for-profit college subsector of higher education is fairly stable. Still, the previous aggregate growth and disproportionate enrollment of underrepresented student groups causes some to argue that for-profit colleges offer unprecedented access to college, while others argue that these patterns indicate greater inequality of access to *legitimate* college educations.

For-profit colleges are often cited as offering occupational training that traditional colleges and universities do not offer. Researchers Guilbert C. Hentschke, Vincente M. Lechuga, and William G. Tierney repeat a common line that attributes the growth of for-profits to their career-focused orientation when they say that for-profits "offer career-oriented programs for which there are proportionately large numbers of workplace vacancies." They are not alone. Of the 33 peer-reviewed academic papers and books about for-profit colleges published between 2000 and 2008, 82 percent of them used some version of this narrative of for-profit colleges' being more attuned to the labor market by offering career-oriented degrees to justify for-profits' rapid growth and popularity. There are largely two ways that academics tend to understand the growth of for-profit colleges. One way says they grew to meet consumer demand that traditional colleges don't meet for various reasons (elitism, financial constraints, politics, and accreditation requirements). Another way to understand this phenomenon is alternately called *credentialing theory* or *credentialism*. This says that something about the unequal distribution of jobs and access to those jobs generates demand for degrees or credentials. We might best understand the rapid growth of a new kind of college by understanding the current inequalities in access to (and returns from) traditional higher education. I subscribe to the latter framework.

For-profit colleges perpetuate long-standing inequalities in gendered work, care work, racial wealth inequalities, and statistical discrimination because they grant credentials that are riskier than most traditional degrees. However, that risk is not entirely their fault. Whether or not its reasons are good or justifiable, traditional higher education has erected barriers between its institutions and for-profit colleges: transfer policies, negative bias in admissions, and hiring practices. While those barriers may serve to protect the students earning traditional college credentials, they trap those with for-profit college credits or credentials in an educational ghetto.

DISCUSSION QUESTIONS

1. Who is Jason? How are the challenges he faces a result of *when and where* he is, rather than just his ability and motivation?

2. What is Lower Ed? How is our economy shaping the educational options available to students?

3. What is *the education gospel*? How is Lower Ed a result of mismatch between the gospel and what actual options people have?

4. What is *the great risk shift* and how is Lower Ed a result of this? How does Lower Ed perpetuate wider social inequalities? Do you think traditional *Higher Ed* might also perpetuate social inequality?

5. Do you think there is any way to design for-profit schools so that they don't perpetuate inequality? What would such schools look like?

The Rest Room and Equal Opportunity

Harvey Molotch

Social structure can be defined as organized patterns of relationships that allow people to form societies and live together. It's these social structures that Mills, in The Sociological Imagination, argues have a profound effect on shaping the lives of individuals. Social structures don't just shape obvious things like education, jobs, income, health, and so on. Social structures also shape the way we interact with each other and how the details of our daily lives are organized and experienced. For example, it's a common sight at sporting events, concerts, airports, and most other places people congregate in any significant number, to see women waiting in line to use the restroom. This is generally attributed to women's propensity to use the bathroom as a place to socialize, fussily fix their appearance, or take their time in answering nature's call. On the surface, who has to wait to relieve themselves and who doesn't seems like a fairly unscholarly topic for study. For one thing, we generally avoid even talking about most natural bodily functions (as I'm doing in this introduction by using euphemisms and more scientific language). But this seemingly mundane detail of daily life provides a telling example of sociological imagination in general and of what sociologists mean when they refer to social structure in particular.

It's important to remember that looking at the influence of social structures is not an argument that people don't have individual agency or that what happens to us is completely determined by social structure. Social structures shape rather than determine our behaviors and life chances. A good analogy for social structure might be the paths available for you to walk on at a park that you visit with a friend. As you get out and start walking on the wide, clearly marked trail from the parking lot, you and your friend start chatting. Odds are that if you are busy enjoying your conversation with your friend, you'll meander on the main trail until you get to some type of junction that forces you to decide which way to go. That doesn't mean that you're not free to pay attention to the smaller, less clearly marked side trails you pass along the way. You certainly could decide to go on those instead, but the main path suggests a route that you're likely to follow, especially if you're not paying attention. Social structure works the same way. It suggests the trajectory of our life chances the same way that a wide, clear path shapes (but does not determine) the route we take on a walk through the woods. We're always free to "trailblaze" whether on a walk or in life, but it tends to take extra attention, effort, and time.

As you read Molotch's article, pay attention to how he describes the various ways that social structures all but ensure that most women will have waiting in line at the restroom become a regular feature of going out in public for them. Why does he think we should care about this seemingly trivial aspect of public life?

A t the risk of appearing disrespectful, let me say that the best way to understand equal opportunity is to use the public toilet. Sometimes a gross approach can best clarify a subtle issue. Through the example of how society is organized to provide men and women with the capacity to relieve themselves, we can understand what it takes, as a more general matter, to provide members of different social groups with authentic equal opportunity.

In many public buildings, the amount of floor area dedicated for the men's room and the women's room is the same. The prevailing public bathroom doctrine in the U.S. is one of segregation among the genders, but with equality the guiding ideology. In some jurisdictions, this square footage equality is enshrined in law. Such an arrangement follows the dictum that equality can be achieved only by policies that are "gender-blind" (or "color-blind" or "ethnic-blind") in the allocation of a public resource. To give less to women (or blacks or Hispanics) would be discrimination; to give more would be "reverse discrimination."[1] Women and men have the same proportion of a building to use as rest rooms. Presumably this should provide members of both genders with equal opportunity for dealing with their bodily needs in a timely and convenient way.

The trouble with this sort of equality is that, being blind, it fails to recognize differences between men as a group and women as a group. These differences are not amenable to easy change. Part of women's demand for bathrooms can not exist for men because only women menstruate. Women make trips to the rest room to secure hygienic and socially appropriate adaptations to this physical fact. And because men's physiology suits them for the use of urinals, a large number of men can be serviced by a relatively small physical space. Women in our society use toilets to urinate, and toilets require a larger area than urinals. By creating men's and women's rooms of the same size, society guarantees that *individual* women will be worse off than individual men. By distributing a resource equally, an unequal result is structurally guaranteed.

The consequences are easily visible at intermission time whenever men and women congregate in theater lobbies. When the house is full, the women form a waiting line in front of the bathroom while the men do their business without delay. Women experience discomfort and are excluded from conversations that occur under more salutary conditions elsewhere in the lobby. If toward the rear of the line, women may experience anxiety that they will miss the curtain rise. Indeed, they may arrive too late to be seated for the opening scene, dance routine, or orchestral movement. Their late arrival is easily taken by others (particularly men) as evidence of characterological slowness or preoccupation with primping and powder room gossip. All these difficulties are built into the structure of the situation. Equality of square feet to the genders delivers women special burdens of physical discomfort, social disadvantage, psychological anxiety, compromised access to the full product (the performance), and public ridicule.

An obvious solution, one I'll call the "liberal" policy, is to make women's rooms larger than men's. Women's bathrooms need to be big enough to get women in and out as quickly as men's bathrooms get men in and out. No more and no less. A little applied sociological research in various types of settings would establish the appropriate ratios needed to accomplish such gender equality.

An alternative solution, one I'll call "conservative," would be for women to change the way they do things, rather than for society to change the structuring of rest room space. There is no need to overturn the principle of equality of square footage among the genders. Instead, women need to use their allotted square footage more efficiently. If women truly want to relieve themselves as efficiently as men, they can take some initiative. Options do exist short of biological alteration.

While women may not be capable of adapting to urinals, they could relieve themselves by squatting over a common trough. This would save some space—perhaps enough to achieve efficiency parity with men. Women are not physically bound to use up so many square feet. It is a cultural issue, and in this case the problem derives from a faulty element of women's culture. It is not physiologically given that each woman should have her own cubicle, much less her own toilet, or that she should sit rather than squat.

This joins the issue well. Should women be forced to change or should the burden be placed on men who may have to give up some of their own square footage so that women might have more? The response from the liberal camp is that even if women's spatial needs are cultural, these needs should be recognized and indulged. Cultural notions of privacy and modes of using toilets were not arrived at by women in isolation from men. Men's conceptions of "decency"—at least as much as women's— encourage women to be physically modest and demure. Men's recurring violence toward women encourages bathroom segregation in the first instance because segregation makes it easier for potential assailants to be spotted as "out of place." Providing women with latched cubicles provides a further bit of security in a world made less secure by men. Thus, prescriptions of dignity and protections from assault come from the common culture produced by women and men. Whatever their origins, these cultural imperatives have become a real force and are sustained by continuing pressures on women's lives. Until this common culture is itself transformed, U.S. women can not become as efficient as Tiwi women in their capacity to urinate in public settings, regardless of the efficiency advantages. On the other hand, altering the spatial allocations for men's and women's bathrooms is relatively simple and inexpensive.

It becomes harder to be a liberal as the weight of cultural imperative seems to lighten. Suppose, for example, that *a part* of the reason for the line in front of the ladies' room is, in fact, a tendency for women to primp longer than men or to gossip among one another at the sinks (although the lines in front of *toilet stalls* would belie such an assumption). Should vanity and sociability be subsidized at the expense of the larger community? But here again, the culture that men and women have produced in common becomes relevant. Perhaps women "take a powder" to escape the oppression of men, using the rest rooms as a refuge from social conditions imposed by the dominant gender? Perhaps the need to look lovely, every moment and in every way, is created by men's need to display a public companion whose make-up is flawless, whose head has every hair in place, and whose body is perfectly scented. Women are driven to decorate themselves as men's commodities and the consequence is bathroom demand. Should men pay for this "service" through sacrificing their own square footage or should women adjust by waiting in line and climbing all over one another for a patch of the vanity mirror?

Again it turns on who should change what. The conservative answer might be for women to give up primping, but that would fly in the face of the demand (also championed by conservatives) that women's cultural role is to be beautiful for their men. Although not because they wished to increase rest room efficiency, radical feminists have argued that women should ease up on their beauty treatments, precisely because it ratifies their subservience to men and deflects them from success in occupational and other realms. But again the liberal view holds appeal: at least until the transition to feminism, the *existing cultural arrangement* necessitates an asymetric distribution of space to provide equality of opportunity among the genders.

As the issues become subtle, reasonable people come to disagree on who should do what and what community expense should be incurred to achieve parity. Such controversy stems from the effort to provide equal opportunity for individuals by taking into account differences among groups. The same problem arises no matter what the issue and no matter what the group. If people commonly get their job leads by word-of-mouth through friends and neighbors, then black people— excluded from the neighborhoods of employers and of those employed in expanding job sectors—will be at labor market disadvantage. Black people's chronically higher unemployment rate stands as evidence of disadvantage: their longer queue for jobs is analogous to the longer line in front of the women's rest room. Blacks can be told to work harder, to use their meager resources more efficiently, to rearrange their lives and cultures to better their job qualifications. Alternatively, their present plight can be understood as *structural*—stemming from a history of enslavement, Jim Crow segregation, and white prejudice that now results in concrete arrangements that hinder individual life changes. One must be color-sighted, rather than color-blind, to deal with these differences. But this is no reverse racism: it rests on perception of social structural locations, not upon inherent inferiority attributed to group membership. Such government mandated policies as open job-searches, ethnic hiring targets, and preference for minority vendors and subcontractors can counteract structural biases that hold down opportunities of women, blacks, and other minorities. Affirmative action programs should be conceived as compensatory efforts to overcome such structured disadvantage (although the legal interpretation of the statutes is usually drawn more narrowly).[2]

Equality is not a matter of arithmetic division, but of social accounting. Figuring out what is equal treatment necessitates—in every instance—a sociological analysis of exactly how it is that structures operate on people's lives. Besides rejecting the conservatives' penchant for blaming the victim, liberal policies need a concrete analytic basis that goes beyond goodhearted sympathy for the downtrodden. As in the rest room case, we need to specify how current patterns of "equal" treatment of groups yield unequal opportunities to individuals. We then should determine exactly what it would take (e.g., square feet to gender ratios) to redress the inequality.

Besides careful analysis, equality also involves a decision as to who is going to change and in what way. These decisions will often take from some and give to others. Thus we have the two-pronged essence of action on behalf of equal opportunity: sociological analysis and political struggle.

DISCUSSION QUESTIONS

1. What are the social structural influences that Molotch argues all but ensure that most women, much of the time, will have to wait in line?

2. What are the two definitions of equality in restroom access that Molotch uses?

3. What are the two options Molotch proposes for remedying women having to wait in line to use the restroom?

4. Why does Molotch think it matters if women have to wait in line to use the restroom?

5. Find someone who is a different gender than you and compare your experiences in accessing restrooms. Ask people who are not the same gender how, if at all, they plan or make accommodations to ensure they will be able to relieve themselves when they need to. Have they ever missed something important to them because they were waiting in line for the restroom?

REFERENCES

Binion, Gayle. "Affirmative Action Reconsidered: Justification, Objectives, Myths and Misconceptions." *Women & Politics.* 7, 1 Spring 1987, pp. 43-62.

Glazer, Nathan, 1975, Affirmative Discrimination: Ethnic Inequality and Public Policy, New York: Basic Books.

NOTES

1. Government acts that provide unequal resources in the name of progressive reform have been denounced in just such terms. See Glazer (1975) for a strong instance.

2. Affirmative action is ordinarily justified as redress for past or present discrimination, rather than necessary actions to bring about future parity. See Binion (1987) for a forceful argument that the proper rationale for affirmative action is *integration* of excluded groups "into the social, political, and economic systems" (Binion, 1987:58).

Damned Lies and Statistics

Untangling Numbers from the Media, Politicians, and Activists

Joel Best

One of the greatest changes in recent history is the exponential increase in the amount of information available to each of us. The growth of the World Wide Web and ever-increasing Internet connectivity gives us access to almost unfathomable amounts of information right at our fingertips. Journalists, activists, social commentators, and researchers are all eager to take advantage of new ways to reach audiences and to use statistics to lend credibility to their stories, opinions, and research. In this article, Joel Best illuminates some of ways that statistics are commonly misused or misinterpreted. He argues that it is a combination of innumeracy (the mathematical equivalent of illiteracy) and mutant statistics (incorrect statistics that are widely propagated) that causes us to believe things about the world that simply are not (and sometimes cannot be) true. Statistics tend to be accepted at face value, particularly if provided by an expert or reputable source, but Best warns us that we should be on the lookout for a whole host of common mistakes, sometimes unintentional and sometimes not, when we turn to numbers to understand the social world. As you read, think about whether you can recall any statistics that you've heard of that sound like they might not be as accurate as they seemed at the time.

The dissertation prospectus began by quoting a statistic—a "grabber" meant to capture the reader's attention. (A dissertation prospectus is a lengthy proposal for a research project leading to a Ph.D. degree—the ultimate credential for a would-be scholar.) The Graduate Student who wrote this prospectus* undoubtedly wanted to seem scholarly to the professors who would read it; they would be supervising the proposed research. And what could be more scholarly than a nice, authoritative statistic, quoted from a professional journal in the Student's field?

So the prospectus began with this (carefully footnoted) quotation: "Every year since 1950, the number of American children gunned down has doubled." I had been invited to serve on the Student's dissertation committee. When I read the quotation, I assumed the Student had made an error in copying it. I went to the library and looked up the article the Student had cited. There, in the journal's 1995 volume, was exactly the same sentence: "Every year since 1950, the number of American children gunned down has doubled."

This quotation is my nomination for a dubious distinction: I think it may be the worst—that is, the most inaccurate—social statistic ever.

What makes this statistic so bad? Just for the sake of argument, let's assume that the "number of American children gunned down" in 1950 was one. If the number doubled each year, there must have been two children gunned down in 1951, four in 1952, eight in 1953, and so on. By 1960, the number would have been 1,024. By 1965, it would have been 32,768 (in 1965, the FBI identified only 9,960 criminal homicides in the entire country, including adult as well as child victims). In 1970, the number would have passed one million; in 1980, *one billion* (more than four times the total U.S. population in that year). Only three years later, in 1983, the number of American children gunned down would have been 8.6 billion (about twice the Earth's population at the time). Another milestone would have been passed in 1987, when the number of gunned-down American children (137 billion) would have surpassed the best estimates for the total human population throughout history (110 billion). By 1995, when the article was published, the annual number of victims would have been over 35 *trillion*—a really big number, of a magnitude you rarely encounter outside economics or astronomy.

Thus my nomination: estimating the number of American child gunshot victims in 1995 at 35 trillion must be as far off—as hilariously, wildly wrong—as a social statistic can be. (If anyone spots a more inaccurate social statistic, I'd love to hear about it.)

Where did the article's Author get this statistic? I wrote the Author, who responded that the statistic came from the Children's Defense Fund (the CDF is a well-known advocacy group for children). The CDF's *The State of America's Children Yearbook—1994* does state: "The number of

---

* For reasons that will become obvious, I have decided not to name the Graduate Student, the Author, or the Journal Editor. They made mistakes, but the mistakes they made were, as this book will show, all too common.

American children killed each year by guns has doubled since 1950." Note the difference in the wording— the CDF claimed there were twice as many deaths in 1994 as in 1950; the article's Author reworded that claim and created a very different meaning.

It is worth examining the history of this statistic. It began with the CDF noting that child gunshot deaths doubled from 1950 to 1994. This is not quite as dramatic an increase as it might seem. Remember that the U.S. population also rose throughout this period; in fact, it grew about 73 percent—or nearly double. Therefore, we might expect all sorts of things—including the number of child gunshot deaths—to increase, to nearly double just because the population grew. Before we can decide whether twice as many deaths indicates that things are getting worse, we'd have to know more.* The CDF statistic raises other issues as well: Where did the statistic come from? Who counts child gun-shot deaths, and how? What do they mean by a "child" (some CDF statistics about violence include everyone under age 25)? What do they mean "killed by guns" (gunshot death statistics often include suicides and accidents, as well as homicides)? But people rarely ask questions of this sort when they encounter statistics. Most of the time, most people simply *accept statistics without question.*

Certainly, the article's Author didn't ask many probing, critical questions about the CDF's claim. Impressed by the statistic, the Author *repeated* it—well, meant to repeat it. Instead, by rewording the CDF's claim, the Author created a *mutant statistic,* one garbled almost beyond recognition.

But people treat mutant statistics just as they do other statistics—that is, they usually accept even the most implausible claims without question.

Statistics, then, have a bad reputation. We suspect that statistics may be wrong, that people who use statistics may be "lying"—trying to manipulate us by using numbers to somehow distort the truth. Yet, at the same time, we need statistics; we depend upon them to summarize and clarify the nature of our complex society. This is particularly true when we talk about social problems. Debates about social problems routinely raise questions that demand statistical answers: Is the problem widespread? How many people—and which people—does it affect? Is it getting worse? What does it cost society? What will it cost to deal with it? Convincing answers to such questions demand evidence, and that usually means numbers, measurements, statistics.

But can't you prove anything with statistics? It depends on what "prove" means. If we want to know, say, how many children are "gunned down" each year, we can't simply guess—pick a number from thin air: one hundred, one

---

*For instance, since only child victims are at issue, a careful analysis would control for the relative sizes of the child population in the two years. We ought to have assurances that the methods of counting child gunshot victims did not change overtime, and so on.

thousand, ten thousand, 35 trillion, whatever. Obviously, there's no reason to consider an arbitrary guess "proof " of anything. However, it might be possible for someone—using records kept by police departments or hospital emergency rooms or coroner—to keep track of children who have been shot; compiling careful, complete records might give us a fairly accurate idea of the number of gunned-down children. If that number seems accurate enough, we might consider it very strong evidence—or proof.

The solution to the problem of bad statistics is not to ignore all statistics, or to assume that every number is false. Some statistics are bad, but others are pretty good, and we need statistics—good statistics—to talk sensibly about social problems. The solution, then, is not to give up on statistics, but to become better judges of the numbers we encounter. We need to think critically about statistics—at least critically enough to suspect that the number of children gunned down hasn't been doubling each year since 1950.

Social statistics describe society, but they are also products of our social arrangements. The people who bring social statistics to our attention have reasons for doing so; they inevitably want something, just as reporters and the other media figures who repeat and publicize statistics have their own goals. Statistics are tools, used for particular purposes. Thinking critically about statistics requires understanding their place in society.

While we may be more suspicious of statistics presented by people with whom we disagree—people who favor different political parties or have different beliefs—bad statistics are used to promote all sorts of causes. Bad statistics come from conservatives on the political right and liberals on the left, from wealthy corporations and powerful government agencies, and from advocates of the poor and the powerless.

Mutant Statistics

Methods for Mangling Numbers

Not all statistics start out bad, but any statistic can be made worse. Numbers—even good numbers—can be misunderstood or misinterpreted. Their meanings can be stretched, twisted, distorted, or mangled. These alterations create what we can call *mutant statistics*—distorted versions of the original figures.

Many mutant statistics have their roots in innumeracy. Remember that innumeracy—difficulties grasping the meanings of numbers and calculations—is widespread. The general public may be innumerate, but often the advocates promoting social problems are not any better. They may become confused about a number's precise meaning; they may misunderstand how the problem has been defined, how it has been measured, or what sort of sampling has been used. At the same time, their commitment to their cause and their enthusiasm for promoting the problem ("After all, it's a big problem!") may lead them to "improve" the statistic, to make the numbers seem more dramatic, even more compelling. Some mutant statistics may be products of advocates' cynicism, of their deliberate attempts to distort information in order to make their claims more convincing; this seems particularly likely when mutation occurs at the hands of large institutions that twist information into the form most favorable to their vested interests. But mutation can also be a product of sincere, albeit muddled interpretations by innumerate advocates.

Once someone utters a mutant statistic, there is a good chance that those who hear it will accept it and repeat it. Innumerate advocates influence their audiences: the media repeat mutant statistics; and the public accepts—or at least does not challenge—whatever numbers the media present. A political leader or a respected commentator may hear a statistic and repeat it, making the number seem even more credible. As statistics gain wide circulation, number laundering occurs. The figures become harder to challenge because everyone has heard them, everyone assumes the numbers must be correct. Particularly when numbers reinforce our beliefs, prejudices, or interests ("Of course that's true!"), we take figures as facts, without subjecting them to criticism.

Once created, *mutant statistics have a good chance of spreading and enduring.* But how and why does mutation occur? This chapter explores four common ways of creating mutant numbers. It begins with the most basic errors—making inappropriate *generalizations* from a statistic. It then turns to *transformations*—taking a number that means one thing and interpreting it to mean something completely different. The third section concerns *confusion*—transformations that involve misunderstanding the meaning of more complicated statistics. Finally, we'll consider *compound errors*—the ways in which bad statistics can be linked to form chains of error. In these four ways, bad statistics not only take on lives of their own, but they do increasing damage as they persist.

Generalization: Elementary Forms of Error

Generalization is an essential step in statistical reasoning. We rarely are able to count all the cases of some social problem. Instead, we collect some evidence, usually from a sample, and generalize from it to the larger problem. The process of generalization involves the basic processes discussed in chapter 2: the problem must be defined, and a means of measurement and a sample must be chosen.

These are elementary steps in social research. The basic principles are known: definitions and measures need to be clear and reasonable;

samples should be representative. But even the most basic principles can be violated and, surprisingly often, no one notices when this happens. Mutant statistics—based on flawed definitions, poor measurements, or bad samples—emerge, and often receive a surprising amount of attention.

Questionable Definitions

Consider the flurry of media coverage about an "epidemic" of fires in African American churches in the South in 1996. Various advocates charged that the fires were the work of a racist conspiracy. Their claims recalled the history of racial terrorism in the South; black churches had often been targets of arson or bombing. Perhaps because 1996 was an election year, politicians—both Democrats (including President Clinton and Vice President Gore) and Republicans—denounced the fires, as did both the liberal National Council of Churches and the conservative Christian Coalition. Virtually everyone spoke out against the wave of arson.

Activists (such as the antiracist Center for Democratic Renewal) tried to document the increased number of fires; they produced lists of church arsons and statistics about the number of suspicious fires as evidence that the problem was serious. However, investigations, first by journalists and later by a federal task force, called these claims into question. While there were certainly some instances in which whites burned black churches out of racist motives, there was no evidence that a conspiracy linked the various fires. Moreover, the definition of a suspicious church fire proved to be unclear; the activists' lists included fires at churches with mostly white congregations, fires known to have been set by blacks, or by teenage vandals, or by mentally disturbed individuals, and fires set in order to collect insurance. And, when journalists checked the records of the fire insurance industry, they discovered not only that the number of fires in 1996 was not unusually high, but that church arsons had been generally declining since at least 1980. The federal task force ultimately failed to find any evidence of either an epidemic of fires or a conspiracy, although the press gave the task force report little coverage and advocates denounced the study's findings.

In short, statistics attempting to demonstrate the existence of an epidemic of church arsons lacked a clear definition of what ought to count as a racially motivated church fire. Nor did advocates define how many fires it would take to constitute an "epidemic" (although it would presumably be some number above the normal annual total of church fires). The absence of any clear definitions made it difficult to assess the evidence. The advocates who offered lists of fires (and asserted that each blaze was evidence of a racist conspiracy) may have been convinced, but those who tried to identify cases using some sort of clear definition failed to find any evidence that the epidemic even existed.

Inadequate Measurement

Clear, precise definitions are not enough. Whatever is defined must also be measured, and meaningless measurements will produce meaningless statistics. For instance, consider recent federal efforts to count hate crimes (crimes motivated by racial, religious, or other prejudice).

In response to growing concern about hate crimes, the federal government began collecting hate-crime statistics. The Federal Bureau of Investigation invited local law enforcement agencies to submit annual reports on hate crimes within their jurisdictions and, beginning in 1991, the bureau began issuing national hate-crime statistics.

Although the FBI had collected data on the incidence of crime from local agencies for decades, counting hate crimes posed special problems. When police record a reported crime—say, a robbery—it is a relatively straightforward process: usually the victim comes forward and tells of being forced to surrender money to the robber; these facts let the police classify the crime as a robbery. But identifying a hate crime requires something more: an assessment of the criminal's *motive*. A robbery might be a hate crime—*if* prejudice motivates the robber—but the crimes committed by robbers with other motives are not hate crimes. There are real disagreements about how to define and measure hate crimes. Not surprisingly, some activists favor broad, inclusive standards that will avoid false negatives; some feminists, for example, argue that rapes automatically should be considered hate crimes (on the grounds that all rape is motivated by gender prejudice). But local officials (who may be reluctant to publicize tensions within their communities) may favor much narrower standards, so that a cross-burning on an African American family's lawn may be classified as a "teenage prank," rather than a hate crime, depending on how police assess the offenders' motives.

While the recordkeeping may improve over time, the hate-crime statistics reported during the program's early years were nearly worthless. The organizational practices for recording hate crimes obviously varied widely among jurisdictions, making meaningful comparisons impossible. Moreover, it should be noted that, as reporting does improve, the numbers of reported hate crimes will almost certainly increase. That is, incidents that previously would not have been counted as hate crimes will be counted, and successive annual reports will show the incidence of hate crime rising. It may be years before measurement becomes sufficiently standardized to permit meaningful comparisons among jurisdictions, or from year to year. Measurement is always important, but this example illustrates why new statistical measures should be handled with special caution.

Bad Samples

Chapter 2 emphasized the importance of generalizing from representative samples. This is a basic principle, but one that is easily lost.

For example, consider a study subtitled "A Survey of 917,410 Images, Descriptions, Short Stories, and Animations Downloaded 8.5 Million Times by Consumers in Over 2000 Cities in Forty Countries, Provinces, and Territories." An undergraduate student published this research in 1995 in a law review; he reported that 83.5 percent of the downloaded images were pornographic. In 1995, the Internet was still a novel phenomenon; people worried that children were frequent users, and that parents did not understand the Internet well enough to protect their children from questionable content. Claims that an extensive research project revealed that a substantial majority of Internet traffic involved pornography generated considerable concern. The huge scope of the study—917,410 images downloaded 8.5 million times—implied that it must be exhaustive.

But, of course, a large sample is not necessarily a good sample. In this case, the researcher did not collect a representative sample of Internet traffic. Rather, he examined postings to only 17 of some 32 Usenet groups that carried image files. Phrased differently, his findings showed that pornographic images accounted for only about 3 percent of Usenet traffic, while Usenet accounted for only about an eighth of the traffic on the entire Internet. In short, the sample of images was drawn from precisely that portion of the Internet where pornographic images were concentrated; it was anything but a representative sample. An alternative way to summarize the study's findings was that only 0.5 percent of Internet traffic involved pornographic images—a markedly lower (and less dramatic) figure than 83.5 percent. This example reminds us that mistaking a large sample for a representative sample can be a serious error.

Transformation: Changing the Meaning of Statistics

Another common form of mutant statistic involves transforming a number's meaning. Usually, this involves someone who tries to repeat a number, but manages to say something different. This chapter's introduction offers an example: recall that 150,000 people with anorexia became 150,000 deaths from anorexia. Of course, not all transformations are as obvious as equating having a disease with dying from it. Often transformations involve more subtle misunderstandings or logical leaps.

Consider the evolution of one critic's estimate that "six percent of America's 52,000 [Roman Catholic] priests are at some point in their adult lives sexually preoccupied with minors." This estimate originated with a psychologist and former priest who treated disturbed clergy and derived the figure from his observations. It was, in short, an educated guess. Still, his claim was often repeated (it was undoubtedly the only statistic available) and, in the process, transformed in at least four important ways. First, some of those who repeated the figure forgot that it was an estimate, and referred to the number as though it were a well-established fact—presumably a finding from a survey of priests. Second, while the psychologist's estimate was based on a sample of priests who had sought psychological treatment (and therefore might well be especially likely to have experienced inappropriate attractions to young people), he generalized to all priests. Third, although the original estimate referred to sexual *attraction*, rather than actual behavior, those who repeated the number often suggested that 6 percent of all priests had had sexual contacts with young people. Fourth, those young people became redefined as "children"; critics charged that 6 percent of priests were pedophiles ("pedophiles" are adults who have sex with prepubescent children). Although the original estimate in fact suggested that twice as many priests were attracted to adolescents as to younger children, this subtlety was lost. Thus, an estimate that perhaps 6 percent of priests in treatment were at some point sexually attracted to young people was transformed into the fact that 6 percent of all priests had had sex with children. Not everyone who repeated the statistic made all four transformations, but the number's original meaning soon became lost in a chorus of claims linking "pedophile priests" to the 6 percent figure.

This example suggests that a single statistic can be transformed in several ways, that it is impossible to predict all the ways a number might be misunderstood and given an entirely new meaning. While it may be especially easy to transform estimates and guesses (because the language of guessing is often vague), even more precisely defined statistics can undergo transformation.

Transformations involve shifts in meaning; advocates convert a statistic about X into a statistic about Y. This is an obvious error. Sometimes transformations are inadvertent; they reflect nothing more than sloppy, imprecise language. In such cases, people try to repeat a statistic, but they accidentally reword a claim in a way that creates a whole new meaning. Of course, other transformations may be deliberate efforts to mislead in order to advance the advocates' cause.

Certainly *transformations often "improve" a claim by making it more dramatic:* the number of anorexics becomes a body count; priests attracted to adolescents become priests having sex with children; homicides of unknown circumstances become serial killings. Such statistics get repeated precisely because they are dramatic, compelling numbers. A transformation that makes a statistic seem less dramatic is likely to be forgotten, but a more dramatic number stands a good chance of being repeated. It is a statistical version of Gresham's Law: *bad statistics drive out good ones.*

Transformation only requires that one person misunderstand a statistic and repeat the number in a way that gives it a new meaning. Once that new meaning— the mutant statistic—is available, many of the ways people may respond to it— accepting it, repeating it, or simply not challenging it—help maintain the error. Even if someone recognizes the mistake and calls attention to it, the error is likely to live on, uncorrected in many people's minds.

Confusion: Garbling Complex Statistics

The examples we've discussed so far in this chapter involve misunderstanding relatively simple, straightforward statistics. But some statistics get mangled because they seem too difficult to grasp, and therefore they are easily confused.

Consider *Workforce 2000*, a 1987 report, commissioned by the U.S. Department of Labor, that projected changes in the American workforce. The population in the workforce is gradually changing for several reasons: most important, a growing proportion of women work, so females account for a growing percentage of workers; in addition, the percentage of workers who are nonwhites is growing (this reflects several developments, including immigration patterns and ethnic differences in birth rates). The combined effect of these changes is gradually to reduce the proportion of white males in the workforce: in 1988 (roughly when *Workforce 2000* appeared), white males accounted for 47.9 percent of all workers; and the report projected that, by 2000, this percentage would fall to 44.8 percent.

However, rather than describing the change in such easily understood terms, the authors of *Workforce 2000* chose to speak of "net additions to the workforce" (see Table 1). What did this term mean? Very simply, the report made predictions about the populations of workers that would enter and leave the workforce (because of death, retirement, and so on) between 1988 and 2000. For example, the authors estimated that 13.5 million white males would join the workforce and 11.3 million would leave during those years. The difference—2.2 million—would be white males' "net addition to the workforce." Because the numbers of female and nonwhite workers are growing faster than those of white males, white males made up a relatively small share—less than 15 percent—of the anticipated total net addition to the workforce.

Rather than describing the gradual decline in white males' proportion of the workforce in terms of a straightforward percentage (47.9 percent in 1988, falling to 44.8 percent in 2000), the authors of *Workforce 2000* chose to use a more obscure measure (net additions to the workforce). That was an unfortunate choice, because it invited confusion. In fact, it even confused the people who prepared the report. *Workforce 2000* came with an "executive summary"—a brief introduction summarizing the report's key points for those too busy to read the entire document. The *Executive Summary to Workforce 2000* mangled the report's findings by claiming: "Only 15 percent of the new entrants to the labor force over the next 13 years will be native white males, compared to 47 percent in that category today." That sentence was wrong for two reasons: first, it confused *net additions* to the labor force (expected to be roughly 15 percent white males) with all *new entrants* to the labor force (white males were expected to be about 32 percent of all those entering the labor force); and, second, it made

Table 1 Projected Net Additions to the Workforce by Ethnicity and Sex, 1988–2000

Worker Category	Projected Net Additions[a]	Percentage
Non-Hispanic white males	2,265,000	11.6
Non-Hispanic white females	6,939,000	35.6
Hispanic males	2,877,000	14.8
Hispanic females	2,464,000	12.7
Black males	1,302,000	6.7
Black females	1,754,000	9.0
Asian & other males	950,000	4.9
Asian & other females	910,000	4.7
Total	19,461,000	100.0

Source: Howard N. Fullerton, "New Labor Force Projections, Spanning 1988 to 2000," Monthly Labor Review 112 (November 1989): 3–11 (Table 7).

Note: The data used in this table are similar to, but not precisely the same as those used to prepare Workforce 2000. Therefore, some of the figures are close to—but not precisely the same as—those quoted from the report.

[a] Projected net additions is a total—the number of workers expected to enter the workforce, minus the number expected to leave through death, retirement, and so on.

a meaningless comparison between the percentage of white males among net workforce entrants and white males' percentage in the existing labor force (roughly 47 percent). The statistical comparison seemed dramatic, but it was pointless.

Unfortunately, the dramatic number captured people's attention. The press fixed on the decline in white male workers as the report's major finding, and they began to repeat the error. Officials at the Department of Labor tried to clarify the confusion, but the mutant statistic predictably took on a life of its own. Politicians, labor and business leaders, and activists all warned that the workplace was about to undergo a sudden change, that white males—historically the typical, the most common category of workers—were an endangered species. The mangled statistic was itself remangled; for example, one official testified before Congress: "By the year 2000, nearly 65% of the total workforce will be women," yet no one asked how or why that might occur. Claims about the vanishing white male worker flourished.

It is easy to see why people repeated these claims; the notion that white males would soon become a small proportion of all workers offered support for very different political ideologies. Liberals saw the coming change as proof that more needed to be done to help women and minorities—who, after all, would be the workers of the future. Liberal proposals based on *Workforce 2000* called for expanded job training for nontraditional (that is, nonwhite or female) workers, additional programs to educate management and workers about the need for diversity in the workplace, and so on. In contrast, conservatives viewed the changing workforce as further evidence that immigration, feminism, and other developments threatened traditional social arrangements. In response to claims that white male workers were disappearing, a wide range of people found it easier to agree ("We knew it! We told you so!") than to ask critical questions about the statistical claims.

The reaction to *Workforce 2000* teaches a disturbing lesson: *complex statistics are prime candidates for mutation.* Not that the statistics in *Workforce 2000* were all that complex—they weren't. But the meaning of "net additions to the workforce" was not obvious, and when people tried to put it in simpler language—such as "new workers"—they mangled the concept. The report's authors made a poor choice when they chose to highlight statistics about net additions; they invited the confusion that followed. They ought to have realized that most people would not grasp this relatively complicated idea. (*Never overestimate the understanding of an innumerate public.*) And, of course, the people who interpreted the report (beginning with the authors of the executive summary!), instead of repeating the statistic, unintentionally mangled it to produce figures with new, wildly distorted meanings. Thus, a correct-but-difficult-to-understand statistic became an easy-to-understand-but-completely-wrong number.

Compound Errors: Creating Chains of Bad Statistics

I have suggested that bad statistics often take on a life of their own. Rarely criticized, they gain widespread acceptance, and they are repeated over and over. Each repetition makes the number seem more credible—after all, everyone agrees that that's the correct figure. And, of course, bad statistics can become worse through mutation: through misuse or misunderstanding, the number becomes further distorted. But that's not the end of the process. Bad statistics can have additional ramifications when they become the basis for calculating still more statistics.

We can think about this process as compounding errors into a chain of bad statistics: one questionable number becomes the basis for a second statistic that is, in turn, flawed; and the process can continue as the second bad number leads to a third, and so on—each number a link in a chain of errors.

Consider, for example, some of the uses to which the Kinsey Reports have been put. During the 1930s and 1940s, the biologist Alfred Kinsey and his colleagues conducted lengthy interviews with several thousand people about their sexual experiences. These interviews became the basis for two books: *Sexual Behavior in the Human Male* (1948) and *Sexual Behavior in the Human Female* (1953), popularly known as the "Kinsey Reports." The books challenged the polite fiction that most sex was confined to marriage; they revealed that many people had experience with a wide range of sexual behaviors, such as masturbation and premarital sex. However, the Kinsey data could not provide accurate estimates for the incidence of different sexual behaviors. While the thousands of interviews constituted a large sample, that sample was not representative, let alone random. The sample contained a much higher proportion of college-educated people than the general population and, in an effort to explore a broad range of sexual experiences, Kinsey deliberately arranged interviews with a substantial number of active homosexuals, as well as with many individuals who had been imprisoned. Nonetheless, commentators sometimes treat the Kinsey findings as though they offer an authoritative, representative portrait of the American population. For example, gay and lesbian activists sometimes argue that one-tenth of the population is homosexual, and they refer to the Kinsey Reports to support this claim.

Rather than define heterosexual and homosexual as a simple dichotomy, the Kinsey Reports described a continuum that ranged from individuals who had never had a homosexual experience, to those who had some incidental homosexual experiences, and so on through those whose sexual experiences had been exclusively homosexual. Still, the male report estimated that "10 per cent of the males are more or less exclusively homosexual... for at least three years between the ages of 16 and 55." (Later surveys, based on more representative samples, have concluded that the one-in-ten estimate exaggerated the amount of homosexuality; typically, they find that 3–6 percent of males [and a lower percentage of females] have had significant homosexual experience at some point in their lives [usually in adolescence or early adulthood], and that the incidence of homosexuality among adults is lower—between 1 and 3 percent.) However, gay and lesbian activists often dispute these lower estimates; they prefer the one-in-ten figure because it suggests that homosexuals are a substantial minority group, roughly equal in number to African Americans—too large to be ignored. Thus, the 10 percent figure lives on, and it is often used in calculating other, new statistics about gays and lesbians.

Consider, for example, claims that one-third of teen suicides—or roughly 1,500 deaths per year—involve gay or lesbian adolescents. Gay activists invoked this statistic to portray the hardships gay and lesbian youth confront; it suggests that stigma and social isolation are severe enough to drive many adolescents to kill themselves.

But how could anyone hope to measure gay teen suicides accurately? Many gays and lesbians try to conceal their sexual orientation, and certainly some teenagers might feel driven to suicide because keeping that secret was becoming a burden. But, given this secrecy, how could anyone know just which teenagers who commit suicide are gay or lesbian? Coroners, after all, do not record sexual orientation on death certificates.

So how did advocates arrive at the statistic that one-third of teenagers who kill themselves are homosexual? The answer is that they constructed a chain of bad statistics. They began with the familiar, Kinsey-based claim that one-tenth of the population—including, presumably, one-tenth of teenagers—were homosexual. Roughly 4,500 teenage deaths are attributed to suicide each year; on average, then, 10 percent of those—450 suicides—should involve gay or lesbian teens. (Note that we have already incorporated our first dubious statistic—derived from Kinsey's questionable sample—that 10 percent of the population is gay or lesbian.)

Next, advocates drew upon various studies that suggested that homosexuals attempted suicide at a rate two to three times higher than heterosexuals. Note that this figure presumes knowledge about the rates of an often secretive behavior in two populations—one itself often hidden. Multiplying 10 percent (the estimated proportion of homosexuals in the population) by 3 (a suicide rate estimated to be three times higher than that of heterosexuals) led to an estimate that gays and lesbians accounted for 30 percent of suicides—and this figure was in turn rounded up to one-third.* Thus, one-third of 4,500 teen suicides—1,500 deaths—involve gay or lesbian youths.

Notice how the final figure depends on the advocates' assumptions. If the proportion of homosexuals among all teenagers is estimated at 3 percent, or 6 percent, the number of gay teen suicides falls. If the rate at which homosexual teens commit suicide is only twice that of heterosexuals, the number falls. (For example, if we instead assume that 3 percent of the adolescent population is gay or lesbian, and that their suicide rate is twice that of heterosexuals, homosexuals would account for less than 6 percent of all teen suicides.) The final figure depends completely on the assumptions used to make the calculations.

This example offers two important lessons. The first is a reminder that bad statistics can live on. Most social scientists consider Kinsey's

---

* There is another innumerate error hidden here. Even if 10 percent of the population is homosexual, and their suicide rate is three times that of heterosexuals, homosexuals should account for only one-quarter—not one-third—of suicides. Let Z be the suicide rate for heterosexuals; if: (.1 [the proportion of the population that is homosexual] x 3Z) + (.9 [the proportion of the population that is heterosexual] x Z) = 4,500 (the total number of teen suicides), then: (.1 x 3Z) = 1,125 = one-quarter of 4,500.

10 percent estimate for homosexuality too high; more recent, more reliable studies have consistently produced lower estimates. Yet some gay and lesbian activists continue to cite the higher figure—precisely because it is the largest available number. In turn, 10 percent often figures into other calculations—not just about gay teen suicides, but also regarding the number of gay voters, the size of the gay population at risk of AIDS, and so on.

The second lesson is perhaps harder to learn. Any claim about the number of gay teen suicides should set off alarm bells. Given the difficulties in learning which deaths are suicides and which teenagers are gay, it obviously would be hard to learn the number of gay teen suicides. It is not unreasonable to ask how the advocates arrived at that number, and which assumptions lay behind their calculations. Those assumptions may be perfectly defensible, but they deserve to be examined. But, of course, such examinations are the exception, not the rule. Once offered, a statistic—such as the claim that gays and lesbians account for one-third of all teen suicides—tends to be repeated, to circulate widely, without confronting questions about its validity.

Compound errors can begin with any of the standard sorts of bad statistics—a guess, a poor sample, an inadvertent transformation, perhaps confusion over the meaning of a complex statistic. People inevitably want to put statistics to use, to explore a number's implications. An estimate for the number of homeless persons can help us predict the costs of social services for the homeless, just as an estimate of the proportion of the population that is homosexual lets us predict the number of gay and lesbian teenagers who may attempt suicide. But, when the original numbers are bad—and we have already explored some of the many ways bad numbers can come into circulation—compound errors can result. Assessing such statistics requires another level of critical thinking: one must ask both how advocates produced the statistic at hand (1,500 gay teen suicides), and whether they based their calculations on earlier numbers that are themselves questionable (e.g., 10 percent of the population is homosexual). The strengths and weaknesses of those original numbers should affect our confidence in the second-generation statistics.

Characteristics of Good Statistics

There is much criticism about the production of bad statistics through guessing, dubious definitions, questionable measurement, and poor sampling. At this point, you may be wondering whether all statistics are bad, nothing more than "damned lies." Are there any good statistics? How can we tell the good numbers from the bad?

The problems identified in this chapter suggest some standards that good statistics meet. First, *good statistics are based on more than guessing.* The most basic question about any statistic is: How did someone arrive at this number? All statistics are imperfect, but some flaws are worse than others. Obviously, we should not place too much confidence in guesses (even educated guesses). Watch for the danger signs of guessing: Do the people offering the statistic have a bias—do they want to show that the problem is common (or rare)? Is the statistic a big, round number? Does the statistic describe an unfamiliar, hidden social problem that probably has a large dark figure (if so, how did the advocates manage to come up with their numbers)?

Second, *good statistics are based on clear, reasonable definitions.* Remember, every statistic has to define its subject. Those definitions ought to be clear and made public. An example—particularly a dramatic, disturbing example, a horror story, a worst case—is not a definition. Anyone presenting a statistic describing a social problem should be able and willing to explain the definition used to create the statistic. Definitions usually are broad: they encompass kinds of cases very different from (and usually less serious than) the examples. We need to ask: How broad? What does the definition include? Again, ask yourself whether the people offering the statistic favor broad (or narrow) definitions, and why. Consider whether their definition might exclude too many false negatives or include too many false positives.

Third, *good statistics are based on clear, reasonable measures.* Again, every statistic involves some sort of measurement; while all measures are imperfect, not all flaws are equally serious. People offering a statistic should be able and willing to explain how they measured the social problem, and their choices should seem reasonable. If the people offering the statistic have some sort of bias (in favor of big—or small—numbers), that bias may be reflected in the way they've measured the problem. For example, they may have worded survey questions to encourage certain responses, or they may interpret responses in peculiar ways. Be suspicious of statistics based on hidden measurements, and consider how measurement choices might shape statistics.

Finally, *good statistics are based on good samples.* Clear, reasonable definitions and clear, reasonable measurements are not enough. Almost all statistics generalize from a sample of cases to a larger population, and the methods of selecting that sample should be explained. Good samples are representative of that larger population; ideally, this means the sample has been selected at random. Watch out for statistics based on small, non-random, convenience samples; such samples are easier and cheaper to study, but they are a poor basis for sweeping generalizations. Ask yourself how the sample chosen might skew the resulting statistics.

One sign of good statistics is that we're given more than a number; we're told something about the definitions, measurement and sampling behind the figure— about how the number emerged. When that information remains concealed, we have every reason to be skeptical.

DISCUSSION QUESTIONS

1. The statistic that each year half of all marriages end in divorce routinely makes the rounds in the media. Using the same logic that Best applied to the example of how many children are gunned down each year, explain why this divorce statistic is really a *mutant statistic*.

2. Why do you think statistics add such an air of credibility and authenticity to claims? Why don't we treat people's nonnumerical observations the same way?

3. Peruse any news outlet that you are familiar with and try to find an example of three statics that sound like they might be problematic. Which of Best's characteristics of mutant statistics do you think is at work with each?

4. If you met someone who promised that he or she could double your chances of winning the Powerball lottery for only $10, should you pay that person the money? Assume that he or she really would double your chances. Why or why not?

Culture, Socialization, and Interaction

Islands of Meaning

Eviatar Zerubavel

If you've ever spent any time around children, you've probably been either amused, grossed out, or both by their lack of appreciation for norms that adults take for granted. Perhaps you've had to explain to a disappointed child why he or she can't order ice cream for dinner, that scissors aren't toys, or why it's OK to jump on the trampoline outside but not on the bed inside. What children have not yet learned are the socially appropriate ways to categorize the world. For example, ice cream belongs in the dessert category, not the dinner category, and trampolines are toys, whereas beds are furniture. In this article, Zerubavel argues that learning the socially appropriate categorization conventions of one's culture is fundamental to creating the reality that we generally take for granted as simply existing objectively out in the physical world. One of the first things that new members of a society must do is learn how to see the islands of meaning (i.e., categories) that are conventionally used in that particular culture.

Zerubavel explains why categorization is so important to the process of socialization, and he describes the different processes used to create these islands of meaning, including lumping, splitting, and creating mental gaps. As you read, pay special attention to the language he uses to describe these processes; the words he uses are very physical in nature. He also uses numerous examples to show how what we tend to perceive as the inherent logic of categorizations are actually simply social conventions that could just as logically be arranged in a different way. If the categorizations were somehow inherent and obvious, children would never ask to have ice cream for dinner.

We transform the natural world into a social one by carving out of it mental chunks we then treat as if they were discrete, totally detached from their surroundings. The way we mark off islands of property is but one example of the general process by which we create meaningful social entities.

In order to endow the things we perceive with meaning, we normally ignore their uniqueness and regard them as typical members of a particular class of objects (a relative, a present), acts (an apology, a crime), or events (a game, a conference). After all, "If each of the many things in the world were taken as distinct, unique, a thing in itself unrelated to any other thing, perception of the world would disintegrate into complete meaninglessness." Indeed, things become meaningful only when placed in some category. A clinical symptom, for instance, is quite meaningless until we find some diagnostic niche (a cold, an allergic reaction) within which to situate and thus make sense of it. Our need to arrange the world around us in categories is so great that, even when we encounter mental odds and ends that do not seem to belong in any conventional category, we nonetheless "bend" them so as to fit them into one anyway, as we usually do with the sexually ambiguous or the truly novel work of art. When such adjustment does not suffice, we even create special categories (avant-garde, others, miscellaneous) for these mental pariahs.

Mental Gaps

Creating islands of meaning entails two rather different mental processes—lumping and splitting. On the other hand, it involves grouping "similar" items together in a single mental cluster—sculptors and filmmakers ("artists"), murder and arson ("felonies"), foxes and camels ("animals"). At the same time, it also involves separating in our mind "different" mental clusters from one another—artists from scientists, felonies from misdemeanors, animals from humans. In order to carve out of the flux surrounding us meaningful entities with distinctive identities, we must experience them as separate from one another.

Separating one island of meaning from another entails the introduction of some mental void between them. As we carve discrete mental chunks out of continuous streams of experience, we normally visualize substantial gaps separating them from one another. Such mental versions of the great divides that split continuous stretches of land following geological upheavals underlie our basic experience of mental entities as situated amid blank stretches of emptiness. It is our perception of the void among these islands of meaning that makes them separate in our mind, and its magnitude reflects the degree of separateness we perceive among them.

Gaps are critical to our ability to experience insular entities. The experiential separateness of the self, for example, is clearly enhanced by the actual gap of "personal space" that normally envelops it. By literally insulating the self from contact with others, such a gap certainly promotes its experience as an insular entity. A similar experience of an island situated in a vacuum often leads us to confine our horizons to, and never venture beyond, our neighborhood, hometown, or country. The great divides we visualize between women and men, children and adults, and blacks and whites likewise promote our perception of such entities as discrete.

Mental gaps are often represented by token partitions. Like the ancient Assyrians, who used mere doorways to demarcate the borders of their empire, we often use a partial wall or a column to create the illusion of a discrete work space or sitting area in a room. And like the ancient Egyptians, who used cartouches to cut off visually the names of monarchs from the rest of the text in which they were embedded, thus substantiating the social gulf that separated royalty from ordinary folk, we often use lines to portray the mental gap between news and commercial ads in newspapers.

Often, however, we represent mental gaps quite literally by blank spaces. When we wish not only to rank entities but also to portray the relative magnitude of the mental distances among them, a visual representation of the latter is of considerable help. I recall, for example, my eight-year-old daughter ranking her favorite restaurants and finding it necessary to "leave some space" between the first two and the third. The ability to visualize mental gaps is even more critical, of course, when we wish to depict the precise magnitude of such intervals.

Often, however, we need more than a blank space or silence to substantiate mental gaps. Along with the rites of passage that help us articulate transitions from one mental entity to another, we also use various "rites of separation" to highlight the gaps we visualize among them. Holidays, reunions, and parties, for example, inevitably dramatize the mental gap separating members who are invited to participate from nonmembers who are excluded. In so doing, they clearly promote our experience of ethnic groups, families, and fraternities as insular entities.

Rites of separation are often designed to dramatize the mental gap between the old and new selves of people whose social identity is radically transformed as a result of crossing some critical mental partition. Thus, for example, as they go through basic military training (in which they become soldiers), puberty rites (in which they officially become adults), and initiations into monastic orders (in which they are symbolically transformed into brides of Christ), recruits, children, and ordinary girls practically undergo a symbolic death. To dramatize the considerable mental gaps (separating civilians from soldiers, childhood from adulthood, and so on) involved in such transformations, they must ritually destroy their old self before they can assume their new identity. Men about to be married thus attend bachelor parties given by their old friends, newly enlisted soldiers relinquish their civilian clothes and much of their hair, and new nuns renounce their entire former life. A ritual name change helps monks, converts, slaves, brides, and adoptees articulate similar symbolic metamorphoses and dramatize the gap between their old identity and the new one.

Mental reality, in short, is deeply embedded in social reality. The gaps we perceive among the supposedly discrete entities that constitute social reality as well as the quantum leaps necessary for crossing them are admittedly mental. Nonetheless, once they are institutionalized, they become seemingly inevitable facts that we can no longer ignore or wish away. Along with the islands of meaning they help delineate, they are the very stuff that our social life is made of. Given their centrality to the way we organize our everyday life, such gaps are therefore quite real in their felt presence. Thus, if we perceive the world as made up of discrete entities, it is because, in a way, they indeed *are* discrete.

The Social Lens

I have thus far drawn a deliberately one-sided picture of reality as an array of insular entities neatly separated from one another by great divides. Such discontinuity, however, is not as inevitable as we normally take it to be. It is a pronouncedly mental scalpel that helps us carve discrete mental slices out of reality: "You get the illusion that [entities] are just there and are being named as they exist. But they can be... organized quite differently depending on how the knife moves.... It is important to see this knife for what it is and not to be fooled into thinking that [entities] are the way they are just because the knife happened to cut it up that way. It is important to concentrate on the knife itself." The scalpel, of course, is a *social* scalpel. It is society that underlies the way we generate meaningful mental entities.

Reality is not made up of insular chunks unambiguously separated from one another by sharp divides, but, rather, of vague, blurred-edge essences that often "spill over" into one another. It normally presents itself not in black and white, but, rather, in subtle shades of gray, with mental twilight zones as well as intermediate essences connecting entities. Segmenting it into discrete islands of meaning usually rests on some social convention, and most boundaries are, therefore, mere social artifacts. As such, they often vary from one society to another as well as across historical periods within each society. Moreover, the precise location—not to mention the very existence—of such mental partitions is often disputed even within any given society.

Culture and Classification

There is more than one way to carve discrete chunks out of a given continuum, and different cultures indeed mold out of the same reality quite different archipelagos of meaning. While all cultures, for example, distinguish the edible from the inedible or the young from the old, they usually differ from one another in where they draw the lines between them. The distinction between the sexually accessible and inaccessible is likewise universal (all cultures, for example, have an incest taboo), yet the specific delineation of those who are considered off limits often varies from one culture to another. Surrounding oneself with a bubble of "personal space," too, is a universal practice, yet, in marked contrast to other species, humans exhibit substantial subspecific cultural variations in where they draw its boundaries. (Along similar lines, the precise delineation of one's "personal" circle of intimates also varies from one culture to another.) By the same token, not everyone who is considered "black" in America would necessarily be classified as such in the West Indies or Brazil.

Languages differ from one another in the way they generate distinct lexical particles, and it is not unusual that a single word in one language would cover the semantic range of several separate words in another. Thus, for example, while there is a single word for both rats and mice in Latin, insects and airplanes in Hopi, and brothers-in-law and grandnephews in the Algonquian language of the Fox, there are separate words for blankets that are folded and spread out, for water in buckets and in lakes, and for dogs that stand and sit in Navajo. Such differences have considerable cognitive implications. After all, it is much easier to isolate a distinct mental entity from its surroundings when one has a word to denote it. That explains why the Navajo, who use different verbs to denote the handling of objects with different shapes, indeed tend to classify objects according to shape much more than English speakers. By the same token, lacking the necessary lexical tools for differentiating, it took me, a native speaker of Hebrew, a long time before I could actually notice the mental gaps—so obvious to English-speakers—that separate jelly from jam or preserves.

While such cross-cultural variability often leads us to look down on other cultures' classificatory schemas as primitive or "confused," it ought to help us recognize and accept the relative validity of our own. Only their ethnocentric blinders prevent those who claim that "savages" fail to notice obvious mental discontinuities from appreciating the highly sophisticated classificatory skills of these people, who clearly do make distinctions, though rarely among the things that we do.

Any notion of logic is valid only within a particular cultural milieu, and our own classifications are no more logical than those of "savages." We must therefore resist the ethnocentric tendency to regard our own way of classifying reality as the only reasonable way to do it. That entails giving up the idea that some ways of classifying are more correct and "logical" than others and, therefore, also reconsidering the standard tests through which we usually measure intelligence. Thus, for example, "a person, asked in what way wood and alcohol are alike [should not be] given a zero score if he answers: 'Both knock you out' [just] because the examiner prefers logical categories of scientific classification." By the same token, nor should we penalize someone who maintains (as did my daughter, when she was five) that the difference between a bus and an airplane lies in the fact that we need not pay the pilot on boarding a plane.

Ways of classifying reality vary not only across cultures but also across historical periods within the same culture. The last couple of centuries, for example, saw substantial shifts in the location of the lines we draw between the sexes, the "races," public and private, family and community.

Only two centuries ago, the mental gap between the sexes was so wide that women were perceived as "closer" to animals than to men and granting them political rights seemed as ludicrous as extending such rights to beasts. That this sounds so utterly absurd today only comes to show that absurdity is a function of where we draw lines, and that mental distances may change over time. Before the Civil War, when blacks were regarded in the United States as objects rather than persons, granting them civil rights would have legally been just as ludicrous. (In fact, public signs as Negroes and Dogs Not Allowed suggest that, until quit recently, they were still perceived in the South as "closer" to animals than to whites.) Only a few decades ago, the idea that homosexuals should be regarded as a distinct political minority would have been as absurd as granting such status to music teachers, baseball fans, or vegetarians. Rights have historically been extended to new social categories (prisoners, noncitizens, children, the insane, the preborn) whose legal standing prior to that would have been inconceivable.

Since it is the very basis of society reality, we often forget that language rests on mere convention and regard such mental entities, which are own creation, as if they were real.

It is society that helps us carve discrete islands of meaning out of our experience. Only English speakers, for example, can "hear" the gaps between the separate words in "perhaps they should have tried it earlier," which everyone else hears as a single chain of sound. Along similar lines, while people who hear jazz for the first time can never understand why a seemingly continuous stretch of music is occasionally interrupted by bursts of applause, jazz connoisseurs can actually "hear" the purely mental divides separating piano, bass, or drum "solos" from mere "accompaniment." Being a member of society entails "seeing" the world through special mental lenses. It is these lenses, which we acquire only through socialization, that allow us to perceive "things." The proverbial Martian cannot see the mental partitions separating Catholics from Protestants, classical from popular music, or the funny from the crude. Like the contours of constellations, we "see" such fine lines only when we learn that we should expect them there. As real as they may feel to us, boundaries are mere figments of our minds. Only the socialized can "see" them. To all cultural outsiders they are totally invisible.

Only through such "glasses" can entities be "seen." As soon as we remove them, boundaries practically disappear and the "things" they delineate fade away. What we then experience is as continuous as is Europe or the Middle East when seen from space or in ancient maps, or our own neighborhood when fog or heavy snow covers curbs and property lines, practically transforming familiar milieus into a visually undifferentiated flux. This is the way reality must appear to the unsocialized—a boundless, unbroken world with no lines. That is the world we would have inhabited were it not for society.

DISCUSSION QUESTIONS

1. Make a list of all the terms that Zerubavel uses to describe the process of categorization that are more conventionally used to describe physical acts. Why do you think he chose to use these types of terms?

2. How are lumping, splitting, and mental gaps part of the process of creating islands of meaning?

3. Zerubavel notes that mental gaps between categories are often reflected in physical gaps. Think about your classroom or where you work. Where do physical gaps reinforce mental gaps?

4. Think about your last trip to the grocery store. How are food items and other supplies generally organized? Have you ever had difficulty finding an item because it was categorized differently (and therefore in a different place in the store) than you thought it would be?

The Presentation of Self in Everyday Life

Erving Goffman

Most of us enter, participate in, and leave countless interactions each day without giving much thought to any of them. In fact, one of the most remarkable things about social interactions is how often they go smoothly. Simply getting to class, buying dinner, or spending time watching TV with friends involves an impressive amount of information gathering, decision making, action, and response. These mundane, often repeated, daily interactions wouldn't seem like they could have anything significant to tell us about the nature of social interaction, but in fact they do.

In this article, Erving Goffman introduces us to dramaturgy, which illuminates the underlying principles that govern just such mundane interactions. Dramaturgy is a theoretical perspective based on the analogy that face-to-face social interactions are like a theatrical performance. Goffman argues that in any face-to-face encounter, the participants engage in "the presentation of self," performing a role (student, employee, friend, significant other, etc.) just as a performer in a stage production would. Successful social actors look the part (appearance), act in a way that matches their role (manner), and play their role in the appropriate place (setting). These are referred to as sign vehicles.

For Goffman, we use sign vehicles to answer the question "What's going on here?" in every face-to-face interaction we have. The agreed upon answer to this question is what he refers to as the definition of the situation, which must be determined every time we enter into an interaction. We tend to only consciously notice this when things don't go as we expected. You probably didn't think too much about class the last time you arrived at your classroom. But imagine instead that you had arrived at your classroom to find all of the chairs pushed to the edges of the room, a disco ball hanging from the ceiling, your professor moonwalking, and 80s music playing from the computer. You would be very likely to ask or at least think, "What's going on here?" In Goffman's terms, the definition of the situation has been called into question. Your teacher's presentation of self does not match what we expect of a teacher in terms of appearance and manner, and the setting has changed significantly.

Importantly, from a dramaturgical perspective, we go through the same process of using sign vehicles to figure out the definition of the situation even when an interaction unfolds exactly as expected and we don't consciously think, "What's going on here." It's a bit like driving on a long stretch of boring road. You may have had the experience of zoning out while driving and suddenly realizing that 20 minutes had passed.[1] It wasn't that you stopped driving; you probably passed a few cars, tapped the brake a few times, and maybe even changed the radio station. But just because you weren't actively attending to the task of driving (as you might when you notice a police officer following behind you) doesn't mean you weren't paying attention and making decisions that are necessary to drive safely. Similarly, just because we don't actively attend to the assumptions and decisions we make about what's going on in most face-to-face interactions doesn't mean we're not still doing the cognitive work to arrive at a definition of the situation based on the sign vehicles we see.

Goffman's dramaturgical ideas are wonderfully easy to apply to your day-to-day life since dramaturgy is a microlevel theory. As you read, think about examples from your own life of the types of behaviors and interactional strategies that he describes.

Preface

The perspective employed in this report is that of the theatrical performances; the principles derived are dramaturgical ones. I shall consider the way in which the individual in ordinary work situations presents himself and his activity to others, the ways in which he guides and controls the impression they form of him, and the kinds of things he may and may not do while sustaining his performance before them.

Introduction

When an individual enters the presence of others, they commonly seek to acquire information about him or to bring into play information about him already possessed. They will be interested in his general socio-economic status, his conception of self, his attitude toward them, his competence, his trustworthiness, etc. Although some of this information seems to be sought almost as an end in itself, there are usually quite practical reasons for acquiring it. Information about the individual helps to define the situation, enabling others to know in advance what he will expect of them and what they may expect of him. Informed in these ways, the others will know how best to act in order to call forth a desired response from him.

For those present, many sources of information become accessible and many carriers (or "sign-vehicles") become available for conveying this information. If unacquainted with the individual, observers can glean clues from his conduct and appearance which allow them to apply their previous experience with individuals roughly similar to the one before them or, more important, to apply untested stereotypes at him. They can also assume from past experience that only individuals of a particular kind are likely to be found in a given social setting. They can rely on what the individual says about himself or on documentary evidence he provides as to who and what he is. If they know, or know of, the individual by virtue of experience prior to the interaction, they can rely on assumptions as to the persistence and generality of psychological traits as a means of predicting his present and future behavior.

Taking communication in both its narrow and broad sense, one finds that when the individual is in the immediate presence of others, his activity will have a promissory character. The others are likely to find that they must accept the individual on faith, offering him a just return while he is present before them in exchange for something whose true value will not be established until after he has left their presence. (Of course, the others also live by inference in their dealings with the physical world, but it is only in the world of social interaction that the objects about which they make inferences will purposely facilitate and hinder this inferential process.) The security that they justifiably feel in making inferences about the individual will vary, of course, depending on such factors as the amount of information they already possess about him, but no amount of such past evidence can entirely obviate the necessity of acting on the basis of inferences.

I have said that when an individual appears before others his actions will influence the definition of the situation which they come to have. Sometimes the individual will act in a thoroughly calculating manner, expressing himself in a given way solely in order to give the kind of impression to others that is likely to evoke from them a specific response he is concerned to obtain. Sometimes the individual will be calculating in his activity but be relatively unaware that this is the case. Sometimes he will intentionally and consciously express himself in a particular way, but chiefly because the tradition of his group or social status require this kind of expression and not because of any particular response (other than vague acceptance or approval) that is likely to be evoked from those impressed by the expression. Sometimes the traditions of an individual's role will lead him to give a well-designed impression of a particular kind and yet he may be neither consciously nor unconsciously disposed to create such an impression. The others, in their turn, may be suitably impressed by the individual's efforts to convey something, or may misunderstand the situation and come to conclusions that are warranted neither by the individual's intent nor by the facts. In any case, in so far as the others act *as if* the individual had conveyed a particular impression, we may take a functional or pragmatic view and say that the individual has "effectively" projected a given definition of the situation and "effectively" fostered the understanding that a given state of affairs obtains.

When we allow that the individual projects a definition of the situation when he appears before others, we must also see that the others, however passive their role may seem to be, will themselves effectively project a definition of the situation by virtue of their response to the individual and by virtue of any lines of action they initiate to him. Ordinarily the definitions of the situation projected by the several different participants are sufficiently attuned to one another so that open contradiction will not occur. I do not mean that there will be the kind of consensus that arises when each individual present candidly expresses what he really feels and honestly agrees with the expressed feelings of the others present. This kind of harmony is an optimistic ideal and in any case not necessary for the smooth working of society. Rather, each participant is expected to suppress his immediate heartfelt feelings, conveying a view of the situation which he feels the others will be able to find at least temporarily acceptable. The maintenance of this surface of agreement, this veneer of consensus, is facilitated by each participant concealing his own wants behind statements which assert values to which everyone present feels obliged to give lip service. Further, there is usually a kind of division of definitional labor. Each participant is allowed to establish the tentative official ruling regarding matters which are vital to him but not immediately important to others, e.g., the rationalizations and justifications by which he accounts for his past activity. In exchange for this courtesy he remains silent or non-committal on matters important to others but not immediately important to him. We have then a kind of interactional *modus vivendi*. Together the participants contribute to a single overall definition of the situation which involves not so much a real agreement as to what exists but rather a real agreement as to whose claims concerning what issues will be temporarily honored. Real agreement will also exist concerning the desirability of avoiding an open conflict of definitions of the situation.[2] I will refer to this level of agreement as a "working consensus." It is to be understood that the working consensus established in one interaction setting will be quite different in content from the working consensus established in a different type of setting

For the purpose of this report, interaction (that is, face-to-face interaction) may be roughly defined as the reciprocal influence of individuals upon one another's actions when in one another's immediate physical presence. *An* interaction may be defined as all the interaction which occurs throughout any one occasion when a given set of individuals are in one another's continuous presence; the term "an encounter" would do as well. A "performance" may be defined as all the activity of a given participant on a given occasion which serves to influence in any way any of the other participants. Taking a particular participant and his performance as a basic point of reference, we may refer to those who contribute the other performances as the audience, observers, or co-participants. The pre-established pattern of action which is unfolded during a performance and which may be presented or played through on other occasions may be called a "part" "routine."[3] These situational terms can easily be related to conventional structural ones. When an individual or performer plays the same part to the same audience on different occasions, a social relationship is likely to arise. Defining social role as the enactment of rights and duties attached to a given status, we can say that a social role will involve one or more parts and that each of these different parts may be presented by the performer on a series of occasions to the same kinds of audience or to an audience of the same persons.

Front

I have been using the term "performance" to refer to all the activity of an individual which occurs during a period marked by his continuous presence before a particular set of observers and which has some influence on the observers. It will be convenient to label as "front" that part of the individual's performance which regularly functions in a general and fixed fashion to define the situation for those who observe the performance. Front, then, is the expressive equipment of a standard kind intentionally or unwittingly employed by the individual during his performance. For preliminary purposes, it will be convenient to distinguish and label what seem to be the standard parts of front.

First, there is the "setting," involving furniture, dècor, physical layout, and other background items which supply the scenery and stage props for the spate of human action played out before, within, or upon it.

If we take the term "setting" to refer to the scenic parts of expressive equipment, one may take the term "personal front" to refer to the other items of expressive equipment, the items that we most intimately identify with the performer himself and that we naturally expect will follow the performer wherever he goes. As part of personal front we may include: insignia of office or rank; clothing; sex, age, and racial characteristics; size and looks; posture; speech patterns; facial expressions; bodily gestures; and the like. Some of these vehicles for conveying signs, such as racial characteristics, are relatively fixed and over a span of time do not vary for the individual from one situation to another. On the other hand, some of these sign vehicles are relatively mobile or transitory, such as facial expression, and can vary during a performance from one moment to the next.

It is sometimes convenient to divide the stimuli which make up personal front into "appearance" and "manner," according to the function performed by the information that these stimuli convey. "Appearance" may be taken to refer to those stimuli which function at the time to tell us of the performer's social statuses. These stimuli also tell us of the individual's temporary ritual state, that is, whether he is engaging in formal social activity, work, or informal recreation, whether or not he is celebrating a new phase in the season cycle or in his life-cycle. "Manner" may be taken to refer to those stimuli which function at the time to warn us of the interaction role the performer will expect to play in the oncoming situation. Thus a haughty, aggressive manner may give the impression that the performer expects to be the one who will initiate the verbal interaction and direct its course. A meek, apologetic manner may give the impression that the performer expects to follow the lead of others, or at least that he can be led to do so.

Regions and Region Behavior

It was suggested earlier that when one's activity occurs in the presence of other persons, some aspects of the activity are expressively accentuated and other aspects, which might discredit the fostered impression, are suppressed. It is clear that accentuated facts make their appearance in what I have called a front region; it should be just as clear that there may be another region—a "back region" or "back-stage"—where the suppressed facts make an appearance.

A back region or backstage may be defined as a place, relative to a given performance, where the impression fostered by the performance is knowingly contradicted as a matter of course. There are, of course, many characteristic functions of such places. It is here that the capacity of a performance to express something beyond itself may be painstakingly fabricated; it is here that illusions and impressions are openly constructed. Here stage props and items of personal front can be stored in a kind of compact collapsing of whole repertoires of actions and characters.[4] Here grades of ceremonial equipment, such as different types of liquor or clothes, can be hidden so that the audience will not be able to see the treatment accorded them in comparison with the treatment that could have been accorded them. Here devices such as the telephone are sequestered so that they can be used "privately." Here costumes and other parts of personal front may be adjusted and scrutinized for flaws. Here the team can run through its performance, checking for offending expressions when no audience is present to be affronted by them; here poor members of the team, who are expressively inept, can be schooled or dropped from the performance. Here the performer can relax; he can drop his front, forgo speaking his lines, and step out of character.

The Role of Expression in Conveying Impressions of Self

Perhaps a moral note can be permitted at the end. In this report the expressive component of social life has been treated as a source of impressions given to or taken by others. Impression, in turn, has been treated as a source of information about unapparent facts and as a means by which the recipients can guide their response to the informant without having to wait for the full consequences of the informant's actions to be felt. Expression, then, has been treated in terms of the communicative role it plays during social interaction and not, for example, in terms of a consumatory or tension-release function it might have in the expresser.[5]

Underlying all social interaction there seems to be a fundamental dialectic. When one individual enters the presence of others, he will want to discover the facts of the situation. Were he to possess this information, he could know, and make allowances for, what will come to happen and he could give the others present as much of their due as is consistent with his enlightened self-interest. To uncover fully the factual nature of the situation, it would be necessary for the individual to know all the relevant social data about the others. It would also be necessary for the individual to know the actual outcome or end product of the activity of the others during the interaction, as well as their innermost feelings concerning him. Full information of this order is rarely available; in its absence, the individual tends to employ substitutes—cues, tests, hints, expressive gestures, status symbols, etc.—as predictive devices. In short, since the reality that the individual is concerned with is unperceivable at the moment, appearances must be relied upon in its stead. And, paradoxically, the more the individual is concerned with the reality that is not available to perception, the more must he concentrate his attention on appearances.

The individual tends to treat the others present on the basis of the impression they give now about the past and the future. It is here that communicative acts are translated into moral ones. The impressions that the others give tend to be treated as claims and promises they have implicitly made, and claims and promises tend to have a moral character. In his mind the individual says: "I am using these impressions of you as a way of checking up on you and your activity, and you ought not to lead me astray." The peculiar thing about this is that the individual tends to take this stand even though he expects the others to be unconscious of many of their expressive behaviors and even though he may expect to exploit the others on the basis of the information he gleans about them. Since the sources of impression used by the observing individual involve a multitude of standards pertaining to politeness and decorum, pertaining both to social intercourse and task-performance, we can appreciate afresh how daily life is enmeshed in moral lines of discrimination.

DISCUSSION QUESTIONS

1. Goffman proposes that in every interaction we are each playing a role and that we must work to present our desired self to our audience. Is he saying that we are all being fake in all of our social interactions?

2. In what kinds of social situations are you most likely to be aware of your impression management efforts?

3. What are some of the examples of the impression management you do each time you are in class?

4. Can you think of an interaction that was either confusing or embarrassing because someone's performance did not go well? Using dramaturgical terms, explain why the interaction was uncomfortable.

5. How might Goffman's ideas be updated or modified to shed light on the ways people use online spaces like Facebook to present a self to the world?

6. Give two examples from your day-to-day life of when you are front stage and when you are backstage.

NOTES

1. Note that this is VERY different from distracted driving, like texting or talking on a cell phone when you really aren't paying attention to the fundamentals

of driving. This example is about distraction-free driving when you might be described as lost in your own thoughts or just listening to music or the radio.

2. An interaction can be purposely set up as a time and place for voicing differences in opinion, but in such cases participants must be careful to agree not to disagree on the proper tone of voice, vocabulary, and degree of seriousness in which all arguments are to be phrased, and upon the mutual respect which disagreeing participants must carefully continue to express toward one another. This debaters' or academic definition of the situation may also be invoked suddenly and judiciously as a way of translating a serious conflict of views into one that can be handled within a framework acceptable to all present.

3. For comments on the importance of distinguishing between a routine of interaction and any particular instance when this routine is played through, see John von Neumann and Oskar Morgenstern, *The Theory of Games and Economic Behaviour* (2nd ed.; Princeton: Princeton University Press, 1947), p.49.

4. As Métraux (*op. cit.*, p. 24) suggests, even the practice of voodoo cults will require such facilities:

   Every case of possession has its theatrical side, as shown in the matter of disguises. The rooms of the sanctuary are not unlike the wings of a theater where the possessed find the necessary accessories. Unlike the hysteric, who reveals his anguish and his desires through symptoms—a personal means of expression—the ritual of possession must conform to the classic image of a mythical personage.

5. A recent treatment of this kind may be found in Talcott Parsons, Robert F. Bales, and Edward A. Shils, *Working Papers in the Theory of Action* (Glencoe, Ill.: The Free Press, 1953), Chap. II, "The Theory of Symbolism in Relation to Action."

American Hookup

Lisa Wade

Socialization is the process of learning culture. One aspect of this is learning the expected behaviors and attitudes that go along with the different roles in that culture. We must learn what behaviors and attitudes are expected of men and women, college students, employees, friends, spouses, student athletes, or musicians just to name a few. Many roles can simply be added to our cultural repertoires, while others require the unlearning of a previous role.

Roles often have particular cultural scripts associated with them and these are an important part of how culture guides how we behave as we interact with one another. One example of this is finding a romantic partner. In the past 20 years, technology has drastically altered the way we connect and communicate with potential partners. In the past, making a stranger aware of your existence and interest generally required being in the same physical location at some point, but online dating sites like Match.com and OkCupid and dating apps like Bumble and Tinder have changed that. The script for meeting potential partners has changed.

Another place that the script for romantic encounters has been altered is on college campuses. Both the media and social scientists have devoted considerable attention to the rise of "hookup culture." Hooking up is an intentionally vague phrase that refers to a physical, romantic encounter that could range anywhere from kissing to having intercourse. Much of the concern about hookup culture is focused on the belief that college students are now having drastically more sex than they used to, but they aren't. Nor are they any less interested in having committed romantic relationships than in the past. As sociologist Lisa Wade points out in this excerpt from her book *American Hookup*, it isn't hookup itself that's a problem, it's hookup culture.

What hookup culture has changed is the script for finding partners. Hooking up and its required partying and drinking is often the predominant means available to meet potential partners. But hookup culture is also self-defeating as a means to find a committed romantic partner because the expression of any type of romantic interest, and even basic kindness, are considered taboo. For this and several other reasons she outlines in this excerpt, Wade describes hookup culture as a fog that has descended on college campuses . . . "an occupying force, coercive and omnipresent" that is neither enjoyable nor beneficial to a majority of students.

As you read, think about what the cultural script for finding romantic or sexual partners looks like at your school. Does the culture she describes sound familiar or alien? If hookup culture exists on your campus, but you chose not to participate, how does this shape your options for dating or other social opportunities?

The New Culture of Sex

"I love it here," Owen said happily, a freshman in college just back from winter break. "Last semester," he told me, "was one of the most interesting, exciting, and strangest times of my life."

Owen had grown up in a farming town in central California, graduating from a high school of about 60 students. Such a small group of peers made puberty awkward. "Everyone knew everything about everyone else," he said, so sexual experimentation was rare and, when indulged in, secretive. He'd had one clandestine affair, which he remembered fondly, but despite his good looks—lean and tallish with a broad, lopsided smile and tousled dark hair—Owen's sexual activities in high school were limited.

College promised to be a whole new world. His campus offered what felt like an endless supply of potential partners and more anonymity than he'd ever dreamed of. In his first semester, he sought casual sexual encounters with what he called *gusto*, and he had his fair share of good luck. "I'm shy and nerdy," he admitted, "but I clean up pretty well." It was everything he'd hoped it would be.

"I'm basically in a paradise full of girls I'm attracted to," he said, exhilarated, "everyone is fucking each other."

As his second semester progressed, though, his excitement started to waver. "A lot of the social life I've experienced," he observed wryly, "is some twisted sort of self-perpetuating vicious cycle of unrealistic expectations, boundless enthusiasm, and copious amounts of alcohol." He complained about mind games, soured friendships, and women who liked him only for his looks. "I can't expect any of the girls I'll meet on a Friday night to care about my personality or my favorite books," he grumbled. "That's just unrealistic." Some only talked to him when they wanted to share his weed. It was discouraging.

He partly blamed himself. "Oftentimes I just flat-out lack grace," he conceded. Other times he wasn't as openhearted as he wanted to be, acting distant or dismissive toward women to avoid being rejected himself. But he also felt like there was something particularly difficult about negotiating casual sex on campus. "I find it especially hard to try to smooth out a relationship with a girl whom I barely know beyond what color underwear she wears," he said, with a characteristic degree of self-deprecation.

As Owen's second semester progressed, he sounded increasingly uncertain, even morbid. "When I think about my sex life," he confessed, "it feels like my insides tie themselves tight together before they boil and rot." He hated the gossip that often followed an encounter. He began doubting himself. Things got dark and he started obsessing. "Worrying about it saps a lot of time and energy from my life," he said in frustration. By the end of the year, despite his initial interest, he had sworn off casual sexual encounters entirely: "I can't handle another negative sexual relationship in my life. My heart might break."

On campuses across America, students are sounding an alarm. They are telling us that they are depressed, anxious, and overwhelmed. Half of first-year students express concern that they are not emotionally healthy, and one in ten say that they frequently feel depressed. The transition from teenager to young adult is rarely easy, but this is more than just youthful angst. Students are less happy and healthy than in previous generations, less so even than just 10 or 20 years ago.

As Owen's transformation suggests, the sexual environment on college campuses is part of why. He anticipated an erotic and carefree life and, at first, that's what college seemed to offer. But, over the course of his first year, he became increasingly disillusioned. The reasons why are related to his specific encounters and are complicated by his personal story, but there is nothing unique about his disappointment.

The idea that college students are having a lot of sex is certainly an enthralling myth. Even students believe it. In Bogle's landmark study, students guessed that their peers were doing it 50 times a year. That's 25 times what the numbers actually show. In Kimmel's *Guyland*, young men figured that 80 percent of college guys were having sex any given weekend; they would have been closer to the truth if they were guessing the percent of men who had *ever* had sex. Students overestimate how much sex their peers are having, and by quite a lot.

In fact, today's students boast no more sexual partners than their parents did at their age. Scholars using the University of Chicago's General Social Survey have shown that they actually report slightly fewer sexual partners than Gen-Xers did. Millennials look more similar to the baby boomer generation than they do to the wild sexual cohort that they are frequently imagined to be.

There are students on campus with active sex lives, of course, but there are plenty with none at all and some with sexual escapades that are, at best, only "slightly less nonexistent" than they were in high school. The average graduating senior reports hooking up just eight times in four years. That amounts to one hookup per semester. Studies looking specifically at the sexual cultures at Duke, Yale, and East Carolina universities, the universities of Georgia and Tennessee, the State University of New York at Geneseo, and UC Berkeley report similar numbers. Not all students are hooking up, and those that do aren't necessarily doing so very often. Neither are students always hopping out of one bed and into another; half of those eight hookups are with someone the student has hooked up with before. Almost a third of students will graduate without hooking up a single time.

Despite the rumors, then, there is no epidemic of casual sexual encounters on college campuses. So, hookups can't be blamed. There just aren't enough of them to account for the malaise. Neither does two sexual encounters every twelve months, possibly with the same person, look like either female empowerment or male domination; if so, it's quite a tepid expression of power. There certainly is no bacchanalian Utopia, poly, queer, or otherwise. Students are too busy not having sex to be enacting the next revolution. The cause of students' unhappiness, then, can't be the hookup. But it is about hooking up, it's hookup *culture*.

Hookup culture is an occupying force, coercive and omnipresent. For those who love it, it's all sunshine, but it isn't for everyone else. Deep in the fog, students often feel dreary, confused, helpless. Many behave in ways they don't like, hurt other people unwillingly, and consent to sexual activity they don't desire.

Campuses of all kinds are in this fog. No matter the size of the college, how heavy a Greek or athletic presence it boasts, its exclusivity, its religious affiliation, or whether it's public or private, hookup culture is there. We find it in all regions of the country, from the Sunshine State of Florida to the sunny state of California. Students all over say so. Hookups are "part of our collegiate culture," writes a representative of the American South in the University of Florida's *Alligator*. If you don't hook up, warns a woman at the University of Georgia, then you're "failing at the college experience." A woman at Tulane puts it succinctly: "Hookup culture," she says, "it's college."

Hooking Up, a How-To

The goal is to look "fuckable," Miranda said, her voice buzzing with excitement. She and her roommate Ruby were tearing through their tiny closets, collecting a pile of "provocative" items to consider wearing to that night's party. The theme was *burlesque*, so they were going for a classy stripper vibe. Bridget offered her two cents as she headed back to her own room: "Lacy bras, corsets, fishnet stockings—anything that hints at being sexy underwear!" Ruby pulled on tights, short shorts, and calf-high boots. On top she wore a bright yellow bra and a see-through white tank top.

Miranda plumped her breasts and contemplated her outfit, a black crop top and a cherry red skirt with a zipper running down the front. She unzipped it a bit from the bottom and, then, a bit more. Ruby finished her "sleepy, drowsy, sexy eye look" with a splash of yellow to match the bra, just as Bridget walked back in balancing three shots of Smirnoff. "Let's get some dick tonight, ladies!" she yelled. They tossed back their shots and headed out. It was approaching midnight.

Across campus, Levi sat down at his computer and googled *burlesque party*, trying to figure out what to wear. The search returned mostly women in corsets. He turned to his friend and motioned to the screen. "It doesn't matter what you wear," his friend said sharply, "you're a guy." So, he put on a pair of "jeans and a nice green button-down shirt" that his mom had given him for Christmas. Satisfied, he looked at his reflection in the tall mirror tacked up on his dorm room closet: "I'd shaved recently, so I looked pretty sharp," he thought. His roommate smeared some gel through his dark hair, tugged on the front of his polo shirt, and swallowed the last of his beer. "Ready?"

Step 1: Pregame

"You don't walk out of the house without your shoes on and you don't walk into a party without a couple of shots of vodka," insisted one of my students. "It's real." The first step in hooking up is to get, as Miranda put it, "shitfaced."

Party-oriented students believe that drinking enhances their experience. Destiny, for example, gushed about how it felt to be a bit drunk at a college-sponsored concert:

> I honestly think I would not have had as much fun as I did if I wasn't intoxicated. . . . I couldn't care less about what people thought about me and felt free enough just to do whatever I wanted and to be bubbly and carefree. That night I didn't have a care in the world and it felt absolutely fantastic.

Students also tend to think that alcohol improves their personality. Getting drunk, they argue, brings out their "intoxicated self," one that is freer, more relaxed, less anxious, and generally more fun to be around. Destiny emphasized how alcohol made her feel carefree three times in as many sentences. Others believe that it gives them confidence. "I rely on mixed drinks and shots," wrote another female student. "They are not lying when they call it 'liquid courage.'"

Step 2: Grind

"If you can't dirty dance," insisted one of my female students, "then you can't dance at all." Grinding is the main activity at most college parties. Women who are willing press their backs and backsides against men's bodies and dance rhythmically. "It is a bestial rubbing of genitals reminiscent of mating zebras," Laura wrote scornfully after attending a party. "Guys were coming up behind women on the dance floor and placing their hands on their hips like two way-ward lobster claws, clamping on and pulling them close."

Because men generally come up to women from behind, sometimes the identity of the man whose penis abuts their backside is a mystery. In that case, instead of turning around—for reasons that will soon become clear—they peer over to their friends for an indication as to whether they should continue. As one of Ronen's students at Stanford observed:

> One woman mouthed to her single friend dancing across from her, "Is he hot?" The female friend motioned back "No" and the woman grimaced. She then gently disentangled herself from the man's hands around her hips and began provocatively dancing with her friend.

It is essential that he be *cute* because the ultimate goal in hookup culture isn't just to hook up, it's to hook up with the right person. Or, more specifically, a *hot* person. Hotness, says one female student, "is the only qualification one needs to be considered for a hookup." "Average guys just don't cut it," another wrote:

> Sure, it's not a social tragedy to hook up with an average-looking guy. But hooking up with someone attractive is a social asset for sure. It raises your standing in the hierarchy of potential partners. It makes you more attractive.

Using indicators like hotness, blondness, fraternity membership, and athletic prowess, students form a working consensus about who is hookup-worthy, and that guides their decisions. "So many hookups," confirmed one student, "are dictated by how our peers view the potential partner." She admitted that she usually asked other people what they thought of guys before getting together with them. "I am unable to separate my opinion from those of my friends," she wrote frankly.

Let me be careful to distinguish this from the idea that people seek sexual contact with others they find attractive. Nominally, at least, this idea acknowledges that people have individual tastes. Beauty, they say, is in the eye of the beholder. In hookup culture, though, beauty is in the eyes of the beholders, plural. A body's value is determined by collective agreement. It's crowdsourced.

Just as hooking up with a hot student can increase one's own popularity, hooking up with one widely considered unattractive can harm it. Because of this, students who are collectively categorized as unhot are sexual hot potatoes. Students fear being burned.

Kendra, for example, quite enjoyed her hookup. "I had fun," she remembered, "and it was a learning experience, and it made me feel good about myself because I felt attractive to someone." But, when she saw him in the harsh light of the cafeteria the next morning, she was suddenly embarrassed: "He wasn't attractive to me. At all. In any way," she wrote, as if squirming with discomfort. "He was scrawny. I mean, really scrawny, with glasses, and just not stereotypically masculine." Revealing that her regret was more about what other people might think than her own experience, she explained, "He wasn't the guy you're *supposed* to hook up with."

When she told her friends later, she exaggerated her level of inebriation, wanting to make "the fact that I hooked up with a relatively unattractive guy okay." By hooking up with someone that others might not approve of, Kendra was doing hookup culture wrong. "Because the point of hookups is to get with someone hot," she insisted, "and if you don't do that, you should have a damn good excuse."

Step 3: Initiate a Hookup

"The classic move to establish that you want to hook up with someone," Miranda's friend Ruby wrote from a woman's perspective, "is to turn around to face him, rather than dance with your back pressed against his front." Initiation can come from behind, too. He may tug on her arm or pull one hip back gently to suggest she spin. Or, he might put his face next to hers, closing the distance between them such that, with the turn of her head, there might be a kiss.

If she spins around, Miranda explained, it *seals the deal*. Turning around isn't just turning around; it's an advance, an invitation to escalate. Once students are face to face, it's *on*. This is why women look to their friends when a guy approaches them from behind instead of taking a look for themselves. Turning around is tantamount to agreeing to a *difmo*—a DFMO, or *dance-floor make-out*.

Back at the burlesque party, Ruby would make exactly that move. The shots of Smirnoff had loosened her inhibitions, and she wasn't alone. "All around me," she wrote, "I saw the same thing happening—female friends of mine meeting guys and flirting, dancing, and then making out." She would join the dance floor shortly and, in the midst of the throbbing crowd, end up dancing with Levi.

They danced for a while, she turned around, and eventually Levi carried her piggyback the two blocks to his dorm. They fell into his bed, laughing, and "suddenly it was happening."

Step 4: Do . . . Something

According to the Online College Social Life Survey, in 40 percent of hookups, Ruby's *it* means intercourse. Another 12 percent include only what we might call foreplay: nudity and some touching of genitals, while 13 percent proceed to oral sex, mostly performed by women on men, but don't include intercourse. A full 35 percent of hookups don't go any further than open-mouth kissing and groping.

This can be confusing. "I sometimes have a hard time distinguishing what a particular person means when mentioning a hookup," reported one of my students. Currier argues that the ambiguity is strategic, allowing students to exaggerate or downplay their encounters depending on what they want others to think. Specifically, she found that it allowed women to "protect their status as 'good girls' (sexual but not promiscuous)" and men to "protect their social status as 'real men' (heterosexual, highly sexually active)." It also has to do with how they feel about the person they hooked up with the next morning. Hookups with high-status people may be exaggerated and those with lower-status people minimized.

In any case, thanks to its ambiguity, the content of any given hookup is mysterious unless the participants get specific or it happens in public. The *purpose* of the hookup, however, is the opposite of ambiguous. Or, at least, it's supposed to be and this is where Ruby worried she might have messed up that night.

Step 5: Establish Meaninglessness

The goal is "fast, random, no-strings-attached sex," Ruby explained, but she wasn't sure that's what had happened with Levi. In fact, they were already quite close friends. Both ran in the popular crowd and were squarely in the *hot* category. Levi had an easy way about him and, though he wasn't a member of a fraternity or an athlete, his time in high school sports had left him able to fit in with the men who were. Ruby was a favorite among the popular boys Levi hung out with. With light brown skin, a heart-shaped face, and wavy brown hair that fell to the small of her back, she had the kind of beauty that others eroticized as *exotic*.

Ruby swore that she'd never thought of him as a potential hookup before that night. So, she was surprised at the turn of events. Uneasy, too. "I don't want hooking up with Levi to mean anything," she confessed nervously. "I don't think seeing someone naked should necessarily drastically change the way you think about them," she wrote, but she was concerned that it might affect their friendship.

> It's mostly me psyching myself out, telling myself that now that we've hooked up our friendship has to change. It doesn't—or at least I really don't want it to. But I can't help feeling so weird every time I see him since then. All I can think is, it didn't mean anything to me . . . but did it to you? Do you hate me now, because you cared and I didn't?

Truly, step 5 is the trickiest. How do two people establish that an intimate moment between them wasn't meaningful?

College students know, then, that the wider culture imbues sexual activity with great emotional significance, and this belief overlaps considerably with what they think characterizes loving, romantic relationships for themselves as well. So, despite the language we have for dismissing the significance of sex in practice, establishing that a hookup was meaningless is a challenging personal and interpersonal task.

If the hookup is going to be understood as meaningless, all of these implications have to be nullified.

This is how they do it.

Step 5a: Be (or Claim to Be) Plastered

When students talk about meaningless sex on college campuses, they are almost always referring to drunk sex. According to the Online College Social Life Survey, most casual sex occurring on college campuses involves alcohol; men have drunk an average of six drinks and women an average of four. "People who hook-up casually are almost always drunk or have at least been drinking," a female student observed. "Thank god for vodka?" Levi asked rhetorically. "I blame it on the Cuervo," countered a student at Marist College. One University of Florida, Gainesville student half-joked, "If you don't remember the sex, it didn't count."

I was first clued into the symbolic function of alcohol in hookup culture while listening to students discuss *sober sex* when I visited campuses and talked to students in small groups. It was the hushed and reverent tone that got my attention. Sober sex is interpreted entirely differently from drunk sex. It's *heavy* with meaning. "A sober hookup indicates one that is more serious," explained a student. About sober hookups, students say things like "shit's getting real" and "it takes a lot of balls." "If you are sober," a female student described in more detail:

> It means you both are particularly attracted to each other and it's not really a one-time thing. When drunk, you can kind of just do it because it's fun and then be able to laugh about it and have it not be awkward or not mean anything.

Step 5b: Cap Your Hookups

"We've only hooked up once," explained a male student, "so . . . it automatically is not a big deal." A second trick for dismissing the significance of hookups is to limit how many times two students hook up together. One hookup, students argue, isn't anything to get serious about. "One and done," is what they say. A female student snorted when asked if she would hook up with a guy a second time. "No way," she said gruffly. She had "no feelings for him," so he was "not a viable hookup ever again." Based on the Online College Social Life Survey, we know that most people only hook up with any given person once and very few hook up more than two or three times.

Students believe that avoiding repeat hookups helps ensure that no one gets the idea that a relationship is on the table. They think this is simply the right thing to do. One insisted that it would be *extremely rude* to hook up with someone a second time if there weren't feelings involved.

Capping hookups also reduces the possibility of someone *catching feelings*. "The number one established rule of hooking up," wrote a woman enrolled at Tufts, is "don't get too attached." It's a real risk, explained a student at Bellarmine University. "Sometimes you actually catch feelings and that's what sucks." Students, then, aim to hook up with someone that they don't particularly like and, from there, retreat.

If the relationship-averse generally agree that repeat hookups with the same person are risky, they're right. The Online College Social Life Survey shows that three-quarters of seniors have been in at least one monogamous relationship lasting six months or more and, even though hookups rarely lead to relationships, most relationships start with hookups. So, one must be vigilant to ensure that expectations for a relationship don't accidentally evolve.

Step 5c: Create Emotional Distance

After it's all over, students confirm that a hookup meant nothing by giving their relationship—whatever it was—a demotion. The rule is to be less close after a hookup than before, at least for a time. If students were good friends, they should act like acquaintances. If they were acquaintances, they should act like strangers. And if they were strangers, they shouldn't acknowledge each other's existence at all. "Unless at the beginning you've made it clear that you want more than a hookup," wrote a male student at Bowdoin, "then the expectation is . . . just to pretend it didn't happen."

The logic gets wacky, but it goes something like this: an unrequited crush will probably be more damaging to a friendship than being temporarily unfriendly. After a hookup, then, when the possibility of romance is a specter that must be eliminated, acting aloof is the best way to ensure that students remain friends. "People act very strangely," one student commented, "to make sure, almost to prove, they're keeping things casual."

Plenty of students feel uncomfortable with this proposition, but hookup culture has a way of enforcing compliance. If the rule is to be unfriendly, then even the slightest kindness—essentially, any effort to connect or reach out—can be interpreted as romantic interest. So, if students are nice after a hookup, they risk making an impression that they don't want to make. As one male student remarked with regret, "I try to stay friends with girls I've hooked up with, or at least stay on a 'don't hate me' basis [but] . . . I've found that, in doing so, you sometimes run into trouble with leading someone on." A second student struggled with how to handle a guy she liked, but not "in that way." She wrote:

> I don't want to be rude by not answering his text messages and not being friendly every time I see him. He doesn't deserve that. But I guess he also doesn't deserve to be led on. . . . I have no idea what to do.

She knew he liked her and it felt terrible to treat him dismissively, but she was advised that "being mean was the best way to handle it." "Many guys I have spoken to," confirmed another student, "admitted to . . . not being nice to the women they hook up with to 'protect' their feelings." The more students value a person's friendship, the more essential they may think it is to be unfriendly after a hookup.

Ruby thought it essential. Since she and Levi had been close friends before their hookup, she temporarily demoted him to acquaintance. A few days later, Ruby filled me in:

> I've seen and interacted with Levi a few times—definitely much less than I would have in a normal three-day span. I've only spent

about ten minutes alone with him, in which we joked and made casual small talk, graciously avoiding the fact that we've had each other's genitals in our mouths.

It worked. A week later, Ruby would happily report, "It's as if it never happened and I am perfectly good with that."

Changing the Culture

Hookup culture is now part of American history, the newest way that young people have come to initiate sexual encounters and form romantic relationships. In some ways, it is a mashup of the best things about the sexual cultures of the last 100 years. Like the gay men of the 1970s, students in hookup culture are inspired by a joyous sense of liberation and the belief that they have the right to indulge their desires and no reason to feel shame. Like the middle-class youth of the 1950s, today's college students get to explore the whole range of sexual options if they want to and, thanks to effective, accessible birth control, they get to do so with much fewer unintended pregnancies and early marriages. Like the young working people who took advantage of the dazzling new nightlife in the cities of the 1920s, students relish novelty and the opportunity to be at least a little unruly. And, like men and women throughout history, and perhaps against all odds, students fall in love. Young people break the rules, as they always have, and out of hookups come committed, lasting, emotionally supportive relationships.

But hookup culture also carries with it some of the worst things about the last 100 years. It is still gripped, for example, by the limiting gender stereotypes that emerged during the Industrial Revolution, that fissuring of love and sex that left us thinking that women's hearts are weak and men's hearts are hard, that men's desires are ablaze and women's barely flicker.

Thanks to these stereotypes, when men pursue sex on campus today it is interpreted as a sign of a healthy, red-blooded masculinity, but we still don't acknowledge a healthy, red-blooded femininity. When women of color are sexual, it's seen as a racial trait; when poor and working-class women are sexual, it's read as *trashy*; and when middle-class white women are sexual, it's interpreted, all too often, as just a proxy for relational yearning. And, since hookup culture demands that students seem uninterested in romance lest they seem desperate, this stereotype ensures that women usually lose the competition over who can care less, if only by default.

These stereotypes also warp what seems possible, making it difficult to advocate for sex that is both casual and kind. As a result, when women express a desire for a caring partner, it's almost always interpreted as desperation for a boyfriend rather than a request to be treated well. And when men stiff-arm their hookup partners after the fact, they are assumed to do so because they want to keep things casual, not because we've decided that it's okay for them to refuse to do the emotional labor that is essential to all respectful interactions.

Hookup culture also continues to uphold the particular strain of gender inequality that took hold in the 1920s, giving men the power to control both love and sex and making women into rivals for male attention. In fact, on campus things may have gotten worse. Competition among women can be especially fierce thanks to the fact that they attend college in higher numbers than men.

College today is oddly like postwar America, those years after so many men were killed in World War II, when the idea that women are greedy for boyfriends took hold.

A woman's sexiness is still held up as a measure of her worth, and men continue to be the arbiters of whether women are sufficiently sexy. It's not altogether unenjoyable for women, but it is often intimidating and emotionally harmful as well. Meanwhile, men are competing for men's approval, too. Some men seek their own orgasms to impress other men and deny them to women for the same reason, while women focus on being hot enough to get guys off in ways that undermine their own pleasure.

Hookup culture has also failed to integrate the best things about gay liberation: people and practices that are wonderfully queer. Instead, it remains hostile or indifferent to non-heterosexual desire, sometimes but rarely setting up environments in which heterosexuality isn't assumed, catered to, and celebrated.

Being sexually active on campus is still dangerous, too. When the young men and women of the 1950s abandoned public dates for private intimacy, students became more vulnerable to sexual predation. Research published in 1957—to my knowledge, the earliest study of sexual assault on campus—found that 21 percent of college women claimed to have been victims of an attempted or completed sexual assault, the same number we find today. Hookup culture continues this ominous tradition by catalyzing sexual aggression among otherwise non-aggressive men and offering camouflage to genuine predators. With pleasure comes danger, and we have yet to fully figure out how to reduce the latter without inhibiting the former.

Feminists tried to change many of these things, to ensure that women and men could engage with one another sexually as equals, but they were only successful in fixing half the problem. They opened doors for women, giving them the opportunity to embrace the part of life that had been given to men during urbanization: the right to work, to pursue male-dominated occupations, to be unabashedly ambitious, and to seek out sex just for fun. And they tried to open doors for men, too—to give them the right to pursue female-dominated occupations or to focus on the home, the right to prioritize nurturance and care and to hold sex close to their hearts—but Americans resisted the latter change more than they have the former. We are still waiting for men to embrace the part of life that was once given exclusively to women, and for the society around them to reward them for doing so.

In hookup culture, we see these dynamics play out clearly. Since the ideal that is held up is a stereotypically masculine way of engaging sexually, both men and women aim to have *meaningless sex*. Expressing emotions is seen as weak. Hookup culture, strongly masculinized, demands carelessness, rewards callousness, and punishes kindness. In this scenario, both men and women have the opportunity to have sex, but neither is entirely free to love.

The majority of students would prefer more meaningful connections with others. They want an easier path toward forming committed, loving relationships. Most would also be glad if their casual relationships were a little less competitive and lot kinder. And while heterosexual men have more orgasms than women, it is at the expense of a full range of sexual expression. Alienated from the pleasure that can come with being desired, and told that it's unmanly and pathetic to seek emotional connection with their sexual partners, men suffer in hookup culture, too.

Students wish they had more options. Some pine for the going-steady lifestyle of the 1950s. Many mourn the antiracist, feminist Utopia that their grandparents envisioned but never saw fully realized. Quite a few would like things to be a lot more queer. Some want a hookup culture that is warmer: where students aren't just poly—hooking up with multiple partners—but poly*amorous*—hooking up with multiple partners who are loving toward them. There are certainly some who would quite like something more akin to college in the 1700s: a lot more studying and whole lot less *fun*.

I think in this is a hint as to what we might hope to see in the coming decades: a diversification of what is possible. We need a more complex and rich cultural life on campus, not just a different one. Students want the opportunity to choose monogamy or not; the right to be treated kindly always; freedom from the rigid constraints on what it means to be a man or woman, including whom we're allowed to desire and whether we want to be male or female at all; and the option to decide whether being sexy—or even sexual—is something one wants in the first place. We need to chip away at hookup culture's dominance and force it to compete with other, more humane sexual cultures that we can envision, and many more that we haven't envisioned yet.

We must transform hookup culture, too, because some students will always prefer hookups. We need to say yes to the opportunity for casual sexual encounters, but no to the absence of care, unfair distribution of pleasure, unrelenting pressure to be hot, and risk of sexual violence. We need to flush out and end racism, sexism, ableism, classism, and other biases. We need a new culture of hooking up, one that keeps the good and roundly rejects the bad.

A campus with lots of healthy, competing sexual cultures is full of opportunity. It requires students to really think about what they want for themselves and from one another. It also requires them to talk to one another instead of assuming (often erroneously) that they know what their peers want. Competing cultures would encourage thoughtfulness, communication, tolerance, and introspection, and all of those things are great for sex.

Seeing what's happening on campus as a culture—recognizing that it's not the hookup itself, but hookup culture that is the problem—is the first step to changing it. Because culture is a type of shared consciousness, change has to happen collectively. And it can. Especially because so many colleges qualify as total institutions, because of the sheer togetherness of the student body, a campus can transform, and faster than you might suspect.

But students need everyone else to change, too. We are all in the fog. We face an onslaught of sexualized messaging designed to make us worry that our sex lives are inadequate. There is an erotic marketplace off campus, too, and it is distorted by prejudice, a fixation on wealth, and a shallow worship of youth and beauty. For certain, there is an orgasm gap between men and women outside of college, and the practices that enhance sexual encounters—communication, creativity, tolerance, confidence, and knowledge—are scarcer than they should be. We all tend to look to men for approval while valuing women's opinions too little. Sexual violence is epidemic everywhere, and unfortunately anyone, male or female, can be cold and cruel.

The corrosive elements of hookup culture are in all of our lives: in our workplaces, in our politics and the media, within our families and friendships, and, yes, in bars and bedrooms. They're even in our marriages. It makes no sense, then, to shake our fingers at college students. They are us. If we want to fix hookup culture, we have to fix American culture. When we do, we can nurture sexualities that are kinder and safer, more pleasurable and authentic, more fun and truly free.

DISCUSSION QUESTIONS

1. What are the steps in hooking up? How do these steps maintain hookup culture?

2. Who is most likely to enjoy and benefit from hookup culture? Who is least likely? Do these differences map to the types of social traits that get privileged in society at large?

3. What role do emotions play in hookups? What strategies do people use to manage their emotions before, during, and after a hookup? How are these problematic?

4. Does the culture she describes sound familiar or alien? If hookup culture exists on your campus, but you chose not to participate, how does this shape your options for dating or other social opportunities?

5. Ask several people in their 50s or older how people went about finding romantic partners when they were younger. Pool your answers with several classmates. What was different? Is there anything that is the same?

Disciplined Preferences

Explaining the (Re)Production of Latino Endogamy

Jessica M. Vasquez

As Lisa Wade demonstrated in her article "American Hookup," our choices in romantic partners and how we interact with them are shaped by our culture. But even who we find attractive or perceive as a potential partner in the first place (for a hookup or sometime more serious) is highly influenced by culture. We implicitly consider a whole host of social characteristics when considering whether someone may be a potential romantic partner; their racial and ethnic background, education level, where they live, gender, age, and religion all play a role.

An examination of dating and marriage patterns shows that we don't like to stray very far, socially speaking. Most people wind up with partners who are socially similar to them, a pattern that social scientists call endogamy. This is remarkable given that in Western culture, sexual attraction and choice of spouse are seen as the most personal and individual of experiences and that belief is safeguarded with considerable vigor—would you let our parents pick who you married or even hooked up with? What about your sociology professor? We want choice, but when we have it we overwhelmingly choose partners in socially predictable ways.

In this reading, Jessica Vasquez accounts for endogamy among Latinos by examining how location, immigrant status, gender, and even skin color all play a role in shaping how Latinos perceive potential partners. Even when individuals describe choosing to only date others like them, she demonstrates how those choices have been socially inscribed. As with most things, we are never far from our culture's influence on how we interpret and interact with others.

While courtship and marriage are often thought of as products of individual agency and "mythic love" (Swidler 2001), legal and social practices circumscribe personal preferences about sexual intimacy.[1] Because families are seen as the foundation of the social order (Moran 2001), their regulation has been "a primary means through which a racially divided and racist society has been maintained" (Dalmage 2000:2). Historically, the state through the legal system orchestrated the marriage and reproductive pool by excluding certain national origin groups from the country (Haney López 1996). Similarly, antimiscegenation laws sought to prevent racial mixing and "to protect whiteness" (Root 2001:35). Although anti-miscegenation laws were struck down in 1967 (Kennedy 2003), intermarriage rates remain low, moving from "nearly nonexistent to merely atypical" (Taylor, Funk, and Craighill 2006:1)

Today, race continues to organize intimate relationships. Despite a decline in racial endogamy in the twentieth century, race persists as the most powerful division in the marriage market (Rosenfeld 2008). Endogamy (intragroup relations) is commonplace, reflected by 87 percent of people in the United States marrying within their own racial category (Bean and Stevens 2003; Lee and Bean 2010).

Persistently low intermarriage rates leads to these questions: Why does high racial endogamy persist in an era without legal proscription? And, how do groups constitute themselves and entrench racial divisions through interactional practices? By drawing on retrospective interviews from racially intermarried and intramarried couples that involve at least one Latino person, I demonstrate the social pressures that bear on intimacy and argue that what we conceive of as personal preferences are actually socially constructed and reinforce the racial hierarchy. My chief argument is that the selection of a marriage partner is circumscribed by what I call disciplined preferences. Disciplined preferences are internalized romantic tastes that are produced through racialized social practices—including violence, threats, censure, and advice—that condition Latinos to date and marry intraracially. Heather Dalmage (2000) uses the term *border patrolling* to denote how mesolevel actors such as families, peers, and the community affect individual choices. I demonstrate how border-patrolling practices are internalized as self-discipline and reproduce endogamy. I also use the concepts of surveillance, punishment, and self-discipline to explain the continued high level of racial endogamy in a social system where intermarriage is legal.[2] The mechanisms that enforce endogamy include: family surveillance, violence or threats from an in-group or out-group, group stereotypes, and notions of cultural fit.

Explaining Endogamy: Border Patrolling by Third Parties

Residential segregation is strongly related to endogamy (Landale, Oropesa, and Bradatan 2006; Rosenfeld 2009; Stevens and Swicegood

1987), dividing populations by race and class, thereby limiting interracial contact and possibilities for romantic liaisons. Due to the "sheer force of propinquity" (Alba and Nee 2003:99), ethnic neighborhoods foster endogamy, whereas intermarried couples are more often located outside of ethnic neighborhoods (Alba, Jiménez, and Marrow 2014; Telles and Ortiz 2008).

Symbolic boundary literature shows that individuals and groups use moral discourses to maintain group worth, to position one group above others, and to guard against the erosion of advantage (Lamont and Molnar 2002; Roth 2012; Sherman 2009). Endogamy is a boundary that maintains social closure, prohibits others' access to valuable resources, and is encoded in representations of social life that construct interracial relations as deviant (Childs 2009). If the objective of boundary work is to differentiate a group from others (Roth 2012), intraracial sexual relations are a powerful tool to enforce social closure and visibly perpetuate, through monoracial families, group cohesion. Endogamy is the ultimate symbolic boundary enforcer in that it "support[s] the social structure by helping to fix social distances . . . between groups" (Merton [1941] 2000:483). I propose that a cogent way to explain endogamy is to link the structural argument of segregation with community-level enactments of boundaries. The question then becomes: How do people enforce and internalize the social edict of intramarriage?

Expanding on the classic explanations of residential segregation and symbolic boundaries, I demonstrate how endogamy is policed through informal, interpersonal border patrolling. *Border patrolling* is a form of discrimination that stems from "the belief that people should stick to their own, taking race and racial categories for granted" (Dalmage 2000:42). Boundary surveillance perpetuates the myth of group homogeneity, punishes boundary crossers, and may be internalized to limit transgressions.

My theoretical proposition is to explain racial endogamy by demonstrating how mesolevel social forces, including family, peer, and community, construct individual subjectivities and actions. Borrowing from social psychologist Kay Deaux (2006:4), the meso level is "a point of focus that links the individual to the social system" where social interaction takes place. Family- and community-enforced surveillance as well as self-discipline—the internalization of societal power—help explain the continued high level of racial endogamy in a social system where intermarriage is legal. Violence and intimidation have been historically effective deterrents to intermarriage as "groups actively police each other to ensure that domination is maintained" by means of "threats of violence or actual violence" (Childs 2009; Collins 2008:267; Hodes 1997). Focusing on the interactional level of analysis is crucial because race is *"performative . . .* [racial and] ethnic boundaries . . . constituted by day-to-day affirmations, reinforcements, and enactments of . . . differences" (Nagel 2000:111, emphasis in original). This article fleshes out the interactional mechanisms by which third parties, such as family, peers, and community, engrave racial and sexual boundaries.

In what follows, I demonstrate how border-patrolling mechanisms (family surveillance and censure, violence and threats of violence, group stereotypes, and ideas about cultural fit) operating at the meso level may vary according to social location and yet produce conformity. Reacting to family and community pressures, most individuals discipline their intimacy preferences and *choose* to abide by the convention of same-race romances.

Methods

This article draws from 70 in-depth, life history interviews with heterosexual Latinos in endogamous and exogamous marriages and their adult children living independently. I include both partners in Latino intramarriages but only Latino partners of intermarriages for, while they married exogamously, their dating histories and counsel to their children concerning marriage is useful information. These data are drawn from a larger comparative project on dating and marriage histories among Latinos and their partners.

There is near parity of interviewees across field sites: 36 interviewees are located in Los Angeles County, California and 34 are located in the northeast region of Kansas (Topeka, Lawrence, and Kansas City). More intramarried Latinos hail from California (32 of 47) whereas more Latinos intermarried with whites reside in Kansas (13 of 16). This unevenness likely reflects the distinct *marriage markets* that ensue from the concentration of Latinos in Los Angeles County and the predominance of whites in northeastern Kansas.

The rationale for selecting California and Kansas is to compare a traditional migration gateway that borders Mexico and boasts a racially diverse population with a predominantly white state distant from the border. California's population is 39.4 percent non-Hispanic white, whereas Kansas' population is 85 percent non-Hispanic white, and the nation's population is 63 percent non-Hispanic white. The nation is comprised of 16.9 percent Hispanic persons (of any race) whereas California, at 38.2 percent Hispanic, is over double that figure and Kansas, at 11 percent Hispanic, is well below the national percentage (U.S. Census 2012). Regional comparisons can yield information concerning the importance of place, from the salience of immigration patterns to race relations (Jiménez 2010; Marrow 2011).

The (Re)Production of Endogamy

Analysis of the data yielded four main findings that collectively demonstrate the production of endogamous partnerships. First, I show how residential segregation limits dating options and shapes preferences by restricting the field of possibilities. Second, I show how Latinos discipline their preferences away from whites by internalizing punishment and interpreting whites as *incompatible* mates. Third, I examine how white parents discourage their children's interracial relationships with Latinos. Finally, I illustrate how Latinos deploy anti-black prejudice to safeguard their position in an intermediate position in the racial hierarchy. I argue that disciplined preference is the result of racialized and gendered treatment of Latinos that punishes interracial intimacy and encourages racial endogamy. Just as this preference is disciplined; so too is it disciplining: this acquired preference shapes the self while simultaneously marginalizing subordinated racial out-groups.

Segregation and Socioeconomic Status

Endogamy is associated with both segregation and socioeconomic status: underclass Mexican Americans who do not attend college—and do not experience expanded marriage pools—but continue to live in segregated ethnic enclaves are unlikely to intermarry (Landale et al. 2006). Due to spatial isolation, neighborhood public schools concentrate racially homogenous communities, delimiting dating options (Alba and Nee 2003; Lichter et al. 2007; Massey and Denton 1993; Rosenfeld 2009). Julia and Lisandro Quinonez, both Mexican American, agree that living in predominantly Latino East LA made endogamous romance seem inevitable. Julia remarked, "Our high school was like 90 percent Latino . . . my [dating] options were pretty limited [laughing] . . . Everybody was Mexican." Lisandro concurred, "Because everybody was Chicano or Latino in high school, it wasn't really a question." Residential segregation is not exclusively a California issue, as 46-year-old Cynthia Herrera-Redgrave from Kansas made clear: "When I was [in] high school I . . . [thought] I was gonna marry somebody who was Mexican. . . That's what I mostly [saw] around me." Neighborhood segregation naturalizes endogamous partnerships, shaping fields of vision in both a practical and cognitive sense. As Cynthia stated, "You wouldn't even think about it."

Thirty-six-year-old Vincent Venegas, who arrived in the United States from Mexico at age seven, lived amongst poor Mexican Americans and African Americans in Los Angeles in his youth. Residential propinquity shaped Vincent's understanding of racial boundaries and attractiveness: "I had several crushes on African Americans and Latinas . . . I didn't perceive the other races to find my race or myself attractive . . . I dated Latina and African American . . . We were close [in social] class. His gang affiliation limited his social circle and disciplined his preferences to include similarly lower-class nonwhite groups: "Since I was a gang member . . . the possibilities are even smaller. You encircle yourself in a little bubble of . . .

gang life: the gang members and the gang girls. I built myself a smaller bubble and it contained me."

One of the poorer interviewees in his youth, who stopped his education at high school, Vincent's segregated adolescence was his *little bubble* that naturalized dating within his socioeconomic stratum. In a social environment that *contained* him, segregation supplanted the need for active discipline and shaped his notions of attractiveness and his marital outcome (he married a local Mexican American *party girl*). Residential segregation curtails dating options, this structural characteristic eradicating the need for mesolevel discipline by making endogamous partnerships seem inevitable.

The least geographically mobile groups are endogamously married and, inversely, intermarriage is most common among the more educated classes (Alba et al. 2014; Kalmijn 1998, 2010; Spickard 1991; Telles and Ortiz 2008). Slightly more than half of my interviewees earned a college degree or higher, this higher educational and class status assuaging third parties' concerns around downward class mobility. College-educated individuals who dated interracially faced less discipline than their lower-educated counterparts. Not only did the college-educated experience expanded dating pools, they were usually removed from their family's sphere of influence, this independence tempering criticism (Rosenfeld 2009). In contrast, interviewees without college education led more segregated lives with fewer opportunities for cross-racial dating. If the less educated crossed the color line, they faced harsher forms of discipline than their higher-educated peers because if dating *up*, their low class status multiplied their disadvantage and unsuitability and if dating *down*, they faced tighter social control by spatially proximate kin and peers.

Learned Incompatibility: Racialized Rebuffs, Failed Romance, and Familial Pressure

Outside of segregated spaces, which structurally limit choice, repeated racializing and disciplining encounters teach Latinos to curtail their romantic options. These racist social forces meant to preserve white privilege accumulate to a *learned incompatibility* with whites, which Latinos nonetheless reinterpret as a *choice* to preserve their agency.[3] Repeated rejection taught Latino men and women to discipline their preferences in socially acceptable ways, and interviewees used a language of defeat ("it'll never work out") to explain their dim prospects with whites.

Latinos' learned incompatibility with whites results from displeasing interracial dating experiences. Omar Zelaya, a 48-year-old U.S.-born son of immigrants, internalized repeated racial messages from women who declined to date him:

I got along with white women fine. I had no problem with them. But, I used to shy away from them a little bit more. . . We couldn't be as readily acceptable to each other. . . Some of these white girls . . . didn't really pay attention to you. . . [they were] stuck up or arrogant. . . Maybe my accent gave me away. . . Some of them were . . . unfriendly [and] had the tendency to . . . brush you off.

Disregard from white women disciplined Omar to avoid situations that would likely incur rejection. Externally imposed discipline converted to internally imposed self-discipline when he withdrew from white potential dates to avoid shame. Mentioning his Spanish accent that may be misinterpreted to indicate foreign-born status (Jiménez 2010), Omar comprehended white women's insouciance as based on race or (incorrect) assumptions about his nativity. Since he *got along fine* with white women, he placed the onus on them for failed romance. When white women rejected him and status contamination in one move, Omar learned that they are not *readily acceptable to each other*. After repeated interactions, Omar internalized the racial order, *shying away* from white women. He ultimately married a less educated Mexican national over whom *he* holds the power advantage.

Awareness of mainstream racism and sexism can inspire preference for intraracial romance (Nemoto 2009), and yet racialized rebuffs from whites function differently for men and women. Varying forms of gendered racialization play out in the dating realm: men are taught to view themselves as unattractive, menacing, and excluded, whereas women's dating encounters consign them to a sexualized, othered, and borderline-acceptable position (Vasquez 2010). Xochitl Velasco, a 39-year-old Mexican American from Kansas who is married to a Bolivian national, asserted that in-marriage avoids racialized and gendered stereotypes that she confronted in interracial romances with white men.[4] Xochitl desired to escape a problematic set of stereotypes white men held about Latinas, this learned incompatibility resulting from failed interracial romances. She found Latino men to be more suitable for her because they offer refuge from disconcerting stereotypes:

I always . . . knew I wanted to be married to a Latino. I always was partial to Latinos, boyfriends and everything. . . [In] college [I] started dating a white guy . . . [and saw] differences between him and I . . . Some white men that are married to my Latina girlfriends . . . like the *Latina spice*. . . They make fun of her accent. They think it's cute. . . They like that exoticness. . . I didn't ever like that. I don't want to be treated as an *other* in my relationship. I knew with Latinos there was never that *other* factor. . . I was just Xochitl

Borges and there was nothing particularly Latina about me—I [did not] have to put on this Latina-ness or take it off . . .

Experience with racialized and gendered stereotypes disciplined Xochitl to conclude that whites were a mismatch and to desire Latinos. She learned from personal experience and observation that white men's exoticization of her would be alienating, her conclusion of incompatibility an acquired perspective. With Latinos, she reasoned, she could avoid being *treated as an* *'other'* in an intimate relationship.

Disciplined preference does not rob individuals of agency. Instead, disciplined preference (whites as incompatible and Latinos as preferable) is self-protective, stemming from the need to preserve racial dignity and avoid misapprehension. Rob Esposito, married to a Mexican American/Native American woman, stated:

> I knew I wasn't going to marry a white girl. I knew I was going to marry a Mexican or Indian girl. . . You . . . dated white girls for one reason and then you had the [Mexican American and Native American] girls you were going to marry (Laugh).

Holding different standards for dating and marriage is notable; some interviewees were adventurous in dating yet restrictive relative to marital prospects (Blackwell and Lichter 2004). Oscar Cota, a 44-year-old Kansan, used similar imagery to explain his dating patterns:

> My [Mexican American] wife says, "You always wanted to go with the white girls because you knew they were easier". I . . . knew that I would marry a Mexican woman. Because when you think of family, being able to raise families, being good wives . . . and maybe [that is] stereotypical—good wives, good cooks—[but] . . . I always knew I would marry a Mexican woman.

Heteronormative sexual stereotypes such as these tap into ethnic cultures' *gender regimes* and are used to evaluate moral value (Nagel 2000:113). Stereotypes about white women as *easy* and Mexican women as *wifely* shape Latino men's marital preferences: these men pursue interracial sexual liaisons before engaging in a *winnowing* process (Blackwell and Lichter 2004) and selecting proper, endogamous marriage partners.

This dichotomous thinking about Mexican and white women is a sexualized way for Latino men to recuperate agency. Use of value-laden ascriptions of *family oriented* and *marriageable* valorize Latina women, denigrate white women who are off-limits, and rationalize the *choice of* endogamy. While dating and marriage are not entirely agent-centered processes, claiming the *choice* of endogamy rhetorically resists the confines of a socially constricted marriage market. Repeated encounters with whites coach Latinos to believe that they are only suitable for other Latinos, reproducing endogamy and maintaining the racial hierarchy.

Preserving White Privilege: Anti-Latino Surveillance and Violence

White parents discriminate against Latinos through violence, threats, and exclusionary tactics in order to preserve their family's white privilege. Racialized and gendered stereotypes mark Latino men as agents of racial taint and white parents attempt to protect their daughters from becoming *unwhitened* (Frankenberg 1993; Twine 2010) whereas they view relations with Latina women as more acceptable (Vasquez 2010, 2011). Accordingly, Latino men are punished more harshly than Latina women when dating whites. White parents' prejudicial (sometimes violent) messages about their children's Latino romantic interests encourage endogamy, this disciplining during adolescence having repercussions in adulthood. For example, in high school, Nathan Lucero, a Mexican American from Lawrence, Kansas, who is now 51 years old, faced threats of bodily harm from his white girlfriend's father:

> [She] was a brunette with green eyes. . . . Her dad hated me. He didn't give me a chance 'cuz I was Mexican. . . I only met [her dad] once. . . . She came out [when I arrived to pick her up] and said, "My dad wants to know if your car can outrun a bullet."

Such threats are an aggressive way to police the symbolic boundary between whites and Latinos. Nathan noted that he was driving a *decent car*, preemptively asserting his financial stability and ruling out class status as the reason for the father's extreme measures. Coming from a similar class status, this interaction highlights the centrality of race, class status not serving as a protection against racism (Feagin and Sikes 1994). While younger cohorts are more racially tolerant than older cohorts (Taylor et al. 2006), white parents vigilantly police racial boundaries through surveillance and violence.

Historically, white women have been vigilantly guarded, their whiteness, reproductive capacity, and symbolic role as mothers of the nation at stake in intimate encounters (Collins 1991; Hodes 1997; Kennedy 2003; Root 2001; Yuval-Davis 1997). In keeping with this gendered rationale, among interviewees, most reported incidents of violence were directed against minority men, mainly by relatives of white women reacting violently to cross-racial intimacy. Fifty-two-year-old Mexican American Rob Esposito, also from Kansas, told a tale similar to Nathan's of white parents' prohibition against interracial dating. In this situation, both the girl and her brother who defended her were injured:

> We were going to go to prom together . . . [but] her dad wouldn't let us date. . . She was pretty adamant about wanting to date me. . . Her dad [threw] her down the stairs . . . when they were fighting about it. [Her brother] intervened and . . . his dad pushed his head through a glass bookcase. All over me—because [her] dad was no way going to let [her] date a Mexican.

While the violence was not directed at a minority male, the action served to discipline romantic tastes and oversee white women's sexuality. Rob did not address whether this violence forced a breakup. In general, he stated, "[the girls] wanted to date me, their fathers were the problem." Given the categorical rejection coming from white girls' parents, he retrospectively called white girls *prohibited fruit*.

White parents considered Rob a threat to their daughters—a source of hypermasculinity and status contamination—yet they lauded him as a star athlete. Collins (2004) argues that the same minority masculinity that is deemed physically and sexually menacing is cheered when displayed as athletic prowess. White girls' parents approved of Rob in sports:

> After a ball game . . . and scoring 25 points . . . I'd go into the local steakhouse . . . [and] parents. . . would order up a hamburger and fries and . . . paid for it . . . Even the parents that didn't want me going out with their daughters were like, "Great game!" Yeah, but when it came down to dating their daughter, it was . . . "we're not going to let you touch our daughters."

Although praised for sports achievement, Rob encountered disapproval when dating white girls. These conflicting reactions—personal discouragement and public congratulations—show how white parents respond to Latino masculinity: they regulate it in the private domain that contains a white daughter's sexuality but applaud it in a public arena that requires sports skill. Especially in the Kansas context where whites drastically outnumber Latinos, border patrolling to prohibit whites from crossing the racial line is marked by threats and violence.

Region matters less for women than for men: while Latino men were victimized by physical, verbal, and symbolic violence in Kansas, women faced milder forms of rejection in California and Kansas. Latina women were subject to surveillance and racial slights by white parents of romantic interests. Forty-one-year-old Californian Corrina Nuñes's Hispanic identity cost her a boyfriend:

> A [white] young man [I was dating] came to school one day and completely avoided me . . . His brother had gotten mad at him . . . told his father that he was dating a Hispanic girl and his dad beat him up.

Parents who police the color line when their children were open to romantic boundary crossing show how age, time period, and generation play a role in boundary maintenance (Taylor et al. 2006).

Region affects attitudes on interracial intimacy: whites resisted Latinos more vigorously in Kansas than in California. Group size impinges upon racial attitudes: families and communities judge whites' interracial dating practices in a largely white context to be a more glaring and punishable offense than in a locale with a limited white dating pool. Racial heterogeneity both increases the chances for interracial romance and decreases the likelihood of sanctions (Kreager 2008). In diverse California, cross-racial dating was perceived as less unlikely and therefore less transgressive.

Two caveats concerning region and generation in the United States deserve mention. First, while Latino families in both sites encouraged endogamy, exogamy with whites was perceived as a reasonable option in Kansas. Because of the small number of Hispanics in the area and because of the value of whiteness, Latinos condoned cross-racial intimacy with whites. Twenty-eight-year-old Liz Downing explained the impact of living in a majority-white town: "It'd kind of be a joke that I couldn't date any people that were Mexican in Lawrence, because we were related to most of the Mexican people in Lawrence [laughs]!" Orlando Puente, from Topeka, explained that he dated white women "mainly because there wasn't [sic] very many Mexican girls to date." Because of supply-side demographics, Latino and white intermarriage was understood as a probable outcome in Kansas.

Second, generational status is influential: immigrants favor endogamy whereas the U.S. born are more open to exogamy. These attitudes follow the noted trend of immigrants marrying co-nationals and later-generation Latinos more likely to marry outside of their racial group (Alba et al. 2014; Chavez 2008; Landale and Oropesa 2007; Murguia 1982; Telles and Ortiz 2008). One woman's immigrant father was *shocked and appalled* when a white boy came to the house: "What was I doing having a [white] boy come to the door and ask for me? [My father thought] . . . I must be doing something [sexually] loose." By depicting minority women as morally superior to dominant culture, immigrant parents reaffirm minority self-worth within a context of subordination (Espiritu 2000; Nagel 2000) and encourage endogamy on cultural grounds.

While both Latino men and women underwent racialized processes of learned incompatibility relative to whites, their experiences varied by gender. Men cited cultural mismatch as the chief reason why white women disregarded them. They disciplined their preferences away from white women and used a cultural explanation of Latina women as suitable and family oriented to legitimate their same-race relations. Women engaged in self-discipline by circumventing objectifying stereotypes white men may have by withdrawing from them. These same women, however, in their turn to Latino men, faced different racialized and gendered preconceptions. The critical difference, however, is that imagery Latino men have of Latina women resonated more with these in-married women's beliefs about themselves. Unlike their intermarried counterparts, in-married Latina women did not complain of domineering fathers or submissive mothers. Instead, endogamously married Latinas had pleasing home lives in their youth and were comfortable with their parents' displays of femininity, masculinity, and culture.

Preserving Relative Group Privilege: Anti-Black Prejudice and Staying in the Racial Middle

Nondominant classes can also protect their relative privilege. Racial discourses influence romantic preferences (Shiao and Tuan 2008), contributing to Latinos' preference to date Latinos or whites more so than blacks (Feliciano, Lee, and Robnett 2011). The aim of anti-black prejudice is to avoid slipping down the racial ladder. Anti-black prejudice among Latinos is expressed in axioms such as *chickens go with chickens*, *stick to your own*, or direction not to *marry down*. As an exertion of power, anti-black prejudice calcifies the boundary between Latinos and blacks and preserves Latinos' relative group privilege.

Less than a quarter of the Latino interviewees dated blacks (two were currently married to biracial blacks) and, of those, women reported more surveillance by family and peer groups than men. The majority of those who dated blacks were darker skinned (skin color code #3 or above), no light-skinned individuals (skin color code #1) reported interracial intimacy with blacks. While black/nonblack relationships elicit strong negative reactions generally (Kreager 2008), nearly all of the interviewees who reported surveillance or punishment regarding romance with blacks were Latinas from Kansas. Region and gender intersect such that families in Kansas guarded Latinas against *downward* racial mixing; cross-racial dating with blacks was viewed as an avoidable norm violation in a locale with a large nonblack population.

Latinas in Kansas who dated black men did so against family counsel. Adriana Guthrie, age 41, recalled lateral surveillance by her cousins: "I did date a black guy. . . My cousins kept saying, 'You're brown and you should be with brown people.'" Forty-three-year-old Lorena Cota dated a black man covertly: "I [wasn't] able to tell my family that I was dating an African American. . . My dad . . . wouldn't have approved. . . Social pressures [were] to date Caucasian and Hispanic . . . only."

Such *social pressures* include peer surveillance from African American women who treated her as if she was *trying to take away their men*. These slights by black women are likely based on black women's expectation of their own endogamy and the lack of *marriageable* black men due to the disappearance of well-paid jobs for black men (Cherlin 2009; Collins 2008) and high rates of incarceration (Pettit 2012; Western 2006). Cassie Hoffman, age 46, who was previously married to a black man, was "a little nervous" to inform her parents of her engagement because, she confessed, "he was black and I didn't know . . . if they would approve or not."

Immigrant parents' expectations of endogamy and anti-black bias compelled 34-year-old Mario Bermudez to conceal his cross-racial romances. Mario, who eventually married a woman with Mexican American and white heritage, likened interracial intimacy to homosexuality to underscore the transgressive quality of such a pairing. Growing up in an ethnic enclave where *everything was Mexican*, Mario explained his self-surveillance when dating non-Mexicans:

> When I used to bring home a . . . black girl. . . I would never bring her around . . . my whole family. . . Just, say a few *tías* [aunts] who I thought were cool, you know? It's almost like you're gay, kinda. Like . . . you're *coming out*. . . The same thing happened with Ana [his half Mexican American, half white wife]: I would only bring her around my three cool *tías* [aunts]. That's not the way it's supposed to be.

For his Mexican immigrant relatives, it was *a big deal* for Mario to date non-Mexicans and he believed that a black woman would never have gained acceptance. While dating a black woman was taboo, marrying a woman with Mexican American descent ensured his *racial authenticity* (Vasquez and Wetzel 2009) within his immigrant family.

Even in nonimmigrant families, Latinos in the *racial middle* (O'Brien 2008) of a three-tiered hierarchy execute anti-black prejudice to safeguard relative privilege and attempt to achieve *honorary white* status (Bonilla-Silva 2003; Haney López 1996). According to Eduardo Bonilla-Silva (2004), "honorary whites may be . . . believing they are better than the 'collective black,'" which would require the development of "white-like racial attitudes befitting their new social position and differentiating (distancing) themselves from the 'collective black'" (p.937).

Skin color is an important dimension to endogamy, as intensity of disciplined preferences varies by skin tone. The darker skinned are more committed to endogamy than the lighter skinned, this stance providing those who are least likely to intermarry with whites (taking a cue from low black/white intermarriage rates [Lee and Bean 2010; Qian 2002; Qian and Lichter 2011]) with a strategy to preserve relative privilege. Darker-skinned parents advocated endogamy for their children, despite their recognition of the social value of whiteness. Oscar Cota, bearing medium-tan skin, counseled his three preteen children on intragroup relations: "Would race play a role? Unfortunately, it would. . . I would [prefer] to have my kids marry a Hispanic, a Latina, or a Mexican. . . I would push to keep . . . a pure bloodline. . . That's . . . a prejudice." Experiencing *daily racisms*, Oscar may have viewed endogamy as a protective device that would shield his children from more integrated social spaces that would make them vulnerable to racial discrimination (Ortiz and Telles 2012). Looking both *up* and *down* from the racial middle, by favoring endogamy, Oscar also guarded against status loss that threatens to accompany interracial intimacy with blacks.

Marriage advice encouraging racial endogamy among darker-skinned Latinos is not gender specific. Noelle Puente, who has medium-tan skin, remarked: "Would I like to have a minority walk through my household? Sure, I would. I can't help that. I do want [my children] to bring somebody home that's Mexican. . . Honestly, I think it's [about] family." This logic hints at not only a racial and color mismatch but also a cultural one, positioning Mexican culture as more family oriented than other racial groups. Similarly, 53-year-old Mexican immigrant Rosalinda Ornales, who also has medium-tan skin and lives in California, remarked: "I would like to see [my children] with somebody Latino. That's my opinion. . . My dad used to say: '*Gallinas se juntan con gallinas.*' Chickens go with chickens. . . You look for your own kind." Coming from darker-skinned Latinos who intramarried, this marital advice suggests prior racializing experiences that disciplined them into abiding by the color line and shaped the disciplining counsel they give to the next generation. Emphasis here is on racial, color, and cultural commensurability. This racialized advice that stresses parity attempts to balance positions of power, disciplinary moves that illuminate how most marriages come to involve partners of relatively equal status (Kalmijn 1998; Rosenfeld 2005; Spickard 1991).

Complementing the finding that darker-skinned Latinos were more committed to endogamy, families pushed lighter-skinned Latinos toward exogamy in order to *whiten* the race. While Xochitl Velasco, discussed above, ultimately married a Bolivian for cultural compatibility and racial/gender comfort reasons, her family communicated that she, as a light-tan-skinned woman, could improve her racial standing through intermarriage with a white person. A perceptible grade lighter than the aforementioned interviewees who practiced and advocated endogamy, Xochitl's family telegraphed a clear message about the racial hierarchy and the potential achievement of higher racial status through intimacy:

> When [my cousins] brought white boyfriends home it was kind of . . . like, *Congratulations!* . . . The white men were considered . . . moving up, successful. . . [It] would never be appreciated to bring an African American man . . . [or] woman home as a boyfriend/ girlfriend. . . And the Mexican men were looked . . . on as . . . status quo and not doing anything really great.

Like commitment to endogamy, familial pressure varies by skin color: darker-skinned Latinos were steered toward endogamy whereas lighter-skinned Latinos were directed toward exogamy with whites. These intra-family, intergenerational messages are laced with implications about who is consigned to racialization versus who is best positioned to escape it. Skin color is an important factor in the construction of disciplined prefer-ences, family counsel pivoting the lighter skinned toward whites, the darker skinned toward Latinos, and all away from blacks.

Intergenerational family advice about the acceptability of other racial groups, a form of surveillance and discipline, extends our understanding of endogamy. *What about the kids* rhetoric is a powerful tool of intrafamil-ial discipline aimed to contain sexual desire within acceptable, endoga-mous limits. Pressure not to *marry down* is intended to entrench symbolic boundaries and preserve relative group privilege. Anti-black prejudice is the means by which Latinos protect their racial status that, while subordi-nate to whites, is superior to blacks, an even less privileged group.

Conclusion: Racial Border Patrolling and Disciplined Preferences Enforce Endogamy

Even as rates of intermarriage modestly increase—approximately 13 percent of American marriages involve persons of different races (Bean and Stevens 2003; Lee and Bean 2004:228)—interracial intimacy remains rare. Studying endogamy brings to light enduring social dynamics that undergird this pattern. Racial endogamy results from macrostructural, family, and community pressures that discipline individuals to prefer specific mates. This article makes three interventions. First, it identifies the practices through which third parties regulate interracial sexuality, biased interactions that demographic studies simply assume are operant. Second, it utilizes intersectionality to reveal how pressures toward endogamy vary by gender, skin color, and region. Third, it moves beyond the literature's focus on black/white couples and examines Latino experiences. This study reveals that what we customarily think of as *personal preferences* are, in fact, socially constructed. Family- and peer-disciplining processes consolidate group position and maintain symbolic boundaries. Surveillance, physical and symbolic violence, and notions of cultural (in)compatibility are all mechanisms of power that support endogamy.

Answering Kalmijn's (1998) question about what *third parties* are actually *doing* to entrench racial homogamy, I find that surveillance and punishment (violence, threats, censure, and advice) imposed from inside and outside of one's racial community that transform into self-discipline are the chief mechanisms enforcing same-race romance. Endogamous pairings do not occur by accident; they are constructed by a racialized social structure whose members police racial boundaries and punish transgressors. Surveillance, punishment, and self-discipline are the regulatory techniques that define acceptability, discipline preferences, and perpetuate endogamy.

Appendix

Table AI   Characteristics of Interviewees

Characteristic	Percent (n)
Ethnic origin	
Mexican American—monoethnic	70 (49)
Mexican American—multiethnic with white	14 (10)
Mexican American—multiethnic with Native American	4 (3)
Other Latin American	11 (8)
Gender	
Men	41 (29)
Women	59 (41)
Age	
20s	11(8)
30s	20 (14)
40s	34 (24)
50s	14 (10)
60s	14 (10)

70s	6 (4)
Region	
California	51 (36)
Kansas	49 (34)
Skin color	
1 (racially white appearance)	33 (13)
2 (light-tan)	27 (19)
3 (medium-tan)	37 (26)
4 (dark-tan)	17 (12)
5 (racially black appearance)	0
Interracial or intraracial marriage[a]	
Intraracial: Latino/Latino	68 (47)
Interracial: Latino/white	23 (16)
Interracial: Latino/non-Latino minority	9 (6)
Education	
Less than high school	3 (2)
High school degree/GED	16 (11)
Some college	29 (20)
College degree	23 (16)
Master's/professional degree	24 (17)
Doctoral degree	6 (4)
Individual income	
Under $30,000	20 (14)
$30,001 – $50,000	31 (22)
$50,001 – $70,000	20 (14)
$70,001 – $150,000+	26 (18)
Not reported	3 (2)

Note: N=70

[a] These counts include current and dissolved marriages (four interviewees are divorced). One single/never married adult is excluded.

DISCUSSION QUESTIONS

1. What is learned incompatibility? What is disciplined preference? How did this play out in the lives of those interviewed?

2. Endogamy was enforced at several different levels. What specific individuals influenced choice of dating partners? How did larger social stereotypes influence these decisions?

3. What role did location play in how likely endogamy was? What about immigrant status? Why do you think these differences existed?

4. Do you feel completely free to marry anyone of any age, gender, race, or religion? How are your dating choices subtly supported, or discouraged, by your culture?

REFERENCES

Alba, Richard, Tomás R Jiménez, and Helen B, Marrow. 2014. "Mexican Americans as a Paradigm for Contemporary Intra-Group Heterogeneity." *Ethnic and Racial Studies* 37(3):446–66.

Alba, Richard D. and Victor Nee. 2003. *Remaking the American Mainstream: Assimilation and Contemporary Immigration.* Cambridge, MA: Harvard University Press.

Bean, Frank D. and Gillian Stevens. 2003. *America's Newcomers and the Dynamics of Diversity.* New York: Russell Sage Foundation.

Blackwell, Debra L. and Daniel T. Lichter. 2004. "Homogamy among Dating, Cohabiting, and Married Couples." *The Sociological Quarterly* 45(4):719–37.

Bonilla-Silva, Eduardo. 2003. *Racism Without Racists: Color-Blind Racism and the Persistence of Racial Inequality in the United States.* Lanham, MD: Rowman & Littlefield.

—. 2004. "From Bi-Racial to Tri-Racial: Towards a New System of Racial Stratification in the USA." *Ethnic and Racial Studies* 27(6):931–50.

Chambliss, Daniel F. and Russell K. Schutt. 2012. *Making Sense of the Social World: Methods of Investigation.* Thousand Oaks, CA: Sage Publications.

Chavez, Leo R 2008. *The Latino Threat: Constructing Immigrants, Citizens, and the Nation.* Stanford, CA: Stanford University Press.

Cherlin, Andrew J. 2009. *The Marriage-Go-Round: The State of Marriage and the Family in America Today.* New York: Vintage.

Childs, Erica Chito. 2005. *Navigating Interracial Borders: Black-White Couples and their Social Worlds.* New Brunswick, NJ: Rutgers University Press.

— 2009. *Fade to Black and White: Interracial Images in Popular Culture.* Lanham, MD: Rowman & Littlefield.

Collins, Patricia Hill. 1991. *Black Feminist Thought.* New York: Routledge.

—. 2004. *Black Sexual Politics: African Americans, Gender, and the New Racism.* New York: Routledge.

—. 2008. *Black Feminist Thought: Knowledge, Consciousness, and the Politics of Empowerment.* New York: Routledge.

Dalmage, Heather M. 2000. *Tripping on the Color Line: Black-White Multiracial Families in a Racially Divided World.* New Brunswick, NJ: Rutgers University Press.

Deaux, Kay. 2006. *To Be an Immigrant.* New York: Russell Sage Foundation.

Espiritu, Yen Le. 2000. "We Don't Sleep Around Like White Girls Do." *Signs* 26(2):415–40.

Feagin, Joe R. and Melvin P. Sikes. 1994. *Living with Racism: The Black Middle-Class Experience.* Boston: Beacon Press.

Feliciano, Cynthia, Rennie Lee, and Belinda Robnett. 2011. "Racial Boundaries among Latinos: Evidence from Internet Daters' Racial Preferences." *Social Problems* 58(2):189–212.

Fiske, Susan T. 2004. *Social Beings: A Core Motives Approach to Social Psychology.* Hoboken, NJ: Wiley.

Foucault, Michel. 1995. *Discipline & Punish: The Birth of the Prison.* New York: Random House.

Frankenberg, Ruth. 1993. *White Women, Race Matters: The Social Construction of Whiteness.* Minneapolis: University of Minnesota Press.

Fu, Vincent Kang. 2001. "Racial Intermarriage Pairings." *Demography* 38(2):147–59.

Gans, Herbert J. 2012. "'Whitening' and the Changing American Racial Hierarchy." *Du Bois Review* 9(2):267–79.

Glaser, Barney G. and Anselm L. Strauss. 1967. *The Discovery of Grounded Theory: Strategies for Qualitative Research.* Hawthorne, NY: Aldine de Gruyter.

Gordon, Milton Myron. 1964. *Assimilation in American Life: The Role of Race, Religion, and National Origins.* New York: Oxford University Press.

Haney López, Ian. 1996. *White by Law: The Legal Construction of Race.* New York: New York University Press.

Hodes, Martha Elizabeth. 1997. *White Women, Black Men: Illicit Sex in the Nineteenth-Century South.* New Haven, CT: Yale University Press.

Jiménez, Tomás R 2010. *Replenished Ethnicity: Mexican Americans, Immigration, and Identity.* Berkeley: University of California Press.

Joyner, Kara and Grace Kao. 2005. "Interracial Relationships and the Transition to Adulthood." *American Sociological Review* 70(4): 563–82.

Kalmijn, Matthijs. 1998. "Intermarriage and Homogamy: Causes, Patterns, Trends." *Annual Review of Sociology* 24:395–421.

—. 2010. "Consequences of Racial Intermarriage for Children's Social Integration." *Sociological Perspectives* 53(2):271–86.

Kennedy, Randall. 2003. *Interracial Intimacies: Sex, Marriage, Identity, and Adoption.* New York: Pantheon.

Kreager, Derek A. 2008. "Guarded Borders: Adolescent Interracial Romance and Peer Trouble at School." *Social Forces* 87(2):887–910.

Lamont, Michele and Virag Molnar. 2002. "The Study of Boundaries in the Social Sciences." *Annual Review of Sociology* (28):167–95.

Landale, N. S., R. S. Oropesa, and C. Bradatan. 2006. "Hispanic Families in the United States: Family Structure and Process in an Era of Family Change." Pp. 138–78 in *Hispanics and the Future of America*, edited by M. Tienda and F. Mitchell. Washington, DC: National Academies Press.

Landale, Nancy S. and R S. Oropesa. 2007. "Hispanic Families: Stability and Change." *Annual Review of Sociology* 33: 381–405.

Lee, Jennifer and Frank P. Bean. 2004. "America's Changing Color Lines: Immigration, Race/Ethnicity, and Multiracial Identification." *Annual Review of Sociology* 30:221–42.

—. 2010. *The Diversity Paradox: Immigration and the Color Line in Twenty-First Century America*. New York: Russell Sage Foundation.

Lichter, Daniel, J. Brian Brown, Qian Zhenchao, and Julie Carmalt. 2007. "Marital Assimilation among Hispanics: Evidence of Declining Cultural and Economic Incorporation?" *Social Science Quarterly* 88(3):745–65.

Lofquist, Daphne, T. Lugaila, M. O'Connell, and S. Feliz. 2012. "Households and Families: 2010." Pp. 1–21 in 2010 *Census Briefs*. Washington, DC: U.S. Census Bureau.

Lopez, Mark Hugo and Daniel Dockterman. 2011. *"U.S. Hispanic Country-of-Origin Counts for Nation, Top 30 Metropolitan Areas."* Washington, DC: Pew Hispanic Center.

Marrow, Helen B. 2011. *New Destination Dreaming: Immigration, Race, and Legal Status in the Rural American South*. Stanford, CA: Stanford University Press.

Massey, Douglas S. and Nancy A Denton. 1993. *American Apartheid: Segregation and the Making of the Underclass*. Cambridge, MA: Harvard University Press.

Merton, Robert K. [1941] 2000. "Intermarriage and the Social Structure: Fact and Theory." Pp. 473–92 in *Interracialism: Black-White Intermarriage in American History, Literature, and Law*, edited by Werner Sollors. New York: Oxford University Press.

Moon, Dawne. 2013. "Powerful Emotions: Symbolic Power and the (Productive and Punitive) Force of Collective Feeling." *Theory and Society* 42:261–94.

Morales, Erica 2012. "Parental Messages Concerning Latino/Black Interracial Dating: An Exploratory Study among Latina/o Young Adults." *Latino Studies* 10(3):314–33.

Moran, Rachel F. 2001. *Interracial Intimacy: The Regulation of Race & Romance*. Chicago: University of Chicago Press.

Murguia, Edward. 1982. *Chicano Intermarriage: A Theoretical and Empirical Study*. San Antonio, TX: Trinity University Press.

Nagel, Joane. 2000. "Ethnicity and Sexuality." *Annual Review of Sociology* 26:107–33.

Nemoto, Kumiko. 2009. *Racing Romance: Love, Power, and Desire among Asian American/ White Couples*. New Brunswick, NJ: Rutgers University Press.

O'Brien, Eileen. 2008. *The Racial Middle: Latinos and Asian Americans Living Beyond the Racial Divide*. New York: New York University Press.

Omi, Michael and Howard Winant. 1994. *Racial Formation in the United States: From the 1960s to the 1990s*. New York: Routledge.

Ortiz, Vilma and Edward Telles. 2012. "Racial Identity and Racial Treatment of Mexican Americans." *Race and Social Problems* 4(1):41–56.

Pascoe, C.J. 2007. *Dude, You're a Fag: Masculinity and Sexuality in High School*. Berkeley: University of California Press.

Passel, Jeffrey, Gretchen Livingston, and D'Vera Cohn. 2012. *"Explaining Why Minority Births Now Outnumber White Births."* Washington, DC: Pew Research Center.

Passel, Jeffrey S., Wendy Wang, and Paul Taylor. 2010. *"Marrying Out: One-in-Seven New U.S. Marriages is Interracial or Interethnic."* Washington, DC: Pew Research Center.

Pettit, Becky. 2012. *Invisible Men: Mass Incarceration and the Myth of Black Progress*. New York: Russell Sage Foundation.

Qian, Zhenchao. 2002. "Race and Social Distance: Intermarriage with Non-Latino Whites." *Race & Society* 5(1):33–47.

Qian, Zhenchao and Daniel T. Lichter. 2007. "Social Boundaries and Marital Assimilation: Interpreting Trends in Racial and Ethnic Intermarriage." *American Sociological Review* 72(1):68–94.

—. 2011. "Changing Patterns of Interracial Marriage in a Multiracial Society." *Journal of Marriage and Family* 73(5): 1065–84.

Rockquemore, Kerry Ann and Loren Henderson. 2010. "Interracial Families in Post-Civil Rights America." Pp. 99–111 in *Families as They Really Are*, edited by Barbara J. Risman. New York: W. W. Norton & Company.

Root, Maria P. P. 2001. *Love's Revolution: Interracial Marriage*. Philadelphia, PA: Temple University Press.

Rosenfeld, Michael. 2002. "Measures of Assimilation in the Marriage Market: Mexican Americans 1970-1990." *Journal of Marriage and the Family* 64(1):152–62.

Rosenfeld Michael J. 2005. "A Critique of Exchange Theory in Mate Selection," *American Journal of Sociology* 110(5): 1284–325.

—. 2008. "Racial, Educational, and Religious Endogamy in the United States: A Comparative Historical Perspective." *Social Forces* 87(1): 1–31.

—. 2009. *The Age of Independence: Interracial Unions, Same-Sex Unions, and the Changing American Family*. Cambridge, MA: Harvard University Press.

Rosenfeld, Michael J. and Byung-Soo Kim. 2005. "The Independence of Young Adults and the Rise of Interracial and Same-Sex Unions." *American Sociological Review* 70(4):541–62.

Roth, Wendy D. 2012. *Race Migrations: Latinos and the Cultural Transformation of Race*. Stanford, CA: Stanford University Press.

Schilt, Kristen and Laurel Westbrook. 2009. "Doing Gender, Doing Heteronormativity: 'Gender Normals,' Transgender People, and the Social Maintenance of Heterosexuality." *Gender & Society* 23(4):440–64.

Sherman, Jennifer. 2009. *Those Who Work, Those Who Don't: Poverty, Morality, and Family in Rural America*. Minneapolis: University of Minnesota Press.

Shiao, Jiannbin Lee and Mia H. Tuan. 2008. "'Some Asian Men are Attractive to Me, but for a Husband . . .' Korean Adoptees and the Salience of Race in Romance." *Du Bois Review* 5(2):259–85.

Spickard, Paul R. 1991. *Mixed Blood: Intermarriage and Ethnic Identity In Twentieth-Century America*. Madison: University of Wisconsin Press.

Steinbugler, Amy C. 2012. *Beyond Loving: Intimate Raceworkin Lesbian, Gay, and Straight Interracial Relationships*. New York: Oxford University Press.

Stevens, Gillian and Gray Swicegood. 1987. "The Linguistic Context of Ethnic Endogamy." *American Sociological Review* 52(1):73–82.

Strauss, Anselm L. 1987. *Qualitative Analysis for Social Scientists*. Cambridge, UK: Cambridge University Press.

Swidler, Ann. 2001. *Talk of Love: How Culture Matters*. Chicago: University of Chicago Press.

Taylor, Paul, Cary Funk, and Peyton Craighill. 2006. "Guess Who's Coming to Dinner: 22% of Americans Have a Relative in a Mixed-Race Marriage." Pew Research Center, Washington, DC.

Telles, Edward and Vilma Ortiz. 2008. *Generations of Exclusion: Mexican Americans, Assimilation, and. Race*. New York: Russell Sage Foundation.

Twine, France Winddance. 2010. *A White Side of Black Britain: Interracial Intimacy and Racial Literacy*. Durham, NC: Duke University Press.

U.S. Census Bureau. 2012. "2012 Population Estimate." Retrieved July 21, 2014 (http://factfinder.census.gov/faces/nav/jsf/pages/index.xhtml).

Vasquez, Jessica M. 2010. "Blurred Borders for Some but not 'Others': Racialization, 'Flexible Ethnicity,' Gender, and Third Generation Mexican American Identity." *Sociological Perspectives* 53(1):45–71.

—. 2011. *Mexican Americans Across Generations: Immigrant Families, Racial Realities*. New York: New York University Press.

Vasquez, Jessica M. and Christopher Wetzel. 2009. "Tradition and the Invention of Racial Selves: Symbolic Boundaries, Collective Authenticity, and Contemporary Struggles for Racial Equality." *Ethnic and Racial Studies* 32(9):1557–75.

Warren, Jonathan W. and France Winddance Twine. 1997. "White Americans, the New Minority?: Non-Blacks and the Ever-Expanding Boundaries of Whiteness." *Journal of Black Studies* 28(2):200–18.

Western, Bruce. 2006. *Punishment and Inequality in America*. New York: Russell Sage.

Yancey, George A 2003. *Who is White?: Latinos, Asians, and the New Black/Nonblack Divide*. Boulder, CO: Lynne Rienner.

Yuval-Davis, Nira. 1997. *Gender & Nation*. Thousand Oaks, CA: Sage Publications.

NOTES

1. While this article concerns heterosexual couples, it is worth noting that heterosexuality itself is highly regulated and rewarded (Schilt and Westbrook 2009) and nonconformity is punished (Pascoe 2007). A study that compares interracial heterosexual and same-sex partnerships suggests that institutional protections benefit interracial straight couples whereas a double minority status (being queer and interracial) can aid connection among cross-racial gay couples (Steinbugler 2012:125, 128).

2. I use Foucault's (1995) concepts of surveillance and discipline as a starting point, though our definitions of discipline vary significantly. Whereas Foucault theorizes that subjectivity is produced through disciplinary power, I maintain that subjects understand external disciplinary actions and restrictions as social facts and largely conform accordingly. In my usage, subjects do not necessarily believe in their circumscribed social power, their subjectivity more removed from the disciplinary process than Foucault theorized.

3. In discussion of spouse selection, most interviewees used the language of *choice*. Although this terminology sounds like a rational choice—as if people weigh potential costs and benefits of romantic partnerships—many said they *just fell in love*.

4. By contrast, Asian American women view intermarriage with white men as a way to repudiate negative stereotypes from their own racial community (Nemoto 2009).

Constructing Deviance and Normality

The Rise of Viagra

Meika Loe

In this article, sociologist Meika Loe maps changing definitions of normal sexual function in men, brought on by the discovery of Viagra. Viagra was a happy accident, discovered by researchers at the pharmaceutical company Pfizer who were trying to find a cure for angina (a condition in which the heart does not get enough blood.) But Pfizer had a marketing problem it had to solve before it could turn Viagra into the best selling drug in the world. The inability to get and maintain an erection was almost always either considered a natural part of aging, the result of stress, or caused by relationships or emotional issues. Only in very rare cases did men have an actual physical condition that led to problems, and many of those were related to lifestyle (smoking, lack of physical exercise, etc.) This condition was referred to as impotence, a term that was highly stigmatized and had significant negative connotations (even today it is grammatically correct to refer to someone who is ineffective in their job as impotent). While this had started to change between 1970 and 1990, it was Pfizer and Viagra that ushered in the widespread medicalization of impotence. Medicalization is the process of redefining a nonmedical condition as a medical one. This started with a name change, impotence became erectile dysfunction (ED); it was followed by an emphasis on physical mechanics of erections (or lack thereof) that intentionally ignored the emotional and social dimensions of the issue. At the same time, Pfizer's marketing of Viagra redefined normal male sexual performance. A healthy man of 60 who occasionally had trouble either getting or maintaining an erection now could be diagnosed with mild ED and prescribed the infamous little blue pill.

As you read, think about the social and cultural context that Viagra and related drugs came from. What ideas and insecurities about masculinity does Viagra play into? Who benefits and who loses from this new definition of men's sexuality?

As a Pfizer Pharmaceuticals sales representative, one of the first things you learn is that erectile dysfunction is a disease. Training manuals counsel that one of the greatest ED myths is that the problem "is all in your mind." A training chart that Pfizer representatives must memorize reveals that "up until the 1970s, erectile dysfunction was deemed 90% psychogenic," or mental, "and 10% organic," or physical. Conversely, the "current medical consensus on erectile dysfunction is 10–30% psychogenic, and 70–90% organic." Today, none of this information sounds strange to us; Pfizer's PR teams and sales representatives have succeeded in converting these "medical facts" into cultural common sense. In fact, most sexual dysfunction reporting takes this organic, or biological, causality "consensus" for granted. But do these sales representatives understand what changed after the 1970s and how these changes created fertile ground for Viagra's debut?

Today, with Viagra offered as a solution, assertions about impotence as an "organic" problem are almost everywhere, with medical practitioners, many of whom were paid researchers or consultants for Pfizer Pharmaceuticals, monopolizing mainstream discussions about impotence. But this wasn't always the case. For most of the twentieth century, sexual problems were attributed to psychological, emotional, relational, and social factors.

Today, most sexual problems are seen as "correctable" physiological problems. How, why, and when this shift towards an "organic model" took place is rarely questioned. What explains the shift in terminology from "impotence" to "erectile dysfunction"? And how do we understand the move from psychologists to urologists as the sex experts of a new era?

The answers to these questions reveal the history of how Viagra came to be. To understand the cultural paradigm shift that occurred between the 1970s and 1990s, one must take into account a changing medical landscape and the rise of social groups that together made this shift possible. As journalist Malcolm Gladwell suggests in his best-selling book, *The Tipping Point,* "Epidemics are a function of the people who transmit infectious agents, the infectious agent itself, and the environment in which the infectious agent is operating." As we will see, in the 1990s, erectile dysfunction took on "epidemic" proportions due to the coordinated efforts of scientific experts and corporations. Specifically, the story of the rise of erectile dysfunction and the emergence of Viagra is a fascinating tale colored by shifting blame, medical accidents, public demonstrations, Puritan intentions, profit motives, vested interests, and medical, scientific, and technological discovery.

The New Emphasis on "Hydraulics"

According to medical historian Robert Aronowitz, the medical profession's large-scale rejection of psychosomatic models for illness can be traced back to a 1933 *JAMA* article, in which medical critic Franz Alexander claimed that medicine's aversion to psycho-social factors harkened back to "the remote days of medicine as sorcery, expelling demons from the body." Alexander claimed that twentieth-century medicine was "dedicated to forgetting its dark, magical past" in favor of "emphasizing exactness and keeping out of field anything that endangers the appearance of science."

In the 1950s, social theorist Talcott Parsons wanted to understand the social function and allure of medicalization. Parsons argued that medical explanations can remove responsibility and blame from the patient. This "sick-role" theory can be applied to the man with sexual failure who is relieved to place blame on his physiology rather than his mind. More recently, sociologists Conrad and Schneider add that medicalization offers optimistic outcomes, such as treatments and cures associated with the prestige of the medical profession.

Clinical psychologist Leonore Tiefer, author of the book *Sex Is Not a Natural Act,* suggests that physiological explanations for impotence fit with the "natural" penile functioning model that men are taught to believe—that the penis is immune when it comes to psychological problems, anxieties, and fears. Biotechnological solutions also allow men to avoid psychological treatments such as marital or sex therapy, which they may find threatening or embarrassing. The trade-off is a potentially embarrassing doctor's visit, which can also be avoided through internet consultations and pharmaceutical purchasing options.

In the 1980s, professional and popular discussions of male sexuality had begun to emphasize physical causes and treatments for sexual problems over and above the earlier respected psychogenic model. Referring to her own experiences working with the Department of Urology at a New York medical center, Tiefer wrote that of the eight hundred men who had been seen since 1981 for erection problems, 90 percent believed their problem to be physical. After examination, only 45 percent of those patients were diagnosed with predominantly medically caused erectile problems. Tiefer was one of the first scholars to question biomedical assumptions, suggesting that they are based on problematic medical models as well as on expectations that normal men must always be interested in sex and that that interest leads easily and directly to erection. Tiefer links these expectations to Masters and Johnson's famous statement that "sex is a natural act," which implies that there is no "natural" reason for decline, so erectile problems must reveal (unnatural) bodily dysfunction, which can be corrected (and bodies restored to normal) with suitable treatment.

Others working in the field of sexual medicine have different explanations for how this paradigm shift came about. Some point to social trends in constant flux, recent influential sex research, or the economic of health care. For example, John Bancroft, former director of the Kinsey Institute for Research on Sex, Gender, and Reproduction, cites a number of factors as crucial to the shift in thinking and practice regarding sexual "function" from psychology to biology: cycles of interest in medicine, changing priorities with increasing technological developments, the need for clinicians to make money, and the high level of involvement of pharmaceutical companies in medical-scientific research and development. Others, like University of Washington psychologist Julia Heiman, explain the change by pointing out the role of researchers Masters and Johnson and the restructuring of health care and coverage in leading the way for a paradigm shift:

> [Medicalization] preceded the Viagra phenomenon. If you think of Masters and Johnson, she was a nurse and he was a medical doctor. They did not do a lot of medicalization for a medical team. They used a much more nonmedical approach. But it favored physiology. Fifteen or twenty years afterwards there's a reaction against this which moves towards the biological. For example, the story of male erection treatment is dominated by medicine. So this is back to the 1970s, when things shifted to the biological. Also, this was part of a larger movement when treatment became considered a medical act. Diagnosis is only available in the DSM, so if you diagnose, this is what you use. Psycho-social diagnoses can be done but they aren't usually because they don't communicate anything to one's colleagues, and there is no reimbursement for that. It's really a guild issue. Anyone doing treatment that is diagnosis related is usually associated with medicine.

Journalistic examples from Viagra media coverage exemplify the seductiveness of medical reasoning in relation to sexual problems. In 1997, two very different publications (to say the least), *JAMA* and *Playboy*, posited similar arguments that: impotence is "mechanical," ignoring psychological dimensions entirely and relying exclusively on biomedical explanations. It is perhaps fair to say that *JAMA* may be invested in promoting the idea that impotence is primarily biological for many reasons, including the fact that this construction is in line with *JAMA* 's regular promotion of medical-science models, as well as the medical community's interest in further developing medical subfields, such as urology. *Playboy*, on the other hand, may have other reasons. Promoting the idea that impotence is a mechanical dysfunction, easily fixed, relieves *Playboy*'s male readership of personal responsibility, blame, or guilt by portraying the condition as one in which the sufferer has no control (but happily, does have access to optimistic outcomes).

In the Viagra era, impotence is no longer blamed on the mind or the wife but, more likely, on human physiology. Locating the problem in the body enables many to benefit, including the patient himself. Lynne Luciano sums up the benefits of medicalizing impotence as follows:

> Transforming impotence into a medical ailment was beneficial not only to physicians but also pharma companies, penile implant manufacturers, and hospitals. Medicalized articles and advertising made information about impotence more acceptable to the mass media by treating it as a scientific issue. Most significantly, medicalization of impotence made men more accepting of it, both because of the centrality of the erections to their self esteem and because modern urology seemed to offer a near-magical technofix—pill, a shot, and not a long session of psychoanalysis. Medical approaches seemed action-oriented. Doctors were doing something about impotence, not just talking about it. In addition, in the 1980s, as health care cutbacks and the proliferation of HMOs eliminated coverage for therapeutic counseling, genuine medical problems were more likely to be covered by insurance. And treating the condition as a medical problem made it more palatable to men by absolving them of blame and failure.

In the 1980s, ideas were changing about who and what to blame for sexual problems. But practitioners and journalists still needed convincing that physiology prevailed over psychology. In 1983, the urologists got their proof.

The "Happy Accident"

The story of Viagra's discovery is a powerful one—a story that Pfizer has carefully crafted for the public. In 1989 the chemical composition of sildenafil existed in Pfizer Pharmaceuticals labs and test tubes as UK-92,480, a cure for angina. In development and then in clinical tests from 1989 to 1994 in Sandwich, England, at Pfizer Pharmaceutical's research headquarters, sildenafil's success in sending blood to the hearts of trial subjects was not realized. Instead, trial subjects and clinicians discovered that sildenafil increased blood flow to the genital region, causing and sustaining erections, and noted this as a common "side-effect." After a preliminary ten-day safety trial for the angina treatment in 1992, one clinician who was running the trials reported common side effects to his supervisor, Allen, at Pfizer.

> He mentioned that at 50 mg taken every 8 hours for 10 days, there were episodes of indigestion [and of] aches in patients' backs and legs. And he said, "Oh, there are some reports of penile erections."

It was not a Eureka moment, as portrayed in some popular accounts, said Allen. It was "just an observation." Obviously, a crucial one.

Overall, the most common Viagra origin story in the mainstream media prior to Viagra's public debut in 1998 recounts the "accidental" discovery of a drug that created and sustained erections and produced intense demand among dumbfounded yet delighted trial subjects. The story generally goes on to suggest that such demand and subsequent public curiosity fueled Pfizer Pharmaceutical's effort to develop and market an impotence drug they later named Viagra.

Such "unanticipated consequence" stories carry public cachet, but only in certain circles. Social scientists Latour and Woolgar argue that scientific accounts are fundamentally about the "creation of order" out of disorder. In this vein, when an article in *JAMA* declared that "better understanding of the mechanisms of erection led to the development of the new oral agent sildenafil," the scientist authors of this article (many of whom worked for Pfizer) predictably tell a more staid version of this story that avoids mention of medical "accidents" and instead favors an ordered, scientific-method approach.

The substitution of science over mischance is repeated by a senior vice president at Pfizer, Dr. David McGibney, in a talk delivered to the Royal Society for the Encouragement of Arts, Manufactures & Commerce in February 1999, one year after Viagra's public debut:

A Nobel prizewinner has said: "Research is the art of seeing what others see, but thinking what others don't think." That was certainly true of one of our recent discoveries, Viagra, with our own preclinical and clinical studies, together with emerging science from academic laboratories, refocusing our therapeutic target from angina to erectile dysfunction.

In Dr. McGibney's narrative, Viagra's discovery is not accidental but the result of creative thinking, research, and "refocusing." Happy clinical trial subjects are nowhere to be found. Dr. McGibney's pride in Viagra one year after its debut also hides Pfizer's initial corporate ambivalence about developing and marketing this drug. By 2001, the "happy accident" story had become popularized enough that Pfizer published and distributed a version of it to Pfizer-affiliated sexual-dysfunction specialists. But it seems that in order to maintain its reputation in the public sphere as a serious company dedicated to drug development and disease treatment, Pfizer continued to develop a corporate strategy and promotional campaign that associated Viagra with debilitating medical dysfunction or disease. And this is exactly what they did, with astounding success.

"Branding" Erectile Dysfunction

By the 1990s, several people and events had set the stage for Viagra. A paradigm shift had taken place in scientific understandings of sexuality, which now located the source of sexual problems in the body, not the mind, the society, or the relationship. Brindley paved the way for the chemical treatment of erections. Urologists were now recognized as the new sex experts, with some poised to become paid consultants to the pharmaceutical industry. A drug for treating impotence was accidentally discovered. Now Pfizer needed a marketing plan that would sanitize and sell sildenafil.

Before starting clinical trials, Pfizer had to solve the problem of how to construct a market for their product and build up public anticipation and practitioner interest. According to philosopher Carl Elliott, author of *Better Than Well*, the industry has learned that the key to selling psychiatric drugs is to sell the illnesses they treat. Doctors treat "patients" and must be convinced that the problem being addressed is a medical disorder. In other words, from a doctor's perspective, Paxil must treat social phobia rather than relieve shyness, and Ritalin must treat attention-deficit disorder rather than improve concentration. The technology in question must treat the proper illness, or else there is no reason why doctors should be obliged to provide it.

One writer in the trade journal *Pharmaceutical Executive* compliments Pfizer on successfully claiming and "branding" ED. To do so, Pfizer had to make sure that from the beginning Viagra and its corresponding medical disorder, ED, were clearly understood and inseparable in the public imagination.

> How many people knew ten years ago that there would be such a term as "erectile dysfunction"? That's brilliant branding. And it's not just about branding the drug; it's branding the condition, and by inference, a branding of the patient....What kind of patient does a blockbuster create? We're creating patient populations just as we're creating medicines, to make sure that products become blockbusters.

Although the diagnostic category "erectile dysfunction" existed prior to Viagra's debut, Pfizer borrowed the term and introduced it and Viagra together in 1998, thus constructing a public association between problem and treatment. According to journalists Stipp and Whitaker writing for *Fortune*, over ten years before Bob Dole made "ED" a house-hold term in television ads as a Viagra spokesperson, erectile dysfunction was a medical category redefined by Irwin Goldstein and his team of researchers in the first federally funded study on impotence, Aging Study (MMAS), which took place from 1987 to 1989. In this important study for the field of urology, impotence was assigned a new name and redefined more broadly. A new subjective and elastic category, "erectile dysfunction" replaced the older stigmatized term "impotence," thereby blurring disease and discontent. Impotence, which is the inability to get an erection, was replaced by ED, which is "the inability to get and maintain an erection adequate for satisfactory sexual performance."

Thus, the MMAS questionnaire characterized erectile potency not as an either/or but as if potency existed on a continuum. Subjects were asked to rate their potency on a scale of one to four: (1) not impotent, (2) minimally impotent, (3) moderately impotent, or (4) completely impotent. These responses were then assigned gradations of erectile dysfunction, ranging from "no ED" to "mild ED (usually able)" to "moderate ED (sometimes able)" to "severe ED (never able)." In other words, men who reported "unsatisfactory sexual performance" or who were "usually able to penetrate partner" were included in the "mild ED" category. Given these flexible definitions, of 1,290 men surveyed, aged forty to seventy, 52 percent fell somewhere in the "mild, moderate, or complete erectile dysfunction" categories. This statistic—that half of men over forty experience ED—is now cited regularly by Pfizer Pharmaceuticals. Thus, by measuring erectile dysfunction both physiologically and subjectively, Pfizer created a "wider range of troubles" to address.

But "diagnostic expansion," or the expansion of medical boundaries and medical categories, may be what is sending record numbers of men to their doctors and spurring record-breaking profits for Pfizer. The big picture of diagnostic augmentation, embedded within a corporate context of market expansion, is that more people are prescribing, selling, taking, and profiting from prescription drugs than ever before. Philosopher and bioethicist Carl Elliot explains,

> Drug companies are not simply making up diseases out of thin air, and psychiatrists are not being gulled into diagnosing well people as sick. No one doubts that some people genuinely suffer from, say, depression...or that the right medications make these disorders better. But surrounding the core of many of these disorders is a wide zone of ambiguity that can be chiseled out and expanded. The bigger the diagnostic category, the more patients who fit within its boundaries, the more psychoactive drugs will be prescribed.

With the change in definition and nomenclature, initial impotence numbers tripled. Pfizer promotional materials for 2000 confusingly pronounce erectile dysfunction a "common condition that's commonly undertreated." In 2001, Pfizer's official website, www.Viagra.com, used the MMAS statistics to claim, "Erectile dysfunction (ED) affects over 30 million men *to some degree* in the United States" (emphasis added). Apparently, erectile dysfunction, while appearing to be a precise, objective measure, is flexible and subjective enough to include almost any male with sexual insecurities, dissatisfaction, concerns, or intermittent erectile "failures."

Disease Mongering and Doctor Salesmen

Pfizer's shifting of medical definitions in what looks like an attempt to create and expand markets is common in contemporary medical marketing. Medical journalist Lynn Payer shares these concerns in her book *The Disease-Mongers*.

> Disease mongering—trying to convince essentially well people that they are sick, or slightly sick, or slightly sick people that they are very ill, is big business. To market drugs to the widest possible audience, pharmaceutical companies must convince people—or their physicians—that they are sick....To tell us about a disease and then to imply that there is a high likelihood that we have it... by citing the fact that huge numbers of Americans do...is to gnaw away at our self-confidence. And that may really make us sick.

> Disease mongering can include turning ordinary ailments into medical problems, seeing mild symptoms as serious, treating personal problems as medical, seeing risks as diseases, and framing prevalence estimates to maximise potential markets.

With the publicity machine in gear and public anticipation high, thanks to the work of Goldstein and other Pfizer consultants, the final phase of preparing America for Viagra required quickly concluding clinical trials, earning fast FDA approval, and associating sildenafil with a name that people would remember. Viagra symbolism and imagery were particularly useful when it came to naming, one of the final stages in the making of the drug.

According to sociologist Joel Best, "naming" is crucial because it "shapes the problem" and the solution. Various journalists have suggested that "Viagra" is a mixture of the words "vigor" and "Niagara"—thus constructing the little blue pill as a powerful, vital, potent, thundering entity, and thereby implying that "the problem" is vulnerability, powerlessness, and helplessness and the solution is the opposite of these states. Such symbolism appears regularly in popular media, as in the *Harper's Bazaar* suggestion, "[Viagra's] name seems meant to evoke the pounding power of Niagara Falls....It's expected to thunder onto the market sometime this year." And this symbolic name is no coincidence. According to Greider, it is common for pharmaceutical companies to hire outside consultants to conduct market research and screen names, because the name is central to "branding" the product.

The product name and inflated statistics infused investors' hopes for the Viagra bull market. Pfizer stocks rose 75 percent in anticipation of the pill that could work on anyone. "Among the ideas that excited some analysts was the possibility that millions of men and women with no medical need for the new drugs would take them to enhance sex, vastly amplifying sales." Pfizer would never officially admit that Viagra was for anyone but those with medical need, but it did profit from the widespread concern with sexual dissatisfaction it helped to create.

Manufacturing Need

As this chapter has shown, the story of Viagra is not just about the manufacture of a little blue pill. It is also about manufacturing "needs," so that every man in America could see himself as a potential Viagra consumer. If nothing else, Pfizer advertisements and expert claims might cause a man to question whether he is young enough, sexual enough, or man enough. While this may seem exaggerated, it is the case that currently most, if not all, American insurance providers pay for Viagra prescriptions, granting legitimacy and value to Viagra and erectile dysfunction, as well as to efforts to normalize male potency and confidence levels, *and* making it possible for all insured men to simply "ask their doctor." It is not accidental that most insurance companies cover Viagra. Kaiser Permanente, the nation's largest HMO, aroused a furor by initially declaring that it would not pay for Viagra, but then backed off. Oxford Health Plans, a Connecticut-based HMO, refused to cover Viagra and became the first insurer to be sued by an irate client. Even the Pentagon agreed to cover the drug once it was estimated that Viagra could eat up one-fifth of the entire pharmaceutical budget of the Veterans Affairs Department, roughly the cost of forty-five Tomahawk Cruise missiles. It is important to note that while insurers tend to cover Viagra, most limit the prescription to six pills a month, with "doctor-diagnosed" erectile dysfunction. Many commentators have pointed out that when the most powerful members of our society or those who control our economy make demands, they are answered. Meanwhile, women's prescriptions such as birth control are still not covered by most insurance plans.[1] Insurance coverage of Viagra and not birth control has spurred a "contraceptive equity movement" nationwide, in which fifteen states have passed contraceptive equity laws that require insurers to cover birth control.

Erectile difficulties are real. But so are the fears that men have about such difficulties, as well as cultural ideals conflating potency, manhood, and individualism. Taken together, those men suffering from erectile problems, those fearful of developing impotence, and those interested in ensuring potency provide Pfizer with a sizeable market for its product. Herein lies the problem for anyone concerned about the construction of normal masculinity and the sexual body. Pfizer and its networks are uniquely positioned to send an important message to men about illness, sexuality, and masculinity—and many will listen. But, the message they have chosen to send is disappointing, for it is the most profitable message they can send: illness in epidemic proportions. The target audience is individual men with aging bodies. And the goal is to get men to their doctors. While this marketing move makes sense, it is oversimplified and highly problematic. Male insecurity may reach epidemic proportions, but the number of men with severe ED is much smaller. By targeting individual men and their dysfunctional bodies, Pfizer obscures the impact that "dysfunctional" social norms or relationships can have on men's insecurities and bodies. Sending men to doctors may be a good thing, but shouldn't they talk with others—such as partners and friends? Pfizer's overemphasis on individuals obscures the sociocultural, medical, relationship-based, and age-related factors that contribute to the concerns and difficulties of men, and it therefore results in mass reinforcement of silence and social insecurity.

DISCUSSION QUESTIONS

1. Viagra is just one example of medicalization. What other nonmedical conditions can you think of that have been redefined over time as medical issues?

2. Viagra is marketed heavily toward middle-aged and older heterosexual men. Why do you think that Viagra isn't marketed to homosexual men?

3. Why might visiting the doctor for a prescription be more appealing to men than going to talk to a counselor or discussing the issue with their partner?

NOTE

1. This changed with the passage of the Affordable Care Act in 2010 which requires health insurance plans on the federal health insurance exchanges to cover women's contraception, although not all options are covered. There have been challenges to this portion of the law by religious organizations.

10

Situational Ethics and College Student Cheating

Emily E. LaBeff, Robert E. Clark, Valerie J. Haines, and George M. Diekhoff

Have you ever cheated on an exam or some other type of schoolwork? If so, you're not alone. The Internet is rife with websites where students can buy term papers, and new digital technologies make it easier than ever to share tests or other work. Some schools even outsource their anticheating efforts by using websites such as Turnitin.com to check student work against that submitted by others. Even an old-fashioned glance at a classmate's test or copying homework before class still happens with impressive frequency. Adults aren't exempt from this either. A recent spate of news stories has revealed that academics, politicians, journalists, and all sorts of other authors plagiarized writing and presented it as their own. Yet as widespread as cheating in various forms may be, it's something that is viewed by the wider society as deviant. If you've ever cheated, you probably didn't drop into your teacher's office or call your parents to brag about how proud you were of how you cheated. People know that cheating is wrong. While people may claim that they didn't realize a behavior counted as cheating, few would argue that they had no idea that cheating itself is wrong.

So how can we explain why cheating is so widespread when it is a form of behavior that is almost universally acknowledged as wrong (i.e., deviant?) In this article, LaBeff et al. provide us with one set of answers. They argue that students who cheat use what they call techniques of neutralization to justify their actions. These rationalizations allow students to reconcile the wider cultural value that cheating is wrong, while simultaneously redefining their actions in such a way that does not feel that they have committed a deviant act.

As you read, think about whether you or those you know have ever used these techniques of neutralization and how they might be applied to behaviors considered deviant other than cheating.

This report examines instances of self-reported cheating engaged in by college students, fifty-four percent of whom reported at least one incidence of cheating. Descriptive responses are analyzed in the context of techniques of neutralization. The neutralizing attitude held by these student cheaters suggests that situational ethics are involved. Although the respondents indicate disapproval of cheating, many students feel justified in cheating under certain circumstances.

Introduction

Studies have shown that cheating in college is epidemic, and some analysts of this problem estimate that fifty percent of college students may engage in such behavior (e.g., Pavela 1976; Baird 1980; Wellborn 1980; Haines, Diekhoff, LaBeff, and Clark 1986). Such studies have examined demographic and social characteristics of students such as age, sex, academic standing, major, classification, extracurricular activity, level of test anxiety, degree of sanctioned threat, and internal social control. Each of these factors has been found to be related, to some extent, to cheating although the relationship of these factors varies considerably from study to study (Bonjean and McGee 1965; Harp and Taietz 1966; Stannord and Bowers 1970; Fakouri 1972; Johnson and Gormly 1972; Bronzaft, Stuart, and Blum 1973; Tittle and Rowe 1973; Liska 1978; Baird 1980; Leming 1980; Barnett and Dalton 1981, Eve and Bromley 1981; Newhouse 1982; Singhal 1982; Haines et al. 1986).

In our freshmen classes, we often informally ask students to discuss whether they have cheated in college and, if so, how. Some students have almost bragged about which of their methods have proven most effective including writing notes on shoes and caps and on the backs of calculators. Rolling up a tiny cheat sheet into a pen cap was mentioned. And one student said he had "incredibly gifted eyes" which allowed him to see the answers of a smart student four rows in front of him. One female student talked about rummaging through the dumpsters at night close to final examination time looking for test dittos. She did find at least one examination. A sorority member informed us that two of her term papers in her freshman year were sent from a sister chapter of the sorority at another university, retyped and submitted to the course professor. Further, many of these students saw nothing wrong with what they were doing, although they verbally agreed with the statement that cheating was unethical.

It appears that students hold qualified guidelines for behavior which are situationally determined. As such, the concept of situational ethics might well describe this college cheating in that rules for behavior may not be considered rigid but depend on the circumstances involved (Norris and

Dodder 1979, p. 545). Joseph Fletcher, in his well known philosophical treatise, *Situation Ethics: The New Morality* (1966), argues that this position is based on the notion that any action may be considered good or bad depending on the social circumstances. In other words, what is wrong in most situations might be considered right or acceptable if the end is defined as appropriate. This concept focuses on contextual appropriateness, not necessarily what is good or right, but what is viewed as fitting, given the circumstances. Central to this process is the idea that situations alter cases, thus altering the rules and principles guiding behavior (Edwards 1967).

Of particular relevance to the present study is the work of Gresham Sykes and David Matza (1957) who first developed the concept of neutralization to explain delinquent behavior. Neutralization theory in the study of delinquency expresses the process of situationally defining deviant behavior. In this view, deviance is based upon "... an unrecognized extension of defenses to crimes, in the form of justifications... seen as valid by the delinquent but not by... society at large" (Sykes and Matza 1957, p. 666). Through neutralization individuals justify violation of accepted behavior. This provides protection "... from self blame and the blame of others..." (Sykes and Matza 1957, p. 666). They do this before, during, and after the act. Such techniques of neutralization are separated into five categories: denial of responsibility, condemnation of condemners, appeal to higher loyalties, denial of victim, and denial of injury. In each case, individuals profess a conviction about a particular law but argue that special circumstances exist which cause them to violate the rules in a particular instance. However, in recent research, only Liska (1978) and Haines et al. (1986) found neutralization to be an important factor in college student cheating.

Methodology

The present analysis is based on a larger project conducted during the 1983–1984 academic year when a 49-item questionnaire about cheating was administered to students at a small southwestern university. The student body (N = 4950) was evenly distributed throughout the university's programs with a disproportionate number (twenty-seven percent) majoring in business administration. In order to achieve a representative sample from a cross-section of the university student body, the questionnaire was administered to students enrolled in courses classified as a part of the university's core curriculum. Freshmen and sophomores were overrepresented (eighty-four percent of the sample versus sixty percent of the university population). Females were also overrepresented (sixty-two percent of the sample versus fifty-five percent of the university population).

There are obvious disadvantages associated with the use of self-administered questionnaires for data-gathering purposes. One such problem is the acceptance of student responses without benefit of contest. To maximize the return rate, questionnaires were administered during regularly scheduled class periods. Participation was on a voluntary basis. In order to establish the validity of responses, students were guaranteed anonymity. Students were also instructed to limit their reponses regarding whether they had cheated to the current academic year.

Previous analysis (e.g., Haines et al. 1986) focused on the quantitative aspects of the questionnaire. The present analysis is intended to assess the narrative responses to the incidence of cheating in three forms, namely on major examinations, quizzes, and class assignments, as well as the perceptions of and attitudes held by students toward cheating and the effectiveness of deterrents to cheating. Students recorded their experiences in their own words. Most students (eighty-seven percent) responded to the open-ended portion of the questionnaire.

Results

Of the 380 undergraduate students who participated in the spring survey, fifty-four percent indicated they had cheated during the previous six month period. Students were requested to indicate whether cheating involved examination, weekly quizzes, and/or homework assignments. Much cheating took the form of looking on someone else's paper, copying homework, and either buying term papers or getting friends to write papers for them. Only five of the 205 students who admitted cheating reported being caught by the professor. However, seven percent (n = 27) of the students reported cheating more than five times during the preceding six month period. Twenty percent (n = 76) indicated that most students openly approved of cheating. Only seventeen students reported they would inform the instructor if they saw another student cheating. Many students, especially older students, indicated they felt resentment toward cheaters, but most also noted that they would not do anything about it (i.e., inform the instructor).

To more fully explore the ways in which students neutralize their behavior, narrative data from admitted student cheaters were examined (n = 149). The narrative responses were easily classified into three of the five techniques described by Sykes and Matza (1957).

Denial of Responsibility

Denial of responsibility was the most often identified response. This technique involves a declaration by the offenders that, in light of circumstances beyond their control, they cannot be held accountable for their actions. Rather than identifying the behavior as "accidental," they attribute wrongdoing to the influence of outside forces. In some instances, students expressed an inability to withstand peer pressure to cheat. Responses show a recognition of cheating as an unacceptable behavior, implying that under different circumstances cheating would not have occurred. One student commented:

> I was working forty plus hours a week and we had a lot to read for that day. I just couldn't get it all in.... I'm not saying cheating is okay, sometimes you just have to.

Another student explained her behavior in the following statement:

> ... I had the flu the week before... had to miss several classes so I had no way of knowing what was going to be on the exam (sic). My grades were good up to that point and I hadn't cheated.... I just couldn't risk it.

It is noteworthy that these statements indicate the recognition that cheating is wrong under normal circumstances.

Other responses demonstrate the attempt by students to succeed through legitimate means (e.g., taking notes and studying) only to experience failure. Accordingly, they were left with no alternative but to cheat. One student commented:

> ... even though I've studied in the past, I've failed the exam (sic) so I cheated on my last test hoping to bring a better grade.

Another student explained his behavior in the following manner:

> I studied for the exam (sic) and I studied hard but the material on the test was different from what I expected.... I had to make a good grade.

In some accounts, students present a unique approach to the denial of responsibility. Upon entering the examination setting, these students had no intention of cheating, but the opportunity presented itself. The following statement by one student provides a clear illustration of this point:

... I was taking the test and someone in another part of the room was telling someone else an answer. I heard it and just couldn't not (sic) write it down.

Although viewing such behavior as dishonest, the blame for any wrongdoing is quickly transferred to those who provide the answers. Another student justified her action in the following manner:

... I didn't mean to cheat but once you get the right answer it's hard, no impossible, not to. How could you ignore an answer that you knew was right?

In addition, some students reported accidentally seeing other students' test papers. In such instances, the cheaters chastised classmates for not covering up their answer sheets. As one student wrote, such temptation simply cannot be overcome:

I studied hard for the exam (sic) and needed an A. I just happened to look up and there was my neighbor's paper uncovered. I found myself checking my answers against his through the whole test.

Appeal to Higher Loyalties

Conflict also arises between peer group expectations and the normative expectations of the larger society. When this occurs, the individual may choose to sacrifice responsibility, thereby maintaining the interest of peers. Such allegiance allows these individuals to supercede moral obligations when special circumstances arise.

Students who invoke this technique of neutralization frequently described their behavior as an attempt to help another. One student stated:

I only cheated because my friend had been sick and she needed help.... it (cheating) wouldn't have happened any other time.

Another student denied any wrongdoing on her part as the following statement illustrates:

I personally have never cheated. I've had friends who asked for help so I let them see my test. Maybe some would consider that to be cheating.

These students recognize the act of cheating is wrong. However, their statements also suggest that in some situations cheating can be overlooked. Loyalty to a friend in need takes precedence over honesty in the classroom. Another student described his situation in the following manner:

> I was tutoring this girl but she just couldn't understand the material.... I felt I had to help her on the test.

Condemnation of Condemners

Cheaters using this technique of neutralization attempt to shift attention from their own actions to the actions of others, most often authority figures. By criticizing those in authority as being unfair or unethical, the behavior of the offender seems less consequential by comparison. Therefore, dishonest behavior occurs in reaction to the perceived dishonesty of the authority figure. Students who utilize this technique wrote about uncaring, unprofessional instructors with negative attitudes who were negligent in their behavior. These incidents were said to be a precursor to their cheating behavior. The following response illustrates this view:

> The teachers here are boring and I dislike this school. The majority of teachers here don't care about the students and are rude when you ask them for help.

In other instances, students cite unfair teaching practices which they perceive to be the reason for their behavior. One student stated:

> Major exams (sic) are very important to your grade and it seems that the majority of instructors make up the exams (sic) to try and trick you instead of testing your knowledge.

In this case, the instructor is thought to engage in a deliberate attempt to fail the students by making the examinations difficult. Also within this category were student accounts which frequently express a complaint of being overworked. As one student wrote:

> One instructor assigns more work than anyone could possibly handle... at least I know I can't, so sometimes cheating is the answer.

Another student described his situation as follows:

Sometimes it seems like these instructors get together and plan to make it difficult.... I had three major tests in one day and very little time to study...

Although less frequently mentioned, perceived parental pressure also serves as a neutralizing factor for dishonesty. One student stated:

During my early years at school my parents constantly pressured me for good grades.... they would have withheld money if grades were bad.

Another student blamed the larger society for his cheating:

In America, we're taught that results aren't achieved through beneficial means, but through the easiest means.

Another stated:

Ted Kennedy has been a modeling (sic) example for many of us.... This society teaches us to survive, to rationalize.... (it) is built on injustice and expediency.

This student went on to say that he cheated throughout a difficult science course so he could spend more time studying for major courses which he enjoyed.

Denial of Injury and Denial of The Victim

Denial of injury and denial of the victim do not appear in the student accounts of their cheating. In denial of injury, the wrongdoer states that no one was harmed or implies that accusations of injury are grossly exaggerated. In the second case, denial of the victim, those who violate norms often portray their targets as legitimate. Due to certain factors such as the societal role, personal characteristics, or lifestyle of the victim, the wrongdoer felt the victim "had it coming."

It is unlikely that students will either deny injury or deny the victim since there are no real targets in cheating. However, attempts to deny injury are possible when the one who is cheating argues that cheating is a personal matter rather than a public one. It is also possible that some students are cognizant of the effect their cheating activities have upon the educational system as a whole and, therefore, choose to neutralize their behavior in ways which allow them to focus on the act rather than the consequences of cheating. By observing their actions from a myopic viewpoint, such students avoid the larger issues of morality.

Conclusion

The purpose of this report was to analyze student responses to cheating in their college coursework. Using Sykes and Matza's model of techniques of neutralization, we found that students rationalized their cheating behavior and do so without challenging the norm of honesty. Student responses fit three of the five techniques of neutralization. The most common technique is a denial of responsibility. Second, students tend to "condemn the condemners," blaming faculty and testing procedures. Finally, students "appeal to higher loyalties" by arguing that it is more important to help a friend than to avoid cheating. The use of these techniques of neutralization conveys the message that students recognize and accept cheating as an undesirable behavior which, nonetheless, can be excused under certain circumstances. Such findings reflect the prevalence of situational ethics.

The situation appears to be one in which students are not caught and disciplined by instructors. Additionally, students who cheat do not concern themselves with overt negative sanctions from other students. In some groups, cheating is planned, expected, and often rewarded in that students may receive better grades That leaves a student's ethical, internalized control as a barrier to cheating. However, the neutralizing attitude allows students to sidestep issues of ethics and guilt by placing the blame for their behavior elsewhere. Neutralization allows them to state their belief that in general cheating is wrong, but in some circumstances cheating is acceptable, even necessary.

Given such widespread acceptance of cheating in the university setting, it may be useful to further test the salience of neutralization and other such factors in more diverse university environments. This study is limited to a small state university. It is important also to extend the research to a wider range of institutions including prestigious private colleges, large state universities, and church-related schools.

Cross-cultural studies of cheating may also prove useful for identifying broader social and cultural forces which underlie situational ethics and cheating behavior. In this regard, the process involved in learning neutralizing attitudes could be integrated with work in the field of deviance in order to expand our understanding of rule breakers along a continuum of minor to major forms of deviance.

DISCUSSION QUESTIONS

1. How does the context in which deviance takes place affect whether a behavior is defined as deviant? Are there people you would openly discuss cheating with but others you would not? What is different about these groups?

2. How might these techniques of neutralization be used by someone who steals office supplies, time, or other things of value from his or her place of work?

3. Do you think that there might be cross-cultural variations in techniques of neutralization? Or might there be more techniques of neutralization from your culture that you could add to this list? How else do we justify deviant acts in ourselves or others?

4. Is sharing work and coordinating intellectual effort with other students always deviant? Under what circumstances is this not only accepted but encouraged by your teacher?

REFERENCES

Baird, John S. 1980. "Current Trends in College Cheating." *Psychology in the Schools* 17:512–522.

Barnett, David C., and J. C. Dalton. 1981. "Why College Students Cheat." *Journal of College Student Personnel* 22:545–551.

Bonjean, Charles M., and Reece McGee. 1965. "Undergraduate Scholastic Dishonesty: A Comparative Analysis of Deviance and Control Systems." *Social Science Quarterly* 65:289–296.

Bronzaft, Arline L., Irving R. Stuart, and Barbara Blum. 1973. "Test Anxiety and Cheating on College Examinations." *Psychological Reports* 32:149–150.

Edwards, Paul 1967. *The Encyclopedia of Philosophy, #3,* edited by Paul Edwards. New York: Macmillan Company and Free Press.

Eve, Raymond, and David G. Bromley. 1981. "Scholastic Dishonesty Among College Undergraduates: A Parallel Test of Two Sociological Explanations." *Youth and Society* 13:629–640.

Fakouri, M. E. 1972. "Achieving Motivation and Cheating." *Psychological Reports* 31:629–640.

Fletcher, Joseph. 1966 *Situation Ethics: The New Morality.* Philadelphia: The Westminster Press.

Haines, Valerie J., George Diekhoff, Emily LaBeff, and Robert Clark. 1986. "College Cheating: Immaturity, Lack of Commitment, and the Neutralizing Attitude." *Research in Higher Education* 25:342–354.

Harp, John, and Philip Taietz. 1966. "Academic Integrity and Social Structure: A Study of Cheating Among College Students." *Social Problems* 13:365–373.

Johnson, Charles D., and John Gormly, 1972. "Academic Cheating: The Contribution of Sex, Personality, and Situational Variables." *Developmental Psychology* 6:320–325.

Leming, James S. 1980. "Cheating Behavior, Subject Variables, and Components of the Internal-External Scale Under High and Low Risk Conditions." *Journal of Education Research* 74:83–87.

Liska, Allen. 1987 "Deviant Involvement, Associations, and Attitudes: Specifying the Underlying Causal Structures." *Sociology and Social Research* 63:73–88.

Newhouse, Robert C. 1982. "Alienation and Cheating Behavior in the School Environment." *Psychology in the Schools* 19:234–237.

Norris, Terry D., and Richard A. Dodder. 1979. "A Behavioral Continuum Synthesizing Neutralization Theory, Situational Ethics and Juvenile Delinquency." *Adolescence* 55:545–555.

Pavela, Gary. 1976, "Cheating on the Campus: Who's Really to Blame?" *Time* 107 (June 7):24.

Singhal, Avinash C. 1982. "Factors in Student Dishonesty." *Psychological Reports* 51:775–780.

Stannord, Charles I., and William J. Bowers. 1970. "College Fraternity as an Opportunity Structure for Meeting Academic Demands." *Social Problems* 17:371–390.

Sykes, Gresham, and David Matza. 1957. "Techniques of Neutralization: A Theory of Delinquency." *American Sociological Review* 22:664–670.

Tittle, Charles, and Alan Rowe. 1973. "Moral Appeal, Sanction Threat, and Deviance: An Experimental Test." *Social Problems* 20:448–498.

Wellborn, Stanley N. 1980. "Cheating in College Becomes Epidemic" *U.S News and World Report* 89 (October 20):39–42.

The New Jim Crow

Michelle Alexander

A caste is a rigid system of stratification within a society. One of the most well-known caste systems is that associated with the Hindu religion, where belief in reincarnation shapes beliefs about how society should be organized. Children inherit the exact same position in society as their parents, without the opportunity for social mobility except in the case of Karma. Options for education, work, friendship, and romantic partners are controlled by strict social sanctions that ensure the members of each caste stay "in their place."

The concept of a caste system is the antithesis to what is commonly referred to as the American Dream—that there is equal opportunity for all Americans and that how far you go in life and where you wind up on the socioeconomic ladder is a reflection of individual ability and effort. The saying "pull yourself up by your bootstraps" is a colloquial way of referring to the idea behind the American Dream.

In a caste system, some segments of the population are not allowed to have bootstraps, or for that matter—boots. The ability to move up (or down) the socioeconomic ladder in a society is, by design, not available to them. In this article, legal scholar Michelle Alexander argues that the American criminal justice system has created a caste system based on race, recreating the overt legal and social barriers faced by African Americans in the Jim Crow era from 1896 to 1965. The problem today is subtler—politicians and those working in the criminal justice system tend to vociferously deny that race plays any role in arrests, incarceration rates, or treatment of criminals after they have served their time. Alexander shows that there are clear statistical and anecdotal biases based on race, and that even the laws surrounding how charges of racial bias can be brought to courts for consideration has contributed to the systematic discrimination and disenfranchisement of blacks in American society. The end result is a racial caste system that is quite the opposite of the American Dream.

How Mass Incarceration Turns People of Color Into Permanent Second-Class Citizens

The first time I encountered the idea that our criminal justice system functions much like a racial caste system, I dismissed the notion. It was more than 10 years ago in Oakland when I was rushing to catch the bus and spotted a bright orange sign stapled to a telephone pole. It screamed in large, bold print: "The Drug War is the New Jim Crow." I scanned the text of the flyer and then muttered something like, "Yeah, the criminal justice system is racist in many ways, but making such an absurd comparison doesn't help. People will just think you're crazy." I then hopped on the bus and headed to my new job as director of the Racial Justice Project for the American Civil Liberties Union of Northern California.

What a difference a decade makes. After years of working on issues of racial profiling, police brutality, and drug-law enforcement in poor communities of color as well as working with former inmates struggling to *reenter* a society that never seemed to have much use for them, I began to suspect that I was wrong about the criminal-justice system. It was not just another institution infected with racial bias but a different beast entirely. The activists who posted the sign on the telephone pole were not crazy, nor were the smattering of lawyers and advocates around the country who were beginning to connect the dots between our current system of mass incarceration and earlier forms of racial control. Quite belatedly, I came to see that mass incarceration in the United States has, in fact, emerged as a comprehensive and well-disguised system of racialized social control that functions in a manner strikingly similar to Jim Crow.

What has changed since the collapse of Jim Crow has less to do with the basic structure of our society than with the language we use to justify severe inequality. In the era of colorblindness, it is no longer socially permissible to use race, explicitly, as justification for discrimination, exclusion, or social contempt. Rather, we use our criminal justice system to associate criminality with people of color and then engage in the prejudiced practices we supposedly left behind. Today, it is legal to discriminate against ex-offenders in ways it was once legal to discriminate against African Americans. Once you're labeled a felon, depending on the state you're in, the old forms of discrimination—employment discrimination, housing discrimination, denial of the right to vote, and exclusion from jury service—are suddenly legal. As a criminal, you have scarcely more rights and arguably less respect than a black man living in Alabama at the height of Jim Crow. We have not ended racial caste in America; we have merely redesigned it.

More than two million African Americans are currently under the control of the criminal-justice system—in prison or jail, on probation or parole. During the past few decades, millions more have cycled in and out of the system; indeed, nearly 70 percent of people released from prison are rearrested within three years. Most people appreciate that millions of African Americans were locked into a second-class status during slavery and Jim Crow, and that these earlier systems of racial control created a legacy of political, social, and economic inequality that our nation is still struggling to overcome. Relatively few, however, seem to appreciate that millions of African Americans are subject to a new system of control—mass incarceration—which also has a devastating effect on families and communities. The harm is greatly intensified when prisoners are released. As criminologist Jeremy Travis has observed, "In this brave new world, punishment for the original offense is no longer enough; one's debt to society is never paid."

The scale of incarceration-related discrimination is astonishing. Ex-offenders are routinely stripped of essential rights. Current felon-disenfranchisement laws bar 13 percent of African American men from casting a vote, thus making mass incarceration an effective tool of voter suppression—one reminiscent of the poll taxes and literacy tests of the Jim Crow era. Employers routinely discriminate against an applicant based on criminal history, as do landlords. In most states, it is also legal to make ex-drug offenders ineligible for food stamps. In some major urban areas, if you take into account prisoners—who are excluded from poverty and unemployment statistics, thus masking the severity of black disadvantage—more than half of working-age African American men have criminal records and are thus subject to legalized discrimination for the rest of their lives. In Chicago, for instance, nearly 80 percent of working-age African American men had criminal records in 2002. These men are permanently locked into an inferior, second-class status, or caste, by law and custom.

The official explanation for this is crime rates. Our prison population increased sevenfold in less than 30 years, going from about 300,000 to more than 2 million, supposedly due to rising crime in poor communities of color.

Crime rates, however, actually have little to do with incarceration rates. Crime rates have fluctuated during the past 30 years and today are at historical lows, but incarceration rates have consistently soared. Most sociologists and criminologists today will acknowledge that crime rates and incarceration rates have moved independently of each other; incarceration rates have skyrocketed regardless of whether crime has gone up or down in any particular community or in the nation as a whole.

What caused the unprecedented explosion in our prison population? It turns out that the activists who posted the sign on the telephone pole were right: The *war on drugs* is the single greatest contributor to mass incarceration in the United States. Drug convictions accounted for about two-thirds of the increase in the federal prison system and more than half of the increase in the state prison system between 1985 and 2000—the period of the U.S. penal system's most dramatic expansion.

Contrary to popular belief, the goal of this war is not to root out violent offenders or drug kingpins. In 2005, for example, four out of five drug arrests were for possession, while only one out five were for sales. A 2007 report from Sentencing Project found that most people in state prison for drug offenses had no history of violence or significant selling activity. Nearly 80 percent of the increase in drug arrests in the 1990s, when the drug war peaked, could be attributed to possession of marijuana, a substance less harmful than alcohol or tobacco and at least as prevalent in middle-class white communities and on college campuses as in poor communities of color.

The drug war, though, has been waged almost exclusively in poor communities of color, despite the fact that studies consistently indicate that people of all races use and sell illegal drugs at remarkably similar rates. This is not what one would guess by peeking inside our nation's prisons and jails, which are overflowing with black and brown drug offenders. In 2000, African Americans made up 80 percent to 90 percent of imprisoned drug offenders in some states.

The extraordinary racial disparities in our criminal justice system would not exist today but for the complicity of the United States Supreme Court. In the failed war on drugs, our Fourth Amendment protections against unreasonable searches and seizures have been eviscerated. Stop-and-frisk operations in poor communities of color are now routine; the arbitrary and discriminatory police practices the framers aimed to prevent are now commonplace. Justice Thurgood Marshall, in a strident dissent in the 1989 case of *Skinner v. Railway Labor Executive Association*, felt compelled to remind the Court that there is *no drug exception* to the Fourth Amendment. His reminder was in vain. The Supreme Court had begun steadily unraveling Fourth Amendment protections against stops, interrogations, and seizures in bus stops, train stations, schools, workplaces, airports, and on sidewalks in a series of cases starting in the early 1980s. These aggressive sweep tactics in poor communities of color are now as accepted as separate water fountains were several decades ago.

If the system is as rife with conscious and unconscious bias, many people often ask, why aren't more lawsuits filed? Why not file class-action lawsuits challenging bias by the police or prosecutors? Doesn't the 14th Amendment guarantee equal protection of the law?

What many don't realize is that the Supreme Court has ruled that in the absence of conscious, intentional bias—tantamount to an admission or a racial slur—you can't present allegations of race discrimination in the criminal justice system. These rulings have created a nearly insurmountable hurdle, as law enforcement officials know better than to admit racial bias out loud, and much of the discrimination that pervades this system is rooted in unconscious racial stereotypes, or *hunches* about certain types of people that come down to race. Because these biases operate unconsciously, the only proof of bias is in the outcomes: how people of different races are treated. The Supreme Court, however, has ruled that no matter how severe the racial disparities, and no matter how overwhelming or compelling the statistical evidence may be, you must have proof of conscious, intentional bias to present a credible case of discrimination. In this way, the system of mass incarceration is now immunized from judicial scrutiny for racial bias, much as slavery and Jim Crow laws were once protected from constitutional challenge.

As a nation, we have managed to create a massive system of control that locks a significant percentage of our population—a group defined largely by race—into a permanent, second-class status. This is not the fault of one political party. It is not merely the fault of biased police, prosecutors, or judges. We have all been complicit in the emergence of mass incarceration in the United States. In the so-called era of colorblindness, we have become blind not so much to race as to the re-emergence of caste in America. We have turned away from those labeled *criminals*, viewing them as *others* unworthy of our concern. Some of us have been complicit by remaining silent, even as we have a sneaking suspicion that something has gone horribly wrong. We must break that silence and awaken to the human rights nightmare that is occurring on our watch.

We, as a nation, can do better than this.

DISCUSSION QUESTIONS

1. What role does language play in allowing the striking racial disparities in the criminal justice system to cause little concern in wider American society?

2. After those convicted of a crime serve their sentences, what additional obstacles do they face? What are the arguments for and against keeping these additional sanctions?

3. How are crime rates and rates of incarceration related? What explains this relationship?

4. What role has the *war on drugs* played in the mass incarceration of African Americans?

5. If the criminal justice system has such widespread racial disparities, why don't activists and lawyers simply bring their evidence to the courts to try to change the system?

Moral Panics

Culture, Politics, and Social Construction

Erich Goode and Nachman Ben-Yehuda

Shortly after taking office, Donald Trump issued an executive order banning travelers from Iraq, Syria, Iran, Libya, Somalia, Sudan and Yemen, all majority-Muslim countries, from entering the United States. That version was blocked by the courts, as was his second travel ban issued six weeks later which blocked non-green card holding travelers from six of the original nine majority Muslim countries.

Those defending the bans point to the need to combat the threat of terrorism, and it is hard to argue that a terrorist attack isn't something to be concerned about given the events of 9/11 and subsequent horrific attacks in Europe. Yet, there is something amiss in this argument. While truly frightening to consider, terrorist attacks are still relatively rare. And if you live in America, statistically speaking a terrorist attack should go very, very low on your list of things to worry about causing you bodily harm. Your odds of dying of heart disease are one in seven, from a car accident your odds are one in 113, and your odds of dying from assault by a gunshot are one in 358. Your odds for being killed by a foreign born terrorist are one in 45,808, and from a terrorist that's in the country illegally, your odds are one in 138,324,873. Statistically speaking, you should eat more vegetables and want more immigrants to come help grow them.

Why then, are so many Americans supportive or at least accepting of spending vast amounts of taxpayer money and risking significant civil rights violations to combat a relatively rare occurrence, while simultaneously supporting or quietly accepting the billion dollar proposed cut to cancer research that is in the latest federal budget? This article provides a useful concept to figure out what's going on. In 1972, sociologist Stanley Cohen coined the term moral panic to refer to "a condition, episode, person, or groups of persons [that emerge] to become defined as a threat to society values and interests." If you pay careful attention to news coverage, editorials, speeches, and debates on people's Facebook walls,

"Moral Panics: Culture, Politics, and Social Construction," by Erich Goode and Nachman Ben-Yehuda, from *Annual Review of Sociology*, 1994, 20: 149–171. Copyright © 1994 by Annual Reviews Inc. Reprinted with permission.

you are very likely to notice that little emphasis is put on the statistical likelihood of a terrorist attack, and a great deal on the type of person we think will commit such an act and how they threaten not just physical safely but also a way of life. This is the hallmark of a moral panic, and recognizing it as such is the first step to making more rational and effective decisions.

Introduction

On the continent of Europe, roughly between 1400 and 1650, hundreds of thousands of people—perhaps as many as half a million, up to 85% of whom were women—were judged to have *consorted with the devil* and were put to death. Much of Europe, especially France, Switzerland, and Germany, was in turmoil with suspicion, accusation, trials, and the punishment of supposed evildoers. A kind of fever—a craze or panic—concerning witchcraft and accusations of witchcraft swept over the land. Once an accusation was made, there was little the accused could do to protect herself. Children, women, and "entire families were sent to the stake. . . . Entire villages were exterminated. . . . Germany was covered with stakes, where witches were burning alive." Said one inquisitor, "I wish [the witches] had but one body, so that we could burn them all at once, in one fire!" (Ben-Yehuda 1985:36, 37).

In 1893, a charismatic religious mystic led a group of faithful followers into a remote mountain valley in the Brazilian state of Bahia and founded the community of Canudos; within two years, the settlement became the second largest city in the state. Canudos was a millennial cult whose adherents believed that the existing order would be overturned with the dawning of a new day. Landowners, the Catholic Church, and political elites resolved to crush the movement. Three military assaults against the settlement were repulsed by tenacious defenders. Finally, in October, 1897, Canudos was encircled by 8000 troops, serving under three generals and Brazil's Minister of War, and was bombarded into submission by heavy artillery. Thousands were killed; the survivors numbered only in the hundreds. Soldiers smashed the skulls of children against trees; the wounded were drawn and quartered, hacked to pieces limb by limb. All 5000 houses in the settlement were "smashed, leveled and burned. . . . The army eradicated the remaining traces of the holy city as if it had housed the devil incarnate" (Levine 1992:190). Throughout the campaign, news of Canudos flooded the Brazilian press; a sense of *public panic* was created. Accounts appeared daily, "almost always on the front page." More than a dozen major newspapers sent war correspondents to the front and "ran daily columns reporting events." "Something about Canudos provoked anxiety, which would be soothed only by evidence that Canudos had been destroyed" (Levine 1992:24).

These historical episodes represent explosions of fear and concern at a particular time and place about a specific perceived threat. In each case, a specific agent was widely felt to be responsible for the threat; in each case, a sober assessment of the evidence concerning the nature of the supposed threat forces the observer to the conclusion that the fear and concern were, in all likelihood, exaggerated or misplaced. Sociologists refer to such episodes as moral panics. They arise as a consequence of specific social forces and dynamics. They arise because, as with all sociological phenomena, threats are culturally and politically constructed, a product of the human imagination.

Social Problems: Objectivism or Constructionism?

Social problems can be approached from either an objectivist or a constructionist perspective. Objectivists argue that what defines a social problem is the existence of an objective, concretely real, damaging, or threatening condition. What makes a condition a problem is that it harms or endangers human life and well-being. Any condition that causes death or disease, that shortens life expectancy, or deteriorates the quality of life on a large scale, must be defined as a social problem (Manis 1974, 1976).

On the other side of the debate, representing the constructionist, *subjectivist*, or *relativist* position, it is argued that what makes a given condition a problem is the *collective definition* of that condition as a problem, that is, the degree of felt concern over a given condition or issue. To the constructionist, social problems do not exist objectively; they are constructed by human mind, called into being or constituted by the definitional process (Spector & Kitsuse 1977, Schneider 1985, Best 1989, Holstein & Miller 1993, Miller & Holstein 1993). The objective existence of a harmful condition does not, by itself or in and of itself, constitute a social problem. Indeed, to the constructionist, a given condition need not even exist to be defined as a social problem (Becker 1966:5)—witness the persecution of witches in Renaissance Europe and colonial New England (Erikson 1966, Ben-Yehuda 1980, 1985). In short, a social problem is "the activities of individuals or groups making assertions of grievances and claims with respect to some putative conditions" (Spector & Kitsuse 1977:75). Definitions of social problems derive from or are produced by specific sociocultural circumstances, group and categories, social structures and societies, historical eras, individuals, or classes.

To the constructionist, it is not necessary for individuals to formulate or use the precise phrase, "X is a social problem in this society." The problemhood of conditions may be expressed in a variety of ways—including expressed attitudes, activism, voting on issues, participation in social movements, rebellion, consuming media stories about certain issues, and so on. More concretely, to the constructionist, the reality of social problems can be measured or manifested in some of the following ways: (i) organized, collective action or campaigns on the part of some of the members of a society to do something about, call attention to, protest, or change (or prevent change in) a given condition—in short, "social problems as social movements" (Mauss 1975, Best 1990:2–3); (ii) the introduction of bills in legislatures to criminalize or otherwise deal with the behavior and the individuals supposedly causing the condition (Becker 1963:135ff, Gusfield 1963, 1981, Best 1990:2–3); (iii) the ranking of a condition or an issue in the public's hierarchy of the most serious problems facing the country (Best, 1990:2–3,151–75, Goode 1993:49–50); and (iv) public discussion of an issue in the media in the form of magazine and newspaper articles and television news stories, commentaries, documentaries, and dramas (Becker 1963:141–43, Best 1990:2–3, 87–111).

To the moderate or contextual constructionists (Best 1989), one of the more intriguing features of social problems is the fact that extremely harmful conditions may not be regarded as serious social problems, while relatively benign ones are. The answer as to why people become concerned about certain conditions cannot be found, at least not entirely, in the realm of objective damage. It is the discrepancy between concern and the concrete threat posed by or damage caused by a given condition that forces us to raise the question, why the concern over one issue but not another? Or, why concern now but not previously? If we insist that we have no right to determine the nature of the threat posed by certain conditions, such questions are not problematic—indeed, they are not even possible.

If public concern is a logical, almost inevitable, product of impending or concrete, inflicted harm, then that concern is not problematic, not a phenomenon necessitating an explanation. If, on the other hand, objective harm and public concern vary in large measure independently of one another, then this concern demands an explanation. How do definitions of social problems come about? Why is a social problem *discovered* in one period rather than another? What steps are taken, and by whom, to remedy this condition but not that, even more harmful, one? Who wins, and who loses, if a given condition is recognized as a social problem? How do groups, classes, or segments of the society struggle to establish their own definition of social problems? How is problemhood established? And by whom? Constructionism forces us to see the social dynamics behind the creation of conditions as problems.

Enter the Moral Panics Concept

On a cold, wet Easter Sunday, 1964, in Clacton, a seaside resort community on England's southern coast, what would normally be regarded as a minor disturbance among young people broke out on the street. Several scuffles and brief rock-throwing incidents took place; motorbikes and motorscooters roared up and down the street; some windows in a dance hall were smashed; several beach huts were damaged; a starter's pistol was fired in the air. The police, unaccustomed to such rowdiness, arrested nearly 100 youths on charges ranging from *abusive behavior* to resisting arrest.

While not exactly raw material for a major story on youth violence, the seaside disturbances nonetheless touched off what can only be described as an orgy of sensationalism in the British media. On Monday, the day following these events, every national newspaper (with the exception of the staid *London Times*) ran a lead story on the Clacton disturbances. "Day of Terror by Scooter Groups," screamed the Daily Telegraph; "Youngsters Beat Up Town" claimed the Daily Express; the Daily Mirror chimed in, "Wild Ones Invade Seaside." On Tuesday, press coverage was much the same. Editorials on the subject of youth violence began to appear. The Home Secretary was urged to take firm action to deal with the problem. Articles begin to appear featuring interviews with Mods and Rockers, the two youth factions current in Britain at the time, who were involved in the scuffles and the vandalism. Theories were articulated in the media, attempting to explain what was referred to as mob violence. Accounts of police and court actions were reported; local residents were interviewed concerning the subject, their views widely publicized. The story was deemed so important that much of the press around the world covered the incident. Youth fights and vandalism at resorts continued to be major theme in the British press for some three years. Each time a disturbance broke out, the same exaggerated, sensationalistic stories were repeated.

The overheated reaction of the police, the media, the public, politicians, and, in time, action group and protosocial movement organizations caught the attention of Stanley Cohen. To Cohen, the major issue was the *fundamentally inappropriate* reaction by key sectors of the society to relatively minor events. The press, especially, had created a horror story practically out of whole cloth. The seriousness of events were exaggerated and distorted—in terms of the number of young people involved, the nature of the violence committed, the amount of damage inflicted, and their impact on the community and the society as a whole. Obviously false stories were repeated as true; unconfirmed rumors were taken as fresh evidence of further atrocities. Once the atrocities were believed to have taken place, a process of sensitization was set in motion, whereby extremely minor disturbances became the focus of press and police attention, captured in the headline at the time: "Seaside Resorts Prepare for the Hooligans' Invasion." And often, Cohen argued, the sensitization process generated an escalation in the disturbances; a minor incident became a more substantial one through overzealous enforcement.

Cohen launched the term *moral panic* to characterize the reactions of the media, the police, the public, politicians, and action groups to the youthful disturbances. Said Cohen, in a moral panic:

A condition, episode, person, or group of persons emerges to become defined as a threat to societal values and interests; its nature is presented in a stylized and stereotypical fashion by the mass media; the moral barricades are manned by editors, bishops, politicians, and other right-thinking people; socially accredited experts pronounce their diagnoses and solutions; ways of coping are evolved or . . . resorted to; the condition then disappears, submerges, or deteriorates and becomes more visible. Sometimes the subject of the panic is quite novel and at other times it is something which has been in existence long enough, but suddenly appears in the limelight. Sometimes the panic passes over and is forgotten, except in folklore and collective memory; at other times it has more serious and long-lasting repercussions and might produce such changes as those in legal and social policy or even in the way society conceives itself (Cohen 1972:9).

In a moral panic, the reactions of the media, law enforcement, politicians, action groups, and the general public are out of proportion to the real and present danger a given threat poses to the society. In response to this exaggerated concern, *folk devils* are created, deviant stereotypes identifying the enemy, the source of the threat, selfish, evil wrongdoers who are responsible for the trouble. The fear and heightened concern are exaggerated, that is, are above and beyond what a sober empirical assessment of its concrete danger would sustain. Thus, they are problematic, a phenomenon in need of an explanation; they are caused by certain social and political conditions that must be identified, understood, and explicated.

To Cohen, in a moral panic, sensitization occurs. Sensitization is the process whereby harm, wrongness, or deviance is attributed to the behavior, condition, or phenomenon that is routinely ignored when the same consequences are caused by or attributed to more conventional conditions. The *cue effect* of the condition or behavior is much greater during the moral panic; supposed effects are noticed and linked to the offending agents that, in ordinary times for ordinary behavior, would have disappeared in the routines and hubbub of everyday life. In addition, the police *escalate* their law enforcement efforts, *diffuse* them from precinct to precinct, and *innovate* new methods of social control (1972:86–97); they operate under the *widening-the-net* principle (1972:94).

If all social fears and concerns entailed reactions to a specific, clearly identifiable, and appropriate or commensurate threat, the magnitude of which can be objectively assessed and readily agreed upon, such reactions would require no explanation. On the other hand, if, as Cohen argues, the reaction is out of proportion to the threat, we are led to ask why it arises. Why is there a moral panic over this supposed threat but not that, potentially even more damaging, one? Why does this cast of characters become incensed by the threat the behavior supposedly poses, but not that cast of characters? Why a moral panic at this time, but not earlier and not later? What role do interests play in the moral panic? What does the moral panic tell us about how society is constituted, how it works, how it changes over time? Cohen's concept introduces the student of society to a wide range of questions and potential explorations.

Moral Panics: Definition and Criteria

What characterizes a moral panic? How do we know when a moral panic has taken hold in a society at a specific time? How may we operationalize the concept? The moral panic is defined by at least five crucial elements or criteria.

CONCERN First, as we saw, there must be a heightened level of concern over the behavior (or supposed behavior) of a certain group or category and the consequences that that behavior presumably causes for the rest of the society. As with social problems, this concern is manifested or measureable in concrete ways, through, for example, public opinion polls, media attention, proposed legislation, action groups, or social movement activity.

HOSTILITY Second, there must be an increased level of hostility toward the category of people seen as engaging in the threatening behavior. Members are collectively designated as the enemy of respectable, law-abiding society; their behavior is seen as harmful or threatening to the values, interests, way of life, possibly the very existence, of the society, or a sizeable segment of that society. These deviants are seen as responsible for the threat. A dichotomization between *them* and *us* takes place, and this includes stereotyping—generating *folk devils* or villains on the one hand, and folk heroes on the other, in this morality play of evil versus good (Cohen 1972:11–12).

CONSENSUS Third, there must be a certain minimal measure of agreement in the society as a whole or in designated segments of the society that the threat is real, serious, and caused by the wrongdoing of group members and their behavior. This sentiment must be fairly widespread, although the proportion of the population who feels this way need not even make up a majority. Differently put: Moral panics come in different sizes—some gripping only certain social categories, groups, or segments, others causing great concern in the majority. In arguing that a measure of consensus is necessary to define a moral panic, we do not mean to imply that panic seizes everyone, or even a majority of the member of a society at a given time. Even during moral panics, public definitions are fought over, and some of them win out among one or another sector of the society, while others do not.

DISPROPORTIONALITY Fourth, there is the implicit assumption in the use of the term *moral panic* that the concern is out of proportion to the nature of the threat, that it is, in fact, considerably greater than that which a sober empirical evaluation could support; in the moral panic, "objective molehills, have been made into subjective mountains" (Jones et al. 1989:4). In moral panics, generating and disseminating numbers is important (Best 1990;45–64)—addicts, deaths, dollars, crimes, victims, injuries, illnesses, total cost—and most of the figures cited by moral panic claims makers are wildly exaggerated.

VOLATILITY And fifth, moral panics are volatile: They erupt fairly suddenly (although they may lie latent for long periods of time and may reappear from time to time), and, nearly as suddenly, they subside. As we'll see, some moral panics may become routinized or institutionalized, while other moral panics vanish—seemingly—without so much as a trace; the legal, cultural, moral, and social fabric of the society after the panic is essentially no different from the way it was before. But whether it has a long-term impact or not, the degree of fear, hostility, and concern generated during a moral panic tends to be fairly limited temporally; the fever pitch that characterizes a society or segments of it during the course of the moral panic is not sustainable over a long stretch of time.

To describe moral panics as volatile and relatively short-lived does not imply that they do not have structural or historical antecedents. The specific issue that generates a particular moral panic may have done so in the past, perhaps even in the not-so-distant past. In fact, moral panics that are sustained over long periods of time are almost certainly conceptual groupings of a series of more or less discrete, more or less localized, more or less short-term panics. Likewise, describing a given concern as volatile does not mean that moral panics do not, or cannot, leave a cultural and institutional legacy. Indeed, elements of panics may be established at one point in time that remain in place and help stimulate incipient concerns later on, at the appropriate time.

Three Theories of Moral Panics

THE GRASSROOTS MODEL The grassroots model argues that panics originate with the general public. The concern about a particular threat is a widespread, genuinely felt—if perhaps mistaken or least exaggerated— concern. The expressions of concern in other sectors (that is, in the media, among politicians, political action groups, and law enforcement) are an expression or a manifestation of more widespread concern. The action of no special group or sector is necessary to generate the public concern that breaks out at a particular time about a specific issue. Instead, the concern may arise more or less spontaneously, although, to be manifested in a public manner, it may require being catalyzed, assisted, guided, or triggered. Thus, if politicians or the media seem to originate or *stir up* concern about a given issue, in reality, the concern must have been latent to begin with. Politicians and the media cannot fabricate concern where none existed initially; all too often, they have tried to stir up concern about a given issue and failed. In the overt expression of the moral panic, a kind of diffuse anxiety or strain simply explodes at the appropriate time, given the requisite triggering event. The panic is simply the outward manifestation of what already existed in less covert form. Politicians give speeches and propose laws they already know will appeal to their constituency, whose views they have already sounded out; the media broadcast stories their representatives know the public, or a segment of the public, is likely to find interesting and about certain topics, troubling. What is central to the grassroots theorist—what explains the outbreak or the existence of the moral panic—is deeply felt attitudes and beliefs on the part of a broad sector of the society, that a given phenomenon represents a real and present threat to their values, their safety, or even their very existence.

THE ELITE-ENGINEERED MODEL The theory that moral panics are elite engineered argues that a small and powerful group or set of groups deliberately and consciously undertakes a campaign to generate and sustain fear, concern, and panic on the part of the public over an issue they recognize not to be terribly harmful to the society as a whole. Typically, this campaign is intended to divert attention away from the real problems in the society, whose genuine solution would threaten or undermine the interests of the elite (Reinarman & Levine 1989). Such a theory is based on the view that elites have immense power over the other members of the society—they dominate the media, determine file content of legislation and the direction of law enforcement, and control much of the resources on which action groups and social movements depend.

INTEREST GROUP THEORY By far, the most widely used perspective on moral panics has been the interest group approach. As we saw, Howard Becker (1963:147–63) argued that rule creators and moral entrepreneurs launch moral crusades—which sometimes turn into panics—to make sure that certain rules take hold and are enforced. In the interest group perspective, as we saw, professional associations, police departments, the media, religious groups, educational organizations, and so on, may have a stake in bringing to the fore an issue which is independent of the interests of the elite. By stating that interest groups have an independent role in generating and sustaining moral panics, we are saying that they are, themselves, active movers and shakers—that elites do not dictate the content, direction, or timing of panics.

The central question asked by the interest group approach is: cui bono?—for whose benefit? Who profits? Who wins out if a given issue is recognized as threatening to the society? To whose advantage is the outbreak of a widespread panic about a given issue, behavior, or phenomenon? Who stands to gain?

Epilogue: Moral Panics, Demise, and Institutionalization

Although the rise of moral panics has received some attention, their demise has been virtually neglected. The question of the demise of moral panics is linked intimately with the issue of their impact: What impact do moral panics have? Do moral panics promote substantial, long-term social change? Or is their impact much like that of fads, which flare up, are popular for a time, and vanish without a legacy or, seemingly, a trace?

The excitement stirred up during a moral panic is strikingly similar to the charisma possessed by certain leaders. This excitement, like charisma is volatile and unstable. The feelings that are generated during its period of influence tend to be intense, passionate. But they do not last. How to translate the vision stimulated during the moral panic into day-by-day, year-by-year normative and institutional policy? How to continue the aims and goals of moral entrepreneurs, action and interest groups, leaders, and much of the public, in *doing something* about the threat that seems to be posed during the moral panic, after the emotional fervor of that panic has died down? What we are suggesting is that, as with charismatic leaders, some moral panics are, almost unwittingly, particularly successful in routinizing the demands for action that are generated during these relatively brief episodes of collective excitement.

Do moral panics have an impact on the society in which they take place by generating formal organizations and institutions; do they, in other words, leave an institutional legacy in the form of laws, agencies, groups, movements, and so on? If so, what is the nature of that legacy? Do moral panics transform the informal normative structure of society? If so, what is the nature of that transformation?

Some panics seem to leave relatively little institutional legacy. The furor generated by the Mods and Rockers in England in the 1960s resulted in no long-term institutional legacy; no new laws were passed (although some were proposed), and the two germinal social movement organizations that emerged in its wake quickly evaporated when the excitement died down.

In contrast, other panics result in laws and other legislation, social movement organizations, action groups, lobbies, normative and behavioral transformations, organizations, government agencies, and so on. For example, the periodic drug panics that have washed over American society for a century continue to deposit institutional sediment in their wake. President Richard Nixon's mini-drug panic of the early 1970s hugely expanded the federal drug budget, placed the drug war on a firm institutional footing, and created several federal agencies empowered to deal with drug abuse in one way or another. The drug panic of the mid- to late-1980s left a substantial institutional legacy in the form of two packages of federal legislation, passed in 1986 and 1988, a substantially larger federal budget, dozens of private social movement organizations, and public sensitization to the drug issue. In this way, not only are successive moral panics built on earlier ones, but even in quieter, nonpanic periods, the institutional legacy that moral panics leave attempts to regulate the behavior that is deemed harmful, unacceptable, criminal, or deviant. The earliest, nineteenth century, drug panics defined drug abuse as deviant and, eventually, criminal; in this sense, they generated social change. The later drug panics, in contrast, reaffirmed the deviant and criminal status of drug abuse after a period of drift toward normalization, and thus they prevented social change.

Even seemingly inconsequential panics leave behind some sort of legacy; even those that produce no institutional, organization, or formal legacy are likely to have had some impact in the informal or attitudinal realm. With the eruption of a given moral panic, the battle lines are redrawn, moral universes are reaffirmed, deviants are paraded before upright citizens and denounced, and society's boundaries are solidified. In Durkheimian terms, society's collective conscience has been strengthened. The message of the moral panic is clear: This is behavior we will not tolerate. Even seemingly transitory panics are not *wasted*: They draw more or less precise moral boundaries. Panics emphasize the contrast between the condition or behavior that is denounced and the correctness of the behavior or position of the righteous folk engaged in the denunciation. The satanic ritual abuse scare, for example, reaffirms the moral correctness of the fundamentalist Christian way of life. The Mods and Rockers scare of 1964 to 1967 prepared the way for a later (early 1970s) moral panic in Britain over juvenile delinquency, street crime, and mugging (Hall et al. 1978). The Canudos massacre reminded Brazilians that they were citizens of a modern, progressive, industrializing, and culturally unified nation.

In short, panics are not like fads, trivial in nature and inconsequential in their impact. Even those panics that seem to end without institutional impact often leave normative or informal traces that prepare us for later panics or other events. Some, for example, leave cultural residue in the form of folklore (Best 1990:131–50; Turner 1993). A close examination of the impact of panics forces us to take a more long-range view of things, to see panics as long-term social process rather than as separate, discrete, time-bound episodes. Moral panics are a crucial element in the fabric of social change. They are not marginal, exotic, trivial phenomena, but one key by which we can unlock the mysteries of social life.

DISCUSSION QUESTIONS

1. What is the difference between the objectivist and social constructionist view of social problems? Which one is more challenging for you to agree with? Why?

2. What is a moral panic? Why do they occur?

3. What are the five criteria for a moral panic?

4. One characteristic of a moral panic is that they come and go. If a moral panic arises, and then disappears, do the authors think there are lasting consequences to this?

5. What role do race, class, and gender play in determining what kind of person and what kind of behavior might be seen as representing a threat to a way of life?

6. What are some other historical or contemporary examples of moral panics?

REFERENCES

Aronson N. 1984. Science as claims-making activity: implications for social problems research. In *Studies in the Sociology of Social Problems*, ed JW Schneider, JI Kitsuse, pp. 1–30. Norwood, NJ: Ablex.

Becker HS. 1963. Outsiders: Studies in the Sociology of Deviance. New York: Free.

Becker HS, ed. 1966. *Social Problems: A Modern Approach*. New York: Wiley.

Ben-Yehuda N. 1980. The European witch craze of the 14th to 17th centuries: a sociological perspective. *Am. J. Sociol* 86:1–31.

Ben-Yehuda N. 1985. *Deviance and Moral Boundaries: Witchcraft and the Occult. Science Fiction, Deviance Sciences and Scientists*. Chicago: Univ. Chicago Press.

Ben-Yehuda N. 1986. The sociology of moral panics: toward a new synthesis. *Sociol Q.* 27:495–513.

Ben-Yehuda N. 1990. *The Politics and Morality of Deviance: Moral Panics, Drug Abuse, Deviant Science, and Reversed Stigmatization*. Albany: State Univ. New York Press.

Best J, ed. 1989. *Images of Issues: Typifying Contemporary Social Problems*. New York: Aldine.

Best J. 1990. *Threatened Children: Rhetoric and Concern About Child-Victims*. Chicago: Univ. Chicago Press.

Cohen S. 1972. *Folk Devils and Moral Panics: The Creation of the Mods and Rockers*. London: MacGibbon &. Kee.

Cohen S. 1980. *Folk Devils and Moral Panics: The Creation of the Mods and Rockers*. New York: St. Martin's Press. 2nd ed.

Erikson KT. 1966. *Wayward Puritans: A Study in the Sociology of Deviance*. New York: Wiley.

Erikson KT. 1990. Toxic reckoning: business faces a new kind of fear. *Harv. Bus. Rev.* 68:118–26.

Goode E. 1993. *Drugs in American Society.* New York: McGraw-Hill. 4th ed.

Goode E. 1994. *Deviant Behavior.* Englewood Cliffs, NJ: Prentice-Hall. 4th ed.

Gusfield JR. 1963. *Symbolic Crusade: Status Politics and the American Temperance Movement.* Urbana: Univ. Illinois Press.

Gusfield JR. 1981. *The Culture of Public Problems: Drinking-Driving and the Symbolic Order.* Chicago: Univ. Chicago Press.

Hagan J. 1980. The legislation of crime and delinquency: a review of theory method, and research. *Law & Society Rev.* 14:603–28.

Hall S, Critcher C Jefferson T, Clarke J, Roberts B. 1978. *Policing the Crisis: Mugging, the State, and Law and Order.* London: Macmillan.

Holstein JA, Miller G, eds. 1993, *Reconsidering Social Constructionism: Debates in Social Problems Theory.* New York: Aldine.

Jenkins P. 1992. *Intimate Enemies: Moral Panics in Contemporary Britain.* New York: Aldine.

Jenkins P, Meier-Katkin D. 1992. Satanism: myth and reality in a contemporary moral panic. *Crime Law & Social Change* 17:53–75.

Jones BJ, Gallagher BJ III McFalls JA Jr. 1989. Toward a unified model for social problems theory. *J. Theory Soc. Behav.* 19:337–57.

Kitsuse JI, Schneider JW. 1989. Preface. In *Images of Issues: Typifying Social Problems,* ed J. Best, pp. xi–xiii. New York: Aldine.

Levine RM. 1992. *Vale of Tears: Revisiting the Canudos Massacre in Northeastern Brazil, 1893–1897.* Berkeley: Univ. Calif. Press.

Liazos A. 1982. *People First: An Introduction to Social Problems.* Boston: Allyn & Bacon.

Manis J. 1974. The concept of social problems: vox populi and sociological analysis. *Soc. Probl.* 21:305–15.

Manis J. 1976. *Analyzing Social Problems.* New York: Praeger.

Mauss AL. 1975. *Social Problems as Social Movements.* Philadelphia: Lippencott.

Merton RK, Nisbet R, eds. 1976. *Contemporary Social Problems.* New York: Harcourt Brace Jovanovich. 4th ed.

Miller G, Holstein JA, eds. 1993. *Constructionist Controversies: Issues in Social Problems Theory.* New York: Aldine.

Perrow C. 1984. *Normal Accidents: Living with High-Risk Technologies.* New York: Basic Books.

Reinarman C, Levine HG. 1989. The crack attack: politics and media in America's latest drug scare. In *Images of Issues: Typifying Contemporary Social Problems,* ed. J Best: 115–37. New York; Aldine.

Richardson JT, Best J, Bromley D, eds. 1991. *The Satanism Scare.* New York: Aldine.

Schneider JW, 1985. Social problems theory. *Annu. Rev. Sociol* 11:209–29.

Slovic P, Layman M, Flynn JH. 1991, Risk perception, trust, and nuclear waste: lessons from Yucca Mountain. *Environment* 33:7–11, 28–30.

Spector M, Kitsuse JI. 1977. *Constructing Social Problems.* Menlo Park, Calif: Cummings.

Turner PA. 1993. *I Heard It Through the Grapevine: Rumor in African-American Culture*. Berkeley: Univ. California Press.

Victor JS. 1993. *Satanic Panic: The Creation of a Contemporary Legend*. Chicago: Open Court.

Waddington PAJ, 1986. Mugging as a moral panic: a question of proportion. *Br. J. Sociol,* 37:245–59.

Zatz MS. 1987, Chicano youth gangs and crime: the creation of a moral panic. *Contemp. Crises* 11:129–58.

Gender

Doing Gender

Candace West and Don H. Zimmerman

Gender is one of the central organizing features of social life. While we have many different roles we play in different contexts (employee, student, friend, significant other), and we each have personality traits that we may turn up in some situations and down in others (shyness, sense of humor, talkativeness), we are always gendered beings. There is not a social option to be genderless, and those that try, such as parents who for 1 year kept their babies gender to themselves, are met with immediate and harsh social sanctions.[1]

Most people think of gender as a trait that someone simply has, much like eye color. On the other hand, many sociologists see gender as a role that people learn rather than something they have. In this article West and Zimmerman argue that gender should be thought of not as a role that we learn but as an accomplishment, something that we actively do and that is a product of our interactions. This outcome of gender is usually seen as justification of institutional arrangements that separate the genders, but West and Zimmerman argue that in fact by doing gender, we create through social interaction the very differences that we think of as being natural and normal. For example, public restrooms, even those with single stalls, are gender segregated and this is seen as a necessity because of the natural biological differences between men and women. Yet bathrooms in homes are not segregated, and men and women quite happily share the same bathrooms with the same setup in their private lives. We don't have separate stalls for women because they need them, we think we need them because there are separate stalls. As you read, think about your own gender performance each day and how it reinforces existing institutional arrangements between men and women.

"Doing gender," by C. West and D. H. Zimmerman, in *Gender and Society*, 1987, 1(2), 125–151.

O ur purpose in this article is to propose an ethnomethodologically informed, and therefore distinctively sociological, understanding of gender as a routine, methodical, and recurring accomplishment. We contend that the "doing" of gender is undertaken by women and men whose competence as members of society is hostage to its production. Doing gender involves a complex of socially guided perceptual, interactional, and micropolitical activities that cast particular pursuits as expressions of masculine and feminine "natures."

When we view gender as an accomplishment, an achieved property of situated conduct, our attention shifts from matters internal to the individual and focuses on interactional and, ultimately, institutional arenas. In one sense, of course, it is individuals who "do" gender. But it is a situated doing, carried out in the virtual or real presence of others who are presumed to be oriented to its production. Rather than as a property of individuals, we conceive of gender as an emergent feature of social situations: both as an outcome of and a rationale for various social arrangements and as a means of legitimating one of the most fundamental divisions of society.

To advance our argument, we undertake a critical examination of what sociologists have meant by *gender,* including its treatment as a role enactment in the conventional sense and as a "display" in Goffman's (1976) terminology. Both *gender role* and *gender display* focus on behavioral aspects of being a woman or a man (as opposed, for example, to biological differences between the two). However, we contend that the notion of gender as a role obscures the work that is involved in producing gender in everyday activities, while the notion of gender as a display relegates it to the periphery of interaction. We argue instead that participants in interaction organize their various and manifold activities to reflect or express gender, and they are disposed to perceive the behavior of others in a similar light.

To elaborate our proposal, we suggest at the outset that important but often overlooked distinctions be observed among *sex, sex category,* and *gender.* Sex is a determination made through the application of socially agreed upon biological criteria for classifying persons as females or males.[2] The criteria for classification can be genitalia at birth or chromosomal typing before birth, and they do not necessarily agree with one another. Placement in a *sex category* is achieved through application of the sex criteria, but in everyday life, categorization is established and sustained by the socially required identificatory displays that proclaim one's membership in one or the other category. In this sense, one's sex category presumes one's sex and stands as proxy for it in many situations, but sex and sex category can vary independently; that is, it is possible to claim membership in a sex category even when the sex criteria are lacking. *Gender,* in contrast, is the activity of managing situated conduct in light of normative conceptions of attitudes and activities appropriate for one's sex category. Gender activities emerge from and bolster claims to membership in a sex category.

We argue that gender is not a set of traits, nor a variable, nor a role, but the product of social doings of some sort. What then is the social doing of gender? It is more than the continuous creation of the meaning of gender through human actions (Gerson and Peiss 1985). We claim that gender itself is constituted through interaction.[3]

Sex, Sex Category, and Gender

Garfinkel's (1967, pp. 118–40) case study of Agnes, a transsexual raised as a boy who adopted a female identity at age 17 and underwent a sex reassignment operation several years later, demonstrates how gender is created through interaction and at the same time structures interaction. Agnes, whom Garfinkel characterized as a "practical methodologist," developed a number of procedures for passing as a "normal, natural female" both prior to and after her surgery. She had the practical task of managing the fact that she possessed male genitalia and that she lacked the social resources a girl's biography would presumably provide in everyday interaction. In short, she needed to display herself as a woman, simultaneously learning what it was to be a woman. Of necessity, this full-time pursuit took place at a time when most people's gender would be well-accredited and routinized. Agnes had to consciously contrive what the vast majority of women do without thinking. She was not "faking" what "real" women do naturally. She was obliged to analyze and figure out how to act within socially structured circumstances and conceptions of femininity that women born with appropriate biological credentials come to take for granted early on. As in the case of others who must "pass," such as transvestites, Kabuki actors, or Dustin Hoffman's "Tootsie," Agnes's case makes visible what culture has made invisible—the accomplishment of gender.

Garfinkel's (1967) discussion of Agnes does not explicitly separate three analytically distinct, although empirically overlapping, concepts— sex, sex category, and gender.

Sex

Agnes did not possess the socially agreed upon biological criteria for classification as a member of the female *sex*. Still, Agnes regarded herself as a female, albeit a female with a penis, which a woman ought not to possess. The penis, she insisted, was a "mistake" in need of remedy (Garfinkel 1967, pp. 126–27, 131–32). Like other competent members of our culture, Agnes honored the notion that there are "essential" biological criteria that unequivocally distinguish females from males. However, if we move away from the commonsense viewpoint, we discover that the reliability of these criteria is not beyond question (Money and Brennan 1968; Money and Ehrhardt 1972; Money and Ogunro 1974; Money and Tucker 1975). Moreover, other cultures have acknowledged the existence of "cross-genders" (Blackwood 1984; Williams 1986) and the possibility of more than two sexes (Hill 1935; Martin and Voorheis 1975, pp. 84–107; but see also Cucchiari 1981, pp. 32–35).

More central to our argument is Kessler and McKenna's (1978, pp. 1–6) point that genitalia are conventionally hidden from public inspection in everyday life; yet we continue through our social rounds to "observe" a world of two naturally, normally sexed persons. It is the *presumption* that essential criteria exist and would or should be there if looked for that provides the basis for sex categorization. Drawing on Garfinkel, Kessler and McKenna argue that "female" and "male" are cultural events—products of what they term the "gender attribution process"— rather than some collection of traits, behaviors, or even physical attributes. Illustratively they cite the child who, viewing a picture of someone clad in a suit and a tie, contends, "It's a man, because he has a pee-pee" (Kessler and McKenna 1978, p. 154). Translation: "He must have a pee-pee [an essential characteristic] because I see the *insignia* of a suit and tie." Neither initial sex assignment (pronouncement at birth as a female or male) nor the actual existence of essential criteria for that assignment (possession of a clitoris and vagina or penis and testicles) has much—if anything—to do with the identification of sex category in everyday life. There, Kessler and McKenna note, we operate with a moral certainty of a world of two sexes. We do not think, "Most persons with penises are men, but some may not be" or "Most persons who dress as men have penises." Rather, we take it for granted that sex and sex category are congruent—that knowing the latter, we can deduce the rest.

Sex Categorization

Agnes's claim to the categorical status of female, which she sustained by appropriate identificatory displays and other characteristics, could be *discredited* before her transsexual operation if her possession of a penis became known and after by her surgically constructed genitalia (see Raymond 1979, pp. 37, 138). In this regard, Agnes had to be continually alert to actual or potential threats to the security of her sex category. Her problem was not so much living up to some prototype of essential femininity but preserving her categorization as female.

This task was made easy for her by a very powerful resource, namely, the process of commonsense categorization in everyday life.

The categorization of members of society into indigenous categories such as "girl" or "boy," or "woman" or "man," operates in a distinctively social way. The act of categorization does not involve a positive test, in the sense of a well-defined set of criteria that must be explicitly satisfied prior to making an identification. Rather, the application of membership categories relies on an "if-can" test in everyday interaction (Sacks 1972, pp. 332–35). This test stipulates that if people *can be seen* as members of relevant categories, *then categorize them that way.* That is, use the category that seems appropriate, except in the presence of discrepant information or obvious features that would rule out its use. This procedure is quite in keeping with the attitude of everyday life, which has us take appearances at face value unless we have special reason to doubt (Schutz 1943; Garfinkel 1967, pp. 272–77; Bernstein 1986).[4] It should be added that it is precisely when we have special reason to doubt that the issue of applying rigorous criteria arises, but it is rare, outside legal or bureaucratic contexts, to encounter insistence on positive tests[5] (Garfinkel 1967, pp. 262–83; Wilson 1970).

Agnes's initial resource was the predisposition of those she encountered to take her appearance (her figure, clothing, hair style, and so on), as the undoubted appearance of a normal female. Her further resource was our cultural perspective on the properties of "natural, normally sexed persons." Garfinkel (1967, pp. 122–28) notes that in everyday life, we live in a world of two—and only two—sexes. This arrangement has a moral status, in that we include ourselves and others in it as "essentially, originally, in the first place, always have been, always will be, once and for all, in the final analysis, either 'male' or 'female'" (Garfinkel 1967, p. 122).

Consider the following case:

> This issue reminds me of a visit I made to a computer store a couple of years ago. The person who answered my questions was truly a salesperson. I could not categorize him/her as a woman or a man. What did I look for? (1) Facial hair: She/he was smooth skinned, but some men have little or no facial hair. (This varies by race, Native Americans and Blacks often have none.) (2) Breasts: She/he was wearing a loose shirt that hung from his/her shoulders. And, as many women who suffered through a 1950s' adolescence know to their shame, women are often flat-chested. (3) Shoulders: His/hers were small and round for a man, broad for a woman. (4) Hands: Long and slender fingers, knuckles a bit large for a woman, small for a man. (5) Voice: Middle range, unexpressive for a woman, not at all the exaggerated tones some gay males affect. (6) His/her treatment of me: Gave off no signs that would let me know if I were of the same or different sex as this person. There were not even any signs that he/she knew his/her sex would be difficult to categorize and I wondered about that even as I did my best to hide these questions so I would not embarrass him/

her while we talked of computer paper. I left still not knowing the sex of my salesperson, and was disturbed by that unanswered question (child of my culture that I am). (Diane Margolis, personal communication)

What can this case tell us about situations such as Agnes's (cf. Morris 1974; Richards 1983) or the process of sex categorization in general? First, we infer from this description that the computer salesclerk's identificatory display was ambiguous, since she or he was not dressed or adorned in an unequivocally female or male fashion. It is when such a display *fails* to provide grounds for categorization that factors such as facial hair or tone of voice are assessed to determine membership in a sex category. Second, beyond the fact that this incident could be recalled after "a couple of years," the customer was not only "disturbed" by the ambiguity of the salesclerk's category but also assumed that to acknowledge this ambiguity would be embarrassing to the salesclerk. Not only do we want to know the sex category of those around us (to see it at a glance, perhaps), but we presume that others are displaying it for us, in as decisive a fashion as they can.

Gender

Agnes attempted to be "120 percent female" (Garfinkel 1967, p. 129), that is, unquestionably in all ways and at all times feminine. She thought she could protect herself from disclosure before and after surgical intervention by comporting herself in a feminine manner, but she also could have given herself away by overdoing her performance. Sex categorization and the accomplishment of gender are not the same. Agnes's categorization could be secure or suspect, but did not depend on whether or not she lived up to some ideal conception of femininity. Women can be seen as unfeminine, but that does not make them "unfemale." Agnes faced an ongoing task of *being* a woman—something beyond style of dress (an identificatory display) or allowing men to light her cigarette (a gender display). Her problem was to produce configurations of behavior that would be seen by others as normative gender behavior.

Agnes's strategy of "secret apprenticeship," through which she learned expected feminine decorum by carefully attending to her fiancé's criticisms of other women, was one means of masking incompetencies and simultaneously acquiring the needed skills (Garfinkel 1967, pp. 146–147). It was through her fiancé that Agnes learned that sunbathing on the lawn in front of her apartment was "offensive" (because it put her on display to other men). She also learned from his critiques of other women that she should not insist on having things her way and that she should not offer her opinions or claim equality with men (Garfinkel 1967, pp. 147–148).

(Like other women in our society, Agnes learned something about power in the course of her "education.")

Popular culture abounds with books and magazines that compile idealized depictions of relations between women and men. Those focused on the etiquette of dating or prevailing standards of feminine comportment are meant to be of practical help in these matters. However, the use of any such source *as a manual of procedure* requires the assumption that doing gender merely involves making use of discrete, well-defined bundles of behavior that can simply be plugged into interactional situations to produce recognizable enactments of masculinity and femininity. The man "does" being masculine by, for example, taking the woman's arm to guide her across a street, and she "does" being feminine by consenting to be guided and not initiating such behavior with a man.

Agnes could perhaps have used such sources as manuals, but, we contend, doing gender is not so easily regimented (Mithers 1982; Morris 1974). Such sources may list and describe the sorts of behaviors that mark or display gender, but they are necessarily incomplete (Garfinkel 1967, pp. 66–75; Wieder 1974, pp. 183–214; Zimmerman and Wieder 1970, pp. 285–98). And to be successful, marking or displaying gender must be finely fitted to situations and modified or transformed as the occasion demands. Doing gender consists of managing such occasions so that, whatever the particulars, the outcome is seen and seeable in context as gender-appropriate or, as the case may be, gender-*in* appropriate, that is, *accountable*.

Resources for Doing Gender

Doing gender means creating differences between girls and boys and women and men, differences that are not natural, essential, or biological. Once the differences have been constructed, they are used to reinforce the "essentialness" of gender. In a delightful account of the "arrangement between the sexes," Goffman (1977) observes the creation of a variety of institutionalized frameworks through which our "natural, normal sexedness" can be enacted. The physical features of social setting provide one obvious resource for the expression of our "essential" differences. For example, the sex segregation of North American public bathrooms distinguishes "ladies" from "gentlemen" in matters held to be fundamentally biological, even though both "are somewhat similar in the question of waste products and their elimination" (Goffman 1977, p. 315). These settings are furnished with dimorphic equipment (such as urinals for men or elaborate grooming facilities for women), even though both sexes may achieve the same ends through the same means (and apparently do so in the privacy of their own homes). To be stressed here is the fact that:

The *functioning* of sex-differentiated organs is involved, but there is nothing in this functioning that biologically recommends segregation; *that* arrangement is a totally cultural matter... toilet segregation is presented as a natural consequence of the difference between the sex-classes when in fact it is a means of honoring, if not producing, this difference. (Goffman 1977, p. 316)

Standardized social occasions also provide stages for evocations of the "essential female and male natures." Goffman cites organized sports as one such institutionalized framework for the expression of manliness. There, those qualities that ought "properly" to be associated with masculinity, such as endurance, strength, and competitive spirit, are celebrated by all parties concerned—participants, who may be seen to demonstrate such traits, and spectators, who applaud their demonstrations from the safety of the sidelines (1977, p. 322).

Assortative mating practices among heterosexual couples afford still further means to create and maintain differences between women and men. For example, even though size, strength, and age tend to be normally distributed among females and males (with considerable overlap between them), selective pairing ensures couples in which boys and men are visibly bigger, stronger, and older (if not "wiser") than the girls and women with whom they are paired. So, should situations emerge in which greater size, strength, or experience is called for, boys and men will be ever ready to display it and girls and women, to appreciate its display (Goffman 1977, p. 321; West and Iritani 1985).

Gender may be routinely fashioned in a variety of situations that seem conventionally expressive to begin with, such as those that present "helpless" women next to heavy objects or flat tires. But, as Goffman notes, heavy, messy, and precarious concerns can be constructed from *any* social situation, "even though by standards set in other settings, this may involve something that is light, clean, and safe" (Goffman 1977, p. 324). Given these resources, it is clear that *any* interactional situation sets the stage for depictions of "essential" sexual natures. In sum, these situations "do not so much allow for the expression of natural differences as for the production of that difference itself " (Goffman 1977, p. 324).

Many situations are not clearly sex categorized to begin with, nor is what transpires within them obviously gender relevant. Yet any social encounter can be pressed into service in the interests of doing gender. Thus, Fishman's (1978) research on casual conversations found an asymmetrical "division of labor" in talk between heterosexual intimates. Women had to ask more questions, fill more silences, and use more attention-getting beginnings in order to be heard. Her conclusions are particularly pertinent here:

Since interactional work is related to what constitutes being a woman, with what a woman *is,* the idea that it *is* work is obscured.

The work is not seen as what women do, but as part of what they are. (Fishman 1978, p. 405)

We would argue that it is precisely such labor that helps to constitute the essential nature of women *as* women in interactional contexts (West and Zimmerman 1983, pp. 109–11; but see also Kollock, Blumstein, and Schwartz 1985).

Individuals have many social identities that may be donned or shed, muted or made more salient, depending on the situation. One may be a friend, spouse, professional, citizen, and many other things to many different people—or, to the same person at different times. But we are always women or men—unless we shift into another sex category. What this means is that our identificatory displays will provide an ever-available resource for doing gender under an infinitely diverse set of circumstances.

Some occasions are organized to routinely display and celebrate behaviors that are conventionally linked to one or the other sex category. On such occasions, everyone knows his or her place in the interactional scheme of things. If an individual identified as a member of one sex category engages in behavior usually associated with the other category, this routinization is challenged. Hughes (1945, p. 356) provides an illustration of such a dilemma:

[A] young woman... became part of that virile profession, engineering. The designer of an airplane is expected to go up on the maiden flight of the first plane built according to the design. He [sic] then gives a dinner to the engineers and workmen who worked on the new plane. The dinner is naturally a stag party. The young woman in question designed a plane. Her co-workers urged her not to take the risk—for which, presumably, men only are fit—of the maiden voyage. They were, in effect, asking her to be a lady instead of an engineer. She chose to be an engineer. She then gave the party and paid for it like a man. After food and the first round of toasts, she left like a lady.

On this occasion, parties reached an accommodation that allowed a woman to engage in presumptively masculine behaviors. However, we note that in the end, this compromise permitted demonstration of her "essential" femininity, through accountably "ladylike" behavior.

Hughes (1945, p. 357) suggests that such contradictions may be countered by managing interactions on a very narrow basis, for example, "keeping the relationship formal and specific." But the heart of the matter is that even—perhaps, especially—if the relationship is a formal one, gender is still something one is accountable for. Thus a woman physician (notice the special qualifier in her case) may be accorded respect for her skill and even addressed by an appropriate title. Nonetheless, she is subject to evaluation in terms of normative conceptions of appropriate attitudes and activities for her sex category and under pressure to prove that she is an "essentially" feminine being, despite appearances to the contrary (West 1984, pp. 97–101). Her sex category is used to discredit her participation in important clinical activities (Lorber 1984, pp. 52–54), while her involvement in medicine is used to discredit her commitment to her responsibilities as a wife and mother (Bourne and Wikler 1978, pp. 435–37). Simultaneously, her exclusion from the physician colleague community is maintained and her accountability *as a woman* is ensured.

In this context, "role conflict" can be viewed as a dynamic aspect of our current "arrangement between the sexes" (Goffman 1977), an arrangement that provides for occasions on which persons of a particular sex category can "see" quite clearly that they are out of place and that if they were not there, their current troubles would not exist. What is at stake is, from the standpoint of interaction, the management of our "essential" natures, and from the standpoint of the individual, the continuing accomplishment of gender. If, as we have argued, sex category is omnirelevant, then any occasion, conflicted or not, offers the resources for doing gender.

We have sought to show that sex category and gender are managed properties of conduct that are contrived with respect to the fact that others will judge and respond to us in particular ways. We have claimed that a person's gender is not simply an aspect of what one is, but, more fundamentally, it is something that one *does*, and does recurrently, in interaction with others.

Gender, Power, and Social Change

Let us return to the question: Can we avoid doing gender? Earlier, we proposed that insofar as sex category is used as a fundamental criterion for differentiation, doing gender is unavoidable. It is unavoidable because of the social consequences of sex-category membership: the allocation of power and resources not only in the domestic, economic, and political domains but also in the broad arena of interpersonal relations. In virtually any situation, one's sex category can be relevant, and one's performance as an incumbent of that category (i.e., gender) can be subjected to evaluation. Maintaining such pervasive and faithful assignment of lifetime status requires legitimation.

But doing gender also renders the social arrangements based on sex category accountable as normal and natural, that is, legitimate ways of organizing social life. Differences between women and men that are created by this process can then be portrayed as fundamental and enduring dispositions. In this light, the institutional arrangements of a society can be seen as responsive to the differences—the social order being merely an accommodation to the natural order. Thus if, in doing gender, men are also doing dominance and women are doing deference (cf. Goffman 1967, pp. 47–95), the resultant social order, which supposedly reflects "natural differences," is a powerful reinforcer and legitimator of hierarchical arrangements. Frye observes:

> For efficient subordination, what's wanted is that the structure not appear to be a cultural artifact kept in place by human decision or custom, but that it appear *natural*—that it appear to be quite a direct consequence of facts about the beast which are beyond the scope of human manipulation.... That we are trained to behave so differently as women and men, and to behave so differently toward women and men, itself contributes mightily to the appearance of extreme dimorphism, but also, the *ways* we act as women and men, and the *ways* we act toward women and men, mold our bodies and our minds to the shape of subordination and dominance. We do become what we practice being. (Frye 1983, p. 34)

If we do gender appropriately, we simultaneously sustain, reproduce, and render legitimate the institutional arrangements that are based on sex category. If we fail to do gender appropriately, we as individuals—not the institutional arrangements—may be called to account (for our character, motives, and predispositions).

Social movements such as feminism can provide the ideology and impetus to question existing arrangements, and the social support for individuals to explore alternatives to them. Legislative changes, such as that proposed by the Equal Rights Amendment, can also weaken the accountability of conduct to sex category, thereby affording the possibility of more widespread loosening of accountability in general. To be sure, equality under the law does not guarantee equality in other arenas. As Lorber (1986, p. 577) points out, assurance of "scrupulous equality of categories of people considered essentially different needs constant monitoring." What such proposed changes *can* do is provide the warrant for asking why, if we wish to treat women and men as equals, there needs to be two sex categories at all (see Lorber 1986, p. 577).

The sex category/gender relationship links the institutional and interactional levels, a coupling that legitimates social arrangements based on sex category and reproduces their asymmetry in face-to-face interaction. Doing gender furnishes the interactional scaffolding of social structure, along with a built-in mechanism of social control. In appreciating the institutional forces that maintain distinctions between women and men, we must not lose sight of the interactional validation of those distinctions that confers upon them their sense of "naturalness" and "rightness."

Social change, then, must be pursued both at the institutional and cultural level of sex category and at the interactional level of gender. Such a conclusion is hardly novel. Nevertheless, we suggest that it is important to recognize that the analytical distinction between institutional and interactional spheres does not pose an either/ or choice when it comes to the question of effecting social change.

DISCUSSION QUESTIONS

1. What do the authors mean when they say that gender is something that we "do"?

2. How do the ideas in this article relate to those in Goffman's *Presentation of Self* article from the last section?

3. How does the act of "doing" gender in face-to-face interactions support and legitimize institutionalized gender differences?

4. Are the authors arguing that gendered differences in interactions are reflections of natural differences between men and women or that gendered differences in interactions have the effect of making what are really social differences appear natural?

5. What is the difference between sex, sex category, and gender? Why do the authors argue these distinctions are important?

6. Can you think of an example of an "institutionalized framework" (p. 149) that facilitates or demands that people "do" gender?

7. How do the institutional arrangements that support a dichotomous gender system (men and women) affect the social interactions of those who do not clearly identify with either gender?

REFERENCES

Bernstein, Richard. 1986. "France Jails 2 in Odd Case of Espionage." *New York Times* (May 11).

Blackwood, Evelyn. 1984. "Sexuality and Gender in Certain Native American Tribes: The Case of Cross-Gender Females." *Signs: Journal of Women in Culture and Society* 10:27–42.

Bourne, Patricia G., and Norma J. Wikler. 1978. "Commitment and the Cultural Mandate: Women in Medicine." *Social Problems* 25:430–40.

Cucchiari, Salvatore. 1981. "The Gender Revolution and the Transition from Bisexual Horde to Patrilocal Band: The Origins of Gender Hierarchy." Pp. 31–79 in *Sexual Meanings: The Cultural Construction of Gender and Sexuality*, edited by S. B. Ortner and H. Whitehead. New York: Cambridge.

Fishman, Pamela. 1978. "Interaction: The Work Women Do." *Social Problems* 25: 397–406.

Frye, Marilyn. 1983. *The Politics of Reality: Essays in Feminist Theory.* Trumansburg, NY: The Crossing Press.

Garfinkel, Harold. 1967. *Studies in Ethnomethodology.* Englewood Cliffs, NJ: Prentice Hall.

Gerson, Judith M., and Kathy Peiss. 1985. "Boundaries, Negotiation, Consciousness: Reconceptualizing Gender Relations." *Social Problems* 32:317–31.

Goffman, Erving. 1967 (1956). "The Nature of Deference and Demeanor." Pp. 47–95 in *Interaction Ritual.* New York: Anchor/Doubleday.

—1976. "Gender Display." *Studies in the Anthropology of Visual Communication* 3:69–77.

—1977. "The Arrangement Between the Sexes." *Theory and Society* 4:301–31.

Henley, Nancy M. 1985. "Psychology and Gender." *Signs: Journal of Women in Culture and Society* 11:101–119.

Hill, W. W. 1935. "The Status of the Hermaphrodite and Transvestite in Navaho Culture." *American Anthropologist* 37:273–79.

Hughes, Everett C. 1945. "Dilemmas and Contradictions of Status." *American Journal of Sociology* 50:353–59.

Kessler, Suzanne J., and Wendy McKenna. 1978. *Gender: An Ethnomethodological Approach.* New York: Wiley.

Kollock, Peter, Philip Blumstein, and Pepper Schwartz. 1985. "Sex and Power in Interaction." *American Sociological Review* 50:34–46.

Lorber, Judith. 1984. *Women Physicians: Careers, Status and Power.* New York: Tavistock.

—1986. "Dismantling Noah's Ark." *Sex Roles* 14:567–80.

Martin, M. Kay, and Barbara Voorheis. 1975. *Female of the Species.* New York: Columbia University Press.

Mithers, Carol L. 1982. "My Life as a Man." *The Village Voice* 27 (October 5):1ff.

Money, John. 1974. "Prenatal Hormones and Postnatal Sexualization in Gender Identity Differentiation." Pp. 221–95 in *Nebraska Symposium on Motivation,*

Vol. 21, edited by J. K. Cole and R. Dienstbier. Lincoln: University of Nebraska Press.

—and John G. Brennan. 1968. "Sexual Dimorphism in the Psychology of Female Transsexuals." *Journal of Nervous and Mental Disease* 147:487–99.

—and Anke, A. Ehrhardt. 1972. *Man and Woman/Boy and Girl.* Baltimore: John Hopkins.

—and Charles Ogunro. 1974. "Behavioral Sexology: Ten Cases of Genetic Male Intersexuality with Impaired Prenatal and Pubertal Androgenization," *Archives of Sexual Behavior* 3:181–206.

—and Patricia Tucker. 1975. *Sexual Signatures.* Boston: Little, Brown.

Morris, Jan. 1974. *Conundrum.* New York: Harcourt Brace Jovanovich.

Raymond, Janice G. 1979. *The Transsexual Empire.* Boston: Beacon.

Richards, Renee (with John Ames). 1983. *Second Serve: The Renee Richards Story.* New York: Stein and Day.

Sacks, Harvey. 1972. "On the Analyzability of Stories by Children." Pp. 325–45 in *Directions in Sociolinguistics,* edited by J. J. Gumperz and D. Hymes. New York: Holt, Rinehart & Winston.

Schutz, Alfred. 1943. "The Problem of Rationality in the Social World." *Economics* 10:130–49.

West, Candace. 1984. "When the Doctor is a 'Lady': Power, Status and Gender in Physician-Patient Encounters." *Symbolic Interaction* 7:87–106.

—and Bonita Iritani. 1985. "Gender Politics in Mate Selection: The Male-Older Norm." Paper presented at the Annual Meeting of the American Sociological Association, August, Washington, DC.

—and Don H. Zimmerman. 1983. "Small Insults: A Study of Interruptions in Conversations Between Unacquainted Persons." Pp. 102–17 in *Language, Gender and Society,* edited by B. Thorne, C. Kramarae, and N. Henley. Rowley, MA: Newbury House.

Wieder, D. Lawrence. 1974. *Language and Social Reality: The Case of Telling the Convict Code.* The Hague: Mouton.

Williams, Walter L. 1986. *The Spirit and the Flesh: Sexual Diversity in American Indian Culture.* Boston: Beacon.

Wilson, Thomas P. 1970. "Conceptions of Interaction and Forms of Sociological Explanation." *American Sociological Review* 35:697–710.

Zimmerman, Don H., and D. Lawrence Wieder. 1970. "Ethnomethodology and the Problem of Order: Comment on Denzin." Pp. 287–95 in *Understanding Everyday Life,* edited by J. Denzin. Chicago: Aldine.

NOTES

1. http://www.dailymail.co.uk/news/article-1389593/Kathy-Witterick-DavidStocker-raising-genderless-baby.html

2. This definition understates many complexities involved in the relationship between biology and culture (Jaggar 1983, pp. 106–13). However, our point is that the determination of an individual's sex classification is a *social* process through and through.

3. This is not to say that gender is a singular "thing," omnipresent in the same form historically or in every situation. Because normative conceptions of appropriate attitudes and activities for sex categories can vary across cultures and historical moments, the management of situated conduct in light of those expectations can take many different forms.

4. Bernstein (1986) reports an unusual case of espionage in which a man passing as a woman convinced a lover that he/she had given birth to "their" child, who, the lover, thought, "looked like" him.

5. For example, in 2009 South African track star Caster Semenya was required to undergo what was dubbed a "gender test" after her appearance and performance in the 800 meter world championships raised doubts about her sex.

AUTHORS' NOTE: *This article is based in part on a paper presented at the Annual Meeting of the American Sociological Association, Chicago, September 1977. For their helpful suggestions and encouragement, we thank Lynda Ames, Bettina Aptheker, Steven Clayman, Judith Gerson, the late Erving Goffman, Marilyn Lester, Judith Lorber, Robin Lloyd, Wayne Mellinger, Beth E. Schneider, Barrie Thorne, Thomas P. Wilson, and most especially, Sarah Fenstermaker Berk.*

Marked

Women in the Workplace

Deborah Tannen

In the previous article, West and Zimmerman note that we are always gendered beings. While other roles such as student, employee, or friend are performed only in certain interactions, there are no social circumstances where we are genderless. Certainly we may not consciously perceive that gender is relevant in an interaction, but that doesn't mean it isn't. The well-known phenomenon of women being judged first on what they look like and second on what they do or say is just one example of this. Yet the social requirement to enact and reproduce gender plays out differently for men and women.

One of the things that shapes our thinking and assumptions about gender is the tendency to leave unmarked things that are masculine or male and to mark that which is feminine or female. This is the phenomenon that linguist Tannen is interested in exploring in this article. As she puts it, "The unmarked form of a word carries the meaning that goes without saying, what you think of when you're not thinking of anything special" (p. 161). Marked words then designate a special category. Sports leagues are a good example of this. The NBA is the National Basketball Association. The WNBA is the Women's National Basketball Association. NBA is unmarked, WMBA is marked.

This is a concept that can also be applied to things like appearance and behavior. As Tannen notes in this piece, women's appearance in public is almost always marked. It means something to be a woman who wears makeup and heels, just as it means something to be a woman who does not. (In fact for a long time the phrase "a woman in comfortable shoes" was a euphemism for a lesbian!) The same, however, is not true for men and their appearance. Men have the option of having their appearance be unmarked.

Being unmarked is a reflection of what's considered normal, and what is normal tends to be both valued more and also reflective of power. The

---

Excerpt from Chapter Four: "Marked: Women in the Workplace" pp. 107-117 from *Talking from 9 to 5: Women and Men at Work* by Deborah Tannen. Copyright © 1994 by Deborah Tannen. Reprinted by permission of HarperCollins Publishers and International Creative Management.

assumptions that markedness brings with it, to the workplace in particular, can not only be individually frustrating for women, but can also reinforce stereotypical assumptions about gender. For women in any type of work or professional setting, "Whatever she wears, whatever she calls herself, however she talks, will be fodder for interpretation about her character and competence" (p. 164). Just look at the attention given to the appearance of female politicians—in 2008 Sarah Palin and Hillary Clinton were both ridiculed for their appearance, one being deemed too attractive and one not attractive enough.[1] But no one used the relative attractiveness of Barack Obama and John McCain or Mitt Romney as a means of critiquing their fitness for political office.

As you read, think about what aspects of your presentation of self are marked or unmarked in your day-to-day activities.

Some years ago I was at a small working conference of four women and eight men. Instead of concentrating on the discussion, I found myself looking at the three other women at the table, thinking how each had a different style and how each style was coherent.

One woman had dark brown hair in a classic style that was a cross between Cleopatra and Plain Jane. The severity of her straight hair was softened by wavy bangs and ends that turned under. Because she was beautiful, the effect was more Cleopatra than plain.

The second woman was older, full of dignity and composure. Her hair was cut in a fashionable style that left her with only one eye, thanks to a side part that let a curtain of hair fall across half her face. As she looked down to read her prepared paper, the hair robbed her of binocular vision and created a barrier between her and the listeners.

The third woman's hair was wild, a frosted blond avalanche falling over and beyond her shoulders. When she spoke, she frequently tossed her head, thus calling attention to her hair and away from her lecture.

Then there was makeup. The first woman wore facial cover that made her skin smooth and pale, a black line under each eye, and mascara that darkened her already dark lashes. The second wore only a light gloss on her lips and a hint of shadow on her eyes. The third had blue bands under her eyes, dark blue shadow, mascara, bright red lipstick, and rouge; her fingernails also flashed red.

I considered the clothes each woman had worn on the three days of the conference: In the first case, man-tailored suits in primary colors with solid-color blouses. In the second, casual but stylish black T-shirt, a floppy collarless jacket and baggy slacks or skirt in neutral colors. The third wore a sexy jumpsuit; tight sleeveless jersey and tight yellow slacks; a dress with gaping armholes and an indulged tendency to fall off one shoulder.

Shoes? The first woman wore string sandals with medium heels; the second, sensible, comfortable walking shoes; the third, pumps with spike heels. You can fill in the jewelry, scarves, shawls, sweaters—or lack of them.

As I amused myself finding patterns and coherence in these styles and choices, I suddenly wondered why I was scrutinizing only the women. I scanned the table to get a fix on the styles of the eight men. And then I knew why I wasn't studying them. The men's styles were unmarked.

The term "marked" is a staple of linguistic theory. It refers to the way language alters the base meaning of a word by adding something—a little linguistic addition that has no meaning on its own. The unmarked form of a word carries the meaning that goes without saying, what you think of when you're not thinking anything special.

The unmarked tense of verbs in English denotes the present—for example, *visit*. To indicate past, you have to mark the verb for "past" by adding *ed* to yield *visited*. For future, you add a word: *will visit*. Nouns are presumed to be singular until marked for plural. To convey the idea of more than one, we typically add something, usually *s* or *es*. More than one *visit* becomes *visits*, and one *dish* becomes two *dishes,* thanks to the plural marking.

The unmarked forms of most English words also convey "male." Being male is the unmarked case. We have endings, such as *ess* and *ette,* to mark words as female. Unfortunately, marking words for female also, by association, tends to mark them for frivolousness. Would you feel safe entrusting your life to a doctorette? This is why many poets and actors who happen to be female object to the marked forms "poetess" and "actress." Alfre Woodard, an Oscar nominee for Best Supporting Actress, says she identifies herself as an actor because actresses worry about eyelashes and cellulite, and women who are actors worry about the characters they are playing. Any marked form can pick up extra meaning beyond what the marking is intended to denote. The extra meanings carried by gender markers reflect the traditional associations with the female gender: not quite serious, often sexual.

I was able to identify the styles and types of the women at the conference because each of us had to make decisions about hair, clothing, makeup and accessories, and each of those decisions carried meaning. Every style available to us was marked. Of course, the men in our group had to make decisions too, but their choices carried far less meaning. The men could have chosen styles that were marked, but they didn't have to, and in this group, none did. Unlike the women, they had the option of being unmarked.

I took account of the men's clothes. There could have been a cowboy shirt with string tie or a three-piece suit or a necklaced hippie in jeans. But there wasn't. All eight men wore brown or blue slacks and standard-style shirts of light colors.

No man wore sandals or boots; their shoes were dark, closed, comfortable, and flat. In short, unmarked.

Although no man wore makeup, you couldn't say the men didn't wear makeup in the sense that you could say a woman didn't wear makeup. For men, no makeup is unmarked. I asked myself what style we women could have adopted that would have been unmarked, like the men's. The answer was: none. There is no unmarked woman.

There is no woman's hairstyle that could be called "standard," that says nothing about her. The range of women's hairstyles is staggering, but if a woman's hair has no particular style, this in itself is taken as a statement that she doesn't care how she looks—an eloquent message that can disqualify a woman for many positions.

Women have to choose between shoes that are comfortable and shoes that are deemed attractive. When our group had to make an unexpected trek, the woman who wore flat laced shoes arrived first. The last to arrive was the woman with spike heels, her shoes in her hand and a handful of men around her.

If a woman's clothes are tight or revealing (in other words, sexy), it sends a message—an intended one of wanting to be attractive but also a possibly unintended one of availability. But if her clothes are not sexy, that too sends a message, lent meaning by the knowledge that they could have been. In her book *Women Lawyers*, Mona Harrington quotes a woman who, despite being a partner in her firm, found herself slipping into this fault line when she got an unexpected call to go to court right away. As she headed out the door, a young (male) associate said to her, "Hadn't you better button your blouse?" She was caught completely off guard. "My blouse wasn't buttoned unusually low," the woman told Harrington. "And this was not a conservative guy. But he thought one more button was necessary for court." And here's the rub: "I started wondering if my authority was being undermined by one button."

A woman wearing bright colors calls attention to herself, but if she avoids bright colors, she has (as my choice of verb in this sentence suggests) avoided something. Heavy makeup calls attention to the wearer as someone who wants to be attractive. Light makeup tries to be attractive without being alluring. There are thousands of products from which makeup must be chosen and myriad ways of applying them. Yet no makeup at all is anything but unmarked. Some men even see it as a hostile refusal to please them. Women who ordinarily do not wear makeup can be surprised by the transforming effect of putting it on. In a book titled *Face Value*, my colleague Robin Lakoff noted the increased attention she got from men when she went forth from a television station still professionally made-up.

Women can't even fill out a form without telling stories about themselves. Most application forms now give four choices for titles. Men have one to choose—"Mr."—so their choice carries no meaning other than to say they are male. But women must choose among three, each of them marked. A woman who checks the box for "Mrs." or "Miss" communicates not only whether she has been married but also that she has conservative tastes in forms of address, and probably other conservative values as well. Checking "Ms." declines to let on about marriage (whereas "Mr." declines nothing since nothing was asked), but it also marks the woman who checks it on her form as either liberated or rebellious, depending on the attitudes and assumptions of the one making the judgment.

I sometimes try to duck these variously marked choices by giving my title as "Dr."—and thereby risk marking myself as either uppity (hence sarcastic responses like "Excuse me!") or an over achiever (hence reactions of congratulatory surprise, like "Good for you!").

All married women's surnames are marked. If a woman takes her husband's name, she announces to the world that she is married and also that she is traditional in her values, according to some observers. To others it will indicate that she is less herself, more identified by her husband's identity. If she does not take her husband's name, this too is marked, seen as worthy of comment: She has done something; she has "kept her own name." Though a man can do exactly the same thing—and usually does— he is never said to have "kept his own name," because it never occurs to anyone that he might have given it up. For him, but not for her, using his own name is unmarked.

A married woman who wants to have her cake and eat it too may use her surname plus his. But this too announces that she is or has been married and often results in a tongue-tying string that makes life miserable for anyone who needs to alphabetize it. In a list (Harvey O'Donovan, Jonathon Feldman, Stephanie Woodbury McGillicutty), the woman's multiple name stands out. It is marked.

Pronouns conspire in this pattern as well. Grammar books tell us that "he" means "he or she" and that "she" is used only if a referent is specifically female. But this touting of "he" as the sex-indefinite pronoun is an innovation introduced into English by grammarians in the eighteenth and nineteenth centuries, according to Peter Miihlhausler and Rom Harre in their book *Pronouns and People.* From at least about the year 1500, the correct sex-indefinite pronoun was "they," as it still is in casual spoken English. In other words, the female was declared by grammarians to be the marked case.

Looking at the men and women sitting around the conference table, I was amazed at how different our worlds were. Though men have to make choices too, and men's clothing styles may be less neutral now than they once were, nonetheless the parameters within which men must choose when dressing for work—the cut, fabric, or shade of jackets, shirts, and pants, and even the one area in which they are able to go a little wild, ties—are much narrower than the riotous range of colors and styles from which women must choose. For women, decisions about whether to wear a skirt, slacks, or a dress is only the start; the length of skirts can range from just above the floor to just below the hips, and the array of colors to choose from would make a rainbow look drab. But even this contrast in the range from which men and women must choose is irrelevant to the crucial point: A man can choose a style that will not attract attention or subject him to any particular interpretation, but a woman can't. Whatever she wears, whatever she calls herself, however she talks, will be fodder for interpretation about her character and competence. In a setting where most of the players are men, there is no unmarked woman.

This does not mean that men have complete freedom when it comes to dress. Quite the contrary—they have much less freedom than women have to express their personalities in their choice of fabrics, colors, styles, and jewelry. But the one freedom they have that women don't is the point of this discussion—the freedom to be unmarked.

That clothing is a metaphor for women's being marked was noticed by David Finkel, a journalist who wrote an article about women in Congress for *The Washington Post Magazine*. He used the contrast between women's and men's dress to open his article by describing the members coming through the doors to the floor of the U.S. House of Representatives:

> So many men, so many suits. Dark suits. Solid suits. Blue suits that look gray, gray suits that look blue. There's Tom Foley—he's in one, and Bob Michel, and Steny Hoyer, and Fred Grandy, and Dick Durbin, and dozens, make that hundreds, more.

> So many suits, so many white shirts. And dark ties. And five o'clock shadows. And short haircuts. And loosening jowls. And big, visible ears.

> So many, many men.

> ...

> And still the members continue to pour through the doors—gray, grayer, grayest—until the moment when, emerging into this humidor, comes a surprise:

> The color red.

> It is Susan Molinari, a first-termer from New York...

> Now, turquoise. It is Barbara Boxer...

> Now, paisley. It is Jill Long...

Embroidering his color-of-clothing metaphor, Finkel, whose article appeared in May 1992, concluded, "Of the 435 members of the House of Representatives, 29 are women, which means that if Congress is a gray flannel suit, the women of Congress are no more than a handful of spots on the lapel."

When is Sexism Realism?

If women are marked in our culture, their very presence in professional roles is, more often than not, marked. Many work settings, just like families, come with ready-made roles prescribed by gender, and the ones women are expected to fill are typically support roles. It was not long ago when medical offices and hospitals were peopled by men who were doctors and orderlies and women who were nurses and clerical workers, just as most offices were composed of men who ran the business and women who served them as receptionists, clerks, and secretaries. All members of Congress were men, and women found in the Capitol Building were aides and staff members. When a woman or man enters a setting in an atypical role, that expectation is always a backdrop to the scene.

All the freshmen women in Congress have had to contend with being mistaken for staff, even though they wear pins on their lapels identifying them as members. For her book A Woman's Place, Congresswoman Marjorie Margolies-Mezvinsky interviewed her female colleagues about their experiences. One congresswoman approached a security checkpoint with two congressmen when a guard stopped only her and told her to go through the metal detector. When Congresswoman Maria Cantwell needed to get into her office after hours, the guard wanted to know which member she worked for. But her press secretary, Larry West, has gone through the gate unthinkingly without being stopped. When Congresswoman Lynn Schenk attended a reception with a male aide, the host graciously held out his hand to the aide and said, "Oh, Congressman Schenk."

You don't have to be in Congress to have experiences like that. A woman who owned her own business found that if she took any man along on business trips, regardless of whether he was her vice president or her assistant, people she met tended to address themselves to him, certain that he must be the one with power and she his helper. A double-bass player had a similar experience when she arrived for an audition with a male accompanist. The people who greeted them assumed she was the accompanist. A woman who heads a research firm and holds a doctorate finds she is frequently addressed as "Mrs.," while her assistant, who holds only a Master's degree, is addressed as "Dr."

One evening after hours, I was working in my office at Georgetown University. Faculty offices in my building are lined up on both sides of a corridor, with cubicles in the corridor for secretaries and graduate-student assistants. Outside each office is a nameplate with the professor's title and last name. The quiet of the after-hours corridor was interrupted when a woman came to my door and asked if she could use my phone. I was surprised but glad to oblige, and explained that she had to dial "9." She made the call, thanked me, and left. A few minutes later, she reappeared and asked if I had any correction fluid. Again surprised, but still happy to be of help, I looked in my desk drawer but had to disappoint her: Since my typewriter was self-correcting, I had none. My patience began to waver, but my puzzlement was banished when the woman bounded into my office for the third and final time to ask if I was Dr. Murphy's secretary, in which case she would like to leave with me the paper she was turning in to him.

I doubt this woman would have imposed on my time and space to use my telephone and borrow correction fluid if she had known I was a professor, even though I would not have minded had she done so. At least she would probably have been more deferential in intruding. And the experience certainly gave me a taste of how hard it must be for receptionists to get any work done, as everyone regards them as perpetually interruptible. But what amused and amazed me was that my being female had overridden so many clues to my position: My office was along the wall, it was fully enclosed like all faculty offices, my name and title were on the door, and I was working after five, the hour when offices close and secretaries go home. But all these clues were nothing next to the master clue of gender: In the university environment, she expected that professors were men and women were secretaries. Statistics were on her side: Of the eighteen members of my department at the time, sixteen were men; of the five members of Dr. Murphy's department, four were men. So she was simply trusting the world to be as she knew it was. It is not particularly ironic or surprising that the student who mistook me for a secretary was female. Women are no less prone to assume that people will adhere to the norm than are men. And this includes women who themselves are exceptions. A woman physician who works in a specialty in which few of her colleagues are female told me of her annoyance when she telephones a colleague, identifies herself as "Dr. Jones calling for Dr. Smith," and is told by Dr. Smith's receptionist, "I'll go get Dr. Smith while you put Dr. Jones on the line." But this same woman catches herself referring to her patients' general practitioners as "he," even though she ought to know better than anyone that a physician could be a woman.

Children seem to pick up norms as surely as adults do. A woman who was not only a doctor but a professor at a medical school was surprised when her five-year-old said to her, "You're not a doctor, Mommy. You're a nurse." Intent on impressing her daughter, she said, "Yes, I am a doctor. In fact, I teach other doctors how to be doctors." The little girl thought about this as she incorporated the knowledge into her worldview. "Oh," she said. "But you only teach women doctors." (Conversely, male nurses must deal with being mistaken for doctors, and men who work as assistants must deal with being mistaken for their boss.)

Another of my favorite stories in this mode is about my colleague who made a plane reservation for herself and replied to the question "Is that Mrs. or Miss?" by giving her title: "It's Dr." So the agent asked, "Will the doctor be needing a rental car when he arrives?" Her attempt to reframe her answer to avoid revealing her marital status resulted in the agent reframing her as a secretary.

I relate these stories not to argue that sexism is rampant and that we should all try to bear in mind that roles are changing, although I believe these statements to be true. I am inclined to be indulgent of such errors, even though I am made uncomfortable when they happen to me, because I myself have been guilty of them. I recall an occasion when I gave a talk to a gathering of women physicians, and then signed books. The woman who organized the signing told me to save one book because she had met a doctor in the elevator who couldn't make it to the talk but asked to have a book signed nonetheless. I was pleased to oblige and asked, pen poised, to whom I should sign the book—and was surprised when I heard a woman's name. Even though I had just spent the evening with a room full of doctors who were all women, in my mind "a doctor" had called up the image of a man.

So long as women are a minority of professional ranks, we cannot be surprised if people assume the world is as it is. I mention these stories to give a sense of what the world is like for people who are exceptions to expectations—every moment they live in the unexpected role, they must struggle against others' assumptions that do not apply to them, much like gay men and lesbians with regard to their sexual orientation, and, as Ellis Cose documents in his book *The Rage of a Privileged Class,* much like middle-class black professionals in most American settings.

One particular burden of this pattern for a woman in a position of authority is that she must deal with incursions on her time, as others make automatic assumptions that her time is more expendable, although she also may benefit from hearing more information because people find her "approachable." There is a sense in which every woman is seen as a receptionist—available to give information and help, perennially inter-ruptible. A woman surgeon complained that although she has very good relations with the nurses in her hospital, they simply do not wait on her the way they wait on her male colleagues. (The very fact that I must say "woman surgeon" and "male nurse" reflects this dilemma: All sur-geons are presumed male, all nurses presumed female, unless proven otherwise. In other words, the unmarked surgeon is male, the unmarked nurse female.

A Braid is a Stronger Rope

Although I describe patterns of women's and men's typical (not universal) styles, and show that styles expected of women can work against them in work settings, I would not advise women to adopt men's style to succeed—although in some cases and in some ways, this might work. In general, that advice is no more practical than advising women to go to work dressed in men's clothes. Instead, I would argue for flexibility and mutual understanding. The frustration of both genders will be reduced, and companies as well as individuals will benefit, if women and men (like Easterners and Southerners, old and young, and people of different classes and ethnic backgrounds) understand each other's styles. Once you understand what is happening to you, you can experiment on your own, trying new ways of behaving to solve your problems. Of course, all problems will not summarily disappear, but the sense of puzzlement and lack of control will at least subside.

Another reason it would be a mistake for women to try to behave like men is that businesses need to communicate with clients of different sorts, including more and more women. For instance, newspapers need to appeal to women as readers in order to sell newspapers, so it would do them no good to hire a slew of women who are just like men. I sometimes give the example of a woman who worked at an appraisal firm. One of her colleagues told her he had just gotten a very strange call from a client. After identifying herself, the client simply told him that she would be going on vacation that week and hung up, without giving him any comprehensible reason for her call. The woman who told me this said she was pretty sure she understood what this was about and called the client back to apologize for the slight delay in the appraisal she had ordered and reassure her that it would be ready when she returned from her vacation.

The appraiser also told me that she had been nonplussed by a client who called her up and began angrily berating her because his appraisal was late. Taken aback by the verbal assault, which seemed to her unacceptable in the context of a business relationship, she had become tongue-tied and unable to give him the assurances she had just given the other client, so she had her colleague call the man back and deal with him. This example shows how pointless it would be to ask which appraiser's style was "best." Each one was best at dealing with certain clients. Rather than trying to determine which style is best and hire a staff with uniform styles, the company clearly is benefiting from having a range of styles among its sales staff.

Will Talk About Gender Differences Polarize?

Some people fear that putting people into two categories by talking about "women" and "men" can drive a wedge between us, polarizing us even more. This is a serious concern. I know of at least one instance in which that is exactly what happened. A female executive at a large accounting firm was so well thought of by her firm that they sent her to a weeklong executive-training seminar at the company's expense. Not surprisingly, considering the small number of women at her level, she was the only woman at the seminar, which was composed of high-ranking executives from a variety of the corporation's wide-ranging divisions. This did not surprise or faze her, since she was used to being the only woman among men.

All went well for the first three days of the seminar. But on the fourth, the leaders turned their attention to issues of gender. Suddenly, everyone who had been looking at her as "one of us" began to look at her differently—as a woman, "one of them." She was repeatedly singled out and asked to relate her experiences and impressions, something she did not feel she could do honestly, since she had no reason to believe they would understand or accept what she was talking about. When they said confidently that they were sure there was no discrimination against women in their company, that if women did not get promoted it was simply because they didn't merit promotion, she did not feel she could object. Worst of all, she had to listen to one after another of her colleagues express what she found to be offensive opinions about women's abilities. By the end of the day, she was so demoralized that she was questioning whether she wanted to continue to work for this company at all. Whereas she had started out feeling completely comfortable, not thinking of herself as different from the men, the discussion of gender issues made her acutely aware of how different she was and convinced her she could never again fit comfortably into this group.

The group in which this occurred was made up of people from far-flung offices, not many of whom were from her own home office. As a result, she was able eventually to get past the experience, and it did not poison her day-to-day relationships at work. If a similar workshop had been held among her daily co-workers, it could have been much more destructive. And the saddest part is that the unfortunate outcome resulted from a program designed to help. As anthropologist Gregory Bateson explained in his work on cybernetics, any time people interfere with a system to change it, they risk making things worse, because they don't understand all the elements in the system and how they interrelate.

But the alternative, doing nothing, is not a viable one, because the situation as it is will have to change. In the case of women in the workplace, the situation is changing, whether we talk about it or not. And the hope that all we had to do was open the doors and let women in has simply not been borne out. Twenty years after women began receiving MBAs and entering businesses where they had not been before, they still make up only a small percentage of higher-level executives. The "pipeline" argument has simply not panned out. Years after women entered the pipeline, they just aren't coming through the other end in proportion to their numbers going in. Instead, more and more women are leaving the corporate world, in greater numbers than men, either to start their own businesses, to be independent contractors, or to do other things entirely. (For example, a 1993 survey of those who received MBAs from Stanford University over the preceding ten-year period found that 22% of the women, as compared to 8% of the men, had left large corporations to start their own businesses.) Some of this may be a privilege that men too would take advantage of if they had the chance. But a lot of women are seeking alternatives simply because they tire of feeling like strangers in a strange land when they go to work each day. In a word they tire of being marked.

Simply opening the doors and letting in women, or any individuals whose styles do not conform to those already in place, is not enough. As the experience of the executive at the training seminar showed, neither are localized efforts at diversity training, though surely these can help if they are done well. Finally, we can't just tell individuals that they should simply talk one way or another, as if ways of talking were hats you can put on when you enter an office and take off when you leave. For one thing, if you try to adopt a style that does not come naturally to you, you leave behind your intuitions and may well behave in ways inappropriate in any style or betray the discomfort you actually feel. Most important, we do not regard the way we talk—how we say what we mean, how we show consideration or frustration to others—as superficial, masks to be donned and doffed at will. Comprehensive training and awareness are needed, until everyone is working to make the workplace a world where differing styles are understood and appreciated.

DISCUSSION QUESTIONS

1. Whatever your school mascot, how does your school refer to men and women's sports teams on campus? Are the female teams marked or unmarked? Why does this matter?

2. Tannen's article is largely about perceptions of men and women in the workplace. Do you think that her observations hold true in a college setting? Are women marked in class by their appearance? What about in dorms or at parties? When, if at all, might men be marked at school?

3. At the end of the article, Tannen says she doesn't think advising women to act more like men is advisable. Do you agree or disagree with her? How might women behaving more assertively and aggressively backfire? How might it be beneficial?

NOTE

1. For an excellent commentary on this phenomenon using humor see http://www .nbc.com/saturday-night-live/video/sarah-palin-and-hillary-clinton-address-thenation/n12287

READING

15

"Out" in the Club
The Down Low, Hip-Hop, and the Architexture of Black Masculinity

Jeffrey Q. McCune, Jr.

The term "coming out of the closet", or in shorthand—"coming out", often refers to an LGBTQ individual making public some aspect of their gender or sexual identity. This is much more common today than it was in the past. American society has changed immensely in its acceptance of homosexuality over the past 30 years. The *Diagnostic Statistical Manual*, or *DSM*, is the official list of mental disorders recognized by the American Psychiatric Association. The *DSM II*, published in 1968, listed homosexuality as a mental disorder. It remained in subsequent revisions to the DSM until 1987. This is one reflection of the widespread attitude and belief that Americans had at the time that homosexuality was immoral, unnatural, and deviant.

Today however, a majority of Americans are accepting of homosexuality and it has lost its taboo, stigmatized status in many (though not all) areas of social life. In 2015, the landmark Supreme Court decision in *Obergefell v. Hodges* legalized same-sex marriage in all 50 states, and a Pew Research poll in June 2017 found that 62% of Americans supported same-sex marriage. That number hides some important differences, however, with older people, conservatives, and certain religious groups tending to remain opposed.

Just as different segments of society feel differently about homosexuality, so do those that are gay often feel differently about their own sexuality. And as always, social characteristics shape the path that individuals must negotiate as they make their way in the world.

In this research, sociologist Jeffrey McCune Jr. explores the intersection of race and sexual identity for black men in a gay hip hop club called The Gate. Negative stereotypes about black men's sexuality are ubiquitous, and for many

"'Out' In the Club: The Down Low, Hip-Hop, and the Architexture of Black Masculinity," by Jeffrey Q. McCune, Jr., in *Text and Performance Quarterly* 28(3): 298–314. July 2008. Reprinted with permission from Taylor & Francis Ltd.

who seek sexual relationships with other men but do not wish to make this desire public find the analogy of "the closet" to be problematic. Instead, they use the term "on the down low" or DL. Gay clubs are one place where they can take on the role (in Goffman's terms) of someone who enjoys sex with men to whatever extent they find comfortable. As McCune says, "most men at The Gate are not 'coming out' but participating in a sort of 'comin' in.' They have arrived at a queer space that welcomes them, but does not require them to become official members." As you read, think about other types of identities that may function in similar ways, becoming more or less salient depending on the geographic and social location that interactions unfold.

> For whom is outness a historically available and affordable option? Is there an unmarked class character to the demand for universal *outness*? Who is represented by which use of the term, and who is excluded? For whom does the term present an impossible conflict between racial, ethnic, or religious affiliation and sexual politics? What kinds of policies are enabled by what kinds of usages and which are backgrounded or erased from view? (Butler 227)

> DL offers a new-school remix of the old-school closet, an improvisation on the coming-out narrative that imagines a low-key way of being in the world. (King 1)

Coming out of the closet has been the contemporary niche phrase to articulate the universal threshold experience of sexual self-discovery and self-fulfillment. Recently, however, we have seen the emergence of black men who have discreet sex with other men, who engage in low-key queer activity and describe themselves as being on the *down low* (DL). These men challenge this overdetermination of the closet as a container of shame, pain, discomfort, and anxiety—offering a counternarrative of discretion as a tactic of survival. As a queer ethnographer committed to understanding the meaning and making of communities, I contend that the closet may be an insufficient trope in critical discussions of the complex sexuality of men of color.[1]

The DL may offer an alternative to the closet—a space where much more happens than black men having sex with wives/girlfriends while having sex with other men—where men actively negotiate issues of race, gender, class, and sexuality. Indeed, if we must accept the idea that black men do play, dwell, or reside in the closet, it is indeed a *quare* one.[2] However, the closet's entanglement with *coming out* often jeopardizes its utility for men of color. As one DL man told me, "There is no closet for us [black men] to go in—neither is it necessary to come out." As these men disidentify with dominant descriptors and performances of sexuality, their lives are often constructed as a black phenomenon of this contemporary moment, even though discreet sexual politics have historically been a part of black male constructions of sexual identity. The DL extends a historical black cultural practice of *quiet as kept* and *be still and know*—adages which have encouraged many black people to safeguard information, not for deceit but survival. DL men are new bodies dancing to an old song.

This essay maps DL presence within "The Gate,"[3] a known gay club in Chicago, and reveals that black masculinity with its diverse textures uniquely enables the possibility for discreet sexual desire. This essay highlights the minoritized subjects' use of masculinity within public space, without having to sacrifice notions of privacy, or the politics of sexual discretion. Here, DL men and black gay men remix the closet, in the act of *queer world-making*.

I focus on the case study, the experience of a 22-year-old man named "Shawn." I met Shawn at a black fraternity informational—where he introduced himself and gave me his number, saying that he was going to "tell me all about the fraternity." Although I trusted his interest in sharing with me the logistics of black fraternal order, the quick passing of his number on a crumpled sheet of paper during our salutatory handshake exchange suggested otherwise. Our phone conversations, which began as an attempt on his part to pique my erotic interest, turned into a series of conversations around discreet sexual behavior and "stories of a DL Hotboi," as Shawn so humbly described his life story. Shawn's centrality in this essay is important, as he was the first of the men with whom I spoke who I witnessed at a queer club. I use his experiences to illuminate, complicate, and outline some of the contradictions and complexities that arise when a DL guy goes *out*. These encounters prompted many questions: How do DL men negotiate their commitment to a heteronormative understanding of self, while participating in homonormative social and sexual activities? What is it about DL subjectivity that allows for such possibilities? What is it about the structures and textures of the club space that invites these performers of discreet sexual identity?

Black Queer World-Making: Going Inside The Gate

The Gate is a gay domain once a week—the Friday night queer outlet for a large hip-hop queer mass. While those who attend The Gate have the option of listening to house or hip-hop, all of the club's advertisements and publicity seems to highlight its hip-hop appeal. Together, those who *kick it* at The Gate partake in what Fiona Buckland describes as *queer world-making*—"a conscious, active way of fashioning the self and the environment, cognitively and physically, through embodied social practices moving through and clustered in the city" (19). While Buckland does not deny the possibility of a racialized subject engaging this practice, her research does not advance a theoretical application that accounts for racial subjectivity. The Gate's patrons were definitely participating in an act of black queer-world making through their appropriation of a traditionally black heterosexual space and transforming it into a space of and for queer desire.

The dynamics of the hip-hop room as a space that lends access to DL positionality is of the utmost interest. Indeed, this space circulates contradictory messages that supercede traditional boundaries of gender and sexuality, where men negotiate their relationship to and their relationship between masculine bravado and black queer culture.

This odd congruence, between hip-hop and queer desire, has *coolness* at its nexus. Here, I wish to discuss coolness as a more general expression, which Marlene Connor understands as a guiding ethic on how to dress, behave, and interact with approval from a largely black and male spectatorship (1–10). Coolness is a theory in practice—an embodied rubric that regulates and monitors what is and is not acceptable among black men under and outside of white surveillance. While I argue that coolness is not a uniquely black expression, it is a modern descriptor for a historical tactic. Most importantly, coolness acts as a way of survival, a coping stance/pose that black men engage, in order to make do with what they do or do not have (4–5). Coolness is a performative utterance and action, whereby men define themselves within and against traditional standards. Indeed, like all performances, it changes depending on those involved, the dimensions of space/place, and who is reading and interpreting the scene of action. The Gate's hip-hop room spilled over with coolness.

This dynamic duo, the combination of hip-hop and queer space (or coolness and queerness), are incongruous at surface level, but a deeper examination can explain this coupling. Historically, hip-hop culture and music have gone against the grain of traditional American music and style—often critiquing dominant structures and modifying other musical forms. Likewise, queerness has also disrupted normative tales of sexuality, restructuring the perceived composition of our society and generally challenging normative sociosexual rules and regulations. Together, they seem to make a *fabulous* pair. These two world-making apparatuses disrupt norms, interrogate new ground, and encourage exploration outside the domains of normativity. Ultimately, the relationship between hip-hop and black queer expression is, in a sense, a meeting of two queers. Thus, hip-hop music's use as a medium for homoerotic engagements is not odd, but almost anticipatory. Furthermore, The Gate as a predominantly black establishment would naturally welcome black forms of musical and cultural expression—its patrons are young black men and consumers of hip-hop in other contexts.

While the relationship between hip-hop and queerdom presents an enthralling question, of most interest here is how black queer subjects utilize hip-hop in queer space. Particularly, how does hip-hop serve as an interlocutor between discreet performances of sexual identity and explicit engagements of queer desire? How do DL men utilize queer space, navigating their desire for discretion and the pleasure of homoerotic engagement? How do these men literally dance down low, while simultaneously remixing the closet? To gain any critical understanding of this process, we must go *in da club*.

In Da Club: Homoerotic Activity in a Heteronormative Playground

It is about 12:45 a.m. on a cold, below-zero, February morning in northwest Chicago. I stand in front of what once was a site of industrialization—a dark brick building with a one-story front and a raised back—now a structure that contains often contradictory architectures of homo and heteronormative performances. The Gate is a parade of contrast. The physical appearances and fashion *looks* are definitely diverse and dynamic. I enter the club, with a huge bouncer behind me yelling, "Have your IDs ready." I scope the never-ending processional, where there are black men and women of all ages, a few whites and Latinos, a couple of drag queens in pumps, and some folks who appear to have got the night *mixed up*. I walk into a small corridor, where plastered on the wall still hangs a sign that announces, "Alternative Lifestyle Night." Near this sign is another that reads "After 1:00 AM, the cover is $12.00." Some of those standing in line scream "Hell, no!" and walk away after they read the sign. I, of course, pay the cover, unsure about what is so special about the 1:00 a.m. hour, yet knowing that there is a rich queer world waiting inside.

Bodies of all ages, sizes, shapes, colors, and fragrances fill both the house and hip-hop spaces. First, as I walk past a bar in the house room, I witness bodies divided across the dance floor by wooden beams in a 20 by 40 foot space of sensuality and sexuality. Indeed, this house was divided, clearly quartering off one *type* from the *others*. There are men over 30 in one quarter, voguers in another, and two quarters contain men and a few women who are under 30 and uninhibited in how they move and groove— who may often be conceived of as the liberal or *queeny* types. As I walk past the divas on the dance floor, I follow a crowd into another space, located in the back of this warehouse—the hip-hop room.

As I look above me, below me, and beside me, I observe physical and facial expressions that recall childhood experiences of *mackin'* and *hollerin'*. These types of poses and approaches were popular when I was a young boy growing up on Chicago's South Side. Men would often stand, in a neutral position, allowing their eyes to do much of the talking. Then, as they approached the person to whom they were attracted, they would quickly perform this *tight* and often *tough guy* posturing. This performance was often accented by a hand on the groin, a smug face almost always absent of any hint of a smile, a cool slouch in the shoulders, and classic concaveness in the chest. A similar aesthetic appreciation is present in The Gate. Interestingly, however, the presence of women in this space is hardly felt. The *mackin'* and *hollerin'* styles of performance are projected onto bodies of the same sex. There is the dancing male butch-femme binary and its ideological counterpart, heterosexual male-female pairing.

As I step down from the passway onto the dance floor, to my surprise, I see Shawn. This 22-year-old college student classifies himself as being on the DL, and previously vowed that he would never "be caught dead in one of those sissy clubs." I am even more surprised when Shawn acknowledges me and proceeds to take my hand and place it on his groin. This is the first time he has ever made such a move, but the time and space encourage him to lose many of his inhibitions and insecurities. When I ask Shawn about the incident, particularly the level of comfort he displayed, he insists that it was due to the alcohol and apologetically says, "I guess I'm becomin' a little bit too comfortable." This statement prompts a longer historical explanation:

> I wasn't always that comfortable. For real. I mean, me and my guy—my best friend—the first time we went to the club in D.C., we practically hid. We wore our hats so far down over our faces; the most you probably could see was my smile and his goatee. We wore real big clothes to conceal our identities. . . . Now I don't know who would have known me in D.C., being that I was from the west suburbs of Chicago.

This admission, clearly marking Shawn's evolution from being very discreet to less discreet in his participation in club life, is informative. While it illuminates a certain level of comfort, it could potentially suggest that Shawn has *come into himself*. However, this comfort within the space of the club does not speak to his behavior in company outside the club. In fact, I observe that Shawn's anxiety over how his fraternity, friends at school, and family would respond to his presence becomes an almost overwhelming concern. Specifically, he articulates a concern for his reputation amongst his *brotherhood* as the *pretty boy, ladies' man*—a title which clearly informs Shawn's general performance of masculinity. The most striking image in this narrative is the costume for concealment, the utilization of hip-hop gear to mask identity. Shawn is astutely aware of the value of clothes in the regulation and monitoring of what is properly masculine. In a sense, Shawn and his friend's clothing is the material mask for their queer desire. His cap is a signifier of hip-hop, while it is also a sign of Shawn's desire to not see and to be seen. All at once, hip-hop is the corroborator and the concealer of queer desire.

Shawn is able not only to be present at The Gate, but also to activate his sexual desires without fear of losing his *masculine* card. My astonishment over Shawn's presence at The Gate, and his behavior therein, is related to his adamant insistence that his identity was *private*, a term that connoted a keen sense of discretion. Typically, the men I had encountered previously would not be seen at an announced *gay* or *alternative* night at any club. Since this encounter, I have seen Shawn at one other gay club that offered a hip-hop fix. Later, he told me, "I can't stand house music—hip-hop is where it's at!" It becomes clear that his ability to engage hip-hop texts and perform a hip-hop brand of masculinity was part of the impetus for his participation in this particular *alternative* Friday at The Gate.

Fifty Cent continues:

I'm that cat by the bar toasting to the good life
You that faggot ass nigga trying to pull me back right?

The last line invokes audience participation. As I deepen the groove of my sway dance, gay men and women shout "faggot ass nigga." Actually, they shout the whole line, but it is this part of the line that throws me. It seems contradictory for these queers of color to engage in such a chant. I turn to a friend, giving him a look of shock and disheartenment, and he says, "It's just like the way we use nigga by itself." However, why would those who, like myself, have endured being called *faggot, sissy,* and *punk,* rearticulate such problematic rhetoric? Why would Shawn, DL men in general, seemingly draw pleasure from this chant of hate and homophobia? As people throw their hands in the air, almost marching to construct a chorus-like concentric circle of *faggot ass nigga,* something tells me this is *cool.*

This performance of heterosexism seems to work in collaboration with a larger desire to be cool. The queer subjects who yell "faggot ass nigga" can feel a part of a larger black masculine sphere—one that usually excludes them. In this masculine imaginary, often the way to affirm one's normality is through participation in homophobic or sexist acts. When one takes possession of the faggot, or the nigga, it reduces the legitimacy of such ascriptions being made upon the speaker's body. In this way, the utterance of the profane empowers the speaker/chanter, affirming his status as appropriately masculine. This chanting moment is emblematic of the *cooling* of the hip-hop room, while also illuminating the ways in which one type of masculinity seems to pose itself as the cool. In this way, the hip-hop room and its patrons, through so-called performances of heterogender, position the hip-hop space as the greater of the two rooms. It is within the hip-hop room that the *real men* reside. Traditional heteromasculine behavior and codes deem this space *hot*. This behavior, though highly problematic, suggests that the *aesthetics of the cool* is always a balancer of the hot (Thompson 85:102). Whereas Thompson is speaking to the literal hotness of bodies, I employ *hot* to align with contemporary black vernacular, where this adjective signifies the place in vogue—the spot—the atmosphere that is most enlivened. Indeed, the men in the hip-hop room understand the hip-hop room as such, while the *room of sissies* is the place less desired—really gay, so to speak.

I also read this instance of hip-hop heterosexual rage in queer face to be a moment where gay men can temporarily *de-queer* themselves. I argue that such a chant may work as a way to set these men apart from the *others* in the space. It is a strategy to disavow one brand of masculinity, while embracing another. In this conceptualization, the *others* who are outside of the traditionally masculine—those ascribed titles such as *femmes, bottoms,* or *punks*—are marked as inferior, less than those who carry traditional masculine codes and behaviors. Shawn explains the Friday chorus by stating, "A faggot is a punk—it's not about what he does in the bedroom, it's what he doesn't do." His perspective suggests that the ability to spout this sexual epithet (*faggot*) is about condemning the feminine male. In addition, Shawn's comment also ridicules those who perform the nondominant role during sex. Like Kathryn Bond Stockton, I am interested in the value given to the role of the sexual "bottom and its relationship to ideas of debasement that extend the bottom beyond sexual positionality." Hence, Shawn's comment "what he doesn't do" interests me greatly—as it signifies a discomfort not only with being the nondominant sex partner, but with those who perform a style of masculinity that signals this sexual preference. Thus, the debasing performance of gender is understood in relation to, and as a result of, sexual performances. Of course, Shawn doesn't understand *bottoms* as masculine, which begs the question: is there a way to masculinize bottoms in this world of queer world-making? Shawn's disavowal of this possibility further accentuates the ways in which femininity "is always already devalued in patriarchal societies, [and] those associated with the feminine are also viewed as inferior" (Johnson 69). There is no room for femininity in the domain of the masculine. A man is considered either masculine or feminine—the different styles of masculinity often remain unaccounted for, or unrecognized. Of course, femininity is the less ideal performance of gender, marking the distinction between who is properly masculine and who is not. Many of these understandings of gender are derived from hegemonic notions which almost always use the effete or feminine to describe *the gay*, setting straight men apart from those who are identified as gay.

This act of devaluation of some gay male bodies is modified in The Gate, as some *masculine* gay men can feel *straight*, while DL men can affirm their allegiance to heterosexuality (read: heteronormativity) through a harsh critique of those who perform queerness, and manliness, differently. Furthermore, it allows some men to carve out the cool, creating an inadvertent hierarchy of masculine performances within The Gate.

It would be dishonest to ignore the ways in which *faggot ass nigga* is something of an inside joke. All those who participate in the *alternative* night at The Gate are aware of their appetite for those of the same sex. Thus, the utterance of the chant also brings with it a reminder that the space is a queer, or *faggot*, terrain. In some ways, the mass chant announces, "We are black faggots, but look who's in possession of these words now?!" In this sense, my friend's comparison of the chanted phrase and the vernacular use of *nigga* is an apt one. Black queer men reappropriate these terms, turn them on their heads, and thereby reduce the power of the terms in constructing their identities. In addition, the overwhelming presence of homoeroticism present in the oft-cited homophobic space of hip-hop is a running joke. In the popular queer imagining, the hip-hop (hyper) homophobe, in this case Fifty Cent, is often read as indicating a propensity towards, not away from, gayness. However, I suggest that this analysis is less applicable to many men on the DL, as they often disidentify with traditional identifications of sexuality in their everyday lives. Many DL men are like the artists, farthest from *faggots*—they are the embodiment of the properly masculine. Thus, their sexuality is less problematic—deemed legitimate because it is not tainted by femininity or faggotry. While this appears to be internal homophobia run amuck, I caution against this interpretation. For these men, the *faggot* and the *feminine* are classifiers of gender performance, rather than reflective of their views on homoerotic desire or male-male sex.

I spend critical time in this essay discussing this moment of hip-hop heterosexist and homophobic chanting because it exposes what I believe is the true pleasure of this queer zone, for black gay men and DL men alike. In this space, performances of gender and sexuality are in flux—men are able to be queer while also acting straight, or even straight while acting queer. Patrons of The Gate are able to realize the treasure of performance that many of us scholars take as given, whereby performance "is a means by which people reflect on their current conditions, define and/or reinvent themselves and their social world, and either reenforce, resist, or subvert prevailing social orders" (Drewal 9). The Gate offers an occasion for black queer men to attain pleasure through the stimulation created by the multiple valences within the hip-hop space. In this unique space of queer world-making, these men can "reenforce, resist, [accept] and subvert" dominant modes of gender and sexuality. While black men can identify and perform their queer desire (resist/subvert), they can still participate in the rituals of patriarchy (reenforce/accept). At the Gate, or any queer world-making space for that matter, bodies produce paradoxical effects which cannot be understood if one tries to force them into a dichotomy of resistance or submission. At The Gate, a belief in a functional system of resist/reenforce/subvert would definitely be inappropriate—ignoring the powerful and provocative presence of the both/and operation, an element of constancy within the hip-hop room. This may be the queerest characteristic of this space—where heterogender, hip-hop, and homoeroticism are married through music and dance. In the hip-hop space, all black queer men can participate and feel *normal*, almost unqueer, as the culture of the space encourages homoerotic desires for each subject, as he dances in the largely heteronormative playground.

It is DL men's physical presence in the queer club that much of the media has misread, as they stake claim to an *out* DL subject. In actuality, most men at The Gate are not *coming out*, but participating in a sort of *comin' in*. They have arrived in a queer space that welcomes them, but does not require them to become official members. The Gate is a black home they can come into, where the relatives understand the fullness of diversity, liberalness, and transgressiveness, and are honest about different forms of desire. The discursive demand that one must be *out* to participate in gay activities ignores the fact that all gay activity does not take place in the public domain; neither does individual participation always guarantee membership. Indeed, DL men are out in the club—in the sense that they are a part of a queer world-making moment. However, outside this club space they live very discreet lives, void of public displays of pleasure and desire for those of the same sex.

The Gate allows DL men to imagine themselves in a sort of utopia (but not quite.) This pleasure, attained through a queer world-making experience, may be the answer to the problematic question: Why are they in a gay club if they are not gay? The answer to this question, I argue here, is all about the structure of the space (its physical frame) and the texture of the space (the ideological frames of gender)—that which I wish to call *architexture*.

The Gate's *architexture* is elastic, but the privileged performance of certain style of masculinity welcomes the presence of DL men. In a sense, The Gate provides a space for DL men to partake in queer desire without having to feel queer (double entendre intended). Most importantly, The Gate teaches us how DL men not only exercise queer play, but inadvertently challenge the quick assumptions we can often make about queer performance in so-called queer space. This project cautions us always to be attentive to the interplay of race, gender, class, and sexuality—as they are often better arbiters of the meanings of space. Judith Butler's rhetorical questions at the outset of this essay, then, are apropos. Racialized queers often do not desire, and cannot afford, to be *out*. Thus, the closet as a threshold apparatus does not fully illustrate the ways in which the patrons of The Gate work through their sexuality. Black queer people have always done queer differently. Symbolically, The Gate, unlike the closet, is not a place of residence, but a place for possibilities to be explored. It is a place where subjects can *come in*, while still recognizing the cultural fabrics of heteronormative black life, which they value and experience, as both a part of and separate from their queer experience. The Gate is a heterogeneous playground whose architexture allows its patrons to explore and enjoy temporal pleasure—through the conjoining of oft-thought disparate traditions. As such, the architexture of The Gate accommodates multiple masculinities, speaking for multiple experiences, while still being attentive to the cross-cutting tropes which attract various bodies to specific cultural spaces.

In this essay, I have attempted to highlight one complicated space that exhibits black queers *making do* within a heteronormative society and white cultural tradition. As DL men *come in* The Gate, they redefine the queer world-making experience, as disrupting not only the heteronorms but also the traditional homonorms of outness as always being predicated upon one's participation in ordained public gay space. This idea of *comin' in* more richly accounts for how it is that many black queer clubs negate and challenge more universal rubrics and force-fitted assertions that queer spaces are always already architextures of outness.

As I sit at my desk, imagining the space of The Gate and the many possibilities within, I am drawn back to Isaac Julien's film *Looking for Langston*. I return to a masterful moment when the film returns to a historic scene, where black men are gathered in a discreet space to party and partake in homoerotic desires. Some stand with drinks, some chat, and some dance with each other—all feeling the pulse of the erotic and the pleasure of this rare opportunity. Dressed in period suits, drinking and tasting the finest of things, these men engage desire on their own terms, in their own way, somewhere *down low* and outside the radar of heteronormative gazes. This moment in film mirrors so much of what I see at The Gate. Black men and black queer men engage desire and use space, style, and music to guide their performances of sexuality. The Gate is no contemporary coincidence; it is a space that resurrects an older, rich tradition. It is a retelling of black queer men, cautiously and creatively, dancing desire. It is an illustration of black queer performance happening outside the closet, but still inside The Gate.

DISCUSSION QUESTIONS

1. What does it mean to be *on the down low*? Why might this be more likely for black men than for white men?

2. Who is Shawn? How does he see and enact his sexual orientation?

3. What is counterintuitive about black men who identify, occasionally or entirely, as queer, embracing and enjoying hip hop music and culture?

4. What does the term *architexture* refer to? How might this term be applied to hook up culture?

REFERENCES

Betsky, Aaron. *Queer Space: Architecture and Same-Sex Desire*. New York: Morrow and Company, 1997.

Boyd, Todd. *Am I Black Enough for You*. Indiana: Indiana U P, 1997.

Buckland, Fiona. *Impossible Dance: Club Culture and Queer World-Making*. Middletown, CT: Wesleyan U P, 2002.

Butler, Judith. Bodies that Matter: *On the Discursive Limits of Sex*. New York: Routledge, 1993.

Connor, Marlene. *What is Cool?: Understanding Black Manhood in America*. New York: Agate, 1995.

de Certeau, Michael. "The Practices of Space." On Signs. Ed. Michael Blonsky. Oxford, UK: Blackwell, 1985. 122–15.

DeFrantz, Thomas. "The Black Beat Made Visible." *Of the Presence of the Body: Essays on Dance and Performance Theory*. Ed. Andre Lepecki. Middletown, CT: Wesleyan U P, 2004. 64–81.

Denizet-Lewis, Benoit. "Double Lives on the Down Low." *New York Times Magazine*, 3 Aug. 2003: sec. 6, 28–33, 48, 52–53.

Drewal, Margaret. "The State of Research on Performance in Africa." *African Studies Review* 34.3 (1991): 1-64.

Halperin, David. *Saint Foucault: Towards a Gay Hagiography*. New York: Oxford U P, 1995.

—. "'Quare' Studies or (Almost) Everything I Know about Queer Studies I Learned from My Grandmother." *Text and Performance Quarterly* 20.1 (January 2001): 1–25.

King, Jason. "Remixing the Closet: The Down-Low Way of Knowledge." *Village Voice*, 25 June 2003: 38–46.

Lefebvre, Henri. *The Production of Space*. Trans. Donald Nicholson-Smith. New York: Basil Blackwell, 1991.

Reddy, Chandan. "Home, House, and Nonidentity. Paris Is Burning." *Burning Down the House: Recycling Domesticity*. Ed. Rosemary George. Boulder, CO: Westview Press, 1998. 355–79. Sedgwick, Eve. *Epistemology of Closet*. Berkeley: U of California P, 1990.

Stockton, Kathryn Bond. *Beautiful Bottom, Beautiful Shame: Where 'Black' Meets 'Queer'*. Durham, NC: Duke U P, 2006.

Thompson, Robert. "Dance and Culture, An Aesthetic of the Cool: West African Dance." *African Forum* 2 Fall 1966: 85–102.

Venable, Malcolm. "A Question of Identity." *Vibe*, July 2001: 98–108.

Warner, Michael. *Fear of a Queer Planet Queer Politics and Social Theory*. Minneapolis: U of Minneapolis: P 1993.

NOTES

1. In my forthcoming book manuscript, tentatively titled *Queering the Closet: Black Masculinity and the Politics of Sexual Passing*, I argue that the closet is a traditionally white paradigm, which has little/limited utility for black men who face issues of sexuality under racialized oppression. America's history of racism, and consequent surveillance of black male bodies, makes the closet an inept signifier/descriptor of black masculine performances of discreet sexuality. Rather, I argue that black men, and others within the black community, have found alternative ways of naming and identifying their discreet desire and practice.

2. The DL, in essence, quares the closet, in that it introduces a racialized understanding of the world, while also drawing attention to the role of intersecting identities in the production of space and time. Here, I draw on E. Patrick Johnson's instructive theoretical and methodological move to account for different *standpoints* and to recognize how intersectional identities affect gender and sexual performances. The DL, as positionality, signifies a location where space is instantiated with homoerotic codes and meanings, with potentially (non) temporal possibilities. Thus, the DL challenges the popular understanding of the closet as always already a dark place with temporary utility.

3. The name of this club has been modified, to secure confidentiality for the men with whom I speak, as well as the club and its other patrons.

16

Doing, Undoing, or Redoing Gender?

Learning from the Workplace Experiences of Transpeople

Catherine Connell

Transgender individuals have started to receive much more public acknowledgement in the past few years. Among the most visible is Caitlyn Jenner, stepfather of Kim and Khloe Kardashian, who transitioned in 2015 and famously came out in part by being photographed for the cover of *Vanity Fair* magazine. One criticism of the cover, showing Caitlyn in full make up, a stereotypically feminine pose and wearing a white corset, is that she was reinforcing the gender binary—the idea that one can only be male or female—rather than challenging societal rules about what gender means and the range of identities that are available.

In "Doing Gender," West and Zimmerman argued that one of these two gender identities, male or female, are unavoidable products of our interactions with each other, and they highlight that being genderless is not an option in contemporary American society. This article questions whether a binary division of gender into male and female is inevitable, or if alternatives are possible. Drawing on interviews with trans individuals about their experiences in the workplace, Catherine Connell tries to understand where the gender identity work of transpeople fits (or doesn't) in West and Zimmerman's widely used theoretical framework about gender.

This article is an excellent example of the collaborative nature of science in action, with one researcher drawing on and challenging the work of another. Connell's goal is not to prove that West and Zimmerman are wrong and therefore "win," but rather to add what her research tells us about meaningful ways to think about gender identity and push for modifications (or even rejection) of previously held beliefs if the evidence is sufficient. As you spend more time reading within a discipline, you'll start to see familiar names pop up in readings as the authors reference work that you are familiar with. It can be a very satisfying experience,

"Doing, Undoing, or Redoing Gender" by Catherine Connell, in *Gender & Society* 24(1), February 2010. Reprinted with permission.

much like bumping in to a friend or acquaintance on the street whose company you particularly enjoy, when you first start encountering references to works that you've read. To set yourself up for that satisfying experience here, take a moment to skim over West and Zimmerman's article at the beginning of this section before you read this one.

West and Zimmerman developed their theory of *doing gender* (1987) to account for the reproduction of gender through interaction. Two decades later, the theory has reached near canonical status in the sociology of gender (Jurik and Siemsen 2009). As doing gender has emerged as the hegemonic theoretical framework for understanding gender inequality, feminist scholars have begun to interrogate the theory's ability to account for social change. A central question in the debate is this: is *undoing gender* possible?

On one side of the debate are those who argue that the gender binary *can* be subverted in interaction (Deutsch 2007; Risman 2009). These scholars criticize the common deployment of doing gender to document the ways gender oppression is maintained, arguing that it is important also to highlight the *undoing* of gender to further the feminist project of dismantling gender inequality (Deutsch 2007). In response, West and Zimmerman (2009) have argued that gender can never be *undone*, but might instead be *redone*. They argue that the accountability structures that maintain gender may shift to accommodate less oppressive ways of doing gender, but are never entirely eradicated (West and Zimmerman 2009).

Thus far, this debate regarding the possibility of undoing gender has remained largely theoretical. This article offers an important contribution to this discussion by empirically investigating the workplace experiences of transgender-identified individuals. Transpeople disrupt the assumption that sex (designation at birth as either *male* or *female*), sex category (social designation as either *male* or *female* in everyday interactions), and gender (management of conduct based on one's assigned sex category) correspond with each other. While cispeople, or nontrans-identified individuals, are assigned a sex at birth, placed in the corresponding sex category, and held accountable to the corresponding gender norms (doing masculinity or doing femininity), the sex category or gender of transpeople does not match up as seamlessly with their sex. Theoretically, this disruption opens up an opportunity to undo or redo gender. Looking at transpeople's experiences allows us to ask the question: When sex, sex category, and gender do not match up, does this result in an undoing of gender? In other words, do transgender people subvert or undermine the gender binary in their daily interactions (Deutsch 2007; Risman 2009)? Alternatively, do transpeople redo gender by expanding or altering the norms associated with gender (West and Zimmerman 2009)?

I interviewed 19 transgender individuals about their negotiation and management of gendered interactions at work, and evaluated how the experiences they disclosed might contribute to doing, undoing, or redoing gender.

The term *transgender* entered the public discourse in the mid-1980s (Elkins and King 1996). It has generally replaced the earlier term *transsexual*, which is now used to refer specifically to people who have had or desire surgical and medical procedures that will match their sex to their gender. *Transgender* usually refers to individuals who deliberately reject their original gender assignment. The term may be used regardless of surgical and medical status. Therefore, the category *transgender* includes transsexual individuals, but also encompasses a wider group than this. Transgender people sometimes label themselves transwomen (or male-to-female), transmen (or female-to-male), or genderqueer. *Genderqueer* generally refers to gender identification other than that of *man* or *woman*. It often involves a politically motivated blending of gendered presentations, pronouns, and self-concepts. *Transpeople* has become the generic category used to describe everyone in these various categories.

Barbara Risman (2009:82) suggests that we might think of *undoing gender* (Deutsch 2007) as occurring "when the essentialism of binary distinctions between people based on sex category is challenged" (Risman 2009:83). In a response to Risman, West and Zimmerman (2009) take issue with the language of *undoing*, claiming that it implies abandonment of accountability to sex category—an abandonment they treat as impossible. They argue that gender is "not so much *undone* as *redone*" (West and Zimmerman 2009:118) through shifts in the accountability structures that sustain gender in interaction. In other words, accountability structures may shift to accommodate challenges to sex category. In this article, I consider whether transpeople's accounts of their gendered work experiences challenge the binary distinctions of sex category and, if so, what this might mean for West and Zimmerman's theory of doing gender. Through an analysis of these experiences, I consider whether transgender workers describe themselves as doing, undoing, or redoing gender.

Method

Because I am interested in questions of meaning making, a qualitative approach was necessary for this research (Esterberg 2002). Since transpeople are located in a variety of jobs, rather than concentrated in any one industry or workplace, ethnography was not suitable for this research project. Ethical concerns about drawing unwanted attention to trans employees by conducting on-the-job observations further precluded an ethnographic account of their individual workplaces. For these reasons, I chose in-depth interviews as my primary research method.

I sought participants from a wide range of racial, ethnic, and class backgrounds. However, my sample is primarily white and, to a lesser degree, middle class. This is in part a function of my snowball sampling technique, which tends to produce demographically similar respondents (Esterberg 2002). Seven of the 19 respondents were involved in a local transgender advocacy group; the remaining 12 were referred through the study participants' personal networks. (Thus, the majority were not members of the advocacy group.)

In the semi-structured interviews, research participants were asked to outline their work histories from their first jobs to their current employment situations. If they transitioned on the job, we discussed that process. I also inquired about interactions with supervisors, coworkers, and clients. After all of the interviews were conducted and transcribed, I coded them by reading through each interview carefully and cataloging each theme. As I cataloged, I kept a journal of patterns, connections, interesting anecdotes, themes, and possible theoretical directions.

The transgender workers I interviewed negotiated their changing gender identities in a variety of ways. A few did *stealth*, meaning that they did not identify themselves as transgender to their coworkers, nor were they perceived as such (as far as they could tell). Others either engaged in an open transition at work or made their transgender status evident through the process of dramatic realization (Goffman 1959), meaning they *came out* as trans.

The decision to be *out* as trans is one that must be individually negotiated based on a number of complex and sometimes contradictory financial, psychological, political, and personal considerations. It must be understood in the socioeconomic context of the individual's life, as well as in the historical context of the violence, stigma, and repression that transpeople have faced. How one navigates this decision in such a repressive environment is not merely a matter of free choice, just as is the case with the gay and lesbian *closet* (Seidman 2002).

My research suggests that the experiences of those performing stealth fit more or less within the theoretical paradigm of doing gender. Out transpeople, on the other hand, described experiences that fit better under either the rubric of undoing gender or of redoing gender. As I will show, they often attempted to meld together masculine and feminine gender performances. At the same time, however, open transpeople often felt they were gender disciplined or reinterpreted according to conventional gender norms. In the following section of this article, I will describe these different kinds of transgender experience and explain how they correspond to the processes of doing, undoing, and redoing of gender in the workplace.

Doing Gender at Work

Of the 19 research participants in this study, five performed *stealth* in the workplace, meaning that they did not identify themselves as transgender, nor were they (at least to their knowledge) *read* as transgender by their coworkers and clientele. These transpeople performed masculinity or femininity in a way that masked discordance between sex and sex category, leaving them subject to the same accountability structures of doing gender that cispeople must negotiate.

Mark, a 64-year-old white transman, had been identifying and living as a man for over 25 years. Because of the lack of legal and social protections at the time of his transition, Mark had always worked stealth. He was able to manage this by changing his name, Social Security information, and driver's license in 1985, before restrictive identification policies made this process more difficult (NCTE 2007). Coworkers questioned his gender early in his transition, because, he said, "as a middle-aged male, there were certain things I didn't know, because I hadn't been raised in the environment and so there were certain things that men expected me to know or be or react to that I didn't." Over time, however, Mark learned to do gender in an *appropriately* masculine way. He eventually "assimilate[d] some of that [*appropriate* masculinity] by being in that community, by having to work in that environment where we have to be one or the other." Here, Mark directly references the gender binary established through the application of sex category in interaction. Mark's on-the-job experiences as a stealth transman are consistent with conventional notions of *doing gender* (West and Zimmerman 1987).

Jessica, a 26-year-old Latina transwoman who works as a customer service representative, was also stealth at work. Unlike Mark, she was not motivated by fears of discrimination; in fact, she invoked her rights under new gender identity legal protections when asked what she would do if her coworkers found out about her transgender status, saying that she would "go straight to HR" with any discrimination or harassment concerns that might arise. Jessica defined her decision to remain stealth as a matter of privacy, explaining, "It's really nobody's business—it's not something that I'm ashamed to talk about, whatever, but in an environment with those people, with ignorant people, it's kind of like, there's no point." Because she felt that her *ignorant* coworkers would misunderstand her transgender status, Jessica chose not to identify herself as trans at work.

When asked how her work experience changed since her transition, which occurred before her current job, Jessica described a newfound accountability to the stringent appearance expectations placed on women in the workplace:

> I put more effort into what I wear. A lot. I mean, I think I always did, period, but I think now in particular it's like—like last night,

oh my gosh! I was trying on different clothes and it took me like an hour and a half just to figure out what I want to wear today for work. Before that wouldn't usually happen. I'd just throw on whatever. Plus there's certain things I have to wear, to take into consideration, like—I want to wear pants, but I can't wear jeans because we're a business casual environment, and if I wear these pants, did I shave my legs? Do I need to shave my legs? Do I need to wear a skirt that doesn't make my tummy stand out too much or not flatter my butt?

Prior feminist analyses of doing gender at work have underscored the pervasive pressures working women face to conform to conventional standards of feminine beauty (Dellinger and Williams 1997). According to Jessica's experience, these same pressures are exerted on stealth transwomen at work. Mark's and Jessica's experiences, as well as those of the other stealth participants in the sample, suggest that transpeople who do not reveal their transgender status remain subject to the same gendered accountability structures as cispeople. From their perspectives, the disruption of sex, gender, and sex category is not apparent in their interactions with their coworkers, thus they participate in the process of doing gender described by West and Zimmerman (1987).

Some of the *out* transgender people I interviewed also described experiences that fit under the rubric of doing gender. The process of transition can sometimes bring transpeople more into alignment with gender norms, thereby possibly easing the anxiety of coworkers and employers who were uncomfortable with their gender transgressive appearance pretransition. Coming out as transgender sometimes mitigates, rather than incurs, ambiguity in gender presentation. This actually allows the transgender subject to be read as more gender normative, thereby making them feel more accepted by others.

This seemed particularly true for the transmen in my study who lived as masculine women before transitioning into men. For example, Bobby, a 47-year-old biracial transman, and Kyle, a 29-year-old white transman, related anecdotes from their previous experiences as women when they were chased out of women's bathrooms for appearing *too masculine* and thereby threatening to the women inside. In particular, Kyle spoke of his prior struggle to *pass* as a woman; work interactions felt easier once his sex category was in line with his gender. He said,

I can just go to court, wear a suit, not have to worry about what bathroom I'm going to go to or what they're going to call me on the stand when I'm testifying, or how my client is going to react to that. I don't have to worry about it anymore—I wear a suit and it's good to go, no question.

Kyle believed that his transition eased tensions at work and smoothed over the possibility that his gender presentation might have a detrimental effect on his clients' court cases. Thus Kyle's transition brought him back in line with the norms of gender presentation at his workplace. He felt that people were more accepting of him because he presented a less controversial spectacle.

Several of the out transpeople in my sample described feeling interpreted in a way that reinforced hegemonic gender dynamics at work. They felt that coworkers, clients, and supervisors often reinterpreted their self-presentations and reinforced hegemonic gender dynamics at work, often in spite of their more transgressive beliefs and practices regarding gender. For instance, Julie, a 31-year-old Latina transwoman, mentioned how, as a customer service representative, customers often tried to make sense of her masculine voice by hearing her name wrong. She explained, "When I said 'This is Julie' on the phone, they would repeat it back to me as 'Julian?' So I started saying 'Juliette' but they still changed it into a guy's name, even less related sounding—'George?' 'Jake?'" Julie felt that her customers were trying to make sense of her masculine vocal presentation by assuming that they misheard her feminine name and translating it into a similar sounding (and even not-so-similar sounding) man's name, thus making her accountable to doing gender. Julie's experiences imply interactional limitations to the possibility of undoing or redoing gender when other participants in the interaction uphold gender accountability by resisting or reinterpreting discordant gender cues.

After announcing his transition and presenting as a man at work, Kurt, a 62-year-old white transman, felt policed by other men in the workplace regarding *appropriate* gender behavior. He recalled, "This one guy—it's kinda funny sometimes, because I'll say, 'I'm gonna slap the crap out of you.' And he says, 'Men do not slap.' And he'll correct me on different things." Kurt's coworker drew the boundary lines for acceptable behavior for men by letting him know that "men do not slap." Consequently, Kurt couldn't express himself without immediately being held accountable to rigid standards of masculine language and actions. To feel accepted as a man, Kurt must learn these *lessons* and adjust himself accordingly. This unbidden *apprenticeship* is a unique consequence of open workplace transitions, in that coworkers feel compelled to teach transpeople the gender normative behaviors they were not socialized into from birth (Schilt and Connell 2007). The experiences of Julie, Kurt, and others suggest that out transpeople are subject to gender accountability in workplace interactions, perhaps even more than cispeople, who may be allowed more room for improvisation in their gender performance.

This finding suggests that simply *being* transgender does not necessarily disrupt doing gender. Those who embody conventional gender presentations find themselves subjected to the accountability structures of doing gender, while those who transgress the rules find themselves corrected or misinterpreted in ways that support the gender binary. However, as the next section of this article shows, the out transgender individuals I interviewed nevertheless resisted these expectations by intentionally disrupting the assumed relationships between sex, gender, and sex category in their workplace interactions. They attempted to undo or redo gender even as their coworkers and clients held them accountable to conventional gender practices.

Undoing or Redoing Gender at Work?

The 13 participants in my sample who were out as transgender intentionally sought to undermine gendered expectations as they began performing their new gender. They were not always successful, because they felt accountable to the conventional gendered practices demanded by their coworkers. However, I found that many resisted these pressures by adapting a hybrid gender style of interacting with others. These acts constitute moments of *chipping away* at the established gender order (Lucal 1999) and, as I will argue, can be interpreted either as *undoing* or *redoing* gender.

Several research participants indicated that they consciously held on to gendered characteristics that did not match their chosen gender presentations. Their reasons for this varied: Some felt that gender-blending had important political meaning, others wanted to maintain parts of themselves that felt authentic even if they didn't perfectly *match* their chosen gender, and still others articulated a combination of both motivations.

For example, Kyle made deliberate decisions to keep certain so-called *feminine* aspects of his work style in his employment as a corrections officer. He did this both to maintain a sense of authenticity and to mitigate the white male privilege that his transition bestowed on him. He described how the style of his interactions with clients differed from that of his male coworkers:

> I tend to take a more female route of "Tell me what you're feeling, tell me where you're at"—that kind of thing, where a lot of our male coworkers are kind of like, in, out, you know, just—these are the boxes I need to check, let's check them. Where I'm, again, I kind of dig into them a little bit more and try to figure out what really is going on. . . . And I know that my clients are just kind of like [eyebrow raised questioningly]. Usually when people meet me they stereotype me as just a straight, white man—but I still talk with my hands, I have a lot of female socialization things that I'm not really willing to compromise because they're part of who I am.

Kyle's relationships with his clients, both in style (talking with his hands) and substance (asking about their feelings), included aspects of his personality that he attributed to his socialization as a woman. Although he perceives these qualities as distinguishing him from other men, he is unwilling to eliminate them from his interactions because they are central to his self-concept. While Kyle's attributes are not innately *female*, as he labels them here, they are attributes that are socially interpreted as such. By maintaining these attributes rather than erasing them wholesale in favor of a more masculine self-presentation, Kyle engages in a hybrid form of gender presentation.

Not only did Kyle maintain these attributes because "they're part of who [he is]," he also conceptualized this choice as a critique of white male domination. He recognized that he is read as a *straight white man*, but he attempted to craft an alternative kind of masculinity that might mitigate the privilege this gave him.

The genderqueer participants in my research were especially committed to hybrid gender performances. For example, Jared, a 23-year-old white genderqueer teaching assistant, articulated an aspect of political critique and resistance in how ze does gender. (I refer to Jared throughout using the pronouns ze prefers—the gender-neutral *ze* and *hir*.) Jared used a masculine name and dressed in men's clothing, yet hir embodiment (short, small, delicate facial features) prevented hir from being read exclusively as a man. As a genderqueer, ze saw this confusing presentation as important to hir identity and political work. In fact, Jared noted that if ze were to become more gender normative (as a result of testosterone use), ze would enact other strategies to maintain the confusion:

> I do think about hormones and I wonder if I start taking hormones—I'm going to pass whether I want to or not . . . I'll get read maybe questioningly still, but I'll probably get read as man. So I suppose if I were to start hormones, I might do more fun, feminine things! . . . I've already told my girlfriend that, you know, if and when I ever get a beard, I'm stealing her skirt!

Rather than try to minimize gender confusion, Jared actively cultivated it because of the way it challenged gender assumptions. Jared's intentional challenge to the gender binary suggest that gender is being undone in hir interactions, according to Risman's (2009) definition of undoing gender. Alternately, Jared can be read as attempting to redo gender, or revising the strictly delineated expectations imposed on men and women.

Agape, a 28-year-old white transwoman, also played with gender ambiguity before and after transitioning. In the period when she worked as a man, she occasionally came into the office in a skirt or dress and wore a dress to the office Christmas party two years in a row. Because of her ambiguous presentation before transition, she noted that her transition was confusing for her coworkers:

> I think the manner of my transition made things harder for people, because it was smooth, rather than abrupt. It wasn't like one day I was male and the next day I was female. It was more like, one day I'm kind of vaguely male-ish, and already pretty androgynous, and then I switch to—from like, slightly masculine androgynous to slightly feminine androgynous. I think it just made it kind of blurry for people.

While she initially felt the need to dress "really girly for a few months," she gradually realized that this presentation was a *façade* and didn't fit her. She explained,

> I tried doing the whole girly girl thing, wearing makeup, wearing pretty clothes, and then I was like, "Eh, this is wrong, this isn't me." But it's a phase I had to go through to get to where I am now.

In both her ambiguous style of transition and her decision not to adhere to a *girly girl* style of gender presentation, Agape tried to demonstrate gender transgression for her coworkers. Her choice of a gender-neutral name (meaning *love*) underscored her opposition to the gender binary, which may either undo or redo gender in her workplace interactions.

Carolina, a 35-year-old Latina transwoman, explained her self-presentation using the creative term *transparency*. Carolina was preparing to leave her engineering career, where she openly identified as trans, to attend law school. When I asked Carolina, who said that she passes most of the time, if she would still be out as transgender in law school, she responded:

> Oh yeah, being out is important to me, period. The only way we'll ever change people's minds is for all of us to be out. It doesn't mean you walk around with a big "T" on your forehead, but you gotta let people know. There's an interesting term I heard recently called *transparency*. I'm gonna be *transparent*. . . . It means that you don't hide or deny who you are, but you don't wear a Transsexual Menace T-shirt everywhere you go. Yeah, it's less in your face, but you also don't deny or hide who you are. Because for me—who I am and where I come from is very important. I like myself, so why am I going to deny that? Why am I going to—there's this idea of *stealth* which is never telling anyone, making up stories about your past. I'm not going to do that, I like who I am.

Carolina refused to start over as stealth in her new life, even though she probably could do so without much difficulty. She said, "I'm going to make [being transgender] an issue. I'm going to always stand up, especially in law school—I'm going to stand up when we start talking about civil rights and challenge people." Carolina planned to use this strategy of transparency to critique legal and social inequalities.

Many of the transgender workers used *outness* as a strategy of political visibility and role modeling in the workplace. Some engaged in acts of dramatic realization (Goffman 1959) to make their trans status apparent in their interactions with others. These moments of dramatic realization can be subtle, such as Carolina's *transparency* strategy, or they can be obvious, such as Jared's use of clashing gender displays to highlight hir genderqueer status.

This politicization of transgender, combined with the efforts at hybridity in their gender performances, could be interpreted as moments of undoing or redoing gender. By blending their current and former gender biographies and drawing attention to their disruption of the relationships between sex, gender, and sex category, these trans people interrupt the gender binary. This is what Risman (2009) would identify as a moment of undoing gender. In documenting these moments of undoing gender, Risman (2009:84) would argue, feminist sociologists are providing guideposts for the ultimate political goal of "mov[ing] to a postgender society."

In contrast, West and Zimmerman (2009) might point to the heightened gender accountability that trans people describe as evidence for the impossibility of gender's undoing. As an alternative to undoing gender, they offer the concept of redoing gender, or revisions to gender accountability that "weaken its utility as a ground for men's hegemony" (West and Zimmerman 2009:117). According to this perspective, by enacting a hybrid gender performance, these transpeople *redo* the accountability structures that maintain the rigid boundaries between men's and women's gender presentations. This redoing may challenge the essentialized notions of masculinity that shore up men's power in society, but it does not eliminate gender as a sorting device in interactional or organizational settings.

Conclusion

Drawing from the perspectives of transpeople, this article finds evidence that they experience the doing and the undoing/redoing of gender. Transpeople are tasked with making sense of a disconnect between sex, gender, and sex category, which they solve in a variety of ways, including through *stealth* representations and through a more transparent blending of characteristics from their former and current gender expressions. I call this constellation of interactive practices *doing transgender*. Regardless of whether they are stealth or out, transgender positionality sensitizes transpeople to gender discrimination, thereby opening up possibilities for the *collective contestation* (Connell 2009) of gendered inequality by transpeople and cisfeminists.

While sociologists have often used doing gender theory to account for stability in gender relations (Deutsch 2007), these findings suggest that interactions may be a site for change as well as stability, at least for this particular group of individuals. This is not to say that all transpeople attempt to undo or redo gender, but rather that they are all always faced with the complex task of negotiating the discordance between sex, gender, and sex category. My interviews with transpeople show that this negotiation often results in moments of interactive resistance to gender stability that deserve careful attention. Future research might investigate other groups for these changes, as proponents of undoing gender have suggested (Deutsch 2007; Risman 2009). Transpeople are not necessarily the only social actors engaged in the undoing or redoing of gender; in fact, the more moments of challenging the gender binary that are identified, the more common ground is uncovered for transpeople and others to oppose gender inequality.

DISCUSSION QUESTIONS

1. What aspects of West and Zimmerman's *doing gender* idea does the author embrace? Which does she think we should reconsider?

2. What were the different ways that her study participants *did* gender at work? What was their motivation for each of these approaches?

3. Watch an episode of the Amazon show Transparent. Do you think Maura is *doing, undoing* or *redoing* gender? What about Caitlyn Jenner on the cover of Vanity Fair? What other kinds of social identities might be said to require *doing, undoing,* or *redoing*?

REFERENCES

Acker, Joan. 1990. Hierarchies, jobs, bodies: A theory of gendered organizations. *Gender & Society* 4 (2): 139–58.

Bolough, Roslyn W. 1992. The promise and failure of ethnomethodology from a feminist perspective: Comment on Rogers. *Gender & Society* 6 (2): 199–206.

Bornstein, Kate. 1995. *Gender outlaw: On men, women, and the rest of us.* New York: Vintage.

Butler, Judith. 1990. *Gender trouble: Feminism and the subversion of identity.* New York: Routledge.

Butler, Judith. 2000. *Undoing Gender.* New York: Routledge.

Collins, Patricia Hill. 2000. *Black feminist thought: Knowledge, consciousness, and the politics of empowerment.* 2nd ed. New York: Routledge.

Connell, R. W. 2006. *Masculinities: Knowledge, power, and social change.* Oxford, UK: Polity.

Connell, Raewyn. 2009. Accountable conduct: "Doing gender" in transsexual and political retrospect. *Gender & Society* 23 (1): 104–11.

Dellinger, K., and C. Williams. 1997. Makeup at work: Negotiating appearance rules in the workplace. *Gender & Society* 11 (2): 151–77.

Denzin, Norman. 1990. Harold and Agnes: A feminist narrative undoing. *Sociological Theory* 8 (2): 198–216.

Deutsch, Frances. 2007. Undoing gender. *Gender & Society* 21 (2): 106–27.

Dozier, Raine. 2005. Beards, breasts, and bodies: Doing sex in a gendered world. *Gender & Society* 19 (3): 297–316.

Elkins, R., and D. King. 1996. *Blending genders: Social aspects of cross-dressing and sex-changing.* London and New York: Routledge.

Eichler, Margrit. 1987. Sex change operations: The last bulwark of the double standard. In *Gender roles: Doing what comes naturally?* Ed. E. D. Salamon & N. Robinson. Toronto: Methuen.

Esterberg, Kristin. 2002. *Qualitative methods in social research.* Boston: McGraw Hill.

Garfinkel, Harold. 1967. *Studies in ethnomethodology.* Englewood Cliffs, NJ: Prentice Hall.

Goffman, Erving. 1959. *Presentation of self in everyday life.* New York: Doubleday.

Gorman, Elizabeth. 2005. Gender stereotypes, same-gender preference, and organizational variation in the hiring of women: Evidence from law firms. *American Sociological Review* 70:702–28.

HRC. 2009. LGBT equality at the Fortune 500. *Human Rights Campaign.* http://www.hrc.org/issues/fortune500.htm (accessed July 17, 2009).

Irvine, Janice. 1990. *Disorder and desire: Sex and gender in modern American sexology.* Philadelphia: Temple University Press.

Jurik, N. C., and C. Simsen. 2009. "Doing gender" as canon or agenda: A symposium on West and Zimmerman. *Gender & Society* 23 (1): 72–75.

Kanter, Rosabeth M. 1977. *Men and women of the corporation.* New York: Basic Books.

Kessler, S. J., and W. McKenna. 1978. *Gender: An ethnomethodological approach.* Chicago: University of Chicago Press.

Lucal, Betsy. 1999. What it means to be gendered me: Life on the boundaries of a dichotomous gender system. *Gender & Society* 13 (6): 781–97.

Martin, Patricia Yancey. 2003. "Said and done" versus "saying and doing": Gendering practices, practicing gender at work. *Gender & Society* 17 (3): 342–66.

Merton, Robert K. 1972. Insiders and outsiders: A chapter in the sociology of knowledge. *American Journal of Sociology* 78:9–47.

Meyerowitz, Joanne. 2002. *How sex changed: A history of transsexuality in the United States*. Cambridge, MA: Harvard University Press.

Mills, C. W. 1940. Situated actions and vocabularies of motive. *American Sociological Review* 5:904–13.

Namaste, Viviane. 2002. *Invisible lives: The erasure of transsexual and transgender people*. Chicago: University of Chicago Press.

National Center for Transgender Equality. 2007. Federal policy changes, http://www .nctequality.org/Issues/federal_documents.html (accessed July 17, 2009).

National Gay and Lesbian Task Force. 2007. One community. One END A. http://www .thetaskforce.org/enda07/enda07.html (accessed July 17, 2009).

Raymond, Janice. 1977. Transsexualism: The ultimate homage to sex-role power. *Chrysalis* 3:11–23.

Raymond, Janice. 1979. *The transsexual empire: The making of the she-male*. London: Women's Press.

Risman, Barbara. 2009. From doing to undoing: Gender as we know it. *Gender & Society* 23 (1): 81–84.

Rogers, Mary. F. 1992. They were all passing: Agnes, Garfinkel, and company. *Gender & Society* 6 (2): 169–91.

Rudacille, Deborah. 2005. *The riddle of gender: Science, activism, and transgender rights*. New York: Pantheon.

Schilt, Kristen. 2006. Making gender visible: Transmen as "outsiders-within" in the workplace. *Gender & Society* 20 (4): 465–90.

Schilt, K. and C. Connell. 2007. Do workplace gender transitions make gender trouble? *Gender, Work, and Organization* 14(6): 596–618.

Seidman, Steven. 2002. *Beyond the closet? The transformation of gay and lesbian life*. New York: Routledge.

Stone, Allucquère Rosanne. 1993. The empire strikes back: A posttransexual manifesto. *Camera Obscura* 10 (2): 150–76.

Stryker, Susan. 1987. Identity theory: Developments and extensions. In *Self and identity: Psychological perspectives*, ed. K. Yardley and T. Holmes. New York: Wiley.

Stryker, Susan. 1995. Transsexuality: The postmodern body and/as technology. *Exposure: The Journal of the Society for Photographic Education* 30:38–50.

Vidal-Ortiz, Salvador. 2008. The figure of the transwoman of color through the lens of "doing gender." *Gender & Society* 23 (10): 99–103.

Vidal-Ortiz, Salvador. 2009. Transgender and transsexual studies: Sociology's influence and future steps. *Sociological Compass* 2 (2): 433–50.

West, C., and D. H. Zimmerman. 1987. Doing gender. *Gender & Society* 1 (2): 125–51.

West, C., and D. H. Zimmerman. 2009. Accounting for doing gender. *Gender & Society* 23 (1): 11–122.

Williams, Christine. 1989. *Gender differences at work: Women and men in non-traditional occupations*. Berkeley: University of California Press.

Williams, Christine. 1995. *Still a man's world*. Berkeley: University of California Press.

Race

17

The Code of the Streets

Elijah Anderson

In this article, Elijah Anderson explains the code of the streets, a set of norms that govern interactions in public spaces in poor, inner-city African American neighborhoods. His insightful analysis sheds light on the social context of the interpersonal violence that plagues many of these neighborhoods. Homicide is the leading cause of death for young African American men, but what is often reported in the news as random or senseless violence likely has its basis in the logic of the code of the streets. Anderson points out that the majority of the residents in these neighborhoods are law-abiding citizens with mainstream values, what he and other residents call decent families. But a small portion of street families also live in these neighborhoods. Street families are marked by more extreme poverty, a lack of consideration for others, less involved parenting, and a belief in the values of the code of the streets.

The main feature of the code of the streets is to display a willingness to use violence to get or maintain respect in interpersonal interactions. Respect is a scarce commodity in communities that lack good job prospects and educational opportunities, so public interactions become an important locale for getting and maintaining respect. Because 'decent' and street families must coexist in the same neighborhood, those from decent families must also adhere to and use the code in order to safely navigate public space. As Anderson insightfully explains, there is much more to the stereotypical image of swaggering, violence-prone, inner city minorities than there appears on the surface.

Of all the problems besetting the poor inner-city black community, none is more pressing than that of interpersonal violence and aggression. It wreaks havoc daily with the lives of community residents and increasingly spills over into downtown and residential middle-class areas. Muggings, burglaries, carjackings, and drug-related shootings, all of which may leave

---

"The Code of the Streets" by Elijah Anderson, The *Atlantic*, May 1, 1994. This essay is further developed in the book, *Code of the Street*, W.W. Norton, 1999. Reprinted by permission of the author.

their victims or innocent bystanders dead, are now common enough to concern all urban and many suburban residents. The inclination to violence springs from the circumstances of life among the ghetto poor—the lack of jobs that pay a living wage, the stigma of race, the fallout from rampant drug use and drug trafficking, and the resulting alienation and lack of hope for the future.

Simply living in such an environment places young people at special risk of falling victim to aggressive behavior. Although there are often forces in the community which can counteract the negative influences, by far the most powerful being a strong, loving, "decent" (as inner-city residents put it) family committed to middle-class values, the despair is pervasive enough to have spawned an oppositional culture, that of "the streets," whose norms are often consciously opposed to those of mainstream society. These two orientations—decent and street—socially organize the community, and their coexistence has important consequences for residents, particularly children growing up in the inner city. Above all, this environment means that even youngsters whose home lives reflect mainstream values—and the majority of homes in the community do—must be able to handle themselves in a street-oriented environment.

This is because the street culture has evolved what may be called a code of the streets, which amounts to a set of informal rules governing interpersonal public behavior, including violence. The rules prescribe both a proper comportment and a proper way to respond if challenged. They regulate the use of violence and so allow those who are inclined to aggression to precipitate violent encounters in an approved way. The rules have been established and are enforced mainly by the street-oriented, but on the streets the distinction between street and decent is often irrelevant; everybody knows that if the rules are violated, there are penalties. Knowledge of the code is thus largely defensive; it is literally necessary for operating in public. Therefore, even though families with a decency orientation are usually opposed to the values of the code, they often reluctantly encourage their children's familiarity with it to enable them to negotiate the inner-city environment.

At the heart of the code is the issue of respect—loosely defined as being treated "right," or granted the deference one deserves. However, in the troublesome public environment of the inner city, as people increasingly feel buffeted by forces beyond their control, what one deserves in the way of respect becomes more and more problematic and uncertain. This in turn further opens the issue of respect to sometimes intense interpersonal negotiation. In the street culture, especially among young people, respect is viewed as almost an external entity that is hard-won but easily lost, and so must constantly be guarded. The rules of the code in fact provide a framework for negotiating respect. The person whose very appearance—including his clothing, demeanor, and way of moving—deters transgressions feels that he possesses, and may be considered by others to possess, a measure of respect. With the right amount of respect, for instance, he can avoid "being bothered" in public. If he is bothered, not only may he be in physical danger but he has been disgraced or "dissed" (disrespected). Many of the forms that dissing can take might seem petty to middle-class people (maintaining eye contact for too long, for example), but to those invested in the street code, these actions become serious indications of the other person's intentions. Consequently, such people become very sensitive to advances and slights, which could well serve as warnings of imminent physical confrontation.

This hard reality can be traced to the profound sense of alienation from mainstream society and its institutions felt by many poor inner-city black people, particularly the young. The code of the streets is actually a cultural adaptation to a profound lack of faith in the police and the judicial system. The police are most often seen as representing the dominant white society and not caring to protect inner-city residents. When called, they may not respond, which is one reason many residents feel they must be prepared to take extraordinary measures to defend themselves and their loved ones against those who are inclined to aggression. Lack of police accountability has in fact been incorporated into the status system: the person who is believed capable of "taking care of himself " is accorded a certain deference, which translates into a sense of physical and psychological control. Thus the street code emerges where the influence of the police ends and personal responsibility for one's safety is felt to begin. Exacerbated by the proliferation of drugs and easy access to guns, this volatile situation results in the ability of the street oriented minority (or those who effectively "go for bad") to dominate the public spaces.

Decent and Street Families

Although almost everyone in poor inner-city neighborhoods is struggling financially and therefore feels a certain distance from the rest of America, the decent and the street family in a real sense represent two poles of value orientation, two contrasting conceptual categories. The labels "decent" and "street," which the residents themselves use, amount to evaluative judgments that confer status on local residents. The labeling is often the result of a social contest among individuals and families of the neighborhood. Individuals of the two orientations often coexist in the same extended family. Decent residents judge themselves to be so while judging others to be of the street, and street individuals often present themselves as decent, drawing distinctions between themselves and other people. In addition, there is quite a bit of circumstantial behavior—that is, one person may at different times exhibit both decent and street orientations, depending on the circumstances. Although these designations result from so much social jockeying, there do exist concrete features that define each conceptual category.

Generally, so-called decent families tend to accept mainstream values more fully and attempt to instill them in their children. Whether married couples with children or single-parent (usually female) households, they are generally "working poor" and so tend to be better off financially than their street-oriented neighbors. They value hard work and self-reliance and are willing to sacrifice for their children. Because they have a certain amount of faith in mainstream society, they harbor hopes for a better future for their children, if not for themselves. Many of them go to church and take a strong interest in their children's schooling. Rather than dwelling on the real hardships and inequities facing them, many such decent people, particularly the increasing number of grandmothers raising grandchildren, see their difficult situation as a test from God and derive great support from their faith and from the church community.

Extremely aware of the problematic and often dangerous environment in which they reside, decent parents tend to be strict in their child-rearing practices, encouraging children to respect authority and walk a straight moral line. They have an almost obsessive concern about trouble of any kind and remind their children to be on the lookout for people and situations that might lead to it. At the same time, they are themselves polite and considerate of others, and teach their children to be the same way. At home, at work, and in church, they strive hard to maintain a positive mental attitude and a spirit of cooperation.

So-called street parents, in contrast, often show a lack of consideration for other people and have a rather superficial sense of family and community. Though they may love their children, many of them are unable to cope with the physical and emotional demands of parenthood, and find it difficult to reconcile their needs with those of their children. These families, who are more fully invested in the code of the streets than the decent people are, may aggressively socialize their children into it in a normative way. They believe in the code and judge themselves and others according to its values.

In fact the overwhelming majority of families in the inner-city community try to approximate the decent-family model, but there are many others who clearly represent the worst fears of the decent family. Not only are their financial resources extremely limited, but what little they have may easily be misused. The lives of the street-oriented are often marked by disorganization. In the most desperate circumstances people frequently have a limited understanding of priorities and consequences, and so frustrations mount over bills, food, and, at times, drink, cigarettes, and drugs. Some tend toward self-destructive behavior; many street-oriented women are crack-addicted ("on the pipe"), alcoholic, or involved in complicated relationships with men who abuse them. In addition, the seeming intractability of their situation, caused in large part by the lack of well-paying jobs and the persistence of racial discrimination, has engendered deep-seated bitterness and anger in many of the most desperate and poorest blacks, especially young people. The need both to exercise a measure of control and to lash out at somebody is often reflected in the adults' relations with their children. At the least, the frustrations of persistent poverty shorten the fuse in such people—contributing to a lack of patience with anyone, child or adult, who irritates them.

In these circumstances a woman—or a man, although men are less consistently present in children's lives—can be quite aggressive with children, yelling at and striking them for the least little infraction of the rules she has set down. Often little if any serious explanation follows the verbal and physical punishment. This response teaches children a particular lesson. They learn that to solve any kind of interpersonal problem one must quickly resort to hitting or other violent behavior. Actual peace and quiet, and also the appearance of calm, respectful children conveyed to her neighbors and friends, are often what the young mother most desires, but at times she will be very aggressive in trying to get them. Thus she may be quick to beat her children, especially if they defy her law, not because she hates them but because this is the way she knows to control them. In fact, many street-oriented women love their children dearly. Many mothers in the community subscribe to the notion that there is a "devil in the boy" that must be beaten out of him or that socially "fast girls need to be whupped." Thus much of what borders on child abuse in the view of social authorities is acceptable parental punishment in the view of these mothers.

Many street-oriented women are sporadic mothers whose children learn to fend for themselves when necessary, foraging for food and money any way they can get it. The children are sometimes employed by drug dealers or become addicted themselves. These children of the street, growing up with little supervision, are said to "come up hard." They often learn to fight at an early age, sometimes using short-tempered adults around them as role models. The street-oriented home may be fraught with anger, verbal disputes, physical aggression, and even mayhem. The children observe these goings-on, learning the lesson that might make right. They quickly learn to hit those who cross them, and the dog-eat-dog mentality prevails. In order to survive, to protect oneself, it is necessary to marshal inner resources and be ready to deal with adversity in a hands-on way. In these circumstances physical prowess takes on great significance.

In some of the most desperate cases, a street-oriented mother may simply leave her young children alone and unattended while she goes out. The most irresponsible women can be found at local bars and crack houses, getting high and socializing with other adults. Sometimes a troubled woman will leave very young children alone for days at a time. Reports of crack addicts abandoning their children have become common in drug infested inner-city communities. Neighbors or relatives discover the abandoned children, often hungry and distraught over the absence of their mother. After repeated absences, a friend or relative, particularly a grandmother, will often step in to care for the young children, sometimes petitioning the authorities to send her, as guardian of the children, the mother's welfare check, if the mother gets one. By this time, however, the children may well have learned the first lesson of the streets: survival itself, let alone respect, cannot be taken for granted; you have to fight for your place in the world.

Campaigning for Respect

These realities of inner-city life are largely absorbed on the streets. At an early age, often even before they start school, children from street oriented homes gravitate to the streets, where they "hang"—socialize with their peers. Children from these generally permissive homes have a great deal of latitude and are allowed to "rip and run" up and down the street. They often come home from school, put their books down, and go right back out the door. On school nights eight- and nine-year-olds remain out until nine or ten o'clock (and teenagers typically come in whenever they want to). On the streets they play in groups that often become the source of their primary social bonds. Children from decent homes tend to be more carefully supervised and are thus likely to have curfews and to be taught how to stay out of trouble.

When decent and street kids come together, a kind of social shuffle occurs in which children have a chance to go either way. Tension builds as a child comes to realize that he must choose an orientation. The kind of home he comes from influences but does not determine the way he will ultimately turn out—although it is unlikely that a child from a thoroughly street oriented family will easily absorb decent values on the streets. Youths who emerge from street-oriented families but develop a decency orientation almost always learn those values in another setting— in school, in a youth group, in church. Often it is the result of their involvement with a caring "old head" (adult role model).

In the street, through their play, children pour their individual life experiences into a common knowledge pool, affirming, confirming, and elaborating on what they have observed in the home and matching their skills against those of others. And they learn to fight. Even small children test one another, pushing and shoving, and are ready to hit other children over circumstances not to their liking. In turn, they are readily hit by other children, and the child who is toughest prevails. Thus the violent resolution of disputes, the hitting and cursing, gains social reinforcement. The child in effect is initiated into a system that is really a way of campaigning for respect.

In addition, younger children witness the disputes of older children, which are often resolved through cursing and abusive talk, if not aggression or outright violence. They see that one child succumbs to the greater physical and mental abilities of the other. They are also alert and attentive witnesses to the verbal and physical fights of adults, after which they compare notes and share their interpretations of the event. In almost every case the victor is the person who physically won the altercation, and this person often enjoys the esteem and respect of onlookers. These experiences reinforce the lessons the children have learned at home: might makes right, and toughness is a virtue, while humility is not. In effect they learn the social meaning of fighting. When it is left virtually unchallenged, this understanding becomes an ever more important part of the child's working conception of the world. Over time the code of the streets becomes refined.

Those street-oriented adults with whom children come in contact— including mothers, fathers, brothers, sisters, boyfriends, cousins, neighbors, and friends— help them along in forming this understanding by verbalizing the messages they are getting through experience: "Watch your back." "Protect yourself." "Don't punk out." "If somebody messes with you, you got to pay them back." "If someone disses you, you got to straighten them out." Many parents actually impose sanctions if a child is not sufficiently aggressive. For example, if a child loses a fight and comes home upset, the parent might respond, "Don't you come in here crying that somebody beat you up; you better get back out there and whup his ass. I didn't raise no punks! Get back out there and whup his ass. If you don't whup his ass, I'll whup your ass when you come home." Thus the child obtains reinforcement for being tough and showing nerve.

While fighting, some children cry as though they are doing something they are ambivalent about. The fight may be against their wishes, yet they may feel constrained to fight or face the consequences—not just from peers but also from caretakers or parents, who may administer another beating if they back down. Some adults recall receiving such lessons from their own parents and justify repeating them to their children as a way to toughen them up. Looking capable of taking care of oneself as a form of self-defense is a dominant theme among both street-oriented and decent adults who worry about the safety of their children. There is thus at times a convergence in their child-rearing practices, although the rationales behind them may differ.

Self-Image Based on "Juice"

By the time they are teenagers, most youths have either internalized the code of the streets or at least learned the need to comport themselves in accordance with its rules, which chiefly have to do with interpersonal communication. The code revolves around the presentation of self. Its basic requirement is the display of a certain predisposition to violence. Accordingly, one's bearing must send the unmistakable if sometimes subtle message to "the next person" in public that one is capable of violence and mayhem when the situation requires it, that one can take care of oneself. The nature of this communication is largely determined by the demands of the circumstances but can include facial expressions, gait, and verbal expressions—all of which are geared mainly to deterring aggression. Physical appearance, including clothes, jewelry, and grooming, also plays an important part in how a person is viewed; to be respected, it is important to have the right look.

Even so, there are no guarantees against challenges, because there are always people around looking for a fight to increase their share of respect—or "juice," as it is sometimes called on the street. Moreover, if a person is assaulted, it is important, not only in the eyes of his opponent but also in the eyes of his "running buddies," for him to avenge himself. Otherwise he risks being "tried" (challenged) or "moved on" by any number of others. To maintain his honor he must show he is not someone to be "messed with" or "dissed." In general, the person must "keep himself straight" by managing his position of respect among others; this involves in part his self-image, which is shaped by what he thinks others are thinking of him in relation to his peers.

Objects play an important and complicated role in establishing self-image. Jackets, sneakers, gold jewelry, reflect not just a person's taste, which tends to be tightly regulated among adolescents of all social classes, but also a willingness to possess things that may require defending. A boy wearing a fashionable, expensive jacket, for example, is vulnerable to attack by another who covets the jacket and either cannot afford to buy one or wants the added satisfaction of depriving someone else of his. However, if the boy forgoes the desirable jacket and wears one that isn't "hip," he runs the risk of being teased and possibly even assaulted as an unworthy person. To be allowed to hang with certain prestigious crowds, a boy must wear a different set of expensive clothes—sneakers and athletic suit—every day. Not to be able to do so might make him appear socially deficient. The youth comes to covet such items—especially when he sees easy prey wearing them.

In acquiring valued things, therefore, a person shores up his identity—but since it is an identity based on having things, it is highly precarious.

This very precariousness gives a heightened sense of urgency to staying even with peers, with whom the person is actually competing. Young men and women who are able to command respect through their presentation of self—by allowing their possessions and their body language to speak for them—may not have to campaign for regard but may, rather, gain it by the force of their manner. Those who are unable to command respect in this way must actively campaign for it—and are thus particularly alive to slights.

One way of campaigning for status is by taking the possessions of others. In this context, seemingly ordinary objects can become trophies imbued with symbolic value that far exceeds their monetary worth. Possession of the trophy can symbolize the ability to violate somebody—to "get in his face," to take something of value from him, to "dis" him, and thus to enhance one's own worth by stealing someone else's. The trophy does not have to be something material. It can be another person's sense of honor, snatched away with a derogatory remark. It can be the outcome of a fight. It can be the imposition of a certain standard, such as a girl's getting herself recognized as the most beautiful. Material things, however, fit easily into the pattern. Sneakers, a pistol, even somebody else's girlfriend, can become a trophy. When a person can take something from another and then flaunt it, he gains a certain regard by being the owner, or the controller, of that thing. But this display of ownership can then provoke other people to challenge him. This game of who controls what is thus constantly being played out on inner-city streets, and the trophy—extrinsic or intrinsic, tangible or intangible—identifies the current winner.

An important aspect of this often violent give-and-take is its zero-sum quality. That is, the extent to which one person can raise himself up depends on his ability to put another person down. This underscores the alienation that permeates the inner-city ghetto community. There is a generalized sense that very little respect is to be had, and therefore everyone competes to get what affirmation he can of the little that is available. The craving for respect that results gives people thin skins. Shows of deference by others can be highly soothing, contributing to a sense of security, comfort, self-confidence, and self-respect. Transgressions by others which go unanswered diminish these feelings and are believed to encourage further transgressions. Hence one must be ever vigilant against the transgressions of others or even appearing as if transgressions will be tolerated. Among young people, whose sense of self-esteem is particularly vulnerable, there is an especially heightened concern with being disrespected. Many inner-city young men in particular crave respect to such a degree that they will risk their lives to attain and maintain it.

The issue of respect is thus closely tied to whether a person has an inclination to be violent, even as a victim. In the wider society people may not feel required to retaliate physically after an attack, even though they are aware that they have been degraded or taken advantage of. They may feel a great need to defend themselves during an attack, or to behave in such a way as to deter aggression (middle-class people certainly can and do become victims of street-oriented youths), but they are much more likely than street-oriented people to feel that they can walk away from a possible altercation with their self-esteem intact. Some people may even have the strength of character to flee, without any thought that their self-respect or esteem will be diminished.

In impoverished inner-city black communities, however, particularly among young males and perhaps increasingly among females, such flight would be extremely difficult. To run away would likely leave one's self-esteem in tatters. Hence people often feel constrained not only to stand up and at least attempt to resist during an assault but also to "pay back"—to seek revenge—after a successful assault on their person. This may include going to get a weapon or even getting relatives involved. Their very identity and self-respect, their honor, is often intricately tied up with the way they perform on the streets during and after such encounters. This outlook reflects the circumscribed opportunities of the inner-city poor. Generally people outside the ghetto have other ways of gaining status and regard, and thus do not feel so dependent on such physical displays.

By Trial of Manhood

On the street, among males these concerns about things and identity have come to be expressed in the concept of "manhood." Manhood in the inner city means taking the prerogatives of men with respect to strangers, other men, and women— being distinguished as a man. It implies physicality and a certain ruthlessness. Regard and respect are associated with this concept in large part because of its practical application: if others have little or no regard for a person's manhood, his very life and those of his loved ones could be in jeopardy. But there is a chicken-and-egg aspect to this situation: one's physical safety is more likely to be jeopardized in public because manhood is associated with respect. In other words, an existential link has been created between the idea of manhood and one's self-esteem, so that it has become hard to say which is primary. For many inner-city youths, manhood and respect are flip sides of the same coin; physical and psychological well-being are inseparable, and both require a sense of control, of being in charge.

The operating assumption is that a man, especially a real man, knows what other men know—the code of the streets. And if one is not a real man, one is somehow diminished as a person, and there are certain valued things one simply does not deserve. There is thus believed to be a certain justice to the code, since it is considered that everyone has the opportunity to know it. Implicit in this is that everybody is held responsible for being familiar with the code. If the victim of a mugging, for example, does not know the code and so responds "wrong," the perpetrator may feel justified even in killing him and may feel no remorse. He may think, "Too bad, but it's his fault. He should have known better."

So when a person ventures outside, he must adopt the code—a kind of shield, really—to prevent others from "messing with" him. In these circumstances it is easy for people to think they are being tried or tested by others even when this is not the case. For it is sensed that something extremely valuable is at stake in every interaction, and people are encouraged to rise to the occasion, particularly with strangers. For people who are unfamiliar with the code—generally people who live outside the inner city—the concern with respect in the most ordinary interactions can be frightening and incomprehensible. But for those who are invested in the code, the clear object of their demeanor is to discourage strangers from even thinking about testing their manhood. And the sense of power that attends the ability to deter others can be alluring even to those who know the code without being heavily invested in it—the decent inner-city youths. Thus a boy who has been leading a basically decent life can, in trying circumstances, suddenly resort to deadly force.

Central to the issue of manhood is the widespread belief that one of the most effective ways of gaining respect is to manifest "nerve." Nerve is shown when one takes another person's possessions (the more valuable the better), "messes with" someone's woman, throws the first punch, "gets in someone's face," or pulls a trigger. Its proper display helps on the spot to check others who would violate one's person and also helps to build a reputation that works to prevent future challenges. But since such a show of nerve is a forceful expression of disrespect toward the person on the receiving end, the victim may be greatly offended and seek to retaliate with equal or greater force. A display of nerve, therefore, can easily provoke a life-threatening response, and the background knowledge of that possibility has often been incorporated into the concept of nerve.

True nerve exposes a lack of fear of dying. Many feel that it is acceptable to risk dying over the principle of respect. In fact, among the hard-core street-oriented, the clear risk of violent death may be preferable to being "dissed" by another. The youths who have internalized this attitude and convincingly display it in their public bearing are among the most threatening people of all, for it is commonly assumed that they fear no man. As the people of the community say, "They are the baddest dudes on the street." They often lead an existential life that may acquire meaning only when they are faced with the possibility of imminent death. Not to be afraid to die is by implication to have few compunctions about taking another's life. Not to be afraid to die is the quid pro quo of being able to take somebody else's life—for the right reasons, if the situation demands it. When others believe this is one's position, it gives one a real sense of power on the streets. Such credibility is what many inner-city youths strive to achieve, whether they are decent or street-oriented, both because of its practical defensive value and because of the positive way it makes them feel about themselves. The difference between the decent and the street-oriented youth is often that the decent youth makes a conscious decision to appear tough and manly; in another setting—with teachers, say, or at his part-time job—he can be polite and deferential. The street-oriented youth, on the other hand, has made the concept of manhood a part of his very identity; he has difficulty manipulating it—it often controls him.

Girls and Boys

Increasingly, teenage girls are mimicking the boys and trying to have their own version of "manhood." Their goal is the same—to get respect, to be recognized as capable of setting or maintaining a certain standard. They try to achieve this end in the ways that have been established by the boys, including posturing, abusive language, and the use of violence to resolve disputes, but the issues for the girls are different. Although conflicts over turf and status exist among the girls, the majority of disputes seem rooted in assessments of beauty (which girl in a group is "the cutest"), competition over boyfriends, and attempts to regulate other people's knowledge of and opinions about a girl's behavior or that of someone close to her, especially her mother.

A major cause of conflicts among girls is "he say, she say." This practice begins in the early school years and continues through high school. It occurs when "people," particularly girls, talk about others, thus putting their "business in the streets." Usually one girl will say something negative about another in the group, most often behind the person's back. The remark will then get back to the person talked about. She may retaliate or her friends may feel required to "take up for" her. In essence this is a form of group gossiping in which individuals are negatively assessed and evaluated. As with much gossip, the things said may or may not be true, but the point is that such imputations can cast aspersions on a person's good name. The accused is required to defend herself against the slander, which can result in arguments and fights, often over little of real substance. Here again is the problem of low self-esteem, which encourages youngsters to be highly sensitive to slights and to be vulnerable to feeling easily "dissed." To avenge the dissing, a fight is usually necessary.

Because boys are believed to control violence, girls tend to defer to them in situations of conflict. Often if a girl is attacked or feels slighted, she will get a brother, uncle, or cousin to do her fighting for her. Increasingly, however, girls are doing their own fighting and are even asking their male relatives to teach them how to fight. Some girls form groups that attack other girls or take things from them. A hard-core segment of inner-city girls inclined toward violence seems to be developing. As one thirteen year-old girl in a detention center for youths who have committed violent acts told me, "To get people to leave you alone, you gotta fight. Talking don't always get you out of stuff." One major difference between girls and boys: girls rarely use guns. Their fights are therefore not life-or-death struggles. Girls are not often willing to put their lives on the line for "manhood." The ultimate form of respect on the male-dominated inner-city street is thus reserved for men.

"Going for Bad"

In the most fearsome youths such a cavalier attitude toward death grows out of a very limited view of life. Many are uncertain about how long they are going to live and believe they could die violently at any time. They accept this fate; they live on the edge. Their manner conveys the message that nothing intimidates them; whatever turn the encounter takes, they maintain their attack—rather like a pit bull, whose spirit many such boys admire. The demonstration of such tenacity "shows heart" and earns their respect.

This fearlessness has implications for law enforcement. Many street oriented boys are much more concerned about the threat of "justice" at the hands of a peer than at the hands of the police. Moreover, many feel not only that they have little to lose by going to prison but that they have something to gain. The toughening-up one experiences in prison can actually enhance one's reputation on the streets. Hence the system loses influence over the hard core who are without jobs, with little perceptible stake in the system. If mainstream society has done nothing for them, they counter by making sure it can do nothing to them.

At the same time, however, a competing view maintains that true nerve consists in backing down, walking away from a fight, and going on with one's business. One fights only in self-defense. This view emerges from the decent philosophy that life is precious, and it is an important part of the socialization process common in decent homes. It discourages violence as the primary means of resolving disputes and encourages youngsters to accept nonviolence and talk as confrontational strategies. But "if the deal goes down," self-defense is greatly encouraged. When there is enough positive support for this orientation, either in the home or among one's peers, then nonviolence has a chance to prevail. But it prevails at the cost of relinquishing a claim to being bad and tough, and therefore sets a young person up as at the very least alienated from street-oriented peers and quite possibly a target of derision or even violence.

Although the nonviolent orientation rarely overcomes the impulse to strike back in an encounter, it does introduce a certain confusion and so can prompt a measure of soul-searching, or even profound ambivalence. Did the person back down with his respect intact or did he back down only to be judged a "punk"—a poison lacking manhood? Should he or she have acted? Should he or she have hit the other person in the mouth? These questions beset many young men and women during public confrontations. What is the "right" thing to do? In the quest for honor, respect, and local status—which few young people are uninterested in—common sense most often prevails, which leads many to opt for the tough approach, enacting their own particular versions of the display of nerve. The presentation of oneself as rough and tough is very often quite acceptable until one is tested. And then that presentation may help the person pass the test, because it will cause fewer questions to be asked about what he did and why. It is hard for a person to explain why he lost the fight or why he backed down. Hence many will strive to appear to "go for bad," while hoping they will never be tested. But when they are tested, the outcome of the situation may quickly be out of their hands, as they become wrapped up in the circumstances of the moment.

An Oppositional Culture

The attitudes of the wider society are deeply implicated in the code of the streets. Most people in inner-city communities are not totally invested in the code, but the significant minority of hard-core street youths who are have to maintain the code in order to establish reputations, because they have—or feel they have—few other ways to assert themselves. For these young people the standards of the street code are the only game in town. The extent to which some children—particularly those who through upbringing have become most alienated and those lacking in strong and conventional social support—experience, feel, and internalize racist rejection and contempt from mainstream society may strongly encourage them to express contempt for the more conventional society in turn. In dealing with this contempt and rejection, some youngsters will consciously invest themselves and their considerable mental resources in what amounts to an oppositional culture to preserve themselves and their self-respect. Once they do, any respect they might be able to garner in the wider system pales in comparison with the respect available in the local system; thus they often lose interest in even attempting to negotiate the mainstream system.

At the same time, many less alienated young blacks have assumed a street-oriented demeanor as a way of expressing their blackness while really embracing a much more moderate way of life; they, too, want a non-violent setting in which to live and raise a family. These decent people are trying hard to be part of the mainstream culture, but the racism, real and perceived, that they encounter helps to legitimate the oppositional culture. And so on occasion they adopt street behavior. In fact, depending on the demands of the situation, many people in the community slip back and forth between decent and street behavior.

A vicious cycle has thus been formed. The hopelessness and alienation many young inner-city black men and women feel, largely as a result of endemic joblessness and persistent racism, fuels the violence they engage in. This violence serves to confirm the negative feelings many whites and some middle-class blacks harbor toward the ghetto poor, further legitimating the oppositional culture and the code of the streets in the eyes of many poor young blacks. Unless this cycle is broken, attitudes on both sides will become increasingly entrenched, and the violence, which claims victims black and white, poor and affluent, will only escalate.

DISCUSSION QUESTIONS

1. Why does use of the code by those from "decent" families make perfect sense according to Anderson?

2. How does enactment of the code of the streets relate to Goffman's ideas from *The Presentation of Self*?

3. If you had to write a code of the campus for your school, what would the rules be? What are the norms and expectations that govern interactions in public spaces where you go to school?

4. What does the code of the streets have in common with bullying that happens in middle-class, mostly White communities?

18

Racial Formation Theory and Systemic Racism in Hip-Hop Fans' Perceptions[1]

Ginger Jacobson[2]

In June 2017, Jay-Z became the first rapper to be inducted into the songwriter's hall of fame. His wife, Beyoncé, has sold over 160 million albums, won 22 Grammies, and has the most nominations of any woman in history. Together, they sit atop the incredibly popular hip-hop and rap genre that has long attracted the interest of researchers. Many sociological inquiries into the genre tend to focus on the lyrics as reflections of both the artist's and the culture's ideas about race, gender, and class. Others explore the somewhat counterintuitive popularity of hip-hop and rap among middle and upper class white youth. While a majority of hip-hop artists are black men, a significant proportion of their fans are nonblack and female.

The racially diverse fan base of hip-hop can be interpreted in several different ways. On the one hand, it can be seen as evidence of progress toward racial equality. Millions of white fans purchasing, supporting, and enthusiastically embracing the artistic work of African American musicians isn't just racial tolerance, but respect and admiration. On the other hand, nonblacks who perform and embrace hip-hop and its associated culture are sometimes accused of cultural appropriation—using elements of a different culture without respect or for gain (social or economic) in ways not available to the original group. Hip-hop is therefore a site of multiple and conflicting interpretations of the state of race relations.

In this article, Ginger Jacobson explores how nonblack, female hip-hop fans interpret the racial meaning of hip-hop music and how they view the problems of racism. She bases her analysis on the concept of racial formation—that racial categories are the product of social, economic, and historical circumstances.

"Racial Formation Theory and Systemic Racism in Hip-Hop Fans' Perceptions," by Ginger Jacobson in *Sociological Forum* Vol. 30, No. 3: 832–851. September 2015. Reprinted with permission from John Wiley & Sons.

She combines this with the concept of a white racial frame through which whites learn to see racial characteristics and experiences in ways that are advantageous to whites. She shows how most of her respondents were aware of the unfortunate position of many African-Americans but failed to recognize the role that systemic racism played in their lives. They employ color blindness as a way of attributing differences in black and white experiences to social class, cultural differences, or generally unfortunate circumstances rather than accounting for the pervasive nature of structural racism. As you read, think of your own tastes in music and how they might reflect your own social characteristics and group membership.

Introduction

Hip-hop music serves as an entry point for discussions related to race, class, sexism, and Black culture (Morgan 1999; Rose 2008). Black and Hispanic men continue to drive the creation and production of hip-hop, and scholars are continually drawn to study how race and gender concepts operate in hip-hop music and culture. This article moves away from the traditional researcher and media analyses of lyrical content and visual representation (Azikwe 2011; Collins 2006a, 2006b; Dyson 2007; Fitts 2005; Goodall 1994; Hunter 2011; Littlefield 2008; Persaud 2006; Rose 1994, 2008; Sharpley-Whiting 2007; Xie et al. 2007) to focus on commentary by people who call themselves fans of hip-hop.

It is important to examine how fans interpret hip-hop music because it is consumed across racial, gender, and socioeconomic barriers. Yet, the artists continue to be predominantly Black men. At a time where color-blind ideology is strong under a Black president (Bonilla-Silva 2010; Omi and Winant 2009), this article explores how nonblack, female fans of hip-hop articulate racial meanings and race relations when discussing hip-hop music and videos. This article contributes empirical research to racial formation theory (RFT) and systemic racism (SR) in order to demonstrate how these theories complement each other (Feagin 2006; Feagin and Elias 2013; Omi and Winant 1994, 2013). While this article focuses on race, I used gender as an entryway to discuss race with participants. Secondary to the discussion of race, this article discusses the relationship between projects of inequality and how they exist in the symbolic interaction process between fans and hip-hop media.

White Americans often have little to no interpersonal contact with people of color (Bonilla-Silva 2010; Feagin 2010a), yet all Americans are exposed to the *white racial frame*. This is a racial framing of society that combines racial stereotypes, racial narratives and interpretations, racial images, language accents, racialized emotions, and inclinations to discriminatory action to maintain a positive orientation to whites and whiteness and a negative orientation to oppressed and exploited nonwhites (Feagin 2010b:10). The white racial frame is proliferated and normalized through the mass media and pressures people of all races to internalize this perspective (Feagin 2010b). Mass media viewers may learn about others through cultural tourism (Xie et al. 2007), looking in on a culture with which they have little unmediated personal interaction. Viewers who are uncritical of larger social forces, no matter their racial identity, may adopt a white racial frame and homogenize groups of people based on mediated interaction. It is important to explore how racial minorities in hip-hop culture are understood within the white racial frame and race theories of racial formation, systemic racism, and color-blind ideology in the United States.[3]

Hip-hop draws criticism for its representations of Blacks and Hispanics, especially concerning the implications these representations have for young people who may wish to emulate those in the media (Dixon et al. 2009; Hurt 2006; Littlefield 2008; Sharpley-Whiting 2007; Stephens and Few 2007; Richardson 2007). Research has not connected fans' understanding of hip-hop's racial representations to the theories of racial formation or systemic racism. I will explain the recent debate between racial formation theory and systemic racism in order to locate hip-hop within them. By connecting these theories with hip-hop, we can learn how hip-hop is a site of racial formation, and how a combination of racial formation theory and systemic racism can explain how viewers understand everyday race relations.

In their seminal book *Racial Formation in the United States*, Omi and Winant (1994) first review three paradigms of race theory: ethnicity/assimilation, class/stratification, and nation/colonialism. Emerging from these theoretical ideas, racial formation theory asserts that the state organizes social structures based on racial meanings and representations through a sociohistorical process. This racial formation occurs through a racial project, which links social structure to representation (Omi and Winant 1994). A racial project is "simultaneously an interpretation, representation, or explanation of racial dynamics, and an effort to reorganize and redistribute resources along particular racial lines" (Omi and Winant 1994:56). The racial project is the anchor of racial formation theory, emphasizing race as the primary stratifying concept whereas other theories have minimized its significance by focusing on ethnicity or nation (Wingfield 2013). Racial formation theory highlights the importance of racial group relations to racial formation, cautions against a Black—white, bipolar race model, and incorporates the political potential for people of color to change the definitions of race (Banton 2013; Omi and Winant 2013). Omi and Winant's work focuses on the importance of understanding how race is constructed and reconstructed before understanding racism (Golash-Boza 2013).

Heavily focused on a bipolar model overlooking racial nuance (Banton 2013; Dennis 2013), systemic racism claims that one way whites maintain this hierarchical organization of racial groups is through the white racial frame. This frame creates racial meanings justifying racial inequality and promotes hegemonic whiteness (Feagin 2010b). Hegemonic whiteness maintains racial cohesion and difference through meanings and practices that (1) appeal to interracial distinctions by essentializing whites as different and superior to nonwhites and (2) intraracial distinctions by marginalizing practices of *being white* that do not exemplify dominant ideals (Hughey 2010; Lewis 2004).

Racial formation theory and systemic racism both help explain American understandings of race so that these theories are more valuable in the way that they complement each other and work together (Golash-Boza 2013). Racial formation theory emphasizes how everyday meanings, ideologies, and biased actions connect to the racial project shaped by the state. Systemic racism takes a structural perspective, emphasizing how the unequal power relations drive an uneven distribution of resources and access to opportunities. Both theories agree that structural forces influence individual thought, with racial formation theory conceptualizing this through the racial project and systemic racism conceptualizing this through the use of the white racial frame. Racial formation is the symbolic interaction of how people interpret representations that occur within the hierarchical structure of systemic racism which ensures that dominant white-skinned Americans are advantaged above others, with dominated darker-skinned Americans at the bottom of the hierarchy (Feagin 2006; Feagin and Elias 2013). Systemic racism and racial formation theory both agree that whites are the agents responsible for constructing racial stratification. Racial formation theory attributes this to political conflict of racial identification while systemic racism assumes a more structural approach (Hughey and Byrd 2013). The hierarchical structure of systemic racism is an institutionalized organization similar to racial formation theory's racial project. The racial project functions at a more individual level of symbolic interaction in which intentions to reorganize and redistribute resources according to race are interpreted in everyday representations and explanations of racial differences (Omi and Winant 1994). This research interrogates how racial formation theory and systemic racism operate together in everyday interactions through hip-hop fans' discussions of race, class, and gender.

Color Blindness

Contemporary American media promotes a postracial paradigm where people are encouraged to believe that race is no longer a structurally embedded obstacle to individual success (Feagin 2010a). This meritocratic belief of color blindness persists despite abundant criticism and research against it that recognizes color blindness as a *new racism* that is more subtly institutionalized (Bonilla-Silva 2010; Collins 2006a; Feagin 2010a; Guinier and Torres 2002; Williams 1995). Those who espouse color-blind ideology perpetuate the racial hierarchy that rewards white privilege while they criticize the morality, values, and work ethic of nonwhites through their use of color-blind language (Bonilla-Silva 2010; Kandaswamy 2012). In this way, the color-blind ideology supports systemic racism by denying that barriers exist in a stratified society. This means that when people talk about race, particularly whites, they choose words carefully, sometimes using coded language. This is what Bonilla-Silva (2010:53) would call *race talk*, which includes "linguistic manners or rhetorical strategies" that allow speakers to deliver storylines or frames concerning race without directly discussing race (see also Bush 2004; Myers 2005). Color blindness allows people to claim that they do not see racial differences while using coded language to indicate the opposite. Color-blind ideology is assumed to be the more progressive stance to race issues, although it is actually regressive, undermining nonwhite experiences and perpetuating existing inequalities. For example, Picca and Feagin (2007) note that *race talk* is carefully used in front-stage encounters, juxtaposed against more explicit language in backstage ones. In this way, people exhibit a *two-faced racism* because interactions are modified based on the racial composition of the audience (Picca and Feagin 2007).

Rooting his work in William Ryan's (1976) *blaming the victim* theory, Bonilla-Silva (2010) uses the term *cultural racism* to refer to culturally based arguments to explain racial minorities' circumstances. Cultural racism shifts causation from biological deficiencies to the malignant nature of poverty, racial difficulties, and all environmental sources so that stigma is socially acquired rather than of genetic origin (Ryan 1976). Speakers espousing cultural racism simultaneously take an interest in the victim's well-being, condemn vague social and environmental conditions that created unfortunate circumstances in the past, and neglect the current stratifying social forces (Ryan 1976). The racial formation of Blacks originally constructed them as biologically inferior, but the contemporary racial formation of Blacks has been rearticulated in terms of cultural inferiority, aligning with the class-based *culture of poverty* theory. The *culture of poverty* theory asserts that the poor share subcultural values and behaviors significantly different from the dominant culture (Roach and Gursslin 1967). Thus cultural racists similarly recognize racial inequalities and assume that Blacks developed a distinct, undeserving subculture from poor social and environmental conditions without acknowledging social structures that have generated and continue to maintain such inequalities. The cultural racism of color blindness justifies the unequal distribution of resources so that systemic racism, and by extension, racial realism persists.

Theorizing Race Intersectionally

This article uses an intersectional analysis to examine how participants perceive overlapping notions of race, class, and gender in hip-hop. Hip-hop is commonly criticized for its narrow conceptualization of gender, propagating misogynist themes and objectification of women, although some researchers assert interpretations of female empowerment (Azikwe 2011; Collins 2006a; Gallo 2003; Goodall 1994; Hunter 2011; Lee 2010; Morgan 1999; Pough 2004; Richardson 2007; Rose 1994; Stephens and Few 2007). Black women in hip-hop often lack agency which reinforces historical and contemporary patterns of paternal ownership and hypersexualization exacerbated by racial stereotypes (Collins 2004, 2006a; Feagin 2010a; Fitts 2005, 2008; Gallo 2003; Hunter 2011; Richardson 2007; Rose 1994, 2008). The music industry and mass media corporations that influence the content of *commercial hip-hop* created for mainstream consumption chose to profit from perpetuating racialized and sexualized images of Black gangstas, pimps, and hoes that appeal to the white racial frame (Rose 2008). The presentation of hip-hop images in music videos may imply existing race, class, and gender stereotypes but these can only be perpetuated if viewers identify and interpret such stereotypes from these images. This study investigates how hip-hop fans associate social concepts of race, class, and gender in the representations of women in music and video.

Methods

Between January and May 2011, I interviewed 23 women between 18 and 24 years old, who self-identified as nonblack. I was open to those who did not identify as Black because a considerable amount of studies have already examined Black women's perceptions of hip-hop music and video (Dixon et al. 2009; Hurt 2006; Littlefield 2008; Peterson et al. 2007; Richardson 2007; Sharpley-Whiting 2007; Stephens and Few 2007; Watkins 2005). I did not quota sample (Bernard 2000) based on race or ethnicity, but did categorize participants by race after the interviews. Twelve identified as white, six as Hispanic, four as Asian American, and one as multiracial.[4]

Semistructured interviews offered the participants flexibility in their responses, allowing diverse, personal interpretations to emerge (Bernard 2000). I followed an interview guide for a systematic approach that increases data reliability (Bernard 2000; Patton 2002). In the interviews, I asked probing questions, first encouraging participants to describe their understanding of hip-hop music and culture. Every interview began with the question: "How would you define hip-hop music?" I then asked about their listening preferences. There was variation in the hip-hop subgenres participants listened to. Some of the interviewees primarily listened to *Top-40* or mainstream hip-hop that was popular on the radio. Others listened primarily to *underground* or *old school* (rap from the 1980s or 1990s) or K-pop (Korean pop music). This article focuses on mainstream hip-hop which was a common point of discussion across the interviews. Thus, artists frequently discussed in the interviews included Chris Brown, Drake, Jay-Z, Kanye West, Lil Wayne, Nicki Minaj, Pharrell, and Waka Flocka Flame with discussion focused on the male artists as they comprise the overwhelming majority of hip-hop artists.

After a brief description of why they listen, their likes and dislikes, and if/how they relate to the music, I asked interviewees to select hip-hop music videos that feature women or have women in them. Some had more difficulty with this than others. If a participant was not familiar with this type of video, I suggested starting with an artist the participant had already mentioned, and looking for a video that was likely to feature women. I asked what the interviewee noticed about the women in the video in terms of their role, appearance, behavior, and purpose. If the participant had not mentioned race by the end of the interview, I asked what was noticed about the race of the women in the videos. In addition to answering these questions, participants often launched into a discussion of broader social issues, artists, or music in general in order to explain their response. Therefore, comments were not always in direct response to, but inspired from, a conversation about a particular artist, song, or video.

Racial Formation and Systemic Racism in Everyday Practice

The interviews yielded rich data indicating how participants perceive the racial project in hip-hop, and related gender and class concepts. On the surface, it seems like participants are critical of social and political issues—class inequality by race, social disapproval of interracial dating, and objectification of women—yet they still understood these issues within the themes of systemic racism and racial formation theory. Participants spoke about a perceived connection between hip-hop and the Black community, often discussing hip-hop culture as a representation of Black culture. They discussed their perceptions of Blacks with color blindness, referring to class characteristics, relationships between Blacks and nonblacks, and how hip-hop may influence cultural tourists' impressions of Blacks, particularly concerned with hypersexualization in the music and video. The findings of this research revealed four major themes: cultural racism, cultural tourism, race relations, and hypersexualization, which were consistent across participants' discussion of hip-hop music and videos. I argue that these themes indicate that fans understand hip-hop music and videos as sites of racial formation and, by using color-blind language, they perpetuate systemic racism.

Cultural Racism

One of the most prominent themes was the cultural racism frame of color blindness. This theme includes instances where interviewees made explicit class-related remarks about Black communities such as deplorable conditions of low-income neighborhoods without acknowledging how systemic racism constructed these conditions. In these instances, participants described assumptions about a uniform Black experience, gathered from their interactions with hip-hop, demonstrating that their views of Black culture and hip-hop culture overlap. Some interviewees claimed that Blacks are uneducated, commonly relating this to the discussion of ignorance in hip-hop music. For example, when responding to the opening interview question, one interviewee stated:

> The lyrics are a lot about drugs, and women, and sex and stuff and the people singing it are not as educated as say someone singing country music. There's not as much meaning to the song as something in country or pop. It's just a bunch of random sentences put together but it produces a good beat and that's why I like it.

To interviewees, the superficial content of hip-hop music, especially in comparison to other genres (with more white artists), implied a lack of education which reflected the artist's background. Participants also referenced the use of slang and nonstandard English in hip-hop music as signals of less education among Blacks.

Participants claimed that Blacks are poorly educated because they are afforded less educational opportunities. Interviewees expressed this belief through cultural racism by blaming conditions which then influence a cultural deficiency of the Black community. This belief was illustrated by one participant when she said:

> The most weak individuals are the most poor. It's not because they're weak in the sense that they don't have the ability to grow strong and they're stupid or anything like that; it's just they weren't given the right tools and the right opportunities. And they're stuck. Some people were born in poverty and they stay in poverty.

. . . People from the ghetto, people who don't have class, or people who don't—the thing is like they don't have class, they're not as educated, they're not as wise, they're trashy, which I don't agree with; I just think it's just different.

Here, the participant described the cycle of poverty with color-blind language. She recognized structural forces of systemic racism without identifying how whites have purposefully denied tools and opportunities to nonwhites, and particularly Blacks. Consistent with cultural racism, this participant describes social structures as unfortunate, dismal circumstances without acknowledging how the hierarchy was created, continues to be maintained, or who this system advantages.

Participants assumed that a low-income class status explained why they think there are more Black and Hispanic women than white women in hip-hop videos. Some participants explained that Black and Hispanic women have less opportunity and they live in environments where drugs and domestic violence are commonplace. As a result, Black and Hispanic women would be more willing than whites to do things that are objectifying or degrading in a music video in order to improve their own circumstances. For example, when discussing a scene in a music video ("Bottoms Up" by Trey Songz) that featured bondage and shadow dancing (a woman dancing seductively behind a screen so that only her shadow is visible), one participant interpreted the bondage as a form of violence. She stated:

I'm not saying white girls are above that. I'm really not, because there's white girls that do this. But I feel like it's so one-sided a lot. Like that's their reality, that's their—a lot of Black people, like Hispanics, other ethnic groups, I feel like that's—they can relate to that. They've lived where there's drugs and there's violence and they've unfortunately been subject to that and domestic violence to them happens every day in a lot of homes. But I mean like, if that's their way out and they make money doing that and they don't buy into—like, it's real, you know? I think that's why. I think producers know that. I think they know that people can relate more.

This participant reasoned that Black and Hispanic women can relate to the violence and sexual objectification of music videos so that producers are more likely to recruit these women over whites. Assumptions about class supported this rationalization of Black and Hispanic women's promiscuous behavior in the videos, consistent with other participant claims. Some interviewees assumed that Blacks and Hispanics experience difficult social circumstances and are afforded limited life opportunities so that participation in sexually exploitative videos is an appealing opportunity even though other types of women also experience the conditions participants describe. Participants who shared this opinion did not believe that the women in the videos necessarily internalized promiscuous behavior but that they comply with such a role because of their personal background.

The participants talked about Blacks and Hispanics with coded language, describing circumstances of class without addressing race, so that speakers could indirectly talk about race by hiding behind color-blind language. Some participants implied a lower-class status when they used the terms *ghetto* or *urban*. Some also used the terms *ghetto*, *urban*, or *ethnic* as code words for Black or Hispanic. One participant explained:

> Well, I guess when you think of someone as ghetto you think of loud, obnoxious, cussing, obviously have some ethnicity or try to be ethnic. I'm not saying ethnic is bad or ethnicity is bad, but usually when you have some type of culture, you have an accent or you dress different, a little different.

When using code words, the interviewees made stereotypical statements about Blacks or Hispanics by assuming that social conditions of poverty create individual behavior and character traits—obnoxiousness, loudness, using profanity, violence, or delinquency—that all Blacks and Hispanics possess. Being ethnic or nonwhite was also associated with living in the *ghetto*, described as having little opportunity, little wealth or income, and routine exposure to domestic violence and drugs. Participants spoke with a white racial frame when using the term *ethnic* to refer to people who are different, as they were conceptualized negatively compared to hegemonic whiteness (Hughey 2010). The practice of espousing white normativity indicated the racial hierarchy of Systemic Racism because interviewees marked and *othered* nonwhites as culturally flawed against the hegemonic ideals of whiteness. Despite intraracial distinction among whites, participants shared a collective understanding of hegemonic whiteness by implying that Blacks and Hispanics are essentially different from and inferior to whites (Hughey 2010) who are educated, classy, and do not struggle with finances, violence, or drugs. By calling upon hegemonic whiteness when making comparisons, participants recognized a shared collectivity of whiteness that supports the stratification of Systemic Racism.

Cultural Tourism

Participants made it clear that they were able to enjoy hip-hop music, watch the videos, and identify themselves as fans without feeling a sense of belonging to hip-hop culture themselves. In this way, they were cultural tourists. They primarily viewed hip-hop as a representation of Black culture to which they did not belong because of their nonblack status. Even though some of the participants recognized racial heterogeneity in hip-hop culture, specifically when referencing dance/b-boying or cypher battles, they still spoke about their place from an outsider's position. In these instances, racial heterogeneity did not make them feel included more so because they were women attempting to participate in masculine spaces.

When nonblacks have little or no personal contact with Blacks, various media sources may contribute to individual perceptions about Blacks as a group (Bonilla-Silva 2010; Feagin 2010a). For example, when I asked where an interviewee's belief about certain racial dynamics originated, she said that it was not from personal experience, explaining, "I dunno. Maybe it's just 'cause I only see it in music videos or something." Some participants referenced other media to demonstrate racial tension between Black and white women. One explanation for this racial tension was the belief that Black women do not want white women to date Black men because they *belong* to the Black community. When participants referenced music or movies rather than personal experience or observation, they demonstrated cultural tourism by assuming that media represent reality. Such statements indicated that cultural tourists acquire explanations for racial tensions between Black and nonblack women through media.

The cultural tourist phenomenon was clearer to some than others. One participant frequented the studio where her aspiring rapper friends recorded. She recognized her positionality:

> Do I personally, as a 23-year-old white, upper-middle-class female relate directly to the music? Maybe not me personally. . . . But honestly, I think it wasn't made for me but I can enjoy it as well as anybody else can as long as I have that—and I do think it's very important—as long as I have that level of respect and understanding, that I know my limits and my barriers and that I know when I'm listening to it as an observer as opposed to a participant.

This statement displays the interviewee's understanding of her place as an outsider who appreciates the music but does not personally relate to it. However, this particular interviewee had exceptional insight compared to the norm of the others.

For many participants, hip-hop culture was synonymous with Black culture so that to know hip-hop music, dance, and culture, you also know Black culture. For example, one white interviewee stated that her knowledge of hip-hop helped foster a relationship between herself and her Black roommates:

I think a lot of times they kind of respect you because you know a little bit about their culture. I lived with Black girls for like three years and even though I was an upper-class white girl, it was, "Oh, she can do the one-two step." They thought it was like the best thing in the world. . . . So I think certain girls will let it get to them, but a lot of them will reach out to you more because they're like, "She's giving our culture and our type of dance a chance, so why shouldn't we give her a chance?"

This participant's experience of relating to Black women through hip-hop confirmed her assumption that hip-hop and blackness are linked. This perspective reasons that nonblacks can learn about Blacks from hip-hop. In another instance, a student of social work said that she was fortunate enough to not have been raised in poverty, but that she uses hip-hop to familiarize herself with real-life situations of poverty. It may be true that hip-hop followers can learn about particular artists' perspectives, but many participants did not acknowledge the heterogeneity of Blacks and other racial groups. Instead, hip-hop images and representations were equated to Black experience and reality, serving as a foundation for ideas about race.

Race Relations

Participants discussed the relationship between different racial groups—Black, white, Asian, and Hispanic—when interviewees compared racial groups or discussed them in relation to each other. When speaking directly about relationships between Blacks and nonblacks, some interviewees interpreted tension between groups but had difficulty elaborating further. For example, a participant commented that artist Kanye West has white girls in his videos and in his song "Gold Digger" he says "then he leaves you for a white girl," which she said made her "feel like there is a lot of tension in that aspect." Consistent with others, this participant could not articulate a theory for the tension she sensed.

When discussing racial dynamics, participants offered descriptions of *ghetto* women in relation to people of other races. Descriptions were based on their personal interactions, their observations of others, or their perceptions from media such as movies and hip-hop music. When discussing Nicki Minaj, a Black female rapper, one Asian American interviewee explained that she was scared of *ghetto* Black girls because they are intentionally intimidating to discourage others from interacting with them:

Like honestly, I'm like very scared of Black girls. Or, some of them. I mean, I used to have, like in middle school like my best friend was like Black. She was really nice, though. But I feel like a lot of the more, like ghetto Black girls set this, they create this, like purposely, they create this like facade you know, where it's like not approachable. You know, they don't want people coming up to them and like talking to them and stuff like that and it works 'cause I'm scared of them. . . . I know they don't want like, especially Asians like coming up to them. I dunno if that's the same or something they feel for like their own race but . . . I dunno sometimes I'll see like them getting along. But they have to be like ghetto Asians. You know, they can't be like, like normal Asian like or Asian-Asian like [fresh-off-the-boat] Asian.

Here, the participant illustrates her perception of Black–Asian interactions, where *ghetto* women are unfriendly to women of other races, especially Asians. This was reflective of other participants' elaborations: *ghetto* women were conceptualized within the white racial frame as Black, unapproachable, unfriendly, confrontational, and abnormal. Black women, particularly low-income Black women, were perceived to be racially exclusive and unwilling to socialize with women who do not share their racial membership. To participants, Black women's identity was linked to their perceptions of representations in the media and framed negatively to support systemic racism.

Some used interracial relationships to explain their understanding of race relations. Participants who discussed interracial relationships stated that they support them, acknowledging that it is more common now but still widely unaccepted. In conflating hip-hop with *ghetto* blackness, one interviewee stated, "I could never see like a [fresh-off-the-boat] Asian with like a ghetto Black guy. Yeah, they have to be like at least, you know, wear like fitted caps and, you know, wear like high-top sneakers, too, for them to get along with each other." For an Asian woman to date a *ghetto* Black man, they would have to at least conform to hip-hop culture, implied here in the style of dress. Again, the assumption is that hip-hop is associated with a *ghetto* Black culture and is therefore a medium to which Blacks can relate, as Blacks are conceptualized as a monolith.

From a white racial frame, and with a culturally racist perspective, Blacks are portrayed negatively and understood as culturally deficient so that participants speaking from this viewpoint suggested that nonblack women dating Black men would have to be deficient in some manner to form a compatible couple. One interviewee said that the pairing of white women and Black men is uncommon, but in interviews participants mentioned that the general nature of hip-hop music is sexual, or more specifically that rappers emphasize having sex with women. Interviewees also indicated hypersexualization when they explained how women in videos insinuated sex through a combination of their clothing, dancing, or behavior, or the way the camera captured women's body parts. Even when speaking about videos generally, interviewees articulated that videos are sexual, indicating that to them, hip-hop has a sexual connotation. For example, one woman said about mainstream hip-hop, "I see that pretty often where the guy is just like rapping and the only interaction between the man and any female is just like sex." When comparing current hip-hop to old school, an interviewee said, "I feel like in most of hip-hop it's all about sex. You can rarely find music that actually talks about life and everything." Another participant noted the visual framing of women in videos: "I feel like in a lot of the videos they won't even show the woman's face; they'll just show their backside." Interviewees noted that hip-hop music stresses sex and women serve a sexual purpose for the male gaze in videos.

Because hip-hop and Black culture are already conceptually linked for participants, hip-hop's focus on sex and women as sexual objects reflected sexuality in Black culture. This is where the gender and racial projects intersect: Black women and men are hypersexual where women are sexual objects for men's desires. This intersection was clear when some of the participants stated that they think hip-hop communicates negative stereotypes about Blacks, citing representations of sexuality as problematic. Participants thought that white hip-hop viewers who have little contact with Blacks (cultural tourists) would develop a negative perception of rappers. For example, one participant argued that white people who viewed hip-hop videos would think Black rappers are "really scary and tough and just bad I guess 'cause they just like rape and have sex with girls." Participants claimed that even though there are probably a lot of white people who admire rappers, the overall message may reinforce stereotypes of violent hypersexual Black men. This stereotype contributes to the racial project because it perpetuates themes of white, heterosexual dominance that fans perceive when gazing upon hip-hop music and culture.

Women were described as sexual objects to complement the male rappers' masculinity. When watching the video for "Buzzin'" by Mann, one interviewee explained, "I think it's supposed to signify his status as a male like I can attract these kinds of beautiful women. So guys should respect him for that and then girls should be attracted to him because of that." Participants noted that the sexual availability of numerous women legitimated the rapper's manhood and desirability. For example, one participant stated: "Sex is a common theme in hip-hop. A lot of videos show a lot of women's skin to get the message across that it's sexual or to make people be like, 'Oh, OK, this is what they're doing, this is the life of a hip-hop artist, have all these women half naked around.'" When watching the video "Lollipop" by Lil Wayne, one commented, "They're all biting their lips like they're jaguars, like they're ready to pounce on him—LOOK SHE'S EVEN WEARING LEOPARD PRINT! They're like animals! Animals that want him. Sex-driven animals . . . It's just a certain lifestyle that's being portrayed." A high female-to-male ratio is perceived to be part of a rapper's lifestyle, as women fulfill a sexual purpose for the men. While the visual focus of videos fixated on the ways women communicated their sexual willingness, this also implied a high sexual desire on behalf of the men whom they surround.

Discussion

This article contributes empirical research to both racial formation theory and systemic racism and also highlights the ways in which these theories complement each other. The symbolic interaction between hip-hop music and video and participants demonstrated how hip-hop is a site of racial formation. Participants demonstrated that they interpreted a representation of a monolithic Black culture, identity, and an explanation for racial dynamics in hip-hop music and video. In this manner, hip-hop contributes to the understanding and construction of race, thereby contributing to racial formation. Participants indirectly, unknowingly referred to systemic racism when they alluded to the hierarchical organization of individuals according to racial group membership, often when comparing groups or discussing how they relate to one another. By using the white racial frame and color blindness, speakers discussed consequences of systemic racism without recognizing the intentional structural organization of social groups. Data revealed four significant themes of participant interpretations: cultural racism, cultural tourism, race relations, and hypersexualization.

In accordance with the cultural racism theme, interviewees described a deficient Black culture, which to them was synonymous with hip-hop. Participants depicted Blacks as uneducated, obnoxious, hypersexual, having little opportunity, and particularly Black women as unfriendly to non-blacks. In purporting cultural racism, interviewees recognized unfortunate conditions but not the social structures that created them. In this way, the data illustrated how systemic racism operates: people are aware of disadvantages that challenge Black communities, but they appear unaware of the underlying system that whites constructed to maintain this order. In recognizing race as an explanation for the unequal distribution of resources (Blacks are afforded less opportunity), participants also indirectly referred to the racial project, linking racial formation theory and systemic racism together.

Racial formation theory stresses that racial group relations are important to understandings of race. The participants identified as fans so that they were insiders of the music, but still felt like outsiders because they were not Black, suggesting a strong association of hip-hop and Blacks. As cultural tourists themselves, participants felt like they learned about Black culture from hip-hop so that it served as a site of racial formation, a way to understand Black folks. Drawing upon hegemonic whiteness, participants felt like other nonblack (particularly white) cultural tourists would interpret negative perceptions about Blacks, perpetuating the white racial frame. In these statements, interviewees suggested that they have had few personal experiences with Blacks and assumed that other nonblacks (particularly whites) might also, which speaks to successful racial stratification and segregation of systemic racism. Racial segregation makes it easier to preserve a white racial frame and assert a hegemonic whiteness. When people of all racial identifications assume a white racial frame and share an understanding of hegemonic whiteness, systemic racism succeeds in pervading mind-sets with various racial perspectives. Both white and non-white participants asserted the white racial frame and drew from a hegemonic whiteness when discussing race relations, indicating that racial formation complements systemic racism.

Participants sensed racial tension between Blacks and others in instances of interracial relationships, and expressed naturalization in observations of self-segregation practices. Interviewees described a pejorative Black identity constructed through cultural racism that was unsuitable for *typical* white mates, reifying hegemonic whiteness. These racial constructions suggest an idealization and normalization of intraracial relationships that maintain segregation of systemic racism. Participants used color-blind language of cultural racism and naturalization to explain micro level social processes. This approach supported the broader social hierarchy and perpetuated systemic racism in their explanations of classed and gendered racial identities.

This research also illustrates how race, class, and gender projects overlap, importantly highlighting how social categories do not operate in isolation. Participants used code words referring to class to signify race. The description of *ghetto* was a color-blind strategy of race talk that referred not only to poor neighborhood conditions but also to undesirable behavior and personal characteristics. Such a pejorative description enacted the white racial frame and clearly placed Blacks and the Black community lower on the racial hierarchy than whites, as purported in systemic racism theory. However, participants suggested that the racial formation of a subordinate Black identity was constructed in conjunction with perceptions of class and gender. Interviewees discussed class concerns to explain why Black women participating in hip-hop videos behave sexually and submissively for male artists. The prominence of these themes in mainstream hip-hop emphasizes that influential corporate powers promote a particular sexualized, racialized, and classed representation of Blacks that, in viewers' minds, contributes to a wider racial formation of Blacks. These data indicate that nonblack hip-hop fans assume the white racial frame in part because the mainstream images and messages support social stratification of systemic racism.

A combination of the cultural racism, cultural tourism, and hyper-sexualization themes revealed perceptions that Black women are promiscuous and Black men are aggressive and hypersexual. Participants also noted Black male artists' use of women to beget status so that the objectification of women for the male gaze signified heterosexual dominance that reinforced their masculinity. Although male rappers display many women to reinforce their male dominance, they inadvertently support white supremacist ideals because the stereotype of the hypersexual Black man (rapper) and woman (as a sexualized person in the video) is reinforced in the viewer's mind. In asserting male dominance, rappers are then unintentionally perpetuating the racial hierarchy.

This research indicates how race, class, and gender projects overlap to create racially constructed identities from a white racial frame. These data illustrate how racial formation occurs as an interaction between individuals and media within the larger social structure of systemic racism. This research suggests that race is a prominent organizing concept that affects how people understand each other. Although this is a small sample of participants, these preliminary data suggest ways that hip-hop music and video can inform perceptions of race among fans. Further research is necessary to make generalizations about particular racial or ethnic groups' perceptions of hip-hop music and video and to substantiate the links discussed in this article.

DISCUSSION QUESTIONS

1. What is racial formation? What is systemic racism? Why are they important to understand in analyzing the reactions and interpretations of white hip-hop fans?

2. What is the *white racial frame* and how does it relate to the concept of color blindness?

3. What explanations did the respondents give for the sexism that was conveyed in many of the lyrics and videos?

4. What role do race and ethnicity play in our tastes, hobbies, and preferences? Does everyone have equal access and *rights* to appreciate, enjoy, or create musical styles? Why or why not?

REFERENCES

Acker, Joan. 2006. *Class Questions: Feminist Answers*. Lanham, MD: Rowman & Littlefield.

Azikwe, Mario D. 2011. "More Than Baby Mamas: Black Mothers and Hip-Hop Feminism." In Gail Dines and Jean M. Humez (eds.), *Gender, Race, and Class in Media: A Critical Reader*, third edition: pp. 137–144. Washington, DC: Sage.

Babbie, Earl. 2007. *The Practice of Social Research*, eleventh edition. Belmont, CA: Thomson Wadsworth.

Banton, Michael. 2013. "In Defence of Mainstream Sociology." *Ethnic and Racial Studies* 36: 6: 1000–1004.

Bernard, Henry R. 2000. *Social Research Methods: Qualitative and Quantitative Approaches*. Thousand Oaks, CA: Sage.

Bonilla-Silva, Eduardo. 2010. *Racism Without Racists: Color-Blind Racism and Racial Inequality in Contemporary America*, third edition. Lanham, MD: Rowman & Littlefield.

Brock, André. 2009. "Life on the Wire: Deconstructing Race on the Internet." *Information, Communication & Society* 12: 3: 344–363.

Brock, André. 2011. "'When Keeping It Real Goes Wrong': Resident Evil 5, Racial Representation, and Gamers." *Games and Culture* 6: 5: 429–452.

Buffington, Daniel, and Todd Fraley. 2011. "Racetalk and Sport: The Color Consciousness of Contemporary Discourse on Basketball." *Sociological Inquiry* 81: 3: 333–352.

Bush, Melanie E. L. 2004. *Breaking the Code of Good Intentions: Everyday Forms of Whiteness*. Lanham, MD: Rowman & Littlefield.

Butler, Judith. 1993. *Bodies that Matter: On the Discursive Limits of " Sex."* New York: Routledge.

Charmaz, Kathy, 2006. *Constructing Grounding Theory: A Practical Guide Through Qualitative Analysis*. Los Angeles, CA: Sage.

Clay, Adreana. 2011. "I Used to Be Scared of the Dick: Queer Women of Color and Hip-Hop Masculinity." In Gwendolyn D. Pough, Elaine Richardson, Aisha Durham and Rachel Raimist (eds.), *Home Girls Make Some Noise!: Hip-Hop Feminism Anthology*; pp. 149–165. Monroe, CA: Parker Publishing.

Collins, Patricia H. 2004. *Black Sexual Politics: African Americans, Gender, and the New Racism*. New York: Routledge.

Collins, Patricia H. 2006a. *From Black Power to Hip Hop: Racism, Nationalism, and Feminism*. Philadelphia, PA: Temple University Press.

Collins, Patricia H. 2006b. "New Commodities, New Consumers: Selling Blackness in a Global Marketplace." *Ethnicities* 6: 3: 297–317.

Dennis, Rutledge M. 2013. "Convergences and Divergences in Race Theorizing: A Critical Assessment of Race Formation Theory and Systemic Racism Theory." *Ethnic and Racial Studies* 36: 6: 982–988.

Dixon, Travis, Yuanyuan Zhang, and Kate Conrad. 2009. "Self-Esteem, Misogyny and Afrocentricity: An Examination of the Relationship Between Rap Music Consumption and African American Perceptions." *Group Processes Intergroup Relations* 12: 3: 345–360.

Dyer, Richard. 1997. *White*. London, UK: Routledge.

Dyson, Michael E. 2007. *Know What I Mean? Reflections on Hip Hop.* New York: Basic Civitas Books.

Feagin, Joe R. 2006. *Systemic Racism: A Theory of Oppression.* New York: Routledge.

Feagin, Joe R. 2010a. *Racist America: Roots, Current Realities and Future Reparations,* second edition. New York: Routledge.

Feagin, Joe R. 2010b. *The White Racial Frame: Centuries of Racial Framing and Counter-Framing.* New York: Routledge.

Feagin, Joe R., and Sean Elias. 2013. "Rethinking Racial Formation Theory: A Systemic Racism Critique." *Ethnic and Racial Studies* 36: 6: 931–960.

Fitts, Mako. 2005. "The Political Economy of Hip Hop and the Cultural Production of Racialized and Gendered Images." Unpublished Ph.D. Dissertation, Arizona State University, Tempe, AZ.

Fitts, Mako. 2008. "'Drop It Like It's Hot': Culture Industry Laborers and Their Perspectives on ap Music Video Production." *Meridians: Feminism, Race, Transnationalism* 8: 211–35.

Froyum, Carissa. 2013. "'For the Betterment of Kids Who Look Like Me': Professional Emotional Labour as a Racial Project." *Ethnic and Racial Studies* 36: 6: 1070–1089.

Gallo, Suzanne. 2003. "Music Preference with an Emphasis on Gangsta Rap: Female Adolescent Identity, Beliefs, and Behavior." Unpublished Ph.D. Dissertation, California Institute of Integral Studies, San Francisco, CA.

George, Nelson. 1998. *Hip Hop America.* New York: Penguin Group.

Golash-Boza, Tanya. 2013. "Does Racial Formation Theory Lack the Conceptual Tools to Understand Racism?" *Ethnic and Racial Studies* 36: 6: 994–999.

Goodall, Nataki H. 1994. "Depend on Myself: T.L.C. and the Evolution of Black Female Rap." *The Journal of Negro History* 79: 1: 85–93.

Gordon, Leonard. 1989. "Racial Theorizing: Is Sociology Ready to Replace Polemic Causation Theory With a New Polemic Model?" *Sociological Perspectives* 32: 1: 129–136.

Guinier, Lani, and Gerald Torres. 2002. *The Miner's Canary: Enlisting Race, Resisting Power, Transforming Democracy.* Cambridge, MA: Harvard University Press.

Hughey, Matthew W. 2010. "The (Dis) Similarities of White Racial Identities: The Conceptual Framework of 'Hegemonic Whiteness.'" *Ethnic and Racial Studies* 33: 8: 1289–1309.

Hughey, Matthew W., and W. Carson Byrd. 2013. "The Souls of White Folk Beyond Formation and Structure: Bound to Identity." *Ethnic and Racial Studies* 36: 6: 974–981.

Hunter, Margaret. 2011. "Shake It, Baby, Shake It: Consumption and the New Gender Relation in Hip-Hop." *Sociological Perspectives* 54: 1: 15–36.

Hurt, Byron (dir.), and S. Nelson (prod.). 2006. *Hip-Hop: Beyond Beats and Rhymes* [Documentary]. Northampton, MA: Media Education Foundation.

Jung, Moon-Kie. 1999. "No Whites, No Asians: Race, Marxism, and Hawai'i's Preemergent Working Class." *Social Science History* 23: 3: 357–393.

Kandaswamy, Priya. 2012. "Gendering Racial Formation." In Daniel M. HoSang, Oneka La Bennett and Laura Pulido (eds.), *Racial Formation in the Twenty-First Century:* pp. 23–43. Berkeley: University of California Press.

Lee, Shayne. 2010. *Erotic Revolutionaries: Black Women, Sexuality, and Popular Culture.* Lanham, MD: Hamilton Books.

Lewis, Amanda E. 2004. "What Group? Studying Whites and Whiteness in the Era of Colorblindness." *Sociological Theory* 22: 4: 623–646.

Lewis, Lisa A. (ed.). 2001. *The Adoring Audience: Fan Culture and Popular Media.* New York: Routledge.

Littlefield, Marci B. 2008. "Media as a System of Racialization: Exploring Images of African American Women and the New Racism." *American Behavioral Scientist* 51:5: 675–685.

Lorber, Judith. 2010. *Gender Inequality: Feminist Theory and Politics.* Oxford, UK: Oxford University Press.

Love, Bettina. 2008. "Don't Judge a Book by Its Cover: An Ethnography About Achievement, Rap Music, Sexuality and Race." Unpublished Ph.D. dissertation, Department of Educational Policy Studies, Georgia State University, Atlanta, GA.

Massey, Douglas S. 2009. "Racial Formation in Theory and Practice: The Case of Mexicans in the United States." *Race and Social Problems* 1:1: 12–26.

Morgan, Joan. 1999. *When Chickenheads Come Home to Roost: My Life as a Hip Hop Feminist.* New York: Simon & Schuster.

Myer, Letrez, and Christine Kleck. 2007. "From Independent to Corporate: A Political Economic Analysis of Rap Billboard Toppers." *Popular Musk and Society* 30: 2: 137–148.

Myers, Kristin A. 2005. *Racetalk: Racism Hiding in Plain Sight.* Lanham, MD: Rowman & Littlefield.

Omi, Michael, and Howard Winant. 1994. *Racial Formation in the United States: From the 1960s to the 1990s.* New York: Routledge.

Omi, Michael, and Howard Winant. 2009. "Thinking Through Race and Racism." *Contemporary Sociology* 38: 2: 121–125.

Omi, Michael, and Howard Winant. 2013. "Resistance Is Futile? A Response to Feagin and Elias." *Ethnic and Racial Studies* 36: 6: 961–973.

Park, Lisa S., and David N. Pellow. 2004. "Racial Formation, Environmental Racism, and the Emergence of Silicon Valley." *Ethnicities* 4: 3: 403–424.

Patton, Michael Q. 2002. *Qualitative Research and Evaluation Methods,* third edition. London, UK: Sage.

Persaud, Elarick R. J. 2006. "Ghetto Echoes: Hip Hop's Subversive Aesthetics." Unpublished Ph.D. Dissertation, York University, Toronto, Canada.

Peterson, Shani H., Gina M. Wingood, Ralph J. DiClemente, K. Kathy Harrington, and Susan Davies. 2007. "Images of Sexual Stereotypes in Rap Videos and the Health of African American Female Adolescents." *Journal of Women's Health* 16: 8: 1157–1164.

Picca, Leslie. H., and Joe R. Feagin. 2007. *Two-Faced Racism: Whites in the Backstage and Frontstage.* New York: Routledge.

Pough, Gwendolyn D. 2004. *Check It While I Wreck It.* Boston, MA: Northeastern University Press.

Richardson, Elaine. 2007. "'She Was Workin' Like Foreal': Critical Literacy and Discourse Practices of African American Females in the Age of Hip Hop." *Discourse Society* 18: 6: 789–810.

Roach, Jack L., and Orville R. Gursslin. 1967. "An Evaluation of the Concept 'Culture of Poverty'." *Social Forces* 45: 3: 383–392.

Rose, Tricia. 1994. *Black Noise: Rap Music and Black Culture in Contemporary America.* Middletown, CT: Wesleyan University Press.

Rose, Tricia. 2008. *The Hip Hop Wars: What We Talk About When We Talk About Hip-Hop—And Why It Matters.* New York: Basic Books.

Ryan, William. 1976. *Blaming the Victim.* New York: Vintage Books.

Saldaña, Johnny. 2013. *The Coding Manual for Qualitative Researchers, second edition.* Los Angeles: Sage.

Sallaz, Jeffrey J. 2010. "Talking Race, Marketing Culture: The Racial Habitus in and out of Apartheid." *Social Problems* 57: 2: 294–314.

Sharpley-Whiting, T. D. 2007. *Pimps Up, Ho's Down: Hip Hop's Hold on Young Black Women.* New York: New York University Press.

Stephens, Dionne P., and April L. Few. 2007. "The Effects of Images of African American Women in Hip Hop on Early Adolescents' Attitudes Toward Physical Attractiveness and Interpersonal Relationships." *Sex Roles* 56: 3–4: 251–264.

Strauss, Anselm L. 1987. *Qualitative Analysis for Social Scientists.* Cambridge, UK: Cambridge University Press.

Watkins, S. Craig. 2005. *Hip Hop Matters.* Boston, MA: Beacon Press.

Williams, Patricia. 1995. *The Rooster's Egg.* Cambridge, MA: Harvard University Press.

Wingfield, Adia H. 2010. "Are Some Emotions Marked 'Whites Only'?: Racialized Feeling Rules in Professional Workplaces." *Social Problems* 57: 2: 251–268.

Wingfield, Adia H. 2013. "Comment on Feagin and Elias." *Ethnic and Racial Studies* 36: 6: 989–993.

Xie, Philip F., Halifu Osumare, and Awad Ibrahim. 2007. "Gazing the Hood: Hip-Hop as Tourism Attraction." *Tourism Management* 28: 2: 452–460.

NOTES

1. I would like to thank my participants for sharing their perspectives as well as Faye Harrison and Milagros Peña for reviewing earlier versions of this paper, I am grateful for all the comments Alison E. Adams has offered on previous drafts of this article. I would also like to thank the Sociological Forum reviewers for their feedback that has led to this publication.

2. Department of Sociology and Anthropology, Nazareth College, 4245 East Avenue, Rochester NY 14618; e-mail: gjacobsonl066@gmail.com.

3. This article's discussion of race follows the participants' perspective of the Black-white, bipolar model of race emphasized by systemic racism by focusing on these two groups, with peripheral discussion of Hispanics and Asians as discussed in the data.

4. The racial categories used throughout (Black, White, Hispanic, Asian) are not meant to imply a monolithic characterization of groups of people. Recognizing the heterogeneity of these groups, these terms are consistent with the language of the participants, who collectively form a group of nonblack women. Although some Hispanic peoples identify as Black, this was not the case for these participants and their reference to Hispanics implied nonblack, nonwhite Hispanics.

19

Being Middle Eastern in the Context of the War on Terror

Amir Marvasti

In his stand-up comedy routine[1], comedian Dean Obeidallah quips that he went to bed on September 10th a white guy, and woke up September 11th an Arab. He then goes on to describe some of the ways that his day-to-day life has changed since the 9/11 attacks, and the constant cloud of suspicion that follows him even in his most mundane interactions in public.

This article tackles the same subject matter, but draws on Erving Goffman's concept of "spoiled identities" to highlight the interactional tactics used by many of Middle Eastern descent as they navigate face-to-face interactions where they are asked to "account" for themselves. To be asked for an "account" is to have someone demand justification for why you should be treated as "normal." Sometimes accounts are prompted by location. A middle school student in the teacher's lounge might be asked, "What are you doing here?" Other times, accounts are requested because of behavior—"Why don't you eat meat" is a request for an account often demanded of vegetarians and vegans. For those of Middle Eastern descent, it is their very appearance or presence that can elicit an account in a myriad of situations. This is both frustrating and dangerous. Violence against Middle Easterners (who are often assumed to be Muslim) has spiked dramatically in the past two years with the heated anti-Muslim rhetoric of many right-wing politicians and media personalities. Donald Trump's anti-immigrant, anti-Muslim speeches and policy proposals further endanger the safety of middle-easterners.[2]

In this article, Amir Marvasti draws on interviews with others and his own experiences to map out different interactional strategies used by those of Middle Eastern heritage to negotiate face-to-face interaction where they are treated with suspicion, hostility, or curiosity. In some cases, humor is used to deflect negative comments or allay suspicions. In other interactions, education and

"Being Middle Eastern American: Identity Negotiation in the Context of the War on Terror," by Amir Marvasti in *Symbolic Interaction* Vol. 28, Issue. 4 (Fall 2005), pp. 525–547. Reprinted with permission from John Wiley & Sons.

explanations are used. In some situations, individuals cower—showing great deference as a way to avoid further suspicion and attention, and in others, they are defiant, challenging the grounds and assumptions that prompted the account in the first place.

What makes this research a valuable contribution to our sociological understanding of the world is not just highlighting the troublesome interactions that Middle Eastern citizens face and how they deal with it. Rather, these strategies are applicable to a wide range of stigmatized identities. Those in the LGBTQ community, those who are differently abled in visible ways, or anyone who might be perceived with suspicion, as someone not "normal" is likely to employ some of these tactics. As you read, think about your own day-to-day life and whether you have used any of these strategies.

About a year after September 11, 2001, I was in a shopping mall in a northeastern city. For the last 30 minutes, I had been acutely aware of a security guard who had been following me around the mall. I was not completely surprised to see him follow me into the restroom. I was, however, taken aback when he moved closer to me near the urinal and looked over my shoulder as I was urinating. I was not sure what to say or do. I thought, "Is he worried that I am going to contaminate the city's water supply with my toxic urine?" I felt violated but did not want to cause a scene. So I started singing, "Chances are, 'cause I wear a silly grin the moment you come into view . . ." I had learned the lyrics from a Taco Bell toy that played the song when you squeezed it. I did not really know the rest of the song, but it did not matter, crowing in English seemed to have done the job. The security guard backed off and left me alone for the rest of my time at the mall.

As this story from my own life shows, September 11th and the ensuing period that has been named the *War on Terror* have significantly changed the daily lives of Middle Eastern Americans. For members of this ethnic group, it was indeed *the day that changed everything*. In the days following September 11th, anything seemed possible, even mass detentions on a scale similar to what Japanese Americans were subjected to after Pearl Harbor. Such fears were so real that on the night of September 11th, I actually packed some of my belongings and essential documents in a small suitcase in preparation for mass detentions. I was, after all, born in Iran and physically resembled the terrorists, whose images were relentlessly displayed in all the mass media.

The extreme measures I feared did not materialize in the aftermath of the terrorist attacks; however, our lives have, in many ways, changed for the worse. In particular, Middle Eastern Americans experience more stereotyping more frequently than before. We are asked to explain our intentions, politics, and personal beliefs, even in the course of the mundane routines of everyday life, such as shopping at a mall. Although prejudice and discrimination against this ethnic group existed for decades before September 11th, the recent intensity and regularity of these demands are unprecedented. As one of my respondents put it, it happened before, "but not with this magnitude, and not with the accusatory tone. . . . Before it was just out of curiosity, and it was incidental, but this is an even more demanding tone of 'Who are you? And why did your people do this?'"

In this article, I investigate how Middle Eastern Americans respond to these disruptions of their daily routines. My original intention was to use interview data as well as my personal experiences as an Iranian immigrant to show how Middle Eastern Americans manage the stigma of their *spoiled identities* (Goffman 1963), especially in the aftermath of September 11th. While working on the first draft, I told my Iranian friend Ahmad,[3] with whom I was having lunch, that I was working on a paper titled "Stigma Management Strategies of Middle Eastern Americans." He nodded with his head down as he swallowed his food. After a short pause, he asked: "Why 'stigma?' What is the stigma?"

I was a little surprised that he failed to see the obvious. I explained, "After September 11th, people from the Middle East, especially Muslims, are treated with suspicion and subjected to ethnic profiling. That's why we are stigmatized."

He replied in a matter-of-fact tone. "Not always. Sitting here with you, talking in this school cafeteria, I don't feel stigmatized."

I began to wonder if this was a case of what Marx would call *false consciousness*. I tried harder to convince him of the gravity of the situation of Middle Eastern Americans in a post-9/11 world. Ahmad did not disagree with the entire argument; he just refused to see himself as someone with a chronic stigma, or a permanent and enduring negative identity.

My friend convinced me that in some situations the stigma of being Middle Eastern goes unnoticed or is altogether nonexistent for all practical purposes. How do we then empirically study stigma or even know if it actually exists? One way to answer this question is to explore differences or similarities between audience and self-perceptions. In other words, we can compare Ahmad's self-image with his audience's perceptions of him and then go on to make certain conclusions about the relation between the two perspectives. For example, we may find that many people do in fact have negative perceptions of Ahmad, but he is fortunate to enjoy a high self-esteem that shields him from any emotional damage. This line of thinking could tell us a good deal about the mental state of both sides, but it offers less insight into everyday practice, or what people actually do when they interact with one another.

Self or audience perception are not fixed; they change in the course of practice. Similarly, the meaning of *stigma* varies situationally. A friend in graduate school jokingly referred to me as "the swarthy Iranian" (I did not find that funny). My same brown complexion apparently evoked a different audience response when a waitress at a Denny's told me, "You have such a nice tan!" (To which I smugly replied, "I was born with it.")

How do I really feel about having a brown complexion? Well, it depends on how it is used. I cannot really discuss it without referring to specific interactions and the social context that made my skin tone relevant. In the same vein, the empirical reality of being Middle Eastern is not just a mental property of the self or audience, but is enacted under the concrete conditions of everyday life. Audience or self-perceptions about stigma become experientially meaningful and accessible when articulated in a specific setting and for a particular purpose.

Thus, to appreciate the complexity of Ahmad's experiences as a Middle Eastern American, it seemed that I needed to attend to situational variations surrounding how individuals define, enact, and cope with stigma in everyday encounters. This article first offers brief discussions of how I conceptualized stigma and everyday practice for the purpose of this study, and then presents my analysis of how Middle Eastern Americans manage their identities in the aftermath of September 11th.

Stigma and the Management of Spoiled Identity

Numerous studies have highlighted how stigmatized individuals employ various resistance and management strategies in response to negative labels (Cahill and Eggleston 1994; Davis 1961; Evans, Forsyth, and Foreman 2003; Feagin and McKinney 2003; Fothergill 2003; Herman 1993; Karp 1992; Riessman 2000; Roschelle and Kaufman 2004; Snow and Anderson 1987). This body of research treats normal deviant interactions as an ongoing drama in which the stigmatized try to create positive identities. As they reveal, individuals use various techniques, such as humor and selective disclosure, to either avoid being stigmatized or soften the impact of the stigma on their *spoiled identity*.

Much of the scholarship cited above is inspired by Goffman's seminal work *Stigma* (1963), in which he states:

> [When a stranger] is present before us, evidence can arise of his possessing an attribute that makes him different from others. . . .
> He is thus reduced in our minds from a whole and usual person to a tainted, discounted one. Such an attribute is a stigma. (Pp. 2–3)

For Goffman, stigma is a variable social construct and not a fixed characteristic of the person. Stigma is bound by social roles and expectations and derives its meaning from particular social contexts. An ascribed status or attribute, such as one's race or ethnicity, is not inherently stigmatizing, but becomes so under a specific set of social rules and social conditions. For example, a number of studies have suggested that recent demographic and sociopolitical trends in North America may gradually lower the rank of whiteness from a preferred racial status to a social stigma (Killian 1985; Kusow 2004; Storrs 1999).

Furthermore, as Link and Phelan's work (2001) notes, stigma is a multifaceted concept. Accordingly, studies of stigma can be classified on the basis of which aspect of the stigmatization process they emphasize. In this article, I am most interested in the *obtrusiveness* of stigma (Goffman 1963:129) and its *disruption* of daily routines (Harvey 2001). Specifically, I focus on encounters that become *incidents* or *scenes* (Goffman 1959:210–12). In such situations, as the norms of *audience tact* and *disattention* are suspended, the stigmatized individuals find themselves caught in the interactional spotlight, forced to explain themselves to others. From the perspective of the stigmatized, these disruptions are especially significant for their *moral careers*—or how they judge themselves and others over time (Goffman 1962:128). As one respondent put it, in such moments "the thin veneer of civility" is stripped away and negative labels are openly applied and contested.

We can view these instances of identity dispute as occasions for eliciting and producing *accounts*. I borrow this term from Lyman and Scott (1989) to refer to encounters in which a person is called to "explain unanticipated or untoward behavior—whether that behavior is his or her own or that of others, and whether the approximate cause of the statement arises from the actor himself or someone else" (p.112). Thus, we give accounts when confronting an unusual situation or individual. In their discussion of stigma, Evans, Forsyth, and Foreman (2003) note that "understanding the way individuals use accounts to construct positive self-identities, in the face of occupying a stigmatized . . . position, is indeed important turf for social science" (p. 373).

This article examines stigma-related accounts as performances that involve both the substance of everyday experience (i.e., *what* is being contested or questioned and under *what* conditions) and the social construction of reality (i.e., *how* it is presented). This view of stigma is consistent with the symbolic interactionist premise that objects are not inherently meaningful; rather, individuals assign meanings in general, and identities in particular, through interaction. Stigma is realized in the reflexive interplay between social conditions and self-presentation. The meaning and practical significance of stigma is interactionally achieved in everyday encounters. To better highlight this reflexive approach to accounts and stigma, the next section discusses interpretive practice as an analytic framework that attends to both the substance of stigma and its dramaturgical management.

Social Context and History

Accounts are conditioned by structural factors. As Lyman and Scott point out (1989), there are patterned differences between those actors who request accounts and those who have to account for themselves. In their words,

> The point with respect to accounts is their right to be requested, their establishment of social identity, and their efficacy to change in accordance with the changing status of the group involved. . . . Situations of account confusion are especially acute when a group in transition from one status position to another is undergoing a collective identity crisis. Racial groups provide numerous examples. Before the 1920s some Japanese in America insisted on their identity as "free white persons" in order to circumvent naturalization and franchise barriers, but found few others would accept this definition of their racial status. (p. 151)

In many ways, the case of Middle Eastern Americans is similar to that of Japanese Americans in the first half of the twentieth century. Political turmoil in the Middle East and terrorism have created an identity crisis for those with ancestral ties to that part of the world. The negative stereotypes of Middle Eastern Americans (*Arabs* in particular) predate the September 11th tragedies. For example,

> An ABC News poll, conducted during the Persian Gulf crisis in February 1991, found 43% of Americans had a high opinion of Arabs while 41% said they had a low opinion. In that poll, majorities of Americans said the following terms applied to Arabs: "religious" (81%), "terrorists" (81%), "violent" (58%) and "religious fanatics" (56%). (Jones 2001:1)

In fact, negative opinions toward Middle Eastern Americans date back at least to the hostage crisis of 1972 in which Palestinian militants took 11 Israeli athletes hostage during the Olympic Games in Munich. The German authorities' attempt to rescue the hostages ended in a massacre that claimed the lives of all eleven hostages and five of the eight terrorists. Shortly after this event, the Federal Bureau of Investigation launched one of its first national campaigns to interview and deport Arab Americans (Marvasti and McKinney 2004:56). Later, the Iranian hostage crisis in 1979, the first Gulf War in 1991, and the 1993 bombing of the World Trade Center all reinforced negative stereotypes of Middle Eastern Americans. Each conflict was followed by a wave of hate crimes and discrimination. Mosques were vandalized, and people were fired from jobs and assaulted on the streets (Feagin and Feagin 2003:327–30; Marvasti and McKinney 2004:53–60; Schaefer 2006:299–302; U.S. Congress 1986).

These backlashes were relatively isolated and episodic until September 11, 2001, when systematic discrimination against Middle Eastern Americans received considerable public support. A *Newsweek* poll conducted shortly after the terrorist attacks, on September 14–15, 2001, indicated that "32% of Americans think Arabs living in this country should be put under special surveillance as Japanese Americans were" (Jones 2001:3–4). Similarly, in June 2002, a Gallup survey of 1,360 American adults showed that "of the five immigrant groups tested [Arabs, Hispanics, Asians, Africans, and Europeans], the public is least accepting of Arab immigrants, as 54% say there are too many entering the United States" (Jones 2002:3).

Since September 11, 2001, accountability has become an everyday reality for Middle Eastern Americans in light of official policies that systematically demand that they explain their every action. Former Attorney General John Ashcroft articulated this state of heightened awareness quite clearly in public addresses by suggesting that if suspected terrorists as much as spit on the sidewalk, they would be arrested (Gorman 2002). The term *suspected terrorists* has become so broadly defined as to include thousands of Middle Eastern men who have been interviewed, arrested, or deported for minor immigration violations.

Interestingly, under U.S. immigration laws, Middle Eastern Americans (officially defined as those with ancestral ties to a region stretching from Turkey to North Africa) are classified as *white*. Indeed, most affirmative action forms specifically instruct people of Middle Eastern descent to identify themselves as *white*. However, the phrase *Middle Eastern-looking*, almost always used in connection with a terrorist threat, has come to connote the same meaning as the words *black suspect*. Their official classification as *white* seems to have no practical relevance in everyday life as Middle Eastern Americans are singled out for antiterrorism measures.

In the post-9/11 era, *Middle Eastern-looking* people, men in particular, have been verbally harassed, physically attacked, and sometimes killed, regardless of their actual nationality or association with Islam or the Middle East.

Furthermore, the current terror warning system, which is intended to alert the public about potential terrorist attacks, acts as an accounting catalyst. As the level of terror is *elevated*, for example, from yellow to orange, public fears and suspicions are equally increased, and subsequently more Middle Eastern people are forced into the position of account-givers. At the same time, terror warnings call on ordinary citizens to be *alert* and report anything *suspicious*—in a sense, deputizing them as semiofficial account-takers. In essence, the terror alert system encourages the suspension of tact and disattention, especially to the detriment of *Middle Eastern-looking* people. To borrow from Goffman (1963), Middle Eastern Americans are suffering *ill-fame* perpetuated by the mass media. In his words, their "public image . . . seems to be constituted from a small selection of facts which . . . are inflated into dramatic newsworthy appearance, and then used as a full picture [of their identity]" (p. 71). Under these circumstances, aspects of one's life that would ordinarily be considered private are routinely subjected to public and official scrutiny in everyday encounters.

However, the outcomes of such encounters are not uniform or predetermined. As Goffman states (1963), and Gubrium and Holstein develop in relation to interpretive practice (2000), stigma is not the property of a person, but of relationships that always unfold through symbolic interaction. Building on these insights, the stigma of being Middle Eastern American is not external to interactions but is constructed or rejected through interaction, accounts, and self-presentational strategies.

Middle Eastern individuals presented or accounted for their selves in disrupted social encounters or *incidents* (Goffman 1959:212). Accounting practices took mainly five forms: humorous accounting, educational accounting, defiant accounting, cowering, and passing. Analyzing these accounting strategies enables us to vividly grasp the interplay between artful self-presentations and obdurate social conditions. Each constitutes a different interpretive practice individuals use to establish a situationally practical and useful Middle-Eastern self.

Humorous Accounting

When questioned about their ethnic identity, respondents sometimes use humor as a way of shifting attention away from the stereotypes that threaten their identities. In this way, they use humor as a diversion technique (Taub, McLorg, and Fanflik 2004). Consider, for example, how Ali accounted for his Middle Eastern-sounding name.

AM: Do you get any reactions about your name? Like people asking you what kind of name is that?

Ali: Sometimes they do; sometimes they don't. Sometimes, if they haven't met me or if they are sending me correspondence, they think it's a lady's name and a lot of correspondence comes in Ms. Ali [last name]. They think I'm either Alison or something like that. Nowadays, when my name comes up [in face-to-face contacts with clients], I use my sense of humor. For example, when they can't spell my name or ask questions about it, I say, "I'm the brother of Muhammad Ali, the boxer."

Ali's deliberate use of associations with the famed boxer places his name in a cultural context his account-takers are familiar with. In this type of accounting, individuals use humor to establish a common ground or "facilitating normalized role-taking" (Davis 1961:128).

Another respondent, whose first name, Ladan (the name of a flower in Persian), brings up unwelcome and troubling associations with the notorious terrorist Osama Bin Laden, tells this story about how she used humor with an inquisitive customer.

AM: With the name Ladan, do you run into any problems?

Ladan: Where I work [at a department store] we all wear nametags, with the name Ladan very clearly spelled out L A D A N. And this old couple, they approached me and I was very friendly with them—I usually chitchat with my customers. And he started asking me all these questions like, "You're so pretty, where're you from?" [I respond,] "I'm from Iran." [He says,] "What?" [I repeat,] "I'm from Iran." So he asks, "What's your name?" And I say, "Ladan." So he bent down to read my nametag and he just looked at me with a funny face and asked, "Are you related to Bin Laden?"

AM: Was he joking?

Ladan: No, he was not. But I did joke back to him and I said, "Yes, he's my cousin and actually he's coming over for dinner tonight." [She chuckles.]

AM: So, when this sort of thing happens, you use humor to deal with it?

Ladan: Yeah, I do, because otherwise, if I don't turn it into a joke or a laughing mood, I get upset. I get really, really offended.

AM: So what was this guy's reaction? Did he laugh with you?

Ladan: When this guy realized my name is Ladan and I'm from Iran, he changed his attitude. He became reserved and he even went one step backward. When I noticed he was uncomfortable, I completed the transaction with his wife and let them leave as soon as they wanted.

In this case, Ladan's use of humor does not necessarily result in the proverbial *happy ending*, or a clearly discernible resolution. The customer turned away and ended the interaction. Whether Ladan remained stigmatized by this encounter or whether the customer walked away feeling that he successfully applied the stigma is unknown, perhaps even for the participants involved in the interaction. What is clearer is that Ladan's account allowed her to highlight the ludicrousness of the account-taker's assumptions and his right to solicit an account. Here, the way of speaking shapes the substance of the identity. Ladan is not giving a specific and accurate account of who she *really* is but is using humor to construct an encounter-specific account that implicitly questions the account-taker's right to ask her questions about her identity.

I also use humor to account for my name. The following encounter took place on Election Day (November 14, 2002) at a voting precinct in a small town in Pennsylvania where I went to cast my vote in the midterm elections. The encounter begins with the examination of my photo identification.

> Election Supervisor: Okay . . . this is a hard one! [squinting at my driver's license] You're ready? [alerting her coworker] It says Amar. . . . It's A . . .

> I wait, silent and motionless, as the three old women probe my ID. I fear that any sudden movement might send people running out of the building screaming for help. "Speak!" I scream in my head. The words finally roll out of my mouth:

AM:	You know, my dad gave me a long name, hoping that it would guarantee my success in life. [They laugh.]
Election Supervisor:	Well, you must be a doctor because you sure sign your name like one.
AM:	[I cannot resist] Actually, I am a doctor . . . So maybe my dad had the right idea after all.

In this case, I use humor as a method of introduction, a way of constructing an identity for the occasion that gives more weight to *how* one speaks rather than *what* one speaks. It was not clear to me what they thought about me, but I sensed that they were still puzzled—I had to account for who I am. The immediate substance of my identity was not in question—they had my photo identification in front of them and most likely could tell from my swarthy appearance that I was not a native Pennsylvanian. Instead, humorous accounting allowed me to shape the broad contours of my identity for the occasion. Namely, I was able to communicate that I come from a *normal* family that aspires to the universal notion of *success in life*, that I am aware that there are concerns about my identity, and am capable of responding to them in a sensible way.

In humorous accounting, the substance of the account is incidental and is deliberately trivialized. The account-giver acknowledges the demands of the encounter while simultaneously undermining the legitimacy and the urgency of the request for an account. How the account-giver handles the substance of the matter shapes the identity in question.

Educational Accounting

Sometimes accounting takes on a deliberate pedagogical form. In such cases, the account-giver assumes the role of an educator, informing and instructing the account-taker about relevant topics. This strategy of *normalization* (Goffman 1963) combats stigma by correcting stereotypes. Unlike humorous accounting, educational accounting centers on the informational substance of the account.

In response to suspicions and antagonism from his neighbors, a Pakistani Muslim, Hassan, conducted a sort of door-to-door educational accounting:

> After September 11th, I walked the street the whole week and talked to every single one of my neighbors. . . . And one of my neighbors—his brother was in Tower Two and he got out, and his mother was there and she was furious with Muslims and me. And we were there for three hours, my wife, my kids, her [the neighbor], her son and her other son that came out of the World Trade Center—he had come down by the time the buildings came down. And I was like, "Look, that's not Islam. That's not who Muslims are. Ask your son, what type of person am I? What type of person is my wife? Do I oppress my wife? Do I beat my wife? Have you ever heard me say anything extreme before?" . . . They all know I don't drink, they all know that I pray five times a day, they all know I fast during the month of Ramadan. At the end of Ramadan, we have a big party and invite everyone over to help celebrate the end of fast. This year, they'll all probably fast one day with me so they can feel what it's like.

Hassan's approach is proactive; it addresses potential questions before they are explicitly asked. In some ways, this form of educational accounting is similar to what Hewitt and Stokes (1975:1–3) call *disclaimers* or a *prospective construction of meaning* that individuals use in an attempt to avoid being categorized in an undesirable way. In this example, Hassan tries to transform the relationship between him, as an account-giver, and the account-takers who suspect him of being an *evildoer*. Unlike humorous accounting, where account-givers deliberately trivialize cultural stereotypes, educational accounting explicitly and diligently addresses them in order to debunk them.

Account-givers have to give considerable attention to deciding which inquiries are worthy of an educational account. For example, an Iranian respondent, Mitra, indicates that she filters inquiries about her culture and identity before answering them:

> If they ask about the government or the senate over there [Iran], I don't know anything about it. I know who the president is, but they ask me about the senate or the name of the senator over there, I don't know. Since I don't know I'm not going to get involved, I'll say I don't know or I'm not interested. If they say, "Oh, you are from that country!" or "You are from the Middle East and you are a terrorist," those kinds of comments I'm not going to get into. I'll just say, "No, I'm not." But if they ask me about the culture I'll tell them, "Alright," and inform them about it—as much as I know.

Although inclined to assume the role of an educator, Mitra is unwilling or unprepared to respond to every question. Part of her educational accounting strategy involves evaluating the degree of her expertise on the subject and the tone of the questions. As she says, if the account-taker begins with accusations, such as "you are a terrorist," the only reasonable reply might be to deny the accusation and end the interaction.

Educational accounting was a common strategy for Middle Eastern Muslim women in my sample, especially those who wear the *hijab*.[4] Many of them were approached by strangers who asked questions such as "Isn't it hot under there?" "Does that come in many colors?" "Why do you wear that?" "Are you going to make *them* [referring to the 10- and 12-year-old girls who were standing in a grocery store line with their mother] wear it too?" These women were literally stopped on the street by strangers who asked questions about the *hijab*, sometimes so directly as to constitute rudeness. My respondents reported that whenever time and circumstances allowed, they provide accounts of their religious practices and beliefs. Some of these answers include "I wear it because it is my culture," "I wear it so that you won't stare at my body when you are talking to me," or a more flippant response such as, "It's cooler under my scarf than you think."

Similarly, as a Middle Eastern sociology professor, I am often asked by my students to explain a wide range of topics about the region and Islam, from customs and culture to the mindset of terrorists. Like Mitra, I evaluate each question before providing an account. For example, a student in an undergraduate criminology seminar began every session with a trivial question about Iran, such as "Do they have trees over there?" At first, I provided a detailed educational account whenever asked to do so, even for seemingly inane items. Given the limited time I had to cover the assigned readings, later in the semester it became necessary to remind the students that I was not paid to educate them about the Middle East. The topic of the course was crime, specifically, the criminogenic aspects of American culture. In place of my personal instructions, I recommended a trip to the library for references on the Middle East and Iran. In this case, educational accounting became unfeasible because it diverted attention from the task at hand.

Defiant Accounting

When prompted to provide an account, Middle Eastern Americans sometimes express righteous indignation. I call this defiant accounting. Similar to humorous accounting, the account-giver exerts agency by challenging the other's right and the rationale to request it. However, whereas humorous accounting entails indirect and fairly conciliatory objections to stigma, in defiant accounting the stigmatized make explicit demands for counter explanations from the *normals*. For example, consider how Alham, a young Iranian woman, describes her experiences with a coworker.

> She [the coworker] would tell me, "I don't know which country you come from but in America we do it like this or that." I let it go because I was older than her and we had to work together. . . . But one day I pulled her aside and I told her, "For your information where I come from has a much older culture. And what I know, you can't even imagine. So why don't you go get some more education. And if you mention this thing again—'my country is this, your country is that'—, I'm going to take it to management and they're going to fire you or they're going to fire me." And that was it.

Alham does not provide an account to repair the interaction or to restore it to a state of equilibrium. On the contrary, she explicitly seeks to challenge the conventional format of the encounter. Instead of aiming for consensus, defiant accounting foregrounds conflicting viewpoints and signals the account-giver's objection to the entire affair. The interaction is explicitly focused on the fairness of the exchange between the account-giver and the account-taker.

Account-givers are especially likely to use defiant strategies when they find the request for an account unfair. Specifically, ethnic minorities who are subjected to profiling may become defiant in response to the practice. For example, when I learned that, unlike myself, my white colleagues were not asked to show ID cards upon entering the campus gym, I felt justified in becoming defiant. In one instance, while pulling out my ID card from my wallet, I asked the woman at the front counter why my white faculty friend, who had just walked in ahead of me, was not asked to present an ID. She explained that she had not noticed the other person entering or she would have asked him to do the same.

This encounter highlights the unpredictability of defiant accounting for both parties involved in the interaction. At its core, this strategy counters an account request with another: they ask for my ID and I ask why

I should be the only one subjected to this rule. In turn, the other side presents its account and so on. This chain of accounts and counter-accounts could result in a formal dispute. Though it is possible that in some cases, when confronted, the account-takers simply back down and cease their efforts, it is just as likely that they intensify their demands, especially when they are backed by policies or other public mandates.

Defiant accounting is a risky approach that can either shield the account-giver from a potentially humiliating process or generate additional requests and demands. In some cases, defiant accounting can become a type of mass resistance, as with African Americans and the passive resistance component of the civil rights movement of the 1960s.

Cowering

Stigma, particularly when endured for a long period, can cause a person to engage in what Goffman (1963:17) calls *defensive cowering*: the stigmatized simply go along with the stereotypical demands of the setting in order to avoid greater harm. With cowering, artful practice and agency take a backseat to external conditions. In encounters of this type, the stigmatized person is virtually powerless in the face of rigid demands of the setting.

Since September 11th, I have been very conscious of this fact when flying. Although I am certain that I have been singled out for security checks, I fear that objecting and confronting these practices would lead to additional hardships (i.e., a direct confrontation with law enforcement agents in which they have the greater authority and likelihood to win). For example, while traveling domestically, my 13-year-old daughter (whose mother is white American but has my Middle Eastern-sounding last name) and I were sent to a separate security line for a *random* screening. From my daughter's perspective this was *a good thing* because it meant going to a shorter line, but for me being searched was both humiliating and threatening. The following is an account of this incident.

> I approach the security gate with my daughter. She goes through. From several feet away, I see them searching her backpack and running a wand over her body as she stands there, still with her arms raised. I am next. I empty my pockets and put the contents on the conveyer belt. A security officer waves me through the gate. The damn thing beeps.

Security Officer One:	Whoa! Back up! [I slowly walk back and await further instructions.]
Security Officer One:	Walk through again. [The machine beeps again.]
Security Officer One:	Undo your belt and turn over the buckle. [She runs the wand over my belt and my waist.]
Security Officer Two:	There's a wallet on the conveyer belt. [My wallet

	was on the other side of the gate on the belt. They had not run it through the x-ray machine because it was not placed in a plastic pan.]
AM:	That's my wallet. [Fearing someone might take my wallet, I walk back through the gate to retrieve it.]
Security Officer Two:	Jesus Christ! You can't do that!
AM:	I meant to get my wallet.
Security Officer Two:	Why did you leave it on the belt?
AM:	I thought I was supposed to put it there.
Security Officer One:	Why didn't you put in a plastic pan?

I raise my shoulders to indicate my confusion. They stare at me, stare at each other, shake their heads and sigh. I am then told sit on a metal chair, take off my shoes, and raise my feet.

Security Officer Three:	Now stand up. [He runs the wand between my legs and down the front of my torso.] Turn around. [He scans my back.] Okay, put on your shoes.
AM:	Can I get my wallet now?
Security Officer Four:	No, we have to search it. [She pulls out the content of the wallet, searches every pocket, and hands it back to me.]
AM:	Can I go now?
Security Office Four:	[Apparently looking for someone to give her approval] Go ahead.

I rejoin my daughter. She smiles at me and we move on.

During this incident, I assumed any kind of *talking back* would draw further unwanted attention and possibly result in hours of interrogation—and a missed flight. I later asked an airline representative at the ticket counter why my daughter and I were so frequently selected for *random* screenings. She responded that we were in fact profiled by a computer program and, for reasons of national security, the airline could not tell us what specific criteria were used for singling us out. After hearing this, I replied, "Thank you for taking the time to speak with me. I am not trying to be difficult, but I think the system is flawed . . . but I am happy to help with whatever it takes to make everyone feel safe. Thanks again."

In another incident, shortly after September 11th, my wife and I were browsing in a video store in Florida. A little boy (maybe about five years old) who was walking in front of us with his parents began frantically tugging at his mother's shirttail with his eyes firmly fixed on me. When his mother finally looked down at him and asked, "What?" the boy said,

"Mommy . . . I thought they were all in jail!" The boy's parents looked at me and pulled their child away. I tried very hard to smile, but my wife was outraged and wanted to confront the parents. I advised against it, fearing that a full-blown confrontation would only highlight and give credibility to the stereotype expressed by the boy.

Similarly, when a man driving by in his truck yelled at me "Ragheads go home!" I had no opportunity to account or choose an accounting strategy. The incident was too shocking, too threatening, and too quick for me to rationally decide on an accounting strategy. I just cowered and tried to make sure the driver did not have the chance to run over me.

My interviewees spoke of similar incidents when they were dumbfounded by the sheer incivility of the attack. For example, a Pakistani man recalled being thrown out of an elevator on a college campus by a student who stated he did not want to be in the same space "with people like him." Several female respondents reported being verbally harassed or physically attacked. One was pelted with spitballs when she was in high school, another reported that her friend's scarf was pulled off by a teenage boy at a grocery store, and another was repeatedly yelled at— "Go home!"—by people in passing cars as she walked to her office on campus.

What these incidents have in common is that they severely limit the agency of the stigmatized; in most cases, the best possible performance is cowering, which is more about *saving body*, or one's physical safety, than *saving face* (Goffman 1959, 1963). In the biographies of the stigmatized, such overt acts of discrimination, however isolated, have great significance as *turning points* or *epiphanies* (Denzin 1989) that define the self as deviant and powerless in relation to normal others.

Passing

The goal of passing (Goffman 1963) is information control and the concealment of stigmatizing attributes from *normals*. As an accounting strategy, passing means eliminating the need for an account (see Lyman and Scott 1989:126–27). How individuals present their identity can potentially eliminate the need for accounting altogether. My respondents accomplished passing by manipulating their appearance. The stereotypical image of a Middle Eastern person roughly translates into someone with dark hair, large facial features, swarthy skin, non-European foreign accent, facial hair on men, and veils and scarves on women. Faced with these stereotypes, some respondents consciously altered their looks to avoid any outside marker that might associate them with these stereotypes. Self-presentation (Goffman 1959), especially attention to clothes and grooming, is an equally important consideration for successful passing. For example, wearing jeans and being clean-shaven draws less attention and leads to fewer occasions for accounting.

Some Middle Eastern Americans try to pass by trading their own ethnic identity for a less controversial one. The simplest way to do this is to move to an ethnically diverse region. The respondents who live in South Florida stated that one reason they did not experience negative episodes of ethnic accounting is because they are perceived as Hispanic. For example, an Iranian woman was asked what kind of Spanish she was speaking when she was having a conversation with her teenage daughter in Farsi at the mall. Another Iranian man tried to pass as Italian by placing an Italian flag vanity license plate on his car. As a general rule, my respondents displayed Western or patriotic symbols (e.g., an American flag) at work, in front of their homes, or on their cars to avoid ethnic accounting. After September 11th, my neighbors gave me an American flag to place outside my apartment. As he put it, "This is for your own safety." In a sense, patriotic symbols are accounting statements in their own right and act as *disidentifiers* (Goffman 1963:93) that help separate *loyal Americans* from suspected terrorists.

Another strategy for passing is to give an ambiguous account in response to ethnic identity questions. For example, asked about his country of origin, an Egyptian man stated that he was Coptic (a pre-Islamic Egyptian culture). He noted that uninformed account-takers typically find it too embarrassing to ask follow-up questions, pretend to know what *Coptic* means, and drop the subject altogether. Iranians create this kind of ambiguity by stating that they are Persians (the designation of ancient Iran). Another way to circumvent accounts is to name one's city of birth instead of country of birth. I once told a college classmate that I was from Tehran. To my astonishment, he asked, "Is that near Paris?"

Changing one's name is another way to pass. Some respondents change their Muslim names (e.g., Akbar) to typical American names (e.g., Michael). When asked why he changed his name, Ahmad explained that he was tired of people slamming down the phone when he made inquiries about jobs. Some change from widely known ethnic-sounding names to lesser known ones as in the change from Hossein to Sina.

Passing strategies pose their own risks for the stigmatized. In particular, the media have constructed passing among Middle Eastern Americans as an extension of the *evil terrorist plot*. After September 11th, it was widely reported that the hijackers were specifically instructed to wear jeans and shave their faces to pass as native born ethnics. Therefore, rather than being viewed as a sign of cultural assimilation, Middle Eastern Americans' conspicuous attempts at passing can be cast as a diabolical plan to form a *sleeper cell* or to disguise *the wolves among us*. These days, when I go to an airport, I am very conscious of how much passing would be considered legitimate. Trying to conceal too much information about oneself can arouse suspicion. In fact, I sometimes wear my gold medallion with its Allah (Arabic for *God*) inscription conspicuously on the outside of my shirt to indicate that I am not attempting to *misrepresent* myself or deceive anyone.

Conclusions: Interpretive Practice and Stigma Management

The case of Middle Eastern Americans' spoiled identities suggests that two sets of empirical observations have to be incorporated into the analysis. One the one hand, there is the reality of the so-called War on Terror and pervasive fear of terrorism, both of which have made Middle Eastern Americans *legitimate* targets of scrutiny in everyday life. Similarly, the political turmoil in the Middle East directly affects their lives in the United States, so much so that there is almost a direct correspondence between the volatility of the region and the instability of Middle Eastern identities in the United States. Every terrorist attack, every hostage taking, and every virulent speech issued from the Middle East triggers a corresponding wave of public scrutiny in the United States. These are the conditions, but how do we get at everyday practices? How do Middle Eastern Americans cope in real life situations? Answering these questions requires wearing a different analytic hat, so to speak.

One way my respondents and I cope with these conditions is by being adaptable and fluid with our self-presentations. We do not enter daily interaction as members of a stigmatized group. Many of us are devout Muslims who practice our religion proudly despite stereotypes and the negative press. To suggest that we are narrowly defined by the stigma of being Middle Eastern is an empirically unfounded claim. It is equally problematic to imply that the majority of Americans are engaged in a mass stigmatization campaign. On a general level, my analysis is informed by the idea that ethnic difference is variable and interactionally achieved (Garfinkel 1967), and suggests that Middle Eastern Americans use a range of interpretive practices to define their ethnic-national identities in the context of everyday life during the War on Terror.

My respondents and I experience being forced into positions where we have to account for our ethnic identities. What triggers these accounting encounters (e.g., genuine interest, fear, or malice) is of secondary relevance. As C. Wright Mills (1939) suggests, the motives for these encounters are themselves situated and discerned in the course, and in the language, of the interaction. In these encounters, account-givers and account-takers monitor each other at every turn and respond accordingly. I have labeled this type of interaction accounting encounters, and have underlined some of the self-presentation strategies Middle Eastern Americans use as they account for their identity (humorous, educational, and defiant accounting, cowering, and passing). Similar questions could be developed about account-takers and the strategies they use to ask for accounts (e.g., how they respond to humor or confrontation in their identity inquiries).

DISCUSSION QUESTIONS

1. What is a stigma? Is a stigma something that is always relevant to someone's identity or does it change with context? How does this relate to Goffman's concept of *presentation of self*?

2. What is an account? What purpose does it serve for a stigmatized individual?

3. What are the various types of accounts used by Middle Eastern Americans? What are the benefits and drawbacks of each?

4. Have you ever been asked to provide an account in an interaction? What were the circumstances and were you perceived as having a stigma? What interactional tactics did you use to combat this?

5. What other groups might need to rely on the interactional accounts described in the article? Are there any types of accounts that you think are widely used but not mentioned in the article?

REFERENCES

Arab American Institute (AAI). 2003. "Arab American Demographics." Retrieved July 30,2003, from www.aaiusa.org/demographics.htm.

Biernacki, Patrick and Dan Waldorf. 1981. "Snowball Sampling: Problems and Techniques of Chain Referral Sampling." *Sociological Methods & Research* 10:141–63.

Brown, Anthony. 2001. "Nervous Pilots Order Off 'Arab' Passengers." *The Observer,* *September* 23, p. 2.

Cahill, Spencer and Robin Eggleston. 1994. "Managing Emotions in Public: The Case of Wheel-chair Users." *Social Psychology Quarterly* 57:300–12.

Carling, Finn. 1962. *And Yet We Are Human*. London: Chatto & Windus.

Cruz, Patricia G. and Angela Brittingham. 2003. *The Arab Population 2000*. Washington, DC: U.S. Census Bureau.

Davis, Fred. 1961. "Deviance Disavowal: The Management of Strained Interaction by the Visibly Handicapped." *Social Problems* 9:121–32.

Delves, Philip. 2001. "New Prejudices Emerge in an Embittered City: New York's Arab Community Is Living in Fear of Attack," *The Daily Telegraph*, September 20, p. 7.

Denzin, Norman. 1989. *Interpretive Biography*. Newbury Park, CA: Sage.

Ellis, Carolyn and Arthur P. Bochner. 2000. "Autoethnography, Personal Narrative, Reflexivity: Researcher as Subject." Pp. 733–68 in *Handbook of Qualitative Research*, 2nd ed., edited by N. Denzin and Y. S. Lincoln. Thousand Oaks, CA: Sage.

Evans, Rhonda D., Craig J. Forsyth, and Rachel A. Foreman. 2003. "Psychic Accounts: Self-Legitimation and the Management of a Spoiled Identity." *Sociological Forum* 23:359–75.

Feagin, Joe and Clairece Feagin. 2003. Racial and Ethnic Relations, 7th ed. Upper Saddle River, NJ: Prentice Hall.

Feagin, Joe and Karyn McKinney. 2003. *The Many Costs of Racism*. Lanham, MD: Rowman and Littlefield.

Fothergill, Alice. 2003. "The Stigma of Charity: Gender, Class, and Disaster Assistance." *Sociological Quarterly* 44:659–80.

Garfinkel, Harold. 1967. *Studies in Ethnomethodology*. Englewood Cliffs, NJ: Prentice Hall.

Goffman, Erving. 1959. *The Presentation of Self in Everyday Life*. Garden City, NY: Doubleday Anchor Books.

——. 1962. *Asylums: Essays on the Social Situation of Mental Patients and Other Inmates*. Garden City, NY: Doubleday Anchor Books.

——. 1963. *Stigma: Notes on the Management of Spoiled Identity*. Englewood Cliffs, NJ: Prentice Hall.

Gorman, Siobhan. 2002. "National Security: The Ashcroft Doctrine." *National Journal* 34:3712–19.

Gubrium, Jaber and James Holstein. 1997. *The New Language of Qualitative Method*. Thousand Oaks, CA: Sage.

——. 2000. "Analyzing Interpretive Practice." Pp. 487–508 in *Handbook of Qualitative Research*, 2nd ed., edited by N. Denzin and Y. S. Lincoln. Thousand Oaks, CA: Sage.

Harvey, Richard D. 2001. "Individual Differences in the Phenomenological Impact of Social Stigma." *The Journal of Social Psychology* 14:174–89.

Hayano, David M. 1979. "Auto-ethnography: Paradigms, Problems, and Prospects." *Human Organizations*, 38:113–20.

Herman, Nancy J. 1993. "Return to Sender: Reintegrative Stigma-Management Strategies of Ex-Psychiatric Patients." *Journal of Contemporary Ethnography* 22:295–330.

Hewitt, John P. and Randall Stokes. 1975. "Disclaimers." *American Sociological Review* 40:1–11.

Hochschild, Arlie. 1983. *The Managed Heart: Commercialization of Human Feeling*. Berkeley: University of California Press.

Holstein, James A. and Jaber Gubrium. 1995. *The Active Interview*. Thousand Oaks, CA: Sage.

Jacobs, Bruce A. 1999. *Race Manners: Navigating the Minefield between Black and White Americans*. New York: Arcade.

Jones, Jeffrey M. 2001. "Americans Felt Uneasy toward Arabs Even before September 11th," *The Gallup Organization* (www.gallup.com).

——. 2002. "Effects of September 11th on Immigration Attitudes Fading but Still Evident," *The Gallup Organization* (www.gallup.com).

Karp, David A. 1992. "Illness Ambiguity and the Search for Meaning: A Case Study of a Self-Help Group for Affective Disorders." *Journal of Contemporary Ethnography* 21:130–70.

Killian, Lewis M. 1985. "The Stigma of Race: Who Now Bears the Mark of Cain?" *Symbolic Interaction* 8:1–14.

Kusow, Abdi M. 2003. "Beyond Indigenous Authenticity: Reflections on the Insider/Outsider Debate in Immigration Research." *Symbolic Interaction* 26:591–99.

—. 2004. "Contesting Stigma: On Goffman's Assumptions of Normative Order." *Symbolic Interaction* 27:179–97.

Lincoln, Yvonna S. and Norman K. Denzin. 1994. "The Fifth Moment." Pp. 575–86 in *Handbook of Qualitative Research*, edited by N. Denzin and Y. S. Lincoln. Thousand Oaks, CA: Sage.

Link, Bruce and Jo Phelan. 2001. "Conceptualizing Stigma." *Annual Review of Sociology* 27:363–85.

Lyman, Stanford and Marvin Scott. 1989. *A Sociology of the Absurd*. Dix Hills, NY: General Hall.

Marvasti, Amir and Karyn McKinney. 2004. *Middle Eastern Lives in America*. New York: Rowman and Littlefield.

Mauthner, Natasha and Andrea Doucet. 2003. "Reflexive Accounts and Accounts of Reflexivity in Qualitative Data Analysis." *Sociology* 37:413–31.

McLellan, David. 2000. *Karl Marx: Selected Writings*. New York: Oxford University Press.

Mills, C. Wright. 1939. "Situated Actions and Vocabularies of Motive." *American Sociological Review* 5:904–13.

Riessman, Catherine K. 2000. "Stigma and Everyday Resistance Practices: Childless Women in South India." *Gender & Society* 14:111–35.

Ronai, Carol R. 1992. "The Reflexive Self through Narrative." Pp. 102–24 in *Investigating Subjectivity*, edited by C. Ellis and M. Flaherty. Newbury Park, CA: Sage.

Roschelle, Anne R. and Peter Kaufman. 2004. "Fitting In and Fighting Back: Stigma Strategies among Homeless Kids." *Symbolic Interaction* 27:23–46.

Said, Edward. 1978. *Orientalism*. New York: Vintage.

Schaefer, Richard T. 2006. *Racial and Ethnic Groups*, 10th ed. Upper Saddle River, NJ: Prentice Hall.

Snow, David and Leon Anderson. 1987. "Identity Work among the Homeless: The Verbal Construction and Avowal of Personal Identities." *American Journal of Sociology* 92:1336–71.

Storrs, Debbie. 1999. "Whiteness as Stigma: Essentialist Identity Work by Mixed Race Women." *Symbolic Interaction* 22:187–212.

Taub, Diane E., Penelope A. McLorg, and Patricia L. Fanflik. 2004. "Stigma Management Strategies among Women with Physical Disabilities: Contrasting Approaches of Downplaying or Claiming Disability Status." *Deviant Behavior* 25:169–90.

Thomas, William I. and Dorothy S. Thomas. 1928. *The Child in America: Behavior Problems and Programs*. New York: Knopf.

U.S. Congress. House of Representatives. Subcommittee on Criminal Justice of the House Judiciary Committee. July 16,1986. *Ethnically Motivated Violence against Arab Americans*. 99th Cong., 2nd sess. Serial no. 135. Washington, DC: U.S. Government Printing Office.

NOTES

1. Axis of Evil Comedy Tour http://www.imdb.com/title/tt1018867/

2. https://www.splcenter.org/fighting-hate/hate-incidents

3. Most names have been fictionalized to protect the identity of the respondents.

Where it is necessary to use an actual first name, every effort has been made to disguise other personal identifying information about a respondent.

4. *Hijab* is the Islamic word for modesty in dress that applies to both men and women. In the case of many Muslim women living in the United States, this means wearing a scarf that covers the hair and the neck, as well as wearing loose-fitting garments so that the outlines of the body are not exaggerated.

"She's Not a Low-Class Dirty Girl!"

Sex Work in Ho Chi Minh City, Vietnam

Kimberly Kay Hoang

Images of sex workers in popular culture shape many of our ideas about who has sex for money and why. From the prostitutes in HBO's *Westworld* to Hulu's *Harlots* to Julia Roberts in *Pretty Woman*, women who work for sex are often portrayed as feisty, enjoying their work, and relatively independent. On the other hand, news stories about sex workers and sex trafficking tend to cast all sex workers as helpless victims working in deplorable conditions who require rescuing from their profession.

Both sets of cultural images fail to use sociological imagination to capture the range and nuances of experiences among different sex workers, and the complicated interplay between gender, race, class, and geography that shapes the experience of each particular individual. In this article, Kimberly Hoang describes the experiences of sex workers in Ho Chi Minh City in Vietnam. She identifies three different tiers of workers who cater to different types of clients and offer different services and relationships that hinge on the race, class, and geography of people involved. Some of the women do indeed engage in sex work because it is the best economic option available to them, and they perform perfunctory sexual acts with and for clients directly for cash, what she calls sexual exchanges. But others cater to primarily white tourists who want to take advantage of a "Third World sexscape" by having romantic relationships with local women. These women often try to parlay these temporary relationships into long term financial support or relationships that would allow them to leave the country. Women in the high-end sector tend to be involved in intimate exchanges that require a particular kind of cultural, economic, and bodily capital. These women are often from upper class families and have no interest in leaving Vietnam or forming long term relationships. They carefully select their clients from overseas Vietnamese men (Viet Kieu) and avoid both locals and white tourists.

"'She's Not a Low Class Dirty Girl': Sex Work in Ho Chi Minh City, Vietnam" by Kimberly Kay Hoang, in *Journal of Contemporary Ethnography* 40(4): 2011. Reprinted with permission.

One of the main differences among the different "tiers" of sex workers in her study is the different types of capital they have at their disposal. She introduces Pierre Bourdieu's concept of cultural capital (the tastes, styles, habits, and dispositions associated with a group) as an important difference among workers and their clients. This compliments the available economic capital (income, assets, and other monetary resources) that each group has. Workers and clients with similar levels of cultural and economic capital tend to wind up together, and these similarities or differences tend to map along racial lines. Interestingly, this is no different than how Western romantic relationships tend to develop—we are most likely to wind up with a romantic partner who is socially, economically, and racially similar to us. As you read, think about how romantic relationships without any overt economic transactions in them may in fact be similar to the types of relationships described in the article.

Introduction

Studies on sex work pay particular attention to the growth of global sex tourism, marked by the production and consumption of sexual services across borders. A recent body of literature uncovers the complexities of stratified sex industries around the world (Bernstein 2007; Zheng 2009). This article extends the literature on the stratification of sex work by comparing three racially and economically diverse sectors of Ho Chi Minh City's (HCMC's) global sex industry: a low-end sector that caters to poor local Vietnamese men, a mid-tier sector that caters to white backpackers, and a high-end sector that caters to overseas Vietnamese (Viet Kieu) men.

Sex Work in Ho Chi Minh City's International Economy

Vietnam is an ideal case for the study of sex work because rapid economic restructuring has triggered new inflows of people and capital, creating a segmented sex market. After the fall of Saigon in 1975, Vietnam effectively closed its doors to foreign relations with most of the international community except the Soviet bloc. In 1986, after a decade of full state management of the economy, heavily subsidized production, and postwar infrastructural instability, the Vietnamese government introduced an extensive economic and administrative renovation policy called Doi Moi (literally *renovation* or *renewal*) that transitioned Vietnam from a socialist to a market economy.

HCMC has a distinctive sex industry with an estimated 200,000 Vietnamese women involved in prostitution CCATW 2005).

The movement of people and capital makes HCMC a critical site where globalization generates new types of inequality, which in turn create new segments of sex work. Unlike studies on sex trafficking that tend to view all women as poor victims in need of rescue, I argue that it is important to examine the social and economic distinctions between sex workers in a stratified economy. Globalization does not create a single market for poor exploited women who cater to wealthy foreigners; rather, I contend that globalization creates diverse markets and new segments that expand already existing inequalities. Structural factors such as women's access to economic, cultural, and bodily resources position them in higher- and lower-paying sectors of sex work with different relations of intimacy.

Sex Work Through the Lens of Capital and Intimate Relations

In this article, I focus on how structural factors such as exchange of different bodily, cultural, and economic capitals lead to a range of short-term and long-term relationships that emerge through client-worker interactions.

First, I turn to Bourdieu's theories of capital to explain how clients and sex workers draw on different economic, cultural, and bodily resources to enter various sectors of HCMC's sex industry. To develop Bourdieu's theories in the context of sex work, I also draw on Zelizer's (2005) concept of intimate relations to illustrate how clients and sex workers mingle sex, money, and intimacy in different ways that correspond to their position in a particular stratum.

Bourdieu defines economic capital as the monetary income, assets, or other financial resources that an actor can access (Bourdieu 1986). Cultural capital refers to actors' dispositions and embodiment in specific social fields. It is the ability to acquire and manipulate a system of embodied, linguistic, or economic markers that carry cultural meaning, especially within a hierarchical social system of status (Bourdieu 1977). Broadly, the relevant demarcations of cultural capital in the world of HCMC's sex industry are the resources, dispositions, and modes of embodiment that allow individuals to position themselves within the particular social field of sex work in HCMC. More specifically, on the client side, I use the term *cultural capital* to draw attention to Viet Kieu clients' understanding of the local culture and their ability to speak Vietnamese when navigating the sex industry in HCMC. For sex workers, I use the term *cultural capital* to refer to the linguistic and discursive abilities needed for communication with clients and also to the sex workers' level of comfort within particular bars and restaurants. In addition, sex workers' cultural capital encompasses the ability to embody and project to clients an imagined nation: Vietnam as nostalgic *home* for Viet Kieu men and, alternatively, Vietnam as foreign and exotic other for Western men (Nguyen-Vo 2008).

I also incorporate Bernstein's (2007) term *body capital*, which she defines as an attractive appearance used to sell sexual services. In this article, I highlight dimensions of body capital such as apparent age, designer clothing, hairstyle, and make-up, as well as strategies to acquire body capital, such as cosmetic surgery. Sex workers' bodies serve as assets that allow them to work as entrepreneurs in bodily capital (Wacquant 1995) to market themselves as attractive and thus more valuable in relation to global men.

Bourdieu (1986) argues that different forms of capital have varied meanings within social fields. A field, in Bourdieu's oeuvre, is a terrain of struggle in which agents strategize to preserve or improve their positions (Bourdieu 1984). While men and women use different forms of capital to enter and maneuver within specific sectors of sex work in HCMC, these various forms of capital are only valued through the relations between men and women in this particular field. In this paper, I highlight the forms of capital that are relevant and valued in relations between clients and sex workers in HCMC's sex industry.

While Bourdieu's (1984) theories of social fields and capital help us to understand the structure of the HCMC's stratified sex industry and the relations within a particular field, his theories inhibit our examination of the product of interactions between clients and sex workers. Zelizer's (2005) concept of intimate relations is more useful because it provides a critical tool for understanding how the exchange of different resources leads to a range of short-term and long-lasting relationships between clients and sex workers.

How does Zelizer (2005) define intimacy and economic activity? Intimacy refers to "the transfer of personal information and wide-ranging, long-term relations which connect and overlap" between people (Zelizer 2005, p. 16). Intimate relations vary over time along a continuum and as people exchange different degrees of physical, informational, and emotional closeness with each other. Economic transactions, in contrast, go beyond the mere use of money. People may use gifts, different forms of compensation, or entitlements as payment, corresponding to the way they define their relationships with one another. They use varied symbols, rituals, practices, and distinguishable forms of money to mark distinct social relations (Zelizer 2004).

Integrating Bourdieu's theories of capital and Zelizer's concept of intimate relations, I argue that sex workers and their clients engage in three types of relationships with varying degrees of intimacy, capital, and duration (see Table 1 below).

Sexual exchanges are swift encounters between clients and sex workers that involve direct sex-for-money exchanges and happen almost entirely in the low-end sector. Although interactions between sex workers and clients are sexually intimate, they are not personal. That is, men and women do not build emotional ties with one another. Relational exchanges, which take place primarily in the mid-tier sector, involve a complex set of intimate and economic arrangements, the exchange of bodily and cultural capitals, as well as short-term client-worker interactions that sometimes develop into long-term boyfriend-girlfriend relationships. Intimate exchanges, which occur mostly in the high-end sector, also involve a complex set of economic and intimate arrangements and the deployment of economic, cultural, and bodily capitals. However, relations between sex workers and clients in the high-end sector are short-term relationships that last only for the duration of the client's visit and rarely develop into long-term remittance relationships.

Table 1 Economic, Relational, and Intimate Exchanges			
	Relations	**Capital at Stake**	**Duration**
Low-end	Sexual exchange (only sex and money are exchanged)	Economic Capital: poor rural and urban women Body capital: lack of access to plastic surgery Cultural capital: lack of cultural and language skills	Short one-time interaction
Mid-tier	Relational exchange (sex, gifts, and money are exchanged)	Economic capital: poor urban women Body capital: plastic surgery, hair, clothing, etc. Cultural capital: ability to speak English and navigate in foreign spaces.	Short-term and long-term remittance relationships that often develop into boyfriend-girlfriend or husband-wife relations
High-end	Intimate exchange (sex, gifts, money, and intimacy are exchanged.	Economic capital: college- or trade-school-educated urban women from wealthy families Body capital: higher-end plastic surgeries, spas, designer clothing Cultural capital: Ability to display comfort in navigating high-end hotels, bars, and restaurants	Short-term intimate relationships where marriage and migration are not the end goal

Note: These typologies are ideal types specific to Ho Chi Minh City's sex industry.

Research Methods

I carried out seven months of ethnographic field research in three intervals between June 2006 and August 2007 in HCMC.

I conducted participant observation in local bars, cafes, sex workers' homes, malls, restaurants, and on the streets. All of the sex workers I studied were women over the age of 18 who chose to enter sex work as independent agents. None of my participants were trafficked or forced into prostitution.

I focused on three sectors of HCMC's sex industry: those catering to poor local Vietnamese men, to white backpackers, and to overseas Vietnamese (Viet Kieu) men. I chose these sectors because together they represent a large portion of the sex work industry in HCMC and because the relations between clients and sex workers in these sectors are largely public and therefore easier to observe. I later returned to Vietnam for 15 months between 2009 and 2010 to examine sex work relationships within private spaces and enclosed karaoke bars that cater to wealthy Vietnamese entrepreneurs and Asian businessmen. Here I focus on the sectors that are more publicly visible because I did not have access to enclosed spaces during 2006 and 2007.

My research began with time spent in local bars and on the streets to meet and develop rapport with various sex workers, clients, and bar owners before asking the women to participate in my project. The second phase of the research process involved intensive participant observation and informal interviews with individual sex workers who agreed to participate in the project. Being an overseas Vietnamese woman helped me gain access to female sex workers because many of them suspected local Vietnamese men who asked them questions of being undercover police. Although all of the women knew that I was a researcher from the United States who would eventually write about their lives, this was not important to them. They cared more about my family history and my life overseas, wanting to situate me in their mental universe.

In my attempt to expand the literature on sex work empirically, I also incorporated male clients into my analysis. All of the clients knew that I was a researcher from the United States. Overseas white backpackers and Viet Kieu clients in my study were much more open with me than local Vietnamese men. White backpackers and Viet Kieu could converse with me in English and relate to me about the context of their lives overseas and the dynamics of their relations in HCMC. I befriended two local motorbike-taxi drivers who introduced me to the low-end sector that catered to local Vietnamese men. Cuong and Loc taught me how to approach men and women in this sector. They also helped ease me into conversations with local male clients. Their assistance was crucial in my understanding of the spatial and structural differences between the local sector and the sectors that cater to overseas male clients.

The Low-End Sector: "Touching Them Makes Me Want To Throw Up!"

Sex workers who catered to local Vietnamese men generally engaged in sexual exchanges that involved direct sex-for-money transactions. These women worked in brothels disguised as barbershops in HCMC's Districts Ten and Four, the Binh Thanh district, and the area surrounding the Tan Son Nhat Airport.

All 12 women in this sector were single mothers between the ages of 29 and 60 who had no more than a grade school education. They were poor, urban women or rural migrants who once worked in the service or manufacturing sectors before entering sex work. Sex workers in this sector provided men with a variety of sexual labors (Boris, Gilmore, and Parrenas 2010), offering a quick orgasm within a 20-minute interaction. Men typically paid three U.S. dollars for this service, and clients and sex workers rarely negotiated these prices. On average, women earned 100 dollars per month, which was 40 to 50 dollars more than they would earn working in local restaurants, legitimate barbershops, or as house cleaners.

I asked Dung, a 34-year-old single mother of two, why she worked for such low pay and why she did not try to find work in District One, the business district, where she could capitalize on the flow of men with overseas money. She said very bluntly:

> I am old. I have a kid. I don't look pretty. I don't speak English or even know how to get to those places [that cater to foreign men]. I don't have the clothes or money to walk around in those kinds of bars so I could never work there. I could never compete with those women. Money is never easy to get from white men.[1]

At beginning of my research, I naively invited some of these women to have lunch or dinner in District One. I quickly realized that they felt extremely uncomfortable, if not illegitimate, in these spaces. True, for example, said:

> I do not go into those restaurants that mostly foreigners go into because I am so afraid that I will sit down, look at the prices on the menu, and panic because I couldn't even afford the cheapest thing there. If I turned around and walked out everyone would laugh at me.

In sum, sex workers' lack of economic and cultural resources placed them in a sector of sex work where they engaged in relations of subordination with poor local men.

In addition to the lack of economic resources and cultural capital that limited them, the women in the low-end sector did not have the body capital to participate in mid-tier or high-end sectors. As Mai, a woman from the Mekong Delta who worked in one of these barbershops, stated, "I am in my mid-30s, I have a child, and I am not good looking. . . . So I don't have a choice but to do this." While women who catered to foreign men reinvested a significant portion of their earnings into their appearance by purchasing cosmetic surgery, clothing, accessories, and make-up, the women in the low-end sector spent all of their earnings on necessities like housing, food, and schooling for their children. As such, the women in the low-end sector typically wore the same plain house-like clothing in both their homes and work places. They did not dress up for work or wear any clothing that marked them in an explicitly sexual way. In fact, these women's bodies resembled the bodies of poor homemakers, sisters, or mothers. They were women who shared similar class dispositions with poor local men.

Although they were not forced into sex work, many entered and continued to do this work as a means to escape poverty. The women in the low-end sector were among the most vulnerable and the most exploited. These women did not have much choice in terms of which clients they would service. In most cases, they served any client, because they needed the money. Mai said:

> What we do is dirty. Old dirty men come in here and they are rough with my body. They don't care about me because to them I am just a worker. When I first started working, I would throw up after each client, but now I am used to it.

Although some women had a set of regular clients, these clients were purchasing a product—an orgasm—and nothing more. Sex workers and clients engaged in direct sex-for-money exchanges where economic and intimate relationships were not closely intertwined.

Mid-Tier Sector: "She's a Smart Woman Who Is Just Trapped in a Poor Country"

The *backpacker* area in HCMC is well known as the central location for people traveling on a budget. Lining the streets are souvenir shops, mini-hotels, tourist agencies, restaurants, cafes, and bars catering to foreigners. The majority of shopkeepers in this area speak some English. I conducted participant observation in seven of the roughly 25 bars located in this area. The clients I met in this sector ranged in age from 22 to 65, and all were white Americans, Europeans, or Australians. White men in the mid-tier sector viewed themselves as savvy travelers who were able to take advantage of a Third-World sexscape (Brennan 2004). They tended to stay in a host of mini-hotels, parching for the *authentic* Vietnamese experience.

Sex workers in this sector exploited the transnational sex market by developing relations with overseas men and engaging in what Smith and Guarnizo (1998) refer to as practices of *transnationalism from below*. While the women in this sector were certainly involved in direct sex-for-money exchanges, they also made use of their cultural capital to feign love and provide their clients with a variety of other services. The following account illustrates how transnationally savvy sex workers create and sustain intimate relations through their English-language skills and their bodies.

I met Linh in June 2006 and continued to maintain ties with her through August 2007. Linh was working in Pink Star, a bar located in the backpacker area of District One. At 5 foot 6 inches, Linh was taller than most Vietnamese women and had a slender body and long legs. She always wore tight pink and black dresses that accentuated her thin legs. Like many of the women working in this sector, Linh invested more than a thousand dollars in a variety of body modifications: breast implants, eyebrow tattoos, Botox injections in her forehead, and liposuction to flatten her stomach. While nearly all of the women in the low-end sector were rural migrants, women like Linh tended to come from urban families that were poor by city standards, but possessed more economic resources than the families of women in the lower-end sector. They were aware of places that catered to overseas white men looking for an authentic Vietnamese experience, and all of them could speak some English. All of these women worked in local bars disguised as bartenders. However, they did not receive a wage for bartending, instead earning money from tips and from their sexual liaisons with their clients. Many of these women learned English by talking to overseas men in the bars, and the more ambitious ones spent their earnings on formal English-language classes. Investing in her body and in English-language skills enabled Linh to initiate and establish ties with white men with economic resources from developed nations.

On one evening, a client named Jeff, a man in his mid-50s from New York, walked in and sat down in Pink Star. Jeff was dressed in khaki shorts, a short-sleeve button-up shirt, and flip-flop sandals. He was sweating, so Linh walked over with a wet towel and wiped down his face, something she frequently did for men to demonstrate her care for them. The two sat and made small talk, despite Linh's limited English skills. They exchanged typical questions including, "Where are you from?" "How long are you here for?" "What do you do?" "How old are you?" "Where does your family live?" After five drinks, Linh moved in, nudged him, and said, "You take me home with you." He smiled and said, "Okay." After which she said, "You pay me 100 dollars?" He laughed and said, "Too much. . . I pay you 50." They smiled silently at each other for several minutes before she said, "Okay, 60." They got up and left.

The next morning, Linh called and asked me to go with her and her daughter to a local amusement park. After several hours of walking through the park, we sat down to eat while her daughter took a short nap. During this time, Linh told me that she used her employment at the bar to meet clients from overseas. With clients she knew were in Vietnam for a short period, she was direct and asked if they wanted to go with her for 50 to 70 dollars a night. However, with clients who visited Vietnam for an extended time, she engaged in relational exchanges in an attempt to develop long-term relationships that sometimes turned into complicated boyfriend-girlfriend relations. Nearly all of the women in this sector had multiple *boyfriends*. When I asked her if she loved any of the men she dated, she said:

> When I first started working, I was young and not so smart. I would fall in love easily and then get hurt when things did not work out. Now, I don't let myself fall in love. I think I can grow to love the man who takes the best care of me in Vietnam or some other country. I want to change my life first and fall in love second.

In both long-term and short-term relations, Linh always attempted to develop remittance relationships after the men left Vietnam. She also dated multiple men as a strategy to migrate abroad: as she reasoned, if one man was unwilling to help her migrate, then she had other men who might take her.

After leaving the amusement park, Linh asked me to translate the first of what turned into more than hundred e-mails between her and James, a 67-year-old Australian man who owned a small business before retiring. She met James in December 2005 at Pink Star while he was on a holiday in Vietnam.

She wanted to build an emotional relationship with James so that he would sympathize with her *struggles* and send her money. James deposited several chunks of money ranging from 500 to 5000 dollars in her bank account to help her through these crises, in addition to monthly remittances of 300 dollars a month to pay for English lessons and beauty school. Through these transactions, by August 2006, she received a monthly remittance of about 700 dollars from three overseas men, two from Australia and one from the United States. Linh convinced all three men that each was the only man in her life. While Linh did take English lessons, she had several men paying for the same set of classes, which provided her with extra money to pay for plastic surgery or purchase nicer clothing and fancier phones. Women like Linh capitalized on global linkages by creating and maintaining a series of fictitious stories about their lives in HCMC.

I first met James that day through Yahoo Messenger, an Internet chat system. Linh introduced me to him as someone studying transnational relationships. To my surprise, James took an interest in my project, and he and I went on to communicate via e-mail, Internet chat, and postal mail more than 60 times between July 2006 and August 2007. In August

2007, I met James in person at a local cafe in District One. The 67-year-old Australian decided that he was going to spend the rest of his life traveling as a backpacker on a budget.

In several conversations that I had with James, he repeatedly described Linh in these terms:

> Linh is an honest person; she is a strong woman with a lot of integrity. You know she only went to school through sixth grade, but she can speak English fairly well. We talk about many things. I love Linh a lot and I want what is best for her. She is a smart and intelligent woman who is just living in a poor country where there aren't very many opportunities. I want to help her start her own small business in Vietnam, you know, so that she can be self-sufficient and not have to work in a bar.

In his e-mails to me, James did not speak of a sex-for-money exchange. Instead, he framed his relationship with Linh as one based on true love. James stated that he was in love with Linh, and that he believed she was truly in love with him. He expressed strong convictions that he was going to be the man who would *save* her from her life as a bar girl. The moral characteristics (Lamont 1992) of honesty, hard work, and personal integrity that James attributed to Linh motivated him to send her large sums of money without questioning her stories of need. He sympathized with her because, as he said, "as a first-world man with so much privilege, I felt that it was important to help."

Linh and James began their relationship as worker and client, and while Linh held on to multiple men until she was able to secure her visa to migrate, she eventually fell in love with James. Vietnam's status as a poor country allowed Linh, and other women in the same position, to represent themselves as victims of global poverty, generating sympathy and regular, large remittances from several men like James. Linh's ability to speak English, navigate foreign spaces, act as a personal tour guide, and induce feelings of love and sympathy in her clients made this relationship possible. Her simultaneous involvement with multiple men across transnational social fields also allowed her to choose whom she would serve, and determine the country to which she would eventually emigrate. Likewise, James drew on moral discourses about global inequality to explain why Linh entered sex work. James and other foreign men like him also made use of the expanded sexual and relational possibilities in a developing country like Vietnam, where they knew their money would both buy more sex and go further to support women they deemed deserving. The stories of men and women like Linh and James demonstrate how seemingly powerless women can exploit global and local systems of oppression by capitalizing on transnational linkages and engaging in relational sex with the hope of migrating to a country with better opportunities, and if they are *lucky*, maybe even falling in love.

High-End Sector: "She's Not a Low-Class Dirty Girl"

Workers and clients in the high end of HCMC sex work engaged in intimate exchanges, blurring the boundaries between economic and intimate relations even further than those in the middle tier.

Clients in the high-end sector engaged in relationships with sex workers who possessed levels of economic and cultural capital similar to them. These men were not looking for poor women whom they could save. Instead, they sought young, desirable women with options. Unlike the women in the mid-tier sector, the women who catered to wealthy Viet Kieu (overseas Vietnamese) did not come from poverty. In fact, many of them came from relatively wealthy families who owned small business and had the social networks and resources to comfortably navigate some of HCMC's most expensive establishments. Although women in the high-end sector often received money from their clients, sex workers and clients both framed the transfer of money as a gift, never as a form of payment, and most definitely not as a way to help save women from poverty.

In the next account, I illustrate the various forms of economic, cultural, and bodily resources that women in this sector possess. I met Ngoc, a tall, slender 24-year-old woman, in May 2007 inside Dragonfly, one of HCMC's most expensive bars.

Ngoc's family owned a small electronics store in District One. She just started a job at Star Capital, an investment company whose global headquarters was based in the United States. She made roughly 600 dollars per month working as an assistant to an account manager. Like Ngoc, most of the women that I studied in this sector had a college or university degree. Along with a well-respected job and a salary that was relatively high by HCMC standards, Ngoc's parents supplemented her income.

Ngoc always dressed in trendy clothing, owned several different designer handbags, and owned multiple cell phones. While spending a day in a local spa together, Ngoc described to me the various surgeries that she underwent to enhance her body. She showed me her breast implants, saying [in Vietnamese]:

> Don't these look good to you? I got them done in Thailand by a doctor who specializes in breast implants for transsexuals: you know, men who want to be women. The doctor told me to stay with a C [size] cup because they would look more natural and my nipples would look better. You don't want to get those cheap implants like a lot of girls in Vietnam get [because] they look fake.

In addition to the breast implants, at the age of 24, Ngoc had nose surgery to create a nose bridge, double eyelid surgery, liposuction from her thighs and stomach, and Botox injections in her forehead. With the exception of the Botox, she completed all of these procedures in Thailand—a mark of distinction that differentiated her from local women who could only afford surgery in Vietnam. These cosmetic alterations cost her more than 12,000 dollars in total. Ngoc also had regular appointments at a local spa, where she got a massage and a facial once a week. She spent several hours in local beauty salons getting her hair and make-up done prior to going out at night. For Ngoc, having plastic surgery, wearing designer clothing, spending days in spas, and getting her hair and nails done at beauty salons distinguished her from poorer Vietnamese women who catered to white men.

Ngoc and I also spent several nights out in cafes, restaurants, and bars where she introduced me to many of her friends, who were local bar and restaurant owners. These men and women often referred clients to Ngoc. On our outings together, rich local men would often proposition Ngoc. She always declined because, as she said, "They would automatically know that I was working, and if something bad happened, everyone would know I was working." I asked her, "What about Western guys?" She said, "Those are for the village girls who want to migrate. If I go with a white guy, everyone will know I'm a working girl." In addition to the rich local Vietnamese clients and white businessmen, she also turned down several Viet Kieu men. When I asked why she turned down so many clients when she had not been with anyone for nearly two weeks, she explained:

> You have to know how to pick out men. Many Viet Kieu men come to Vietnam and they show off, but they are actually poor men. You can tell the difference between rich and poor men by the kind of clothes they wear, their watches, and the kinds of places where they hang out. Poorer Viet Kieu men will eat at places that don't cost much, but men with money, know about good restaurants.

While overseas Viet Kieu men certainly leverage the power of the dollar to consume more in Vietnam than they could in the United States, Ngoc used the consumption patterns of male clients to distinguish richer Viet Kieu men from working-class Viet Kieu men. Women like Ngoc avoided men whom they thought were *working-class Viet Kieu* because these women had no desire to develop relationships that would result in marriage and migration. As Ngoc said:

> I love Vietnam and I am comfortable here. I don't want to live anywhere else. In Vietnam, when you have money, you can afford everything. I have aunts and uncles in America, and you know in America people have to clean their own houses, buy their own food, and cook it themselves. I speak English, but I know that I could never get a job overseas that will pay me enough to live

like this. Life here is just so much easier if you have money. If my family was poor, I think I would want to marry someone who will take me to the U.S., so that I could live a better life. I am not poor. Why would I give up this life?

Ngoc's ability to live a high-end lifestyle year round kept her in short term, noncommittal relationships with several Viet Kieu men, who spent large sums of money on her while they were in Vietnam. She was aware that immigrants from Vietnam to first-world countries rarely find coveted jobs in the primary labor market, often ending up with low-status, low-paying jobs instead (Thai 2008). She had no desire to marry and migrate abroad, because the possibility of downward mobility was too great. On another occasion, I asked Ngoc, "If you have the money already, and you don't want to live in the U.S., why do you spend your time with these men?" She responded [in English]:

I am 26 years old and I don't want to settle down yet. Marriage here is not easy. I see so many husbands cheat on their wives with younger, more attractive women and I want to have fun for as long as I can. It's temporary: these men will eventually go back home, and it is nice to be spoiled with nice gifts and extra money. I have fun doing it. I'm young, so why not, right? I can't do this when I'm in my 30s, so that's when I'll get married.

Ngoc's social, cultural, economic, and physical advantages allowed her to move with ease in spaces where high-end Viet Kieu men spent their time and money. Her body capital, economic resources, and ability to convey a high-class image enabled her to exert power over her clients.

In June 2007, Ngoc introduced me to Tuan, a Viet Kieu from France who had worked as an orthodontist for 15 years in France before returning to Vietnam to open a practice. During one of four informal interviews with Tuan over coffee, he remarked:

I am 39, almost 40 years old, and I am not ready to settle down with anyone, but I don't want to spend my days alone either. This is a fun city to go out in at night. I don't want to be tied down, so I spend my time with girls who are sort of working. I mean, I know that I have to buy her things and spend money on her. Otherwise, she won't waste her time with me. I can't be with just any girl, either. I need to be with someone who is young and beautiful. When you go out in Vietnam, people see you. If you have money, you can't have a cheap girl.

Viet Kieu men looked for intimate relationships with local women that involved more than just sex. These men purchased the services of women whose skills and looks distinguished them from the lower-class sex workers who accompanied white men. Men like Tuan wanted to be around women who helped them display their masculinity in very public places (Allison 1994). High-end sex workers were better than women in other tiers at disguising the nature of their relationships as boyfriend-girlfriend relations rather than client-worker relations, because they did not work as disguised bartenders. Instead, they could afford to pay for drinks and services in the high-end bars and cafes that cater to foreigners.

Moreover, while relations of intimacy certainly involved sex in private spaces, the relationships took place in very public places like local bars, cafes, restaurants, hotels, and on the streets. The multiple sites of intimate labors went hand in hand with the multiple forms of compensation. These clients often spent large sums of money on expensive cellular phones, motorbikes, and designer handbags and clothing for the sex workers, all of which served as markers of distinction. The clients were often willing to spend liberally on gifts for their women because—as Thanh, a computer technician from Paris, explained—"I don't go to those low-class dirty girls, you know? These girls are young and pretty, and other men want them. You know they are smart, they speak English, and they come from good families." In short, the purchase of intimacy from high-end sex workers involved the deployment of economic, cultural, and bodily capital. In return, high-end clients compensated women with expensive gifts and cash. However, the cash was always framed as a gift and not, as in the middle and lower sectors, a way of fulfilling a need.

Viet Kieu men also sought relations with local women who embodied their ideals of Vietnamese femininity. When I asked Tuan why he preferred local Vietnamese women to Viet Kieu women, he said:

The women whom I dated back in France all had careers. One was a lawyer. [She] loved me a lot, but she was too independent, and as a man, I just wanted to feel like I could protect her. I didn't feel that way. I didn't feel like a man who could take care of her, because she was just too independent.

As Tuan stated, Vietnamese women could make men like him feel good because, unlike women in the West, they knew how to foreground their dependence on men and shunt their autonomy into the background in a way that made men feel important.

Viet Kieu men, unlike white men, had the linguistic and cultural resources to participate in the high-end sector. Whereas in the low-end and mid-tier sectors clients and sex workers talked more directly and explicitly about forms of payment, relations between men and women in the high-end sector often involved more indirect and discreet exchanges. In fact, because so many of the high-end sex workers disguised their labor so skillfully, many of the white men in my study could not figure out how to engage in relations with high-end women. In contrast, Viet Kieu men were comfortable participating in the oblique, elaborate pas de deux that high-end sex workers expected. This was most evident in moments of rupture, when relationships between clients and sex workers in the high-end sector grew precarious. Clients understood that they needed to compensate the women in some way; otherwise, their relationships would dissolve.

In my conversations with high-end sex workers and clients, the physical act of sex served both as a way for sex workers to distinguish themselves as upscale women and to make clients feel more intimately involved. These women often withheld sex from their clients, projecting the image that they were not *easy* girls who would go with just anyone.

Economic and intimate relations in this sector were closely intertwined, as both clients and sex workers went to great lengths to distinguish themselves as high-end. The consumption practices of high-end women enabled men like Tuan to distinguish themselves from the white men who participated in the mid-tier market. While some white men spent just as much money in their relations with mid-tier sex workers, they justified their consumption practices in different ways. White men engaged in relations with women who *needed* help, while Viet Kieu men engaged in relations with women who helped them assert a particular class status in public. This cultural logic of desire (Constable 2003) is embedded not only in a client's ability to engage in relations with high-end women but also in the sex worker's ability to distinguish herself from mid-tier and low-end sex workers who do not have her bodily, cultural, social, and symbolic capital. Women like Ngoc are among the most sophisticated workers because they have the money, skill, and looks to mask their work. Clients in the high-end sector pay for intimate relationships characterized by a hidden set of intimate labors that are intertwined with a complex set of economic arrangements. While low-end women provide their clients mainly with sexual services, women in the high-end sector provide their clients with short-term physical, sexual, and emotionally intimate encounters.

DISCUSSION QUESTIONS

1. What role did race and ethnicity play in the sexual marketplace in Ho Chi Minh City? What other factors intersected with race and ethnicity to shape the types of clients that the women had?

2. What are the different types of capital discussed in the article? In what aspect of your own life do these types of capital play a role?

3. Are there any similarities between the three different tiers of sexual markets in Ho Chi Minh City and the different types of sexual experiences that college students have?

4. What role does globalization play in shaping the sex industry in Vietnam? How might globalization play a role in your choice of romantic partner?

REFERENCES

Allison, Anne. 1994. Nightwork: Sexuality, pleasure, and corporate masculinity in a Tokyo hostess club. Chicago: University of Chicago Press.

Bernstein, Elizabeth. 2007. Temporarily yours: Intimacy, authenticity, and the commerce of sex. Chicago: University of Chicago Press.

Boris, Eileen, Stephanie Gilmore, and Rhacel Parrenas. 2010. Sexual labors: Interdisciplinary perspectives toward sex as work. Sexualities 23:131–37.

Bourdieu, Pierre. 1977. Outline of a theory of practice. Cambridge: Cambridge University Press.

Bourdieu, Pierre. 1984. Distinction: A social critique of the judgment of taste. Cambridge, MA: Harvard University Press.

Bourdieu, Pierre. 1986. The forms of capital. In Handbook of theory and research for the sociology of education, edited by J. Richardson. New York: Greenwood.

Bourdieu, Pierre, and Loic Wacquant. 1992. An invitation to reflexive sociology. Chicago: University of Chicago Press.

Brennan, Denise. 2004. What's love got to do with it? Transnational desires and sex tourism in the Dominican Republic. Durham: Duke University Press.

Cabezas, Amalia. 2009. Economies of desire: Sex and tourism in Cuba and the Dominican Republic. Philadelphia: Temple University Press.

Coalition against Trafficking in Women (CATW). 2005. Trafficking and prostitution in Asia and the Pacific, http://www.catw-ap.org/programs/research-documentation-publications/facts-and-statistics/.

Constable, Nicole. 2003. Romance on a global stage: Pen pals, virtual ethnography, and "mail-order" marriages. Berkeley: University of California Press.

Hayton, Bill. 2010. Vietnam: Rising dragon. New Haven: Yale University Press.

Hoang, Kimberly Kay. 2010. Economies of emotion, familiarity fantasy and desire: Emotional labor in Ho Chi Minh City's sex industry. Sexualities 13: 255–72.

Hoogvelt, Ankie. 1997. Globalization and the postcolonial world: The new political economy of development. Hampshire: Macmillan.

Lamont, Michele. 1992. Money, morals and manners: The culture of the French and the American upper-middle class. Chicago: University of Chicago Press.

MacKinnon, Catharine. 1982. Feminism, Marxism, method, and the state: An agenda for theory. Signs 7: 515–44.

Nguyen-Vo, Thu-Huong. 2008. The ironies of freedom sex, culture, and neoliberal governance in Vietnam. Seattle: University of Washington Press.

Pateman, Carole. 1988. The sexual contract. Stanford: Stanford University Press.

Pham, Chi Do. 2003. The Vietnamese economy: Awakening the dormant dragon. New York: Routledge.

Rosen, Eva, and Sudhir Venkatesh. 2008. A "perversion" of choice: Sex work offers just enough in Chicago's urban ghetto. Journal of Contemporary Ethnography 37:417–41.

Sassen, Saskia. 2001. The global city: New York, London, Tokyo. Princeton: Princeton University Press.

Sassen, Saskia. 2002. Global cities and survival circuits. In Global woman: Nannies, maids, and sex workers in the new economy, edited by B. Ehrenreich and A. Hochschild. Edited by New York: Metropolitan Books.

Smith, Michael Peter, and Luis Eduardo Guarnizo. 1998. Transnationalism from below. New Brunswick: Transaction Publishers.

Thai, Hung. 2008. For better or for worse: Vietnamese international marriages in the new global economy. New York: Rutgers University Press.

Truong, Thanh-Dan. 1990. Sex, money and morality: Prostitution and tourism in Southeast Asia. London: Zed Books.

Wacquant, Loic. 1995. Pugs at work: Bodily capital and bodily labour among professional boxers. Body & Society 1: 65–93.

Weitzer, Ronald. 2010. The ethnography of prostitution: New international perspectives. Contemporary Sociology 39: 262–69.

Wonders, Nancy, and Raymond Michalowski. 2001. Bodies, borders and sex tourism in a globalized world: A tale of two cities—Amsterdam and Havana. Social Problems 48: 545–71.

WTO. 2006. General council approves Vietnam's membership. WTO: 2006 Press Releases, vol. Press/455.

Zelizer, Viviana. 2004. The social meaning of money. New York: Basic Books.

Zelizer, Viviana. 2005. The purchase of intimacy. Princeton: Princeton University Press.

Zheng, Tiantian. 2009. Red lights: The lives of sex workers in postsocialist china. Minneapolis: University of Minnesota Press.

NOTE

1. All of the conversations that I had with the women in the low-end sector took place in Vietnamese. The quotations are my English translations.

Social Class

The Uses of Poverty

The Poor Pay All

Herbert J. Gans

Efforts to significantly reduce or eliminate the number of people living in poverty have been underway for decades. While the approach has varied, from Roosevelt's New Deal in the 1930s to the welfare reforms enacted by Bill Clinton in 1996, poverty has remained stubbornly on the American landscape. In 2013, over 46 million Americans, about 15% of the population, lived below the poverty line. In this article, Herbert Gans proposes a very different explanation of why poverty is so hard to get rid of. Relying on the functionalist perspective, he argues that having a group of people who are poor serves many useful social functions. These functions benefit and stabilize society at large in many ways. It's important to note that he isn't arguing that poverty is good or enjoyable for those who live in it. Rather, he is arguing that because having people who are poor has benefits for those who are not poor, it's unlikely to disappear anytime soon. As you read, think about how Gans' perspective differs from how the causes of poverty is typically discussed on the news or among your family and friends.

S ome twenty years ago Robert K. Merton applied the notion of functional analysis to explain the continuing though maligned existence of the urban political machine: if it continued to exist, perhaps it fulfilled latent - unintended or unrecognized - positive functions. Clearly it did. Merton pointed out how the political machine provided central authority to get things done when a decentralized local government could not act, humanized the services of the impersonal bureaucracy for fearful citizens, offered concrete help (rather than abstract law or justice) to the poor, and otherwise performed services needed or demanded by many people but considered unconventional or even illegal by formal public agencies.

"The Uses of Poverty: The Poor Pay All," by Herbert J. Gans from *Social Policy*, July/August 1971. Reprinted with permission from Social Policy Magazine.

Today, poverty is more maligned than the political machine ever was; yet it, too, is a persistent social phenomenon. Consequently, there may be some merit in applying functional analysis to poverty, in asking whether it also has positive functions that explain its persistence.

Merton defined functions as "those observed consequences [of a phenomenon] which make for the adaptation or adjustment of a given [social] system." I shall use a slightly different definition; instead of identifying functions for an entire social system, I shall identify them for the interest groups, socio-economic classes, and other population aggregates with shared values that 'inhabit' a social system. I suspect that in a modern heterogeneous society, few phenomena are functional or dysfunctional for the society as a whole, and that most result in benefits to some groups and costs to others. Nor are any phenomena indispensable; in most instances, one can suggest what Merton calls "functional alternatives" or equivalents for them, i.e., other social patterns or policies that achieve the same positive functions but avoid the dysfunctions.

Associating poverty with positive functions seems at first glance to be unimaginable. Of course, the slumlord and the loan shark are commonly known to profit from the existence of poverty, but they are viewed as evil men, so their activities are classified among the dysfunctions of poverty. However, what is less often recognized, at least by the conventional wisdom, is that poverty also makes possible the existence or expansion of respectable professions and occupations, for example, penology, criminology, social work, and public health. More recently, the poor have provided jobs for professional and para-professional "poverty warriors," and for journalists and social scientists, this author included, who have supplied the information demanded by the revival of public interest in poverty.

Clearly, then, poverty and the poor may well satisfy a number of positive functions for many nonpoor groups in American society. I shall describe thirteen such functions - economic, social and political - that seem to me most significant.

The Functions of Poverty

First, the existence of poverty ensures that society's "dirty work" will be done. Every society has such work: physically dirty or dangerous, temporary, dead-end and underpaid, undignified and menial jobs. Society can fill these jobs by paying higher wages than for "clean" work, or it can force people who have no other choice to do the dirty work - and at low wages. In America, poverty functions to provide a low-wage labor pool that is willing - or rather, unable to be unwilling - to perform dirty work at low cost. Indeed, this function of the poor is so important that in some Southern states, welfare payments have been cut off during the summer months when the poor are needed to work in the fields. Moreover, much of the debate about the Negative Income Tax and the Family Assistance Plan [welfare programs] has concerned their impact on the work incentive, by which is actually meant the incentive of the poor to do the needed dirty work if the wages therefrom are no larger than the income grant. Many economic activities that involve dirty work depend on the poor for their existence: restaurants, hospitals, parts of the garment industry, and "truck farming," among others, could not persist in their present form without the poor.

Second, because the poor are required to work at low wages, they subsidize a variety of economic activities that benefit the affluent. For example, domestics subsidize the upper middle and upper classes, making life easier for their employers and freeing affluent women for a variety of professional, cultural, civic and partying activities. Similarly, because the poor pay a higher proportion of their income in property and sales taxes, among others, they subsidize many state and local governmental services that benefit more affluent groups. In addition, the poor support innovation in medical practice as patients in teaching and research hospitals and as guinea pigs in medical experiments.

Third, poverty creates jobs for a number of occupations and professions that serve or "service" the poor, or protect the rest of society from them. As already noted, penology would be minuscule without the poor, as would the police. Other activities and groups that flourish because of the existence of poverty are the numbers game, the sale of heroin and cheap wines and liquors, Pentecostal ministers, faith healers, prostitutes, pawn shops, and the peacetime army, which recruits its enlisted men mainly from among the poor.

Fourth, the poor buy goods others do not want and thus prolong the economic usefulness of such goods - day-old bread, fruit and vegetables that otherwise would have to be thrown out, secondhand clothes, and deteriorating automobiles and buildings. They also provide incomes for doctors, lawyers, teachers, and others who are too old, poorly trained or incompetent to attract more affluent clients.

In addition to economic functions, the poor perform a number of social functions: Fifth, the poor can be identified and punished as alleged or real deviants in order to uphold the legitimacy of conventional norms. To justify the desirability of hard work, thrift, honesty, and monogamy, for example, the defenders of these norms must be able to find people who can be accused of being lazy, spendthrift, dishonest, and promiscuous. Although there is some evidence that the poor are about as moral and law-abiding as anyone else, they are more likely than middle-class transgressors to be caught and punished when they participate in deviant acts. Moreover, they lack the political and cultural power to correct the stereotypes that other people hold of them and thus continue to be thought of as lazy, spendthrift, etc., by those who need living proof that moral deviance does not pay.

Sixth, and conversely, the poor offer vicarious participation to the rest of the population in the uninhibited sexual, alcoholic, and narcotic behavior in which they are alleged to participate and which, being freed from the constraints of affluence, they are often thought to enjoy more than the middle classes. Thus many people, some social scientists included, believe that the poor not only are more given to uninhibited behavior (which may be true, although it is often motivated by despair more than by lack of inhibition) but derive more pleasure from it than affluent people (which research by Lee Rainwater, Walter Miller and others shows to be patently untrue). However, whether the poor actually have more sex and enjoy it more is irrelevant; so long as middle-class people believe this to be true, they can participate in it vicariously when instances are reported in factual or fictional form.

Seventh, the poor also serve a direct cultural function when culture created by or for them is adopted by the more affluent. The rich often collect artifacts from extinct folk cultures of poor people; and almost all Americans listen to the blues, Negro spirituals, and country music, which originated among the Southern poor. Recently they have enjoyed the rock styles that were born, like the Beatles, in the slums, and in the last year, poetry written by ghetto children has become popular in literary circles. The poor also serve as culture heroes, particularly, of course, to the Left; but the hobo, the cowboy, the hipster, and the mythical prostitute with a heart of gold have performed this function for a variety of groups.

Eighth, poverty helps to guarantee the status of those who are not poor. In every hierarchical society, someone has to be at the bottom; but in American society, in which social mobility is an important goal for many and people need to know where they stand, the poor function as a reliable and relatively permanent measuring rod for status comparisons. This is particularly true for the working class, whose politics is influenced by the need to maintain status distinctions between themselves and the poor, much as the aristocracy must find ways of distinguishing itself from the nouveaux riches.

Ninth, the poor also aid the upward mobility of groups just above them in the class hierarchy. Thus a goodly number of Americans have entered the middle class through the profits earned from the provision of goods and services in the slums, including illegal or nonrespectable ones that upper-class and upper-middle-class businessmen shun because of their low prestige. As a result, members of almost every immigrant group have financed their upward mobility by providing slum housing, entertainment, gambling, narcotics, etc., to later arrivals - most recently to Blacks and Puerto Ricans.

Tenth, the poor help to keep the aristocracy busy, thus justifying its continued existence. "Society" uses the poor as clients of settlement houses and beneficiaries of charity affairs; indeed, the aristocracy must have the poor to demonstrate its superiority over other elites who devote themselves to earning money.

Eleventh, the poor, being powerless, can be made to absorb the costs of change and growth in American society. During the nineteenth century, they did the backbreaking work that built the cities; today, they are pushed out of their neighborhoods to make room for "progress." Urban renewal projects to hold middle-class taxpayers in the city and expressways to enable suburbanites to commute downtown have typically been located in poor neighborhoods, since no other group will allow itself to be displaced. For the same reason, universities, hospitals, and civic centers also expand into land occupied by the poor. The major costs of the industrialization of agriculture have been borne by the poor, who are pushed off the land without recompense; and they have paid a large share of the human cost of the growth of American power overseas, for they have provided many of the foot soldiers for Vietnam and other wars.

Twelfth, the poor facilitate and stabilize the American political process. Because they vote and participate in politics less than other groups, the political system is often free to ignore them. Moreover, since they can rarely support Republicans, they often provide the Democrats with a captive constituency that has no other place to go. As a result, the Democrats can count on their votes, and be more responsive to voters - for example, the white working class - who might otherwise switch to the Republicans.

Thirteenth, the role of the poor in upholding conventional norms (see the fifth point, above) also has a significant political function. An economy based on the ideology of laissez faire requires a deprived population that is allegedly unwilling to work or that can be considered inferior because it must accept charity or welfare in order to survive. Not only does the alleged moral deviancy of the poor reduce the moral pressure on the present political economy to eliminate poverty but socialist alternatives can be made to look quite unattractive if those who will benefit most from them can be described as lazy, spendthrift, dishonest and promiscuous.

The Alternatives

I have described thirteen of the more important functions poverty and the poor satisfy in American society, enough to support the functionalist thesis that poverty, like any other social phenomenon, survives in part because it is useful to society or some of its parts. This analysis is not intended to suggest that because it is often functional, poverty should exist, or that it must exist. For one thing, poverty has many more dysfunctions that functions; for another, it is possible to suggest functional alternatives.

For example, society's dirty work could be done without poverty, either by automation or by paying "dirty workers" decent wages. Nor is it necessary for the poor to subsidize the many activities they support through their low-wage jobs. This would, however, drive up the costs of these activities, which would result in higher prices to their customers and clients. Similarly, many of the professionals who flourish because of the poor could be given other roles. Social workers could provide counseling to the affluent, as they prefer to do anyway; and the police could devote themselves to traffic and organized crime. Other roles would have to be found for badly trained or incompetent professionals now relegated to serving the poor, and someone else would have to pay their salaries. Fewer penologists would be employable, however. And Pentecostal religion probably could not survive without the poor - nor would parts of the second- and third-hand goods market. And in many cities, "used" housing that no one else wants would then have to be torn down at public expense.

Alternatives for the cultural functions of the poor could be found more easily and cheaply. Indeed, entertainers, hippies, and adolescents are already serving as the deviants needed to uphold traditional morality and as devotees of orgies to "staff " the fantasies of vicarious participation. The status functions of the poor are another matter. In a hierarchical society, some people must be defined as inferior to everyone else with respect to a variety of attributes, but they need not be poor in the absolute sense. One could conceive of a society in which the "lower class," though last in the pecking order, received 75 percent of the median income, rather than 15-40 percent, as is now the case. Needless to say, this would require considerable income redistribution.

The contribution the poor make to the upward mobility of the groups that provide them with goods and services could also be maintained without the poor's having such low incomes. However, it is true that if the poor were more affluent, they would have access to enough capital to take over the provider role, thus competing with and perhaps rejecting the "outsiders." (Indeed, owing in part to antipoverty programs, this is already happening in a number of ghettos, where white storeowners are being replaced by Blacks.) Similarly, if the poor were more affluent, they would make less willing clients for upper-class philanthropy, although some would still use settlement houses to achieve upward mobility, as they do now. Thus "Society" could continue to run its philanthropic activities.

The political functions of the poor would be more difficult to replace. With increased affluence the poor would probably obtain more political power and be more active politically. With higher incomes and more political power, the poor would be likely to resist paying the costs of growth and change. Of course, it is possible to imagine urban renewal and highway projects that properly reimbursed the displaced people, but such projects would then become considerably more expensive, and many might never be built. This, in turn, would reduce the comfort and convenience of those who now benefit from urban renewal and expressways. Finally, hippies could serve also as more deviants to justify the existing political economy - as they already do. Presumably, however, if poverty were eliminated, there would be fewer attacks on that economy. In sum, then, many of the functions served by the poor could be replaced if poverty were eliminated, but almost always at higher costs to others, particularly more affluent others. Consequently, a functional analysis must conclude that poverty persists not only because it fulfills a number of positive functions but also because many of the functional alternatives to poverty would be quite dysfunctional for the affluent members of society. A functional analysis thus ultimately arrives at much the same conclusion as radical sociology, except that radical thinkers treat as manifest what I describe as latent: that social phenomena that are functional for affluent or powerful groups and dysfunctional for poor or powerless ones persist; that when the elimination of such phenomena through functional alternatives would generate dysfunctions for the affluent or powerful, they will continue to persist; and that phenomena like poverty can be eliminated only when they become dysfunctional for the affluent or powerful, or when the powerless can obtain enough power to change society.

DISCUSSION QUESTIONS

1. What are some of the useful functions of poverty Gans lists? Do you benefit from any of these functions?

2. Does Gans think that it is impossible to get rid of poverty or just that it is unlikely it will happen? What is his reasoning?

3. How might Gans's argument about the role of poverty in society be related to the difficulty of stemming illegal immigration into the United States?

Unequal Childhoods

Class, Race, and Family Life

Annette Lareau

Much attention has been paid to how experiences in childhood shape us as adults. A great deal of this research focuses on how formative experiences affect our personalities and the types of relationships we have as adults. While it is well established that the social class of your parents is an excellent predictor of your future social class, exactly how this happens isn't as straightforward as it seems. Certainly the amount of wealth a family has contributes to things like quality of education (via neighborhood), social contacts, and formative experiences (attending sailing camp as opposed to playing in the neighborhood vacant lot for example). But there are even more subtle ways that social class influences our life chances. In this article, Annette Lareau uses a sociological approach to examine how social class is reproduced through different parenting styles. The results of her careful ethnographic study reveal general differences in the approach and philosophy of parenting by working-class versus middle-class parents, what she terms the natural growth approach and the concerted cultivation approach. Each has clear benefits and drawbacks for kids, but it is the concerted cultivation approach that middle-class parents use that implicitly teaches children how to negotiate and navigate in social interactions in a way that opens more doors of opportunity and leads to greater rewards.

As you read, think about your own childhood experience. Which approach most closely describes your experience? How do you think you would have benefited if you had grown up in a family that used the other approach?

Laughing and yelling, a white fourth-grader named Garrett Tallinger splashes around in the swimming pool in the backyard of his four-bedroom home in the suburbs on a late spring afternoon. As on most evenings, after a quick dinner his father drives him to soccer practice. This is only one of Garrett's many activities. His brother has a baseball game at a different location. There are evenings when the boys' parents relax, sipping a glass of wine. Tonight is not one of them. As they rush to change out of their work clothes and get the children ready for practice, Mr. and Mrs. Tallinger are harried.

Only ten minutes away, a Black fourth-grader, Alexander Williams, is riding home from a school open house.[1] His mother is driving their beige, leather-upholstered Lexus. It is 9:00 P.M. on a Wednesday evening. Ms. Williams is tired from work and has a long Thursday ahead of her. She will get up at 4:45 A.M. to go out of town on business and will not return before 9:00 P.M. On Saturday morning, she will chauffeur Alexander to a private piano lesson at 8:15 A.M., which will be followed by a choir rehearsal and then a soccer game. As they ride in the dark, Alexander's mother, in a quiet voice, talks with her son, asking him questions and eliciting his opinions. In interactions with professionals, the Williamses, like some other middle-class parents in the study, seem relaxed and communicative. They want Alex to feel this way too, so they teach him how to be an informed, assertive client. On one hot summer afternoon, Ms. Williams uses a doctor visit as an opportunity for this kind of instruction. During the drive to the doctor's office, the field-worker listens as Ms. Williams prepares Alexander to be assertive during his regular checkup: As we enter Park Lane, [Christina] says quietly to Alex, "Alexander you should be thinking of questions you might want to ask the doctor. You can ask him anything you want. Don't be shy. You can ask anything." Alex thinks for a minute, then says, "I have some bumps under my arms from my deodorant. Christina: "Really? You mean from your new deodorant?" Alex: "Yes." Christina: "Well, you should ask the doctor."

Alex's mother is teaching him that he has the right to speak up (e.g., "don't be shy"; "you can ask anything"). Most important, she is role modeling the idea that he should prepare for an encounter with a person in a position of authority by gathering his thoughts ahead of time

Discussions between parents and children are a hallmark of middle-class child rearing. Like many middle-class parents, Ms. Williams and her husband see themselves as "developing" Alexander to cultivate his talents in a concerted fashion. Organized activities, established and controlled by mothers and fathers, dominate the lives of middle-class children such as Garrett and Alexander. By making certain their children have these and other experiences, middle-class parents engage in a process of *concerted cultivation*. From this, a robust sense of entitlement takes root in the children: This sense of entitlement plays an especially important role in institutional settings, where middle-class children learn to question adults and address them as relative equals.

Only twenty minutes away, in blue-collar neighborhoods, and slightly farther away, in public housing projects, childhood looks different. Mr. Yanelji, a white working-class father, picks up his son Little Billy, a fourth-grader, from an after-school program. They come home and Mr. Yanelli drinks a beer while Little Billy first watches television, then rides his bike and plays in the street. Other nights, he and his Dad sit on the sidewalk outside their house and play cards. At about 5:30 P.M. Billy's mother gets home from her job as a house cleaner. She fixes dinner and the entire family sits down to eat together. Extended family are a prominent part of their lives. Ms. Yanelli touches base with her "entire family every day" by phone. Many nights Little Billy's uncle stops by, sometimes bringing Little Billy's youngest cousin. In the spring, Little Billy plays baseball on a local team. Unlike for Garrett and Alexander, who have at least four activities a week, for Little Billy, baseball is his only organized activity outside of school during the entire year. Down the road, a white working-class girl, Wendy Driver, also spends the evening with her girl cousins, as they watch a video and eat popcorn, crowded together on the living room floor.

Farther away, a Black fourth-grade boy, Harold McAllister, plays outside on a summer evening in the public housing project in which he lives. His two male cousins are there that night, as they often are. After an afternoon spent unsuccessfully searching for a ball so they could play basketball, the boys had resorted to watching sports on television. Now they head outdoors for a twilight water balloon fight. Harold tries to get his neighbor, Miss Latifa, wet. People sit in white plastic lawn chairs outside the row of apartments. Music and television sounds waft through the open windows and doors.

The adults in the lives of Billy, Wendy, and Harold want the best for them. Formidable economic constraints make it a major life task for these parents to put food on the table, arrange for housing, negotiate unsafe neighborhoods, take children to the doctor (often waiting for city buses that do not come), clean children's clothes, and get children to bed and have them ready for school the next morning. But unlike middle-class parents, these adults do not consider the concerted development of children, particularly through organized leisure activities, an essential aspect of good parenting. Unlike the Tallingers and Williamses, these mothers and fathers do not focus on concerted cultivation. For them, the crucial responsibilities of parenthood do not lie in eliciting their children's feelings, opinions, and thoughts. Rather, they see a clear boundary between adults and children. Parents tend to use directives: they tell their children what to do rather than persuading them with reasoning. Unlike their middle-class counterparts, who have a steady diet of adult organized activities, the working-class and poor children have more control over the character of their leisure activities. Most children are free to go out and play with friends and relatives who typically live close by. Their parents and guardians facilitate the *accomplishment of natural growth*.[2] Yet these children and their parents interact with central institutions in the society, such as schools, which firmly and

Table 22.1 Typology of Differences in Child Rearing

	Child-Rearing Approach	
	Concerted Cultivation	Accomplishment of Natural Growth
Key Elements	Parent actively fosters and assesses child's talents opinions, and skills	Parent cares for child and allows child to grow
Organization of Daily Life	Multiple child leisure activities orchestrated by adults	"Hanging out," particularly with kin, by child
Language Use	Reasoning/directives; child contestation of adult statements; extended negotiations between parents and child	Directives; rare questioning or challenging of adults by child; general acceptance by child of directives
Interventions in Institutions	Criticisms and interventions on behalf of child; training of child to take on this role	Dependence on institutions; sense of powerlessness and frustration; conflict between child-rearing practices at home and at school
Consequences	Emerging sense of entitlement on the part of the child	Emerging sense of constraint on the part of the child

decisively promote strategies of concerted cultivation in child rearing. For working-class and poor families, the cultural logic of child rearing at home is out of synch with the standards of institutions. As a result, while children whose parents adopt strategies of concerted cultivation appear to gain a sense of entitlement, children such as Billy Yanelli, Wendy Driver, and Harold McAllister appear to gain an emerging sense of distance, distrust, and constraint in their institutional experiences.

What is the outcome of these different philosophies and approaches to child rearing? Quite simply, they appear to lead to the transmission of differential advantages to children. In this study, there was quite a bit more talking in middle-class homes than in working-class and poor homes, leading to the development of greater verbal agility, larger vocabularies, more comfort with authority figures, and more familiarity with abstract concepts. Importantly, children also developed skill differences in interacting with authority figures in institutions and at home. Middle-class children such as Garrett Tallinger and Alexander Williams learn, as young boys, to shake the hands of adults and look them in the eye. In studies of job interviews, investigators have found that potential employees have less than one minute to make a good impression. Researchers stress the importance of eye contact, firm handshakes, and displaying comfort with bosses during the interview. In poor families like Harold McAllister's, however, family members usually do not look each other in the eye when conversing. In addition, as Elijah Anderson points out, they live in neighborhoods where it can be dangerous to look people in the eye too long.[3] The types of social competence transmitted in the McAllister family are valuable, but they are potentially less valuable (in employment interviews, for example) than those learned by Garrett Tallinger and Alexander Williams.

The white and Black middle-class children in this study also exhibited an emergent version of the sense of entitlement characteristic of the middle-class. They acted as though they had a right to pursue their own individual preferences and to actively manage interactions in institutional settings. They appeared comfortable in these settings; they were open to sharing information and asking for attention. Although some children were more outgoing than others, it was common practice among middle-class children to shift interactions to suit their preferences. Alexander Williams knew how to get the doctor to listen to his concerns (about the bumps under his arm from his new deodorant). His mother explicitly trained and encouraged him to speak up with the doctor. Similarly, a Black middle-class girl, Stacey Marshall, was taught by her mother to expect the gymnastics teacher to accommodate her individual learning style. Thus, middle-class children were trained in "the rules of the game" that govern interactions with institutional representatives. They were not conversant in other important social skills, however, such as organizing their time for hours on end during weekends and summers, spending long periods of time away from adults, or hanging out with adults in a nonobtrusive, subordinate fashion. Middle-class children also learned (by imitation and by direct training) how to make the rules work in their favor. Here, the enormous stress on reasoning and negotiation in the home also has a potential advantage for future institutional negotiations. Additionally, those in authority responded positively to such interactions. Even in fourth grade, middle-class children appeared to be acting on their own behalf to gain advantages. They made special requests of teachers and doctors to adjust procedures to accommodate their desires.

The working-class and poor children, by contrast, showed an emerging sense of constraint in their interactions in institutional settings. They were less likely to try to customize interactions to suit their own preferences. Like their parents, the children accepted the actions of persons in authority (although at times they also covertly resisted them). Working-class and poor parents sometimes were not as aware of their children's school situation (as when their children were not doing homework). Other times, they dismissed the school rules as unreasonable. For example, Wendy Driver's mother told her to "punch" a boy who was pestering her in class; Billy Yanelli's parents were proud of him when he "beat up" another boy on the playground, even though Billy was then suspended from school. Parents also had trouble getting "the school" to respond to their concerns. When Ms. Yanelli complained that she "hates" the school, she gave her son a lesson in powerlessness and frustration in the face of an important institution. Middle-class children such as Stacey Marshall learned to make demands on professionals, and when they succeeded in making the rules work in their favor they augmented their "cultural capital" (i.e., skills individuals inherit that can then be translated into different forms of value as they move through various institutions) for the future.[4] When working-class and poor children confronted institutions, however, they generally were unable to make the rules work in their favor nor did they obtain capital for adulthood. Because of these patterns of legitimization, children raised according to the logic of concerted cultivation can gain advantages, in the form of an emerging sense of entitlement, while children raised according to the logic of natural growth tend to develop an emerging sense of constraint.[5]

How Does It Matter?

Both concerted cultivation and the accomplishment of natural growth offer intrinsic benefits (and burdens) for parents and their children. Nevertheless, these practices are accorded different social values by important social institutions. There are signs that some family cultural practices, notably those associated with concerted cultivation, give children advantages that other cultural practices do not.

In terms of the rhythms of daily life, both concerted cultivation and the accomplishment of natural growth have advantages and disadvantages. Middle-class children learn to develop and value an individualized sense of self. Middle-class children are allowed to participate in a variety of coveted activities: gymnastics, soccer, summer camps, and so on. These activities improve their skills and teach them, as Mr. Tallinger noted, to be better athletes than their parents were at comparable ages. They learn to handle moments of humiliation on the field as well as moments of glory. Middle-class children learn, as Mr. Williams noted, the difference between baroque and classical music. They learn to perform. They learn to present themselves. But this cultivation has a cost. Family schedules are disrupted.

Dinner hours are very hard to arrange. Siblings such as Spencer and Sam Tallinger spend dreary hours waiting at athletic fields and riding in the car going from one event to another. Family life, despite quiet interludes, is frequently frenetic. Parents, especially mothers, must reconcile conflicting priorities, juggling events whose deadlines are much tighter than the deadlines connected to serving meals or getting children ready for bed. The domination of children's activities can take a toll on families. At times, everyone in the middle-class families—including ten-year-old children—seemed exhausted. Thus, there are formidable costs, as well as benefits to this child-rearing approach.

Working-class and poor children also had advantages, as well as costs, from the cultural logic of child rearing they experienced. Working-class and poor children learned to entertain themselves. They played outside, creating their own games, as Tyrec Taylor did with his friends. They did not complain of being bored. Working-class and poor children also appeared to have boundless energy. They did not have the exhaustion that we saw in middle-class children the same age. Some working-class and poor children longed to be in organized activities—Katie Brindle wanted to take ballet and Harold McAllister wanted to play football. When finances, a lack of transportation, and limited availability of programs conspired to prevent or limit their participation, they were disappointed. Many were also deeply aware of the economic constraints and the limited consumption permitted by their family's budget. Living spaces were small, and often there was not much privacy. The television was almost always on and, like many middle-class children growing up in the 1950s, working-class and poor children watched unrestricted amounts of television. As a result, family members spent more time together in shared space than occurred in middle-class homes. Indeed, family ties were very strong, particularly among siblings. Working-class and poor children also developed very close ties with their cousins and other extended family members.

Within the home, these two approaches to child rearing each have identifiable strengths and weaknesses. When we turn to examining institutional dynamics outside the home, however, the unequal benefits of middle-class children's lives compared to working-class and poor children's lives become clearer. In crucial ways, middle-class family members appeared reasonably comfortable and entitled, while working-class and poor family members appeared uncomfortable and constrained. For example, neither Harold nor his mother seemed as comfortable as Alexander and his mother had been as they interacted with their physician. Alexander was used to extensive conversation at home; with the doctor, he was at ease initiating questions. Harold, who was used to responding to directives at home, primarily answered questions from the doctor, rather than posing his own. Unlike Ms. Williams, Ms. McAllister did not see the enthusiastic efforts of her daughter Alexis to share information about her birthmark as appropriate behavior. Ms. Williams not only permitted Alexander to hop up and down on the stool to express his enthusiasm; she explicitly trained him to be assertive and well prepared for his encounter with the doctor. Harold was reserved. He did not show an emerging sense of entitlement, as Alexander and other middle-class children did. Absorbing his mother's apparent need to conceal the truth about the range of foods in his diet, Harold appeared cautious, displaying an emerging sense of constraint.

This pattern occurred in school interactions, as well. Some working-class and poor parents had warm and friendly relations with educators. Overall, however, working-class and poor parents in this study had much more distance or separation from the school than did middle-class mothers. At home, Ms. McAllister could be quite assertive, but at school she was subdued. The parent-teacher conference yielded Ms. McAllister few insights into her son's educational experience.[6]

Other working-class and poor parents also appeared baffled, intimidated, and subdued in parent-teacher conferences. Ms. Driver, frantically worried because Wendy, a fourth-grader, was not yet able to read, resisted intervening, saying, "I don't want to jump into anything and find it is the wrong thing." When working-class and poor parents did try to intervene in their children's educational experiences, they often felt ineffectual. Billy Yanelli's mother appeared relaxed and chatty when she interacted with service personnel, such as the person who sold her lottery tickets on Saturday morning. With "the school," however, she was very apprehensive. She distrusted school personnel. She felt bullied and powerless.

There were also moments in which parents encouraged children to outwardly comply with school officials but, at the same time, urged them to resist school authority. Although well aware of school rules prohibiting fighting, the Yanellis directly trained their son to "beat up" a boy who was bothering him. Similarly, when Wendy Driver complained about a boy who pestered her and pulled her ponytail, and the teacher did not respond, her mother advised her to "punch him." Ms. Driver's boyfriend added, "Hit him when the teacher isn't looking."[7]

The unequal level of trust, as well as differences in the amount and quality of information divulged, can yield unequal profits during a historical period such as ours, when professionals applaud assertiveness and reject passivity as an inappropriate parenting strategy.[8] Middle-class children and parents often (but not always) accrued advantages or profits from their efforts. Alexander Williams succeeded in having the doctor take his medical concerns seriously. The Marshall children ended up in the gifted program, even though they did not qualify.

Overall, the routine rituals of family life are not equally legitimized in the broader society. Parents' efforts to reason with children (even two-year-olds) are seen as more educationally valuable than parents' use of directives. Spending time playing soccer or baseball is deemed by professionals as more valuable than time spent watching television. Moreover, differences in the cultural logic of child rearing are attached to unequal currency in the broader society. The middle-class strategy of concerted cultivation appears to have greater promise of being capitalized into social profits than does the strategy of the accomplishment of natural growth found in working-class and poor homes. Alexander Williams's vocabulary grew at home, in the evenings, as he bantered with his parents about plagiarism and copyright as well as about the X-Men. Harold McAllister, Billy Yanelli, and Wendy Driver learned how to manage their own time, play without the direction of adults, and occupy themselves for long periods of time without being bored. Although these are important life skills, they do not have the same payoff on standardized achievement tests as the experiences of Alexander Williams.

These potential benefits for middle-class children, and costs for working-class and poor children, are necessarily speculative, since at the end of the study, the children were still in elementary school. Still, there are important signs of hidden advantages being sown at early ages. The middle-class children have extensive experience with adults in their lives with whom they have a relatively contained, bureaucratically regulated, and somewhat superficial relationship. As children spend eight weeks playing soccer, baseball, basketball, and other activities, they meet and interact with adults acting as coaches, assistant coaches, car pool drivers, and so on. This contact with relative strangers, although of a different quality than contact with cousins, aunts, and uncles, provides work-related skills. For instance, as Garrett shakes the hand of a stranger and looks him or her in the eye, he is being groomed, in an effortless fashion, for job interviews he will have as an adult (employment experts stress the importance of good eye contact). In the McAllister home, family members have great affection and warmth toward one another, but they do not generally look each other in the eye when they speak; this training is likely to be a liability in job interviews. In settings as varied as health care and gymnastics, middle-class children learn at a young age to be assertive and demanding. They expect, as did Stacey Marshall, for institutions to be responsive to them and to accommodate their individual needs. By contrast, when Wendy Driver is told to hit the boy who is pestering her (when the teacher isn't looking) or Billy Yanelli is told to physically defend himself, despite school rules, they are not learning how to make bureaucratic institutions work to their advantage. Instead, they are being given lessons in frustration and powerlessness.

DISCUSSION QUESTIONS

1. Which of these styles was closest to your own childhood experience? Do you think there is perhaps a third or fourth model of parenting that should be examined?

2. How does concerted cultivation prepare middle-class and upper-class children for success later in life?

3. What are the advantages of the natural growth approach? What are the downsides of concerted cultivation?

4. In recent years the "helicopter parent" phenomenon has gotten a fair bit of attention. Which parenting style is this associated with? What do you think motivates parents to engage in this behavior?

5. How can parents try to balance both of these approaches to child rearing to maximize the benefits of each? What about the way our social institutions are set up would have to change in order to accommodate parents who wish to use both approaches?

NOTES

1. Choosing words to describe social groups also becomes a source of worry, especially over the possibility of reinforcing negative stereotypes. I found the available terms to describe members of racial and ethnic groups to be problematic in one way or another. The families I visited uniformly described themselves as "Black." Recognizing that some readers have strong views that Black should be capitalized, I have followed that convention, despite the lack of symmetry with the term white. In sum, this book alternates among the terms "Black," "Black American," "African American," and "white," with the understanding that "white" here refers to the subgroup of non-Hispanic whites.

2. Some readers have expressed concern that this phrase, "the accomplishment of natural growth," underemphasizes all the labor that mothers and fathers do to take care of children. They correctly note that working-class and poor parents themselves would be unlikely to use such a term to describe the process of caring for children. These concerns are important. As I stress in the text (especially in the chapter on Katie Brindle, Chapter 5) it does take an enormous amount of work for parents, especially mothers, of all classes to take care of children. But poor and working-class mothers have fewer resources with which to negotiate these demands. Those whose lives the research assistants and I studied approached the task somewhat differently than did middle-class parents. They did not seem to view children's leisure time as their responsibility; nor did they see themselves as responsible for assertively intervening in their children's school experiences. Rather, the working-class and poor parents carried out their chores,

drew boundaries and restrictions around their children, and then, within these limits, allowed their children to carry out their lives. It is in this sense that I use the term "the accomplishment of natural growth."

3. Elijah Anderson, *Code of the Street;* see especially Chapter 2.

4. For a more extensive discussion of the work of Pierre Bourdieu see the theoretical appendix; see also David Swartz's excellent book *Culture and Power*

5. I did not study the full range of families in American society, including elite families of tremendous wealth, nor, at the other end of the spectrum, homeless families. In addition, I have a purposively drawn sample. Thus, I cannot state whether there are other forms of child rearing corresponding to other cultural logics. Still, data from quantitative studies based on nationally representative data support the patterns I observed. For differences by parents' social class position and children's time use, see especially Sandra Hofferth and John Sandberg, "Changes in American Children's Time, 1981–1997." Patterns of language use with children are harder to capture in national surveys, but the work of Melvin Kohn and Carmi Schooler, especially *Work and Personality,* shows differences in parents' child-rearing values. Duane Alwin's studies of parents' desires are generally consistent with the results reported here. See Duane Alwin, "Trends in Parental Socialization Values." For differences in interventions in institutions, there is extensive work showing social class differences in parent involvement in education. See the U. S. Department of Education, *The Condition of Education, 2001,* p.175.

6. Of course, some middle-class parents also appeared slightly anxious during parent-teacher meetings. But overall, middle-class parents spoke more, and they asked educators more questions, including more critical and penetrating ones, than did working-class and poor parents.

7. Working-class and poor children often resisted and tested school rules, but they did not seem to be engaged in the same process of seeking an accommodation by educators to their own *individual* preferences that I witnessed among middle-class children. Working-class and poor children tended to react to adults' offers or, at times, plead with educators to repeat previous experiences, such as reading a particular story, watching a movie, or going to the computer room. In these interactions, the boundaries between adults and children were firmer and clearer than those with middle-class children.

8. Carol Heimer and Lisa Staffen, *For the Sake of the Children.*

The (Mis)Education of Monica and Karen

Laura Hamilton and Elizabeth A. Armstrong

A college education presents a tricky financial paradox for students and their families. On the one hand, a college education is very likely to result in higher levels of income later on in life. College graduates earn, on average, about 40 percent more than those with only a high school diploma. Even some college is associated with about 15 percent more income later on in life.[1] On the other hand, about 70 percent of college students graduate with debt, and the average amount of debt in 2015 was about 30,000 dollars.[2]

Based on these types of numbers, it might seem that deciding whether to go to college and where to go could simply be reduced to a cost benefit analysis. But as Laura Hamilton and Elizabeth Armstrong show in this article, not all students benefit from college in the same way. The majority of students who attend college do NOT go directly from high school, live on campus, attend full time, graduate in four years, and enjoy a thriving party scene while doing so. While this may be the image conjured by MTV Spring Break coverage, or worried newspapers articles about the prevalence of hooking up, successfully making it through college on this "party pathway" is mostly reserved for academically gifted, wealthy students.

Hamilton and Armstrong followed a group of women at a large, Midwest flagship public university over five years. In this article, they focus on two students, Karen and Monica, who are more accurate representatives of "typical" students. Neither is wealthy, and for both the school is academically and socially challenging. They note that many easy majors popular with those on the "party path" require particular types of cultural and social capital (habits, looks, and connections) in order to translate into job offers. These types of majors do not serve students from middle and lower classes well. They argue that these students benefit more from following a "mobility" pathway through college, where they are carefully guided into majors that are more directly skill and credential based.

[Source line. See permissions log.] To Come

Hamilton and Armstrong highlight the importance of a good fit between students and the social and structural features of their school to make college pay off financially. Of particular note is how important campus culture is to student success. Much of what students learn and how their college experience is shaped takes place outside of the classroom. They find that smaller, less prestigious state schools without Greek systems (and hence less social emphasis on partying) and with strong advising programs are most likely to lead to success for students.

As you read, think about your own school and how you're experiencing college. Was your choice of school constrained in any way or did you have lots of options? What role do you think your race, class, or gender might have played in where you wound up going to school?

M onica grew up in a small, struggling Midwestern community, population 3,000, which was once a booming factory town.

She was from a working-class family, and paid for most of her education at Midwest U, a *moderately selective* residential university, herself. She worked two jobs, sometimes over 40 hours a week, to afford in-state tuition. Going out-of-state, or to a pricey private school, was simply out of the question without a large scholarship. Attending MU was even a stretch; one year there cost as much as four years at the regional campus near her hometown.

Karen grew up in the same small town as Monica, but in a solidly middle-class family. Her college-educated parents could afford to provide more financial assistance. But even though MU was only three hours away, her father *wasn't too thrilled* about her going so far from home. He had attended a small religious school that was only 10 minutes away.

Neither Karen nor Monica was academically well prepared for college. Both had good, but not stellar, grades and passable SAT scores, which made admission to a more selective school unlikely. Given the lower cost, ease of admission, and opportunity to commute from home, they might have started at the regional campus. However, MU offered, as Monica's mother put it, a chance to "go away and experience college life." Karen refused to look at any other school because she wanted to leave home. As she noted, "I really don't think I'm a small town girl." Monica's family was betting on MU as the best place for her to launch her dream career as a doctor.

Karen and Monica's stories offer us a glimpse into the college experiences of average, in-state students at large, mid-tier public universities. Though they struggled to gain entrance to the flagship campus, they soon found that the structure of social and academic life there served them poorly—and had deleterious effects.

The Great Mismatch

There is a great gap between what the vast majority of Americans need and what four-year institutions offer them.

Most four-year residential colleges and universities in the United States are designed to serve well-funded students, who have minimal (if any) caretaking responsibilities, and who attend college full-time after they graduate from high school.

Yet only a minority of individuals who pursue postsecondary education in the United States fit this profile. There is a great gap between what the vast majority of Americans need and what four-year institutions offer them.

This mismatch is acutely visible at Midwest U, where Karen and Monica started their college careers. Almost half of those attending four-year colleges find themselves at schools like this one. Students from modest backgrounds who have above average, but not exceptional, academic profiles attend state flagship universities because they believe such schools offer a surefire route to economic security.

Public universities were founded to enable mobility, especially among in-state populations of students—which contributes to their legitimacy in the eyes of the public. In an era of declining state funding, schools like Midwest U have raised tuition and recruited more out-of-state students. They especially covet academically accomplished, ambitious children of affluent families.

As sociologist Mitchell Stevens describes in *Creating a Class*, elite institutions also pursue such students. While observing a small, private school, Stevens overhead an admissions officer describe an ideal applicant: "He's got great SATs [and] he's free [not requiring any financial aid]. . . . He helps us in every way that's quantifiable." Once private colleges skim off affluent, high-performing students, large, middle-tier, public universities are left to compete for the tuition dollars of less studious students from wealthy families.

How, we wondered, do in-state students fare in this context? To find out, for over five years we followed a dormitory floor of female students through their college careers and into the workforce, conducted an ethnography of the floor, and interviewed the women and their parents. What we found is that schools like MU only serve a segment of their student body well—affluent, socially-oriented, state students—to the detriment of typical in-state students like Karen and Monica.

"I'm Supposed to Get Drunk"

Monica and Karen approached the housing application process with little information, and were unprepared for what they encountered when they were assigned to a room in a *party dorm*. At MU, over a third of the freshman class is housed in such dorms. Though minimal partying actually took place in the heavily policed residence halls, many residents partied off-site, typically at fraternities, returning in the wee hours drunk and loud. Affluent students—both in and out-of-state—often requested rooms in party dorms, based on the recommendations of their similarly social siblings and friends.

Party dorms are a pipeline to the Greek system, which dominates campus life. Less than 20 percent of the student body at MU is involved in a fraternity or sorority, but these predominately white organizations enjoy a great deal of power. They own space in central campus areas, across from academic buildings and sports arenas. They monopolize the social life of first-year students, offering underage drinkers massive, free supplies of alcohol, with virtual legal impunity. They even enjoy special ties to administrators, with officers sitting on a special advisory board to the dean of students.

Over 40 percent of Monica and Karen's floor joined sororities their first year. The pressure to rush was so intense that one roommate pair who opted out posted a disclaimer on their door, asking people to stop bugging them about it. The entire campus—including academic functions—often revolved around the schedule of Greek life. When a math test for a large, required class conflicted with women's rush, rather than excusing a group of women from a few rush events, the test itself was rescheduled.

Monica, like most economically disadvantaged students, chose not to rush a sorority, discouraged by the mandatory 60 dollar T-shirt, as well as by the costly membership fees. Karen, who was middle class, had just enough funds to make rushing possible. However, she came to realize that Greek houses implicitly screen for social class. She pulled out her boots—practical rain boots that pegged her as a small town, in-state girl instead of an affluent, out-of-state student with money and the right taste in clothing. They were a *dead give-away*, she said. She soon dropped out of rush.

Like all but a few students on the 53-person floor, Monica and Karen chose to participate in the party scene. Neither drank much in high school. Nor did they arrive armed with shot glasses or party-themed posters, as some students did. They partied because, as a woman from a similar background put it, "I'm supposed to get drunk every weekend. I'm supposed to go to parties every weekend." With little party experience, and few contacts in the Greek system, Monica and Karen were easy targets for fraternity men's sexual disrespect. Heavy alcohol consumption helped to put them at ease in otherwise uncomfortable situations. "I pretty much became an alcoholic," said Monica. "I was craving alcohol all the time."

Their forced attempts to participate in the party scene showed how poorly it suited their needs. "I tried so hard to fit in with what everybody else was doing here," Monica explained. "I think one morning I just woke up and realized that this isn't me at all; I don't like the way I am right now." She felt it forced her to become more immature. "Growing up to me isn't going out and getting smashed and sleeping around," she lamented. Partying is particularly costly for students of lesser means, who need to grow up sooner, cannot afford to be financially irresponsible, and need the credentials and skills that college offers.

Academic Struggles and "Exotic" Majors

Partying also takes its toll on academic performance, and Monica's poor grades quickly squelched her pre-med dreams. Karen, who hoped to become a teacher, also found it hard to keep up. "I did really bad in that math class, the first elementary ed math class," one of three that were required. Rather than retake the class, Karen changed her major to one that was popular among affluent, socially-oriented students on the floor: sports broadcasting.

She explained, "I'm from a really small town and it's just all I ever really knew was jobs that were around me, and most of those are teachers." A woman on her floor was majoring in sports broadcasting, which Karen had never considered. "I would have never thought about that. And so I saw hers, and I was like that's something that I really like. One of my interests is sports, watching them, playing them," she reasoned. "I could be a sportscaster on ESPN if I really wanted to."

As Monica and Karen's stories suggest, students are not necessarily better served by attending the most selective college they can get into.

Karen's experience shows the seductive appeal of certain *easy majors*. These are occupational and professional programs that are often housed in their own schools and colleges. They are associated with a higher overall GPA and, as sociologists Richard Arum and Josipa Roksa report in *Academically Adrift*, lower levels of learning than majors in the more challenging sciences and humanities housed in colleges of arts and sciences.

In many easy majors, career success also depends on personal characteristics (such as appearance, personality, and aesthetic taste) that are developed outside of the classroom—often prior to entering college. Socially-oriented students flock to fields like communications, fashion, tourism, recreation, fitness, and numerous *business-lite* options, which are often linked to sports or the arts, rather than the competitive business school. About a third of the student body majored in business, management, marketing, communications, journalism, and related subfields.

Karen's switch to sports broadcasting gave her more time to socialize. But education is a more practical major that translates directly into a career;

hiring rests largely on the credential. In contrast, success in sports broadcasting is dependent on class-based characteristics—such as family social ties to industry insiders. Several of Karen's wealthier peers secured plum internships in big cities because their parents made phone calls for them; Karen could not even land an unpaid internship with the Triple-A baseball team located 25 minutes from her house.

No one Karen encountered on campus helped her to assess the practicality of a career in this field. Her parents were frustrated that she had been persuaded not to graduate with a recognizable marketable skill. As her mother explained, "She gets down there and you start hearing all these exotic sounding majors. . . . I'm not sure quite what jobs they're going to end up with." Her mother was frustrated that Karen "went to see the advisor to make plans for her sophomore year, and they're going, 'Well, what's your passion?'" Her mother was not impressed. "How many people do their passion? To me, that's more what you do for a hobby. . . . I mean most people, that's not what their job is."

Halfway through college, when Karen realized she could not get an internship, much less a job, in sports broadcasting, her parents told her to switch back to education. The switch was costly: it was going to take her two more years to complete. As her mother complained, "When you're going through the orientation . . . they're going, 'oh, most people change their major five times.' And they make it sound like it's no big deal. But yeah, they're making big bucks by kids changing."

Leaving Midwest U Behind

Monica left MU after her first year. "I was afraid if I continued down there that I would just go crazy and either not finish school, or get myself in trouble," she explained. "And I just didn't want to do that." She immediately enrolled in a beauty school near her home. Dissatisfied with the income she earned as a hairstylist, she later entered a community college to complete an associate degree in nursing. She paid for her nursing classes as she studied, but had 10,000 dollars in student loan debt from her time at MU. Still, her debt burden was substantially smaller than if she had stayed there; some of her MU peers had amassed over 50,000 dollars in loans by graduation.

While we were concerned that the in-state leavers, most of whom were moving down the ladder of prestige to regional campuses, would suffer, they actually did better than in-state women from less privileged families who stayed at MU.

Because her GPA was too low to return to elementary education at MU, Karen transferred to a regional college during her fourth year. Since the classes she took for sports broadcasting did not fulfill any requirements, it took her six years to graduate. Karen's parents, who reported that they spent the first 10 years of their married life paying off their own loans, took out loans to cover most of the cost, and anticipated spending even longer to finance their daughter's education.

Monica and Karen were not the only ones on their dormitory floor to leave MU. Nine other in-state women, the majority of whom were from working-class or lower-middle-class backgrounds, did as well. The only out-of-state student who transferred left for a higher-ranked institution. While we were concerned that the in-state leavers, most of whom were moving down the ladder of prestige to regional campuses, would suffer, they actually did better than in-state women from less privileged families who stayed at MU. Their GPAs improved, they selected majors with a more direct payoff, and they were happier overall.

The institutions to which women moved played a large role in this transformation. As one leaver described the regional campus to which she transferred, it "doesn't have any fraternities or sororities. It only has, like, 10 buildings." But, she said, "I just really love it." One of the things she loved was that nobody cared about partying. "They're there just to graduate and get through." It prioritized the needs of a different type of student: "Kids who have lower social economic status, who work for their school."

Without the social pressures of MU, it was possible to, as Karen put it, "get away from going out all the time, and refocus on what my goal was for this part of my life." Few majors like sports broadcasting and fashion merchandising were available, reducing the possible ways to go astray academically. Those who attended regional or community colleges trained to become accountants, teachers, social workers, nurses or other health professionals. At the conclusion of our study, they had better employment prospects than those from similar backgrounds who stayed at MU.

The Importance of Institutional Context

It is tempting to assume that academic success is determined, in large part, by what students bring with them—different ability levels, resources, and orientations to college life. But Monica and Karen's stories demonstrate that what students get out of college is also organizationally produced. Students who were far more academically gifted than Monica or Karen sometimes floundered at MU, while others who were considerably less motivated breezed through college. The best predictor of success was whether there was a good fit between a given student's resources and agendas, and the structure of the university.

Monica and Karen's struggles at MU can be attributed, in part, to the dominance of a *party pathway* at that institution. These organizational arrangements—a robust, university-supported Greek system, and an array of easy majors—are designed to attract and serve affluent, socially-oriented students. The party pathway is not a hard sell; the idea that college is about fun and partying is celebrated in popular culture and actively promoted by leisure and alcohol industries. The problem is that this pathway often appeals to students for whom it is ill suited.

Regardless of what they might want, students from different class backgrounds require different things. What Monica and Karen needed was a *mobility pathway*. When resources are limited, mistakes—whether a semester of grades lost to partying, or courses that do not count toward a credential—can be very costly. Monica and Karen needed every course to move them toward a degree that would translate directly into a job.

They also needed more financial aid than they received—grants, not loans—and much better advising. A skilled advisor who understood Karen's background and her abilities might have helped her realize that changing majors was a bad idea. But while most public universities provide such advising support for disadvantaged students, these programs are often small, and admit only the best and brightest of the disadvantaged—not run-of-the-mill students like Monica and Karen.

Monica, Karen, and others like them did not find a mobility pathway at MU. Since university resources are finite, catering to one population of students often comes at a cost to others, especially if their needs are at odds with one another. When a party pathway is the most accessible avenue through a university, it is easy to stumble upon, hard to avoid, and it crowds out other pathways.

As Monica and Karen's stories suggest, students are not necessarily better served by attending the most selective college they can get into. The structure of the pathways available at a given school greatly influences success. When selecting a college or university, families should consider much more than institutional selectivity. They should also assess whether the school fits the particular student's needs.

Students and parents with limited financial resources should look for schools with high retention rates among minority and first-generation students, where there are large and accessible student services for these populations. Visible Greek systems and reputations as party schools, in contrast, should be red flags.

Families should investigate what majors are available, whether they require prerequisites, and, to the extent it is possible, what additional investments are required to translate a particular major into a job. Are internships required? Will the school link the student to job opportunities, or are families expected to do so on their own? These are some questions they should ask.

Collectively, the priorities of public universities and other higher education institutions that support *party pathways* should be challenged. Reducing the number of easy majors, pulling university support from the Greek system, and expanding academic advising for less privileged students would help. At federal and state levels, greater commitment to the funding of higher education is necessary. If public universities are forced to rely on tuition and donations for funding, they will continue to appeal to those who can pay full freight. Without these changes, the mismatch between what universities offer and what most postsecondary students need is likely to continue.

DISCUSSION QUESTIONS

1. What are the *party path* and the *mobility path* through college? What types of students do they each benefit?

2. How is it possible for two students to have the same major, with the same GPA, yet for one to be very successful at finding a job and the other unable to?

3. How did you decide where to go to college? Was your choice of school constrained in anyway or did you have lots of options? What role do you think your race, class, or gender might have played in where you wound up going to school?

4. Listen to Episode 5: Food Fight of Malcolm Gladwell's podcast Revisionist History. http://revisionisthistory.com/episodes/05-food-fight. What is his criticism of how colleges spend their money on their students? Do you think Armstrong and Hamilton would agree or disagree with him?

5. Contact your college's admissions or institutional research office and find out what type of data about enrollment is available. What proportion of students at your school receives financial aid? What is the distribution of high school GPAs or SAT scores among this year's freshman class? How many students graduate within four years? Compare what you find out to the schools described in the article. What type of student do you think is most likely to benefit from attending your school? Is that type of student who the school admitted in this year's freshman class?

RECOMMENDED RESOURCES

Arum, Richard, and Josipa Roksa. *Academically Adrift: Limited Learning on College Campuses* (University of Chicago Press, 2011). Uses survey data from 24 institutions to offer an evaluation of what students are really learning during their time at college.

Bowen, William G., Matthew M. Chingos, and Michael S. McPherson. *Crossing the Finish Line: Completing College at America's Public Universities* (Princeton University Press, 2009). Offers a systematic analysis of the factors shaping college completion at American public universities.

Brint, Steven (ed.). *The Future of the City of Intellect: The Changing American University* (Stanford University Press, 2002). Provides an assessment of how postsecondary education is changing, the forces behind such change, and the future prospects for the sector from top scholars of higher education.

Deil-Amen, Regina. "The 'Traditional' College Student: A Smaller and Smaller Minority and Its Implications for Diversity and Access Institutions," paper prepared for the Mapping Broad-Access Higher Education conference (2011). Available online at cepa.stanford.edu. Discusses the diverse group of non-traditional college students who are marginalized despite forming a majority of the college-going population.

Stevens, Mitchell. *Creating a Class: College Admissions and the Education of Elites* (Harvard University Press, 2007). Provides an inside perspective on how admissions officers at elite private colleges construct an incoming class.

Stuber, Jenny. *Inside the College Gates: How Class and Culture Matter in Higher Education* (Lexington Books, 2011). Offers a comparison of how college social life and extra-curricular activities contribute to social class inequities at a large public and small private institution.

NOTES

1. https://www.bls.gov/emp/ep_chart_001.htm
2. http://ticas.org/posd/map-state-data#

How Homeownership Became the Engine of American Inequality

Matthew Desmond

In 2017, sociologist Matthew Desmond won a Pulitzer Prize for his book *Evicted*, which highlighted the plight of poor Americans who routinely must spend more than half of their income on housing and are frequently evicted when even the smallest of unexpected expenses arise. In this article, Desmond highlights the role of homeownership and its associated tax benefits in perpetuating the divide between the poor and the well off in America.

At the center of his criticism is the mortgage-interest deduction (MID). Homeowners can deduct the interest they pay on their mortgage on their taxes, lowering their overall taxable income. The more expensive the house, the larger the tax break. The MID resulted in a 71 billion dollars' worth of subsidies to homeowners in 2015. Far from a public outcry about this taxpayer subsidy (71 billion dollars is more than the budget of the Departments of Education, Justice, and Energy combined), the MID is one of the most popular features of the tax code and any attempts to modify it are widely regarded as political suicide. Contrast this with public attention to those who receive what we think of as "welfare"—food stamps, payments to the disabled or those who are very poor and have children. The poor are often cast as lazy free loaders who don't deserve to be supported by someone else's tax dollars. Yet that's exactly what the MID is—a public housing subsidy to the middle and upper class. Donald Trump's preliminary 2018 budget contains significant cuts to the very programs that assist the poor in obtaining housing, but the MID will remain in place.

Home ownership is one of the primary ways that wealth is transferred from one generation to the next. The difference in home ownership rates are one of the biggest factors in the racial wealth gap. The median wealth of white households is 13 times more (141,900 dollars) than the median wealth of black families

(11,000 dollars), and is 10 times more than the median wealth of Hispanic families (13,700 dollars)[1]. Much of this difference can be traced directly to racist housing policies in the past that in various forms either prevented or discouraged home ownership among minorities. This initial disparity has compounded over time, so that even the elimination of overt racial barriers to home ownership does little to fix the disparity. In addition to inheritance, parents who own homes are more likely to be able to assist their children in making a down payment on their own home, when they will then be able to take advantage of the MID. Meanwhile, the poor face cuts to the already comparatively paltry programs that subsidize housing, and live under the constant threat of eviction, which brings with it a whole host of additional financial and practical hardships.

As you read, think about how poverty and eviction are not just individual problems, but rather those created by the way we have chosen to set up our society. Is the American Dream of good job and home ownership equally available to everyone who works hard? How do our political policies and cultural images of poverty impact the day-to-day lives of the wealthy and poor?

The son of a minister, Ohene Asare grew up poor. His family emigrated from Ghana when he was eight and settled down in West Bridgewater, Mass., a town 30 miles south of Boston, where he was one of the few black students at the local public school. "It was us and this Jewish family," Asare remembered. "It was a field day." His white classmates bullied him, sometimes using racial slurs. His father transferred Asare when he was 14 to Milton Academy, which awarded Asare a scholarship that covered tuition and board. His parents still had to take out loans worth about 20,000 dollars for his living expenses. But the academy set Asare up for future success. He and his wife, Régine Jean-Charles, whom he got to know at Milton, are in their late 30s. She is a tenured professor of romance languages and literature at Boston College and Asare is a founder of Aesara, a consulting and technology company.

Two years ago, the couple bought a new home. Set on a half-acre lot that backs up to conservation land in Milton, Mass., the 2,350-square-foot split-level has four bedrooms, three bathrooms, an open-concept kitchen and dining area, a finished basement, hardwood floors, and beautiful touches throughout, like the Tennessee marble fireplace and hearth. It cost 665,000 dollars. "This is the nicest house I've ever lived in," Asare told me.

Asare and Jean-Charles have four children and earn roughly 290,000 dollars a year, which puts them in the top 5 percent of household incomes in the country. After renting for the first years of their marriage, they participated in a home buyers' program administered by the nonprofit

Neighborhood Assistance Corporation of America. The program allowed Asare and Jean-Charles to purchase their first home in 2009 for 360,000 dollars with a 10 percent down payment, half of what is typically required. In 2015, they sold it for 430,000 dollars. There is a reason so many Americans choose to develop their net worth through homeownership: it is a proven wealth builder and savings compeller. The average homeowner boasts a net worth (195,400 dollars) that is 36 times that of the average renter (5,400 dollars).

Asare serves on the advisory board for HomeStart, a nonprofit focused on ending and preventing homelessness. Like most organizations, HomeStart is made up of people at various rungs on the economic ladder. Asare sits near the top; his salary exceeds that of anyone on staff at the nonprofit he helps advise. When Crisaliz Diaz was a staff member at HomeStart, she was at the other end of the ladder. She earned 38,000 dollars a year, putting her near the bottom third of American household incomes. A 26-year-old Latina with thick-rimmed glasses, Diaz rents a small two-bedroom apartment in Braintree, Mass., an outer suburb of Boston. Her two sons, Xzayvior and Mayson—Zay and May, she calls them—share a room plastered with Lego posters and Mickey Mouse stickers. Her apartment is spare and clean, with ceiling tiles you can push up and views of the parking lot and busy street.

When Diaz moved in four years ago, the rent was 1,195 dollars a month, heat included, but her landlord has since raised the rent to 1,385 dollars a month, which takes 44 percent of her paycheck. Even with child-support payments and side jobs, she still doesn't bring in enough to pay her regular bills. She goes without a savings account and regularly relies on credit cards to buy toilet paper and soap. "There's no stop to it," she told me. "It's just a consistent thing."

Diaz receives no housing assistance. She has applied to several programs, but nothing has come through. The last time Boston accepted new applications for rental-assistance Section 8 vouchers was nine years ago, when for a few precious weeks you were allowed to place your name on a very long waiting list. Boston is not atypical in that way. In Los Angeles, the estimated wait time for a Section 8 voucher is 11 years. In Washington, the waiting list for housing vouchers is closed indefinitely, and over 40,000 people have applied for public housing alone. While many Americans assume that most poor families live in subsidized housing, the opposite is true; nationwide, only one in four households that qualifies for rental assistance receives it. Most are like Diaz, struggling without government help in the private rental market, where housing costs claim larger and larger chunks of their income.

Almost a decade removed from the foreclosure crisis that began in 2008, the nation is facing one of the worst affordable-housing shortages in generations. The standard of *affordable* housing is that which costs roughly 30 percent or less of a family's income. Because of rising housing costs and stagnant wages, slightly more than half of all poor renting families in the country spend more than 50 percent of their income on housing costs, and at least one in four spends more than 70 percent. Yet America's national housing policy gives affluent homeowners large benefits; middle-class homeowners, smaller benefits; and most renters, who are disproportionately poor, nothing. It is difficult to think of another social policy that more successfully multiplies America's inequality in such a sweeping fashion.

Consider Asare and Diaz. As a homeowner, Asare benefits from tax breaks that Diaz does not, the biggest being the mortgage-interest deduction—or MID, in wonk-speak. All homeowners in America may deduct mortgage interest on their first and second homes. In 2015, Asare and Jean-Charles claimed 21,686 dollars in home interest and other real estate deductions, which saved them 470 dollars a month. That's roughly 15 percent of Diaz's monthly income. That same year, the federal government dedicated nearly 134 billion dollars to homeowner subsidies. The MID accounted for the biggest chunk of the total, 71 billion dollars, with real estate tax deductions, capital gains exclusions, and other expenditures accounting for the rest. That number, 134 billion dollars, was larger than the entire budgets of the Departments of Education, Justice and Energy combined for that year. It is a figure that exceeds half the entire gross domestic product of countries like Chile, New Zealand, and Portugal.

Recently, Gary Cohn, the chief economic adviser to President Trump, heralded his boss's first tax plan as a "once-in-a-generation opportunity to do something really big." And indeed, Trump's plan represents a radical transformation in how we will fund the government, with its biggest winners being corporations and wealthy families. But no one in his administration, and only a small (albeit growing) group of people in either party, is pushing to reform what may very well be the most regressive piece of social policy in America. Perhaps that's because the mortgage-interest deduction overwhelmingly benefits the sorts of upper-middle-class voters who make up the donor base of both parties and who generally fail to acknowledge themselves to be beneficiaries of federal largess. "Today, as in the past," writes the historian Molly Michelmore in her book *Tax and Spend*, "most of the recipients of federal aid are not the suspect 'welfare queens' of the popular imagination but rather middle-class homeowners, salaried professionals and retirees." A 15-story public housing tower and a mortgaged suburban home are both government-subsidized, but only one looks (and feels) that way. It is only by recognizing this fact that we can begin to understand why there is so much poverty in the United States today.

When we think of entitlement programs, Social Security and Medicare immediately come to mind. But by any fair standard, the holy trinity of United States social policy should also include the mortgage-interest deduction—an enormous benefit that has also become politically untouchable.

The MID came into being in 1913, not to spur homeownership but simply as part of a general policy allowing businesses to deduct interest payments from loans. At that time, most Americans didn't own their homes and only the rich paid income tax, so the effects of the mortgage deduction on the nation's tax proceeds were fairly trivial. That began to change in the second half of the twentieth century, though, because of two huge transformations in American life. First, income tax was converted from an elite tax to a mass tax: in 1932, the Bureau of Internal Revenue (precursor to the IRS) processed fewer than two million individual tax returns, but 11 years later, it processed over 40 million. At the same time, the federal government began subsidizing homeownership through large-scale initiatives like the G.I. Bill and mortgage insurance. Homeownership grew rapidly in the postwar period and so did the MID.

By the time policy makers realized how extravagant the MID had become, it was too late to do much about it without facing significant backlash. Millions of voters had begun to count on getting that money back. Even President Ronald Reagan, who oversaw drastic cuts to housing programs benefiting low-income Americans, let the MID be. Subsequent politicians followed suit, often eager to discuss reforms to Social Security and Medicare but reluctant to touch the MID, even as the program continued to grow more costly: by 2019, MID expenditures are expected to exceed 96 billion dollars.

"Once we're in a world with a MID," says Todd Sinai, a professor of real estate and public policy at the University of Pennsylvania's Wharton School, "it is very hard to get to a world without the MID." That's in part because the benefit helps to prop up home values. It's impossible to say how much, but a widely cited 1996 study estimated that eliminating the MID and property-tax deductions would result in a 13 to 17 percent reduction in housing prices nationwide, though that estimate varies widely by region and more recent analyses have found smaller effects. The MID allows home buyers to collect more after-tax savings if they take on more mortgage debt, which incentivizes them to pay more for properties than they could have otherwise. By inflating home values, the MID benefits Americans who already own homes—and makes joining their ranks harder.

The owner-renter divide is as salient as any other in this nation, and this divide is a historical result of statecraft designed to protect and promote inequality. Ours was not always a nation of homeowners; the New Deal fashioned it so, particularly through the G.I. Bill of Rights. The G.I. Bill was enormous, consuming 15 percent of the federal budget in 1948, and remains unmatched by any other single social policy in the scope and depth of its provisions, which included things like college tuition benefits and small-business loans. The G.I. Bill brought a rollout of veterans' mortgages, padded with modest interest rates and down payments waived for loans up to 30 years. Returning soldiers lined up and bought new homes by the millions. In the years immediately following World War II, veterans' mortgages accounted for over 40 percent of all home loans.

But both in its design and its application, the G.I. Bill excluded a large number of citizens. To get the New Deal through Congress, Franklin Roosevelt needed to appease the Southern arm of the Democratic Party. So he acquiesced when Congress blocked many nonwhites, particularly African Americans, from accessing his newly created ladders of opportunity. Farm work, housekeeping, and other jobs disproportionately staffed by African Americans were omitted from programs like Social Security and unemployment insurance. Local Veterans Affairs centers and other entities loyal to Jim Crow did their parts as well, systematically denying nonwhite veterans access to the G.I. Bill. If those veterans got past the VA, they still had to contend with the banks, which denied loan applications in nonwhite neighborhoods because the Federal Housing Administration refused to insure mortgages there. From 1934 to 1968, the official FHA policy of redlining made homeownership virtually impossible in black communities. "The consequences proved profound," writes the historian Ira Katznelson in his perfectly titled book, *When Affirmative Action Was White*. "By 1984, when G.I. Bill mortgages had mainly matured, the median white household had a net worth of 39,135 dollars; the comparable figure for black households was only 3,397 dollars, or just 9 percent of white holdings. Most of this difference was accounted for by the absence of homeownership."

This legacy has been passed down to subsequent generations. Today a majority of first-time home buyers get down payment help from their parents; many of those parents pitch in by refinancing their own homes. As black homeowners, Asare and Jean-Charles are exceptions to the national trend: while most white families own a home, a majority of black and Latino families do not. Differences in homeownership rates remain the prime driver of the nation's racial wealth gap. In 2011, the median white household had a net worth of 111,146 dollars, compared with 7,113 dollars for the median black household and 8,348 dollars for the median Hispanic household. If black and Hispanic families owned homes at rates similar to whites, the racial wealth gap would be reduced by almost a third.

Racial exclusion was Roosevelt's first concession to pass the New Deal; his second, to avoid a tax revolt, was to rely on regressive and largely hidden payroll taxes to fund generous social-welfare programs. A result, the historian Michelmore observes, is that we "never asked ordinary taxpayers to pay for the economic security many soon came to expect as a matter of right." In providing millions of middle-class families stealth benefits, the American government rendered itself invisible to those families, who soon came to see their success as wholly self-made. We forgot because we were not meant to remember.

We tend to speak about the poor as if they didn't live in the same society, as if our gains and their losses weren't intertwined. Conservatives explain poverty by pointing to *individual factors*, like bad decisions or the rise of single-parent families; liberals refer to *structural causes*, like the decline of manufacturing or the historical legacies of racial discrimination. Usually pitted against each other, each perspective serves a similar function: letting us off the hook by asserting that there is a deep-rooted, troubling problem—more than one in six Americans does not make enough to afford basic necessities—that most of us bear no responsibility for.

It's around this point that the conversation gets snagged in the weeds with questions about home prices, political ramifications or the administrative hurdles of reform—escape routes that allow us to lose sight of people like Cris Diaz, low-income renters who are not entitled to any housing assistance and who are giving most of their income to landlords and utility companies. To drive down poverty and promote economic mobility, the United States will need to make a major investment in affordable housing. You don't need to reform the MID to pay for that—there are plenty of other ways to raise revenue—but you have to pay for it somehow. Whatever our position on homeowner tax benefits, we should have an answer for people like Diaz.

Trump's preliminary 2018 budget includes a 13.2 percent reduction to the Department of Housing and Urban Development and the elimination of the Interagency Council on Homelessness, cuts that will almost certainly result in the loss of hundreds of thousands of housing vouchers and leave more families rent-burdened and homeless. President Barack Obama's 2017 budget proposal estimated that it would take 1 billion dollars a year over the next 10 years to eliminate family homelessness in America—not decrease it or slice it in half, but end it. That's less than 1 percent of what we currently spend on homeowner subsidies. And yet a bill designed to provide every child in America with a home was pronounced dead on arrival in Congress. Up to this point, bills proposing modest reforms to the mortgage-interest deduction have met the same fate.

Poverty and homelessness are political creations. Their amelioration is within our grasp and budget. But those of us most likely to vote and contribute to political campaigns are least likely to support MID reform—either because it wouldn't affect our lives or because it would, by asking us to take less so that millions of Americans could be given the opportunity to climb out of poverty. It's just that we usually don't dial our elected officials when our less-fortunate neighbors are hurting, because we are not.

And yet over the course of our history, there have been times when Americans embraced a politics of sacrifice. During World War II, families volunteered to pay more taxes, ration food, and give blood to serve a higher purpose. And even today, in what can feel like an age of insecurity and self-preservation, some Americans have shown a willingness to take a personal financial hit to promote social mobility and equality. Take the people of Seattle: for 36 years, they have agreed to be taxed more to raise revenue for affordable-housing programs. Last August, 70 percent of Seattle voters agreed to the largest housing levy yet, one expected to raise 290 million dollars over the next seven years. Contributions to the levy are based on home values; a family living in a 480,000 dollar home (the city's median value in 2015) pays an additional 122 dollars a year in taxes. With that money, Seattle will fund emergency rental assistance, loans to first-time home buyers and the construction of housing units that must remain affordable for at least 50 years. Previous housing levies have generated over 13,000 affordable apartment units and enabled 900 low-income families to buy homes. The 2016 Housing Levy will do more because the residents of Seattle decided to invest in economic diversity and residential stability, sacrificing a pinch to help those in need.

Asare and Jean-Charles would welcome MID reform, even if it meant that they would have less in the bank at the end of the year. "There are people who sacrificed for me to be here," Asare told me. One of them was a boy named Chris Jackson, whom Asare met during his tormented years in the West Bridgewater school system. When Asare wouldn't fight back, Jackson, a fellow black student, would stick up for him. "I watched him fight and fight, get into trouble," Asare remembers. "And I'd be like, 'No, stop.' But he wouldn't, because what was right was right." Asare paused to collect himself, a hand fingering the space above his freshly shaved head. "That kind of compassion, that kind of brotherhood, is what I would ask of people: that we don't give according to what people are willing to receive; we give according to the standard for what they should have."

In February, Diaz's landlord increased her rent by 65 dollars a month, to 1,450 dollars. The timing couldn't have been worse: Diaz had recently taken a new job as a leasing consultant at a small property management firm. The pay wasn't better, but she had reduced her commute to 30 minutes from two hours. "I get to see my kids before it gets dark," she said. But transitioning between the jobs caused her to go without income for a couple of weeks. With no savings to fall back on, she couldn't pay the increased rent and was summoned to eviction court. A month later, Diaz walked through the metal detector at the Quincy District Courthouse. "Where do you go for evictions?" she asked a clerk, who pointed to a crowd of tenants shuffling toward the same room. Some wore heavy-heeled work boots and worn jeans; some leaned on canes and walkers; some bounced babies. Diaz took a seat on a long wooden bench and looked at the clock. She had had to use her lunch break to make court and only had 45 minutes.

Once a rarity in America, eviction has become commonplace in our cities, disrupting families, schools, and entire neighborhoods. Forty people a day are evicted in Milwaukee; each day in New York City brings 60 marshal evictions. An eviction could plunge Diaz and her boys into homelessness and poverty. Studies have found that evicted families lose not only their homes but their jobs, possessions, and neighbors too; they relocate to substandard housing in distressed communities; they have higher rates of depression and suicide. Even if poor families avoid eviction, they still suffer, because so much of their money goes to housing costs, forcing them to buy fewer school supplies, clothes, books—and food.

In some markets, there are virtually no affordable units left. The median annual rent for a two-bedroom apartment is currently 39,600 dollars in Boston, 49,200 dollars in New York City, and 54,720 dollars in San Francisco. Families priced out of large cities have moved to smaller ones, and now those cities are experiencing some of the steepest rent increases in the nation. The poor used to live on the other side of the tracks. Now they live in different towns and counties entirely.

And yet we continue to give the most help to those who least need it—affluent homeowners—while providing nothing to most rent-burdened tenants. If this is our design, our social contract, then we should at least own up to it; we should at least stand up and profess, "Yes, this is the kind of nation we want." Before us, there are two honest choices: we can endorse this inequality-maximizing arrangement, or we can reject it. What we cannot do is look a mother like Diaz in the face and say, "We'd love to help you, but we just can't afford to." Because that is, quite simply, a lie.

After her name was called, Diaz stepped outside the courtroom to talk with her landlord's attorney, a white man in wire glasses. She had secured emergency assistance from the state. It wasn't enough. But the lawyer told Diaz that if she *zeroed out* by next month, paying all her back rent and April's rent in full, he would dismiss the case. Diaz wrote out a check for 583 dollars—a start, and what amounted to 357 dollars less than what Asare and Jean-Charles receive from the MID in two months—and raced back to work. In April, she was let go.

Thinking about the long, hard road ahead for Diaz, I remembered a conversation I had with her six months earlier. Around her small dining table, Diaz and I had calculated her monthly budget, which left her with -221 dollars after all the bills were paid. The process seemed to reduce her to a sadder, emptied-out version of herself. "Eventually I'm going to have to figure something out," she said softly, "whether it's a second job or a third job. I don't know."

I looked down at my empty plate, smeared with tomato sauce from the meatball sub Diaz had made me. "Do you know what the mortgage-interest deduction is?" I asked.

"I don't," she said. "I'm sorry."

After I explained what it is, she asked, "Why don't they spend it on lower-income housing?" I shrugged. After a moment, I asked, "What would you do if you only had to pay 30 percent of your income on rent?"

Diaz looked around. Her eyes paused on one of Zay's homework assignments stuck to the refrigerator. Titled "Someone Special," its words wiggled forward in a child's handwriting: "My mom is special because she helps me figure out addition and subtraction. We always cook together. We cook some spaghetti." On the other side of the fridge, held up by a clown fish magnet, was a bill from the Massachusetts Registry of Motor Vehicles.

"That would be life," she said.

DISCUSSION QUESTIONS

1. What is the MID and how does it work? Does it benefit all homeowners equally? Who gets the most benefit from it?

2. What other benefits do homeowners get other than the MID? How does home ownership help families acquire and pass down wealth?

3. Why do politicians view any attempt to get rid of the MID as political suicide? Whose interests are at stake and how does that influence what our tax code looks like?

4. What are your plans for home ownership? If you want to own a home, what obstacles or advantages do you think you will have in making that dream a reality?

NOTE

1. http://www.pewresearch.org/fact-tank/2014/12/12/racial-wealth-gaps-great-recession/